Collaborative Information Behavior:
User Engagement and Communication Sharing

Jonathan Foster
University of Sheffield, UK

INFORMATION SCIENCE REFERENCE

Hershey · New York

Director of Editorial Content:	Kristin Klinger
Director of Book Publications:	Julia Mosemann
Acquisitions Editor:	Lindsay Johnston
Development Editor:	Christine Bufton
Publishing Assistant:	Deanna Jo Zombro
Typesetter:	Deanna Jo Zombro
Production Editor:	Jamie Snavely
Cover Design:	Lisa Tosheff
Printed at:	Yurchak Printing Inc.

Published in the United States of America by
Information Science Reference (an imprint of IGI Global)
701 E. Chocolate Avenue
Hershey PA 17033
Tel: 717-533-8845
Fax: 717-533-8661
E-mail: cust@igi-global.com
Web site: http://www.igi-global.com

Library of Congress Cataloging-in-Publication Data

Collaborative information behavior : user engagement and communication sharing / Jonathan Foster, editor.
    p. cm.
  Includes bibliographical references and index.
  Summary: "This book coordinates and integrates current research and practices in the area of collaborative information behavior, providing information on empirical research findings, theoretical frameworks, and models relevant to understanding collaborative information behavior"--Provided by publisher.
  ISBN 978-1-61520-797-8 -- ISBN 978-1-61520-798-5 (ebook) 1. Information behavior. 2. Group work in research. 3. Virtual work teams. I. Foster, Jonathan, 1965-
  ZA3075.C65 2010
  025.5'24--dc22
                        2009040556British Cataloguing in Publication Data

A Cataloguing in Publication record for this book is available from the British Library.

Table of Contents

Section 1
Collaborative Information Behavior in Large Groups

Section 2
Collaborative Information Behavior in Small Groups

Section 3
Language and Communication in Collaborative Information Behavior

Detailed Table of Contents

Section 1
Collaborative Information Behavior in Large Groups

Chapter 1

Wolf R. Richter, Oxford Internet Institute, UK
David A. Bray, Massachusetts Institute of Technology, USA
William H. Dutton, Oxford Internet Institute, UK

The Internet and related digital networking platforms facilitate searches for information and the sharing of information and expertise among individuals. In recent years, these behaviours evolved from focusing on information retrieval and sharing to include facilitation and coordination of collaborative problem-solving efforts and distributed co-creation of services and products. Such collaborations, supported by digital networks, often extend beyond the traditional boundaries of organizations and institutions, the social networks of small groups, the subjects of specific disciplines, and the geographic borders of nations. Consequently, they raise concerns over how to best manage networked individuals and realize the potential utility of their activities. This chapter builds on the findings of a series of case studies designed to explore such questions. From the results of these case studies the authors propose a framework for categorizing 'Collaborative Network Organizations' (CNOs); one that suggests that value emerges as a result of cultivating particular kinds of relationships and activities within these networks. The authors employ the term 'cultivation', instead of management, as the case studies indicated that such efforts often fail if managed too precisely or too restrictively in a "top-down" fashion. Instead, the provision of greater latitude and "bottom-up" autonomy to the individuals involved characterized the more successful CNOs we studied. In addition, the success of CNOs depended on how such efforts reconfigured information and communication flows in ways that supported distributed sharing, generation, or co-creation of content within a wide variety of collaborative contexts, ranging from the conduct of scientific research to problem-solving in business and everyday life. Directly attempting to manage or control CNOs can undermine these networks, whereas indirectly influencing and cultivating desired behaviours and activities can encourage the expansion of productive networking. The authors offer this theoretical framework as a means for better capturing the mechanisms governing collaborative behaviour.

This chapter considers the collective information behavior of the poor in Bangladesh. It examines the mobile phone as the central node and seeks to understand the construction of collectiveness by examining the collective-mediated learning, sharing and experimenting among the poor. Three brief cases provide the background and illustrate the elements of a Learn, Share and Experiment model. Against this tapestry of multiple perspectives, collective-mediated learning, sharing and experimenting enable the poor to be cost-efficient and socially productive. In conclusion there is an urgent need for all researchers to reexamine and rethink the poor's collective information behavior as new media technology spreads deeper into their lives. Without it, we may miss the opportunity to discover something useful that will eventually lift them out of poverty.

The long-term sustainability of online communities depends on the active participation and contribution of its members, but we have limited knowledge about why individuals do not post and how online communities can differ. This chapter presents an exploratory case study of contribution rates and lurking in a professional international online community that focuses on architecture and design in the Islamic world. The purpose of this study was to gain a deeper understanding of the community and the lurking behavior of its members. Using a web-based survey and log files, it asked three primary questions: Who contributes? Where do they contribute? And what reasons do members give for not contributing?

The last 30 years have seen the creation of a variety of electronic collaboration tools for science and business. Some of the best-known collaboration tools support text editing (e.g., wikis). Wikipedia's success shows that large-scale collaboration can produce highly valuable content. Meanwhile much structured data is being collected and made publicly available. We have never had access to more powerful databases and statistical packages. Is large-scale collaborative data analysis now possible? Using a quantitative analysis of Web 2.0 data visualization sites, the authors find evidence that at least moderate open collaboration occurs. The authors then explore some of the limiting factors of collaboration over data.

Section 2
Collaborative Information Behavior in Small Groups

Chapter 5

Madhu C. Reddy, The Pennsylvania State University, USA
Bernard J. Jansen, The Pennsylvania State University, USA
Patricia R. Spence, The Pennsylvania State University, USA

Collaborative information behavior is an important and growing area of research in the field of information behavior. Although collaboration is a key component of work in organizational and other settings, most research has primarily focused on individual information behavior and not the collaborative aspects of information behavior. Consequently, there is a pressing need to understand both the conceptual features of this type of behavior and the technical approaches to support these collaborative activities. In this chapter, the authors describe current research in this area and what we are learning about collaboration and coordination during these activities. In particular, the authors present details of ethnographic field studies that are starting to uncover the characteristics of collaborative information behavior. They also discuss a preliminary collaborative information behavior model and some technical explorations that they are conducting in this space.

Chapter 6

Nozomi Ikeya, Palo Alto Research Center, USA
*Norihisa Awamura, Keio University and Research Fellow of the Japan Society for the Promotion
    of Science, Japan*
Shinichiro Sakai, Rikkyo University, Japan

In order to study collaborative information behaviour (e.g. information search, creation, and sharing) in the work environment, it is important that we take into consideration its embedded nature in collaborative work, however not many studies have actually taken this into consideration. In conducting fieldwork, we studied group task management in the work of IT product hardware designers. The study shows how understanding the details of information activities embedded in task management allowed us to generate some ideas for transforming task management into a more collaborative activity, and for *re*embedding task management more thoroughly into their work practices together with the practitioners. The paper discusses how taking an ethnomethodological approach can be fruitful for researchers who want to gain a close understanding of actual collaborative information activities and their embedded nature in work, and how understandings of this kind can be important for developing ideas for transforming practice, both with or without the introduction of technology.

Chapter 7

Sean Goggins, Drexel University, USA
Sanda Erdelez, University of Missouri, USA

This chapter situates collaborative information behavior in completely online groups as a phenomenon distinct from prior work understanding collaborative information behavior in face-to-face groups, free and open source software groups and Wikipedia groups. The unexpected diversity of information resources utilized by completely online group members is analyzed through Sonnenwald's Information Horizons theory. Information practices of completely online group members are described, and the key themes of groups as information resources, the influence of tool change on collaborative information behavior online, and the focusing potential of collaborative information tools for completely online group work are explicated. Future research directions that explore the potential of COGs for distributed innovation; new types of collaborative information behavior and breaking down the digital divide are reviewed.

Chapter 8

Typically education is a process that is done to students. The work reported here relates to students who collaborate in the education process so that they become educators of later students. This collaboration takes the form of development of re-usable learning objects (RLOs) that are firstly used to assess each student's understanding, but which are then to be used for the education of subsequent cohorts. This approach is based on a range of pedagogic concerns with motivational and social aspects of teaching. Students are given the options of producing a written or a video assignment. They make this decision in the knowledge that their work will be used to instruct students who will come after them. The video is relatively short at 5 – 10 minutes in length. Once assessed the video is added to a library for later use. Students report that they enjoy these assessments and that it is valuable to see the work of previous students.

Chapter 9

The last 30 years have seen the creation of a variety of electronic collaboration tools for science and business. Some of the best-known collaboration tools support text editing (e.g., wikis). Wikipedia's success shows that large-scale collaboration can produce highly valuable content. Meanwhile much structured data is being collected and made publicly available. We have never had access to more powerful databases and statistical packages. Is large-scale collaborative data analysis now possible? Using a quantitative analysis of Web 2.0 data visualization sites, the authors find evidence that at least moderate open collaboration occurs. The authors then explore some of the limiting factors of collaboration over data.

Section 3
Language and Communication in Collaborative Information Behavior

Chapter 10

This chapter describes the cross-disciplinary conceptual frameworks used to examine a popular American entertainment website that employs a virtual newsroom utilizing instant messaging as its primary means of communication. This computer-mediated communication reconfigures the standard place-based newsroom arrangements and significantly influences the group's organizational dynamics and culture. Because of the distinctive content and unconventional organizational structure of this site, no single theoretical perspective can be applied to its organizational context and content. Therefore a combination of organization theory (Schein, 2004), and newsroom sociology theoretical frameworks articulates an emerging dynamic represented by such a medium's evolution from hierarchical to networked organization. This chapter exemplifies the potential for new media researchers to adopt a cross-disciplinary approach to their analysis. As old models for understanding media cease to support the complex structures of new organizations we must look to other frameworks for additional guidance.

The chapter presents findings from recent studies that feature a model of doctor-patient collaboration called Video Intervention/Prevention Assessment (VIA), a research methodology that engages patient-participants in sharing their life stories on video, communicating their concerns and teaching their doctors what it means to live with a chronic illness. Patients are collaborators in creating a comprehensive understanding of illness that expands the medical community's definition of disease. This chapter focuses on visual narratives made by young patients with Cystic Fibrosis and Spina Bifida as they experience their transitions from pediatric to adult-oriented medicine care. Collaboration in research facilitates more effective ownership of and accountability for their illness, facilitating adherence to treatment plans and improved quality of life. Our chapter concludes with an evaluation of the pros and cons of VIA as a collaborative information methodology.

The concept of "traces" is useful for understanding the collaborative practices of informing. Readers of documents leave traces of their use, and institutional talk embeds traces of collaborative work, including work done and elsewhere and at other times. This chapter employs a multifaceted qualitative strategy of analytic bracketing to analyze traces in midwives' and clients' discussions of clinical results. Results are used to identify and evaluate trends in relation to the current case or to universal norms. Conflicting forms of evidence may need to be negotiated. Barriers may arise when results or sources are inadequate or unavailable. Midwives and women manage these barriers by flexibly assigning the role of information provider in official and unofficial ways. The analysis of traces provides insight into the *hows* and *whats* of collaborative work and reveals it to be a complex set of practices that go well beyond the immediately visible contributions of others.

Chapter 13

This chapter presents a coding guide for the analysis of peer talk during educational information seeking. The guide is an outcome of a structuring content analysis of learners' dialogues as they seek, evaluate, and use information on a collaborative basis. The analysis is informed by a language-based theory of learning and the sequential organization of spoken discourse. The generic steps of a structuring content analysis are described first; before each step, sequence, exchange, and move type identified in the dialogues are described. Illustrative examples of each unit and type of talk are provided, so as to aid in the precise and reliable assignment of the categories and codes in further studies. The chapter concludes with implications of the coding guide, and the broader study of which it is a part, for research in educational information seeking.

Preface

In what is commonly received to be a defining moment for the field of information behavior an article by Dervin and Nilan (1986) crystallized what has become known as a user-based approach to the study of information needs, seeking and use. During the 1980s and throughout much of the 1990s user studies were almost exclusively focused on the information needs, seeking, and uses of the individual user. During the mid-to-late 1990s society witnessed the large-scale diffusion and take-up of the World Wide Web, and the emergence of a digital infrastructure that acts as a platform for widespread data and information sharing, electronic communications and transactions. These developments led in turn to an interest in what can be called collaborative information behavior. Collaborative information behavior can be defined as the study of collaboration with, through, and in relation to information; along with the systems and practices that support this. Collaboration can be explicit (e.g. in the purposive sharing and generating of information in support of work or learning activity); or implicit (e.g. exploiting the traces of the informational activity of others); or automated (e.g. recommender systems). Collaboration can also involve and lead to the co-production of information goods or services (e.g. Wikipedia). Collaborative information behavior can occur in face-to-face settings where language plays a preeminent role in the interaction, or in settings in which technology acts to mediate the interaction across space and time. Collaboration also involves, although not exclusively, an intensification of the relations between peers. A situation brought about latterly by the sharing of a common communications medium, i.e. the Internet, and the emergence of a technologically networked society. Studying collaboration with, through, and in relation to information is not the exclusive preserve of researchers in information studies. The sheer pervasiveness and relevance of information and communication networks to professional and everyday life make it a topic of interest to at least the following fields and beyond: computer-supported cooperative work, human-computer interaction, Internet research, and new media.

The structure of the book is as follows. Although it is not an absolute distinction, a difference of scale is made between the collaborative information behavior of large and small groups. In large groups the relations between the individual members tends to be weaker than in small groups. As a consequence knowledge in large groups will tend to be more widely dispersed than in small group; and as a result the mechanisms used to aggregate the knowledge of a large group, and coordinates its activities, may receive greater attention than in a small group. The first section on collaborative information behavior in large groups contains chapters on for example collaborative network organizations, communities, and collaborative data processing; while the second section on collaborative information behavior in small groups contains chapters on information sharing in work teams and learning groups for example. A final section contains chapters focusing on one of the primary tools used to aggregate the knowledge of a group and coordinate its activities: language and communication. This section contains one chapter on computer-mediated communication; and three chapters that take language and communication as a starting-point for their investigations in collaborative information behavior.

In a chapter that pays homage to James Surowiecki's influential book *The Wisdom of Crowds*, Richter Bray and Dutton define the concept of a collaborative network organization (CNO). A CNO is a socio-technical form of organization defined by its members' engagement in one or more of these activities: information sharing, content generation, or collaboration in the co-creation of a product or service. Using a case study approach a framework is developed in which three types of CNOs are identified and characterized. CNO 1.0: sharing, in which a network (e.g. the WWW) enables the transmission and linking of objects in a distributed context; CNO 2.0: contributing, in which group and social networking applications (e.g. social news websites) reshape the information and communications shared among its contributors; and CNO 3.0: co-creating, in which the network functions to facilitate cooperative work among its members in the service of a shared goal. The framework is illustrated by case studies of users who display medium to high engagement in a CNO. These are: *Sermo* (CNO 2.0) which is a platform that enables a community of medical practitioners to share their knowledge and expertise via conversations and social networking applications; and *A Swarm of Angels* (CNO 3.0), which is an open source feature film and participatory filmmaking community consisting of an online discussion forum, wiki platform, and web-based polling system. In discussing these cases Richter, Bray and Dutton also address their governance structures, decision-making processes, models for collecting and distributing resources, and legal frameworks. The chapter concludes by arguing that among other conditions a key ingredient in the effectiveness of CNOs is an ethos of cultivation rather than of management.

Mobile communications are, besides the Internet, one of the primary means by which people search for and communicate information. Wong presents a group of case studies that illustrate the collective process by which the mobile phone is appropriated and used by the poor in Bangladesh. Wong argues that because the information available to the poor is often neither comprehensive nor actionable, the processes of information seeking and use consequently become problematical. In response to this problematical situation, Wong describes how a form of collective information behavior arises where the use made of mobile communications is embedded in a collective process of peer learning, sharing, and experimenting. Three case examples of mobile communications sharing are presented that act as a starting-point for understanding and learning how the poor can be connected to a digitally networked world, and what the effective means are for doing this; and common aspects of the cases lead to the development of the learning, sharing, and experimenting model-a form of behavior that contributes to cost savings and risk reduction on the part of the poor and functions to domesticate mobile communications into their lives.

While a shared communications environment is one condition for effective collaborative information behavior, a further is the active and sustained engagement of users. Beamish presents the findings of a survey conducted to understand the contribution rates and obstacles to participation within an online community. Known obstacles to information sharing e.g. medium, content, individual social-cultural factors are reviewed first; before the data collection and data collection methods for the study are described. Data were collected via site activity reports, and a web-based survey organized into sections on demographics, participation, contribution, information seeking, and overall satisfaction with the online community. Findings relate to who contributes to the site and where they contribute; and any reasons members give for not contributing. These findings are also cross-tabulated with the demographic data. In respect of who contributes findings are comparable with typical participation patterns in other online communities, i.e. intense (by staff), active (by a core group of members), and peripheral (by the majority). In respect of where members contribute, an imbalance was found in the contributions posted to private vs. public areas of the site, with the former attracting more contributions than the latter. In respect to obstacles to participation and reasons for lurking, a combination of individual factors (e.g. time, interest only in reading/browsing) and social-cultural factors (e.g. a lack of active encouragement, the large size and public nature of the site) were the most prominent. The chapter concludes by highlighting some of the conditions that would enable more active participation in the online community and greater user engagement with its resources; including reminders, interaction, functionality, and content.

Large-scale data sets are one of the major resources that are currently being published on the Internet; for use both by the general public and by specialized communities. The types of resources that are being made available include data repositories, open online databases, open source projects and open access journals; as well collaborative data analysis sites and public datasets. Although the open availability of these resources is a necessary step towards widespread collaborative data processing, Noel and Lemire argue that it is not a sufficient one, if the resources are to be fully exploited; and the chapter therefore investigates some of the promise and current limits of large-scale collaborative data processing. Current tools available to handle and interact with structured data are reviewed first, e.g. databases, spreadsheets, and visualization tools; before the findings of a survey evaluating current collaborative data analysis tools are discussed. The survey's main conclusion is that current collaborative data analysis tools can be deemed collaborative to the extent that more prolific users tend to contribute only half of the content. This implies that such tools attract a broader base of participation than situations where the majority of the contributions are made by a minority of users. The chapter concludes with examining some of the conditions that need to be addressed if greater engagement with these types of resources is to occur e.g. motivation; credit; data sharing; flexible semantics; task specialization; usability; concurrent access and asynchronicity; along with further developments in data visualization tools.

The second section is on collaborative information behavior in small groups. These are groups where relations between the individual members tends to be stronger than in large groups; and where two or more members of the group engage in one or more of the following tasks: creating, identifying, seeking, retrieving, organizing, distributing or using information in support of the group's activity.

Reddy, Jansen and Spence review the research they have conducted into collaboration and coordination during information seeking and retrieval. Conceptual and technical perspectives on collaborative information behavior are reviewed first before the methods used in and findings from their research are presented. The methods used to collect have been primarily those associated with ethnographic field-work, with data analyses informed by a grounded theory approach. Findings relate to the collaborative information behavior of patient care teams in the Surgical Intensive Care Unit of a large urban teaching hospital, and of personnel in the Emergency Department of a small rural non-teaching hospital. They discuss how collaborative information behavior occurs when there are breakdowns in information flow that trigger a need for information (e.g. unavailability of anticipated information, incorrect or incomplete information, or information delivered to the wrong person). The reasons for why people collaborate in responding to this need include: the complexity of the need, a lack of immediately accessible information, a lack of domain expertise, and fragmented information resources. The roles of communication and of technological support in collaborative information behavior are also highlighted. A collaborative information behavior model is presented, and an evaluation of a prototype collaborative information retrieval system discussed. The chapter concludes with outlining the lessons learnt from their research.

Information sharing is deemed a positive feature of an organization's information culture. Reference to information sharing is often rhetorical however. Ikeya, Awamura and Sakai's chapter provides a detailed empirical example of how a work practice can be first investigated and then transformed by re-designing the methods used to share information. Collaborative in relation to information can often lie hidden, embedded and unobserved in broader activities and tasks. Adopting a naturalistic approach informed by ethnomethodology, the authors describe, model, and transform the task-based information sharing activities of a group of IT product hardware designers. Data for the study were collected from transcripts of the group's weekly meetings. The authors first describe the management-designed and initiated model of information sharing that they encountered, which they called a document-based individual task management model. This model was found to be ineffective in a number of ways including insufficient embedding of information sharing in the work practices of the team's members; its occurrence within the context of a reporting relationship between worker and group leader; and an individualized method of task status updating that was problematic for coordinating information sharing at the weekly meetings. The authors describe how users were engaged in the re-design of their work practice and the implementation of a collaborative task management model. This included the utilization of communication sharing tools such as whiteboards and self-adhesive paper sheets for public display; a shift from reporting information to actively seeking and eliciting information from other participants; and a change in meeting style from an individual task management model to a sharing-and-coordinating-the-plan-of-the-day style. Through seeing information sharing from the team members' point of view and by engaging users in the re-design of their work practice the authors demonstrate how more effective information sharing can result.

Teams can operate of course in both face-to-face and online environments. Goggins and Erdelez address the information practices of completely online groups (COGs). In doing so they differentiate COGs from other types of groups, e.g. face-to-face groups FOSS groups and Wikipedia groups, hypothesizing that the opportunities for exchanging social information will be more constrained; that differences will exist in what coordination information is used; and that their often dispersed membership will mean that it is likely that different social networks and different sets of information sources will be accessed. The authors describe a study of collaborative information behavior during an online graduate student course on Computer Supported Collaborative Learning that utilized the Sakai collaboration and learning environment. Participants were forty-two students in eight groups and the methodology was informed by Information Horizons theory. Data for the study was collected via a combination of serial and critical incident interviews; and students were asked to describe their main sources of information and their experiences of finding information within and outside the course management system. On the basis of these interviews a taxonomy of information resources was drawn up that underpinned a further survey that participants to rank the significance of the information sources. Four collaborative information behavior themes were identified from their analysis: (i) groups as information resources in COGs (ii) tools to control collaboration (iii) rapid tool changes diffuse collaborative information behavior (iv) tools to constrain and focus collaboration. Goggins and Erdelez discuss their findings in relation to the collaborative information behavior of each and all groups; with the most commonly used resources ranked. The chapter concludes with identifying areas for future research into collaborative information behavior in COGs.

The investigation of collaboration and information in an educational context continues with Scown, who reports on a classroom innovation in which learners and tutor collaborate on the production of a video podcast. In doing so students also collaborate implicitly with other students in the generation and re-use of a digital educational library of learning objects. The topics of blended learning and podcast production are reviewed first, before some features of the broader university educational context relevant to the initiative (e.g. technologies, assessment, student competencies) are discussed. An innovative assignment that enables students to engage in the production of a video podcast is then introduced. Students were required to produce an original, focused, podcast of five to ten minutes in duration. Assumed benefits of the innovation included increased engagement with the subject; higher achievement; and a digital library of re-usable learning objects that is accessible by future cohorts of students. In evaluating the intervention, the reported benefits include a higher mean grade for those undertaking the podcast assignment compared to other assignments on the module; along with student feedback that indicated greater interest and engagement with the material, and increased an awareness of the communication possibilities when using podcasts. The chapter concludes with considering future research directions, and how the formation of a digital library can act as the basis for a learning community.

The chapter by Shah provides a review of concepts, design guidelines and tools relevant to developing systems that can support collaborative information seeking. Drawing on literature in computer-supported cooperative work, he proceeds to develop design guidelines for collaborative information seeking systems that are based on the notions of space-time, control, communication, and awareness. The costs and challenges of collaborative information seeking and their implications for systems designers are also discussed. Shah argues that a shift from individual to collaborative information seeking entails addressing not only some of the issues that previous research has identified in the design of groupware systems but also issues relating to collaborative costs, cognitive load, adaptation and learning. Criteria for evaluating collaborative information seeking are presented; and current systems implementations are reviewed e.g. *Ariadne*, *SearchTogether*, and *Coagmento*. The chapter concludes with identifying future challenges and research directions in the design of systems to support collaborative information seeking.

The final section contains chapters that explicitly address the role of language and communication in collaborative information behavior. In each chapter language and communication plays a preeminent role in the interaction; and is the main means through which collaboration and information sharing takes place. Hendrickson's chapter presents a case study of the use of computer-mediated communication in web-based journalism. Perspectives from organization theory, newsroom sociology, and new media are combined to provide a multi-theoretical approach to the values and interpersonal dynamics of a 'virtual newsroom'. Data for the study were gathered via observations, interviews, memos, and instant messages sent between editorial staff. Hendrickson reports how a move towards a virtual newsroom entails a shift in the way information is gathered for news stories, and how the informal use of instant messaging can promote greater creativity and community among journalists. She also recognizes that while some organizational routines are carried over from place-based to virtual newsrooms (e.g. accountability for stories, and deadlines), there appears to be greater scope for the promotion of personal values in the latter than in the former. A greater sense of flexibility and ethical norms also appears to be in play; factors that appear to derive more from the prior collective experience of the editors involved than any formal organizational structures. In sum, her chapter illustrates how a cross-disciplinary approach can be utilized to analyze the culture and communication relevant to coordinating the work of a virtual newsroom.

The chapter by Chalfen and Rich is one of two contributions relating to information sharing in the medical domain. As the authors explain the ideal collaboration between patient and doctor is one that leads to a common understanding of illness and shared responsibility for treatment plans and outcomes; a form of collaboration that is underpinned among other conditions by mutual requests for sharing information. The current state of medical economics and informatics is tipping the balance however towards a different mode of information gathering; one that improves the collection of medical data but sacrifices the gathering of important psychological and socio-cultural information that can also play a role in a patient's treatment plan and outcomes. The authors review previous collaborative and participative approaches to the use of media and its implementation in the medical domain. They then describe the protocols and methods of a collaborative approach to medical diagnosis and treatment called Video

Intervention/Prevention Assessment (VIA). In VIA the patient uses a video camera to record a personal narrative that acts as a window onto the patient's subjective experience of their illness, treatment, and wellbeing. While in non-participative methods the patient acts as a passive supplicant; in VIA the patient acts as a co-producer of a symbolic world of information shared by both patient and doctor. Evaluations of the VIA methodology from patient, carer, and doctor perspectives are also provided. The chapter concludes with demonstrating how VIA can inform the development of a more collaborative, and less paternalistic, relationship between doctor and patient-a relationship that benefits both parties as they work together to co-create a strategy for wellness.

Mckenzie's chapter provides a further contribution to understanding practices of information sharing within the medical domain. The chapter introduces the notion of interactional traces defined as "direct and indirect reference to people, organizations or interests outside the confines of the here-and-now clinical interaction". Mckenzie explains how these interactional traces serve a dual purpose; acting as resources for participants and as evidence for researchers to analyze the institutionally mandated 'whats' and interactional 'hows' of collaborative informing within a clinical setting. She then proceeds to demonstrate the value of an interpretive approach called 'analytic bracketing' that allows the researcher to draw simultaneously on a range of analytic strategies. The approach is illustrated by the use of analytic bracketing applied to practical examples taken from a data set of audio-recordings of the interactions of 40 midwife-client pairs. A multi-perspectival analysis of the interactional traces that occur in clinical talk results; one that oscillates between and plays off the different analytic strategies. The chapter concludes with future research directions in analyzing the whats and hows of institutionally mandated informing.

The systematic development of a coding schema consisting of a set of categories and codes that can be assigned to empirical examples of talk is a pivotal activity in the analysis of any study of language and communication. In doing so the researcher is able to generalize from empirical patterns and develop theoretical propositions. Foster discusses the development of a coding guide used for analyzing talk that occurs during educational information seeking. The chapter is organized around the steps of a structuring content analysis conducted in order to analysis the functions and forms of talk that occurred as learners discussed information sought and retrieved as part of cooperative learning activity called group investigation. These steps include the determination of materials, the application and characterization main and individual content-related categories; the construction of definitions, root examples and coding rules; empirical coding; if appropriate revision and amendment of the category system in the light of the empirical data; paraphrasing and summarization. The categories and characteristics of a language-based theory of learning, along with the types of collaborative talk that occurred, are described. The chapter contains empirical examples of each theoretically informed category relevant to a sequential analysis of the talk that occurs during educational information seeking. The coding guide therefore functions to enable the precise and reliable assignment of codes and categories for any future analyses. The chapter concludes with considering the implications of the guide for research in educational information seeking.

In summary, the reader will find that the chapters in the book explore a number of themes relevant to collaboration with, through, and in relation to information; and the systems and practices that support this. Key conditions for collaborative information behavior to occur include the sharing of a common information and communications environment and increasing levels of user engagement in information processes and production. Understanding how these conditions contribute to the collaborative information behavior that occurs in particular contexts is what the individual chapters now address.

REFERENCES

Case, D.O. (2007). *Looking for information*: *A survey of research on information seeking, needs, and behavior*, Second edition. London: Academic Press.

Dervin, B. & Nilan, M. (1986). "Information needs and uses". In: Williams, M.E. (Ed.) *Annual Review of Information Science and Technology*, 21, 3-33.

Sunstein, C.R. (2006). *Infotopia*: *How many minds produce knowledge*. Oxford: Oxford University Press.

Surowiecki, J. (2005). *The Wisdom of crowds*: *Why the many are smarter than the few*. London: Abacus.

Acknowledgment

The chapters in this collection provide evidence in support of the fact that collaborative information behavior is a theme of current interest to researchers and practitioners from a number of different fields. Contributors to this collection work for example in the fields of information studies, computer-supported cooperative work, education, human-computer interaction, journalism, medicine, and internet research. Since the objective of the book was to co-ordinate contributions from a number of fields in order to support a more common understanding of the issues, problems, and opportunities of studying collaborative information behavior, I am very grateful to the chapter authors, and reviewers for taking the plunge,and setting sail in cross-disciplinary and interdisciplinary waters. If the book goes some way to providing others with some of the conceptual, methodological, analytical, and technical tools that can be used to navigate these waters then it will have fulfilled its purpose. I would also like to thank IGI Global for their efficiency in bringing the collection to publication.

Jonathan Foster
University of Sheffield, UK

Section 1
Collaborative Information Behavior in Large Groups

Chapter 1
Cultivating the Value of Networked Individuals

Wolf R. Richter
University of Oxford, UK

David A. Bray
Massachusetts Institute of Technology, USA

William H. Dutton
University of Oxford, UK

ABSTRACT

The Internet and related digital networking platforms facilitate searches for information and the sharing of information and expertise among individuals. In recent years, these behaviours evolved from focusing on information retrieval and sharing to include facilitation and coordination of collaborative problem-solving efforts and distributed co-creation of services and products. Such collaborations, supported by digital networks, often extend beyond the traditional boundaries of organizations and institutions, the social networks of small groups, the subjects of specific disciplines, and the geographic borders of nations. Consequently, they raise concerns over how to best manage networked individuals and realize the potential utility of their activities. This chapter builds on the findings of a series of case studies designed to explore such questions. From the results of these case studies the authors propose a framework for categorizing 'Collaborative Network Organizations' (CNOs); one that suggests that value emerges as a result of cultivating particular kinds of relationships and activities within these networks. The authors employ the term 'cultivation', instead of management, as the case studies indicated that such efforts often fail if managed too precisely or too restrictively in a "top-down" fashion. Instead, the provision of greater latitude and "bottom-up" autonomy to the individuals involved characterized the more successful CNOs we studied. In addition, the success of CNOs depended on how such efforts reconfigured information and communication flows in ways that supported distributed sharing, generation, or co-creation of content within a wide variety of collaborative contexts, ranging from the conduct of scientific research to problem-solving in business and everyday life. Directly attempting to manage or control CNOs can undermine these networks, whereas indirectly influencing and cultivating desired behaviours and activities can encourage the expansion of productive networking. The authors offer this theoretical framework as a means for better capturing the mechanisms governing collaborative behaviour.

DOI: 10.4018/978-1-61520-797-8.ch001

INTRODUCTION: UNDERSTANDING THE VALUE OF NETWORKED INDIVIDUALS

The adoption and diffusion of the Internet and Web and related applications has greatly expanded the opportunities for distributed collaboration among individuals by facilitating the sharing of information and expertise across geographical and organizational boundaries. The collaborative creation of Wikipedia to a level comparable in quality to the *Encyclopaedia Britannica,* illustrates the potential for open co-production of a new product. Another prominent example is provided by 'open source software' (OSS) development, where individual programmers collaborate in producing software without receiving immediate financial rewards (Weber 2004). This productive activity defies conventional wisdom about the necessary incentive structures required for the production of high-quality computer software. Yet not all OSS efforts succeed. There have been major successes (e.g. the Linux operating system) and many failures.

A growing number of researchers view these kinds of developments as illustrating, in part, the value of tapping into the 'wisdom of crowds' – the idea that instances can occur where a large number of 'ordinary' people can outperform a few experts by sharing information and solving problems together (Surowiecki 2004). Our research sought to assess critically such a premise through a series of case studies designed to examine a wide spectrum of what we initially dubbed 'distributed problem-solving networks' and later, after a series of collaborative workshops to assess critically the analysis and comparative effectiveness of the different networks, dubbed CNOs (Chui et al 2009). Our case studies focused on identifying: (1) the governance and incentive structures inherent in the design of these networks, (2) the appropriation mechanisms for the distributed value produced by the networked participants, and (3) success of such networks in terms of various performance

measurements. A key objective for our studies included development of a model linking the structure, incentives, and processes of these networks to their associated performance outcomes, so that we could then assess when and where the activities of a metaphorical 'crowd' translated into outcomes of value to key participants.

This chapter starts by examining historical precedents to the new socio-technical organizational forms identified in our research, which we have called Collaborative Network Organizations or CNOs (Dutton 2008). We define a typology formulated through retrospective analysis of our case studies, followed by an outline defining how each case study fits into this framework. The findings emphasize the important role played by forms of governance in gaining value from CNOs. Our chapter concludes by developing two themes that arose from the case studies: (1) 'cultivating the wisdom of networked individuals' represents a more significant metaphorical lens than the notion of the wisdom of crowds; and (2) governance approaches of CNOs depend on the ways CNOs reconfigure access to information and people – i.e., the type of CNO they define.

HISTORICAL PRECEDENTS FOR COLLABORATIVE NETWORK ORGANIZATIONS

The emergence of CNOs represents the latest stage in a forty-year thread of initiatives using computer-based systems to harness distributed expertise. For example, the RAND Corporation developed Delphi techniques in the 1960s to reduce the bias created by influential individuals in the social dynamics of co-located face-to-face groups of experts. Difficulties in soliciting thoughtful responses from experts undermined the perceived value of such techniques, but they remain in use in a variety of contexts.

The potential for computer-based communication networks to enable the sharing of expertise accelerated the drive towards distributed collaboration in the 1970s, to include computer conferencing (Hiltz and Turoff 1978), group decision-support systems, and later initiatives around computer-supported cooperative work (CSCW). The diffusion of personal computers across organizations also led to conceptions of 'groupware', computer-supported collaborative work and other digital applications to network individuals and personal computers within and across organizations in the 1980s and 1990s (Johansen 1988; Grudin 1995; and Sproull and Kiesler 1995).

Since 1995, rapid adoption and diffusion of the Internet has expanded the range of opportunities for distributed working and the sharing of information and expertise, leading to increasing confidence in the potential benefits of collaborative networking. For instance, 'Web 2.0' applications include a wide range of proposals for employing 'user-generated content' and greater collaboration across a number of sectors, from social networking to corporate communication and scientific research. However, since these networks of individuals often span and seldom conform to organizational and institutional boundaries (Dutton and Eynon 2009), many organizations have questioned whether or not they can capture real value from these networks.

THE RESEARCH METHODOLOGY: EXPLORATORY CASE STUDIES

To address these performance issues, we conducted a series of case studies in a wide variety of fields, including high-energy physics, biomedical sciences, IT software, and filmed entertainment, among others. These case studies sought to provide empirical evidence to ground debate over the performance of CNOs and the merit behind increasing practitioner support of such collaborations.

We began by identifying projects, such as Wikipedia, widely associated with peer-produced, distributed problem-solving. We then sought novel cases that employed different approaches in other

areas of application, ranging from scientific collaboration to film production. For example, after scanning the horizon for an overview of distributed co-creation in global media and entertainment industries, we focused on one case that we could explore in depth.

Grouping the cases into categories of approaches to 'distributed problem-solving', our initial conceptualization, represented a critical step. Assessing the performance of these networks led us to a conceptual framework and our methodology. A six-month exploratory study linked a review of extant literature to our case studies and employed a series of collaborative workshops to assess critically the analysis and comparative effectiveness of the different networks, which we reconceptualised as CNOs.

All the case studies of this research project involved original research by members of the research team. The team had direct access to the initiators of the respective CNOs and used a range of methods including elite interviews, participatory observation, and quantitative analysis of forum posts for data collection. The goal of each case study was to identify performance indicators, quantify them if possible, and relate the observations on the CNO's structure to the findings on its performance (Dutton 2008; Chui et al 2009).

A FRAMEWORK FOR COLLABORATIVE NETWORK ORGANIZATIONS

Each CNO we studied reconfigured how individuals connected with one another; specifically who communicated what, to whom, and when, within the network. This represented a prominent design feature across all CNOs that emerged from our analyses. The case studies also demonstrated less value in viewing participants as a 'crowd', since CNOs regulated interactions among networked individuals. Such regulation occurred, in part, through the architecture of the network.

In most of these networks, a small minority of 'core participants' made a majority of activities within the network. Consequentially, characterizing these networks by the activities they supported, rather than the purposes they served – which were many and shifting – represented a better way to categorize different CNOs (which explains why we refer to them as 'Collaborative Network Organizations', instead of our original view of as 'distributed problem-solving networks').

Our resulting framework distinguishes three types of CNO characterized by: (1) the type of information shared, (2) the tools used for collaboration, (3) the management structures inherent in these networks, and (4) the locus of the Intellectual Property Rights (IPR). Table 1 summarizes the three categories of CNOs we identified, although most networks blend aspects of each ideal type.

CASE STUDIES

This section describes two of the twelve case studies conducted within our project as a means for demonstrating the various features of the three network categories. Given a significant amount of extant research regarding CNO 1.0 organizations, which focus on sharing information, we focus our discussion on one type CNO 2.0 example and one type CNO 3.0 example, placing particular emphasis on the governance strategies found in the

networks. We find that the governance strategies differ significantly regarding CNO Architecture, Openness, Control, and Modularization.

- Sermo represents a platform for medical practitioners, who share medical knowledge and information. Sermo exemplifies primarily a CNO 2.0 approach, employing social networking tools to elicit responses from and facilitate interaction among the community.
- A Swarm of Angels (ASOA) represents a project led by Brighton-based film producer Matt Hanson, who gathered a community to co-author and co-produce a full-length feature film. ASOA's exemplifies a CNO 3.0 approach, mediating discussions about the production and the sharing and co-creation of its components through a set of collaboration tools.

SERMO

Sermo facilitates the development of a community of physicians to both contribute and filter professional expertise. In addition, pharmaceutical firms, insurance companies, government agencies, or other potential problem-holders can pay to ask questions, and to see the answers their own questions and to questions raised independently

Table 1. Three categories of CNOs, adapted from Dutton (2008)

Type	Characteristic
CNO 1.0	*Sharing:* Transmitting and linking of objects in a distributed network context, thereby reconfiguring access to information. Tim Berners-Lee's invention of the Web to share documents at CERN exemplifies such an enabling network. Of note, the idea of a 'semantic Web' to support more intelligent search, linkage, and retrieval of information further advances the conceived abilities of such a network.
CNO 2.0	*Contributing:* Employing group and social networking applications of the Web to facilitate communication, thereby reshaping who contributes information to the collective group. The aggregation of judgments in information markets or joint rating systems like Digg News represent typical examples for this type of network.
CNO 3.0	*Co-creating:* Collaborating through networks that facilitate cooperative work toward shared goals, thereby reconfiguring the sequencing, composition, and role of contributors. Joint writing and editing of Wikipedia exemplifies such an enabling network.

by community members. Participating physicians remain anonymous but other physicians can 'peer-review' postings by providing qualitative comments and quantitative scores, creating a reputation assessment for each participant linked to her or his contribution. Figure 1 illustrates Sermo's model.

Sermo's Governance Structure

As of February 2009, any U.S. physician could join Sermo (Latin for 'conversation'). The company asked those who wished to join the network to provide information that enabled Sermo to authenticate the individual as a legally registered physician. By vetting prospective community members, Sermo represented an Internet-enabled, closed-community of experts within their specific field. In terms of an instrumental aim, Sermo has sought to facilitate valuable conversations – the sharing of observations and knowledge – about healthcare and medical practices. At the same time, in terms of a social aim, Sermo sought to foster a distributed group sense of a 'community of peers' among participating physicians. Through our research, we found this shared sense of a 'community of peers' critical to Sermo's successful growth and continued community participation.

Extant research has found that closed-communities of experts can exceed the performance of more open or more democratic communities when identifying previously unknown solutions to relevant problems (Galbraith 1982; March 1991). That said, this body of research also demonstrates the need for a requisite level of diversity within a complex adaptive system if the system confronts emergent, unforeseen concerns (Daft and Wiginton 1979; Weick and Roberts 1993; Anderson 1999). Balancing the closed nature of its medical community with a need for diversity of insights represented one governance challenge for the Sermo community model. This echoes a

Figure 1. Sermo's information flow model (Source: www.sermo.com)

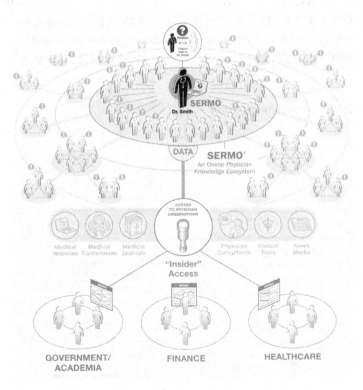

similar need for a diversity of opinion suggested by Surowiecki (2004), however Sermo differs in that it does preclude the opinions of physicians from being influenced by other physicians.

Sermo's Decision Making

As of February 2009, Sermo continued to grow at a rate of more than 700 new members per week. An average of 15-20% of members participated on a weekly basis, with active users averaging more than one hour on the site per week. As recorded by client company posts, Sermo had more than once succeeded at generating more than 1,000 physician responses (out of their current company of about 25,000) in less than four hours (Bray et al. 2008).

When starting a question or survey within Sermo, a participating physician would post a general text introduction and then generate a series of survey questions (check one, check all that apply, etc.), as per Figure 2. Using a 'folksonomy' of user-generated tags, the poster would select appropriate tags for the article, which allowed Sermo to search across different posts related to similar symptoms, diseases, drugs, or other topical themes. The poster would also pick a category from a pre-defined list of topics. Sermo did not charge a physician to post or answer a question; but did charge third parties to post questions or view answers to questions. Our interviews and observation of the site suggested that physicians chose to participate through a multiple set of incentive mechanisms, which included: (1) the perceived value of the information they could gain through access to the site, (2) a sense of enjoyment through interacting with peers, (3) profit from rewards offered by Sermo, (4) a normative sense of community among their fellow participating physicians, and (5) through self-interest gained by demonstrating knowledge within their field – even though Sermo employed the use of pseudonyms among participating physicians.

Sermo's Model for Collecting and Distributing Resources

All physicians on the network could view and respond during a set two-week period (which started with the posting of a survey question). Options for physicians responding included: answering the survey questions directly by clicking on a set of multiple choice responses, writing a more descriptive comment as a textual narrative (visible to all who view the question in real-time), perform-

Figure 2. Composing a sample survey question

ing both actions, or opting to ignore the survey completely. Sermo tracked physician comments by the pseudonym of the physician responding, enabling someone to link back to the personal profile of the responding physicians, along with their specialties, reported areas of expertise and interest, the date and time they joined, and previous posts to the Sermo network. Of note, the participating third parties, distinct from the community of physicians, could not vote, post comments, or respond to surveys.

Physician surveys would end after the two-week period, at which time all participants on Sermo could view the results of the survey. While the community would not see the results of the survey until the end of the two-week period, the posting physician would receive real time feedback as other physicians posted responses, enabling them to obtain almost immediate knowledgeable feedback.

Extant research into decision-support systems demonstrates that the early answers posited by experts do not represent necessarily the best answer to a problem – moreover, if others in a closed system see these early answers, their own answers may skew towards this initial answer, at the risk of sacrificing a better, different answer (Eisenhardt 1989; Kling 1991). Sermo confronted this challenge of an "information cascade bias" by not disclosing the results of the survey until the end of the two-week period. Nevertheless, the immediate response to the poster provided early reward to those taking the time to post questions.

In addition to answering queries, physicians could rate any post (a question or a response), indicating their perceived importance and interest in the post. Sermo asked physicians to give high ratings to "well written, unique, [and] illuminating" posts; conversely that physicians would give low ratings to "redundant [or] inappropriate" posts. This mechanism allowed community members to filter and weight knowledge of the CNO in ways that could help users to discern valuable signals from noise. Additionally, physicians could post

general discussion items to include conversations relating to a journal or news-related article or debates relating to medicine and healthcare issues (to include policy-related as well as political concerns). These posts, too, allowed physicians to provide votes, comments, and ratings.

Sermo's Legal Framework

Sermo services raised normative and ethical concerns over knowledge aggregation and discussion. For example, physicians could attempt to profit from their participation in Sermo, such as by promoting a specific interest or client company. Therefore, Sermo asked its participants to disclose any conflicts of interest when participating in the community. This included the requirement that physicians posting to the Sermo forum should disclose any potential for bias or financial conflict of interest to allow physicians to consider this background when forming their medical decisions; for example, when considering any proposed "off-label" uses of medication. Sermo stressed to community members that full disclosure of all biases or conflicts help assure that doctors prescribing "off-label" treatments would exercise independently informed medical judgment.

An additional concern included the responsibility of physicians both to protect the anonymity of their patients and to report diseases to local and state health departments as required, not only to Sermo. The CNO advised all participants not to discuss identifying patient information with other physicians online, which U.S. physicians already knew not to do. Sermo also advised all participants to "file all legally required forms with local health authorities." For example, if a physician observed a communicable disease that legally required reporting to public health authorities, Sermo advised them to do so. Reporting an infectious disease on Sermo would not satisfy any public reporting requirements.

Lastly, with regard to malpractice concerns, Sermo asked those accessing information through the CNO to recognize it as a forum for the free exchange of scientific information, but that physicians must assume full responsibility for their use of the information.

A SWARM OF ANGELS

A Swarm of Angels (ASOA) represents an 'open source' movie project (Cassarino and Geuner 2008, Cassarino and Richter 2008). ASOA aims to create and distribute a £1 million feature film using the Internet to engage a global community of members. Matt Hanson, a film director based in Brighton, UK, started the project in January 2006. He sought to gather people from around the world who wished to take part in making a movie. His artistic focus was on "creativity/passion/curiosity" oriented participation, as opposed to realizing a profit or ownership of a film. Moreover, he sought to distribute the final film 'for free' in the Richard Stallman sense of 'free' as in 'free speech' not as in 'free beer': His model allowed everybody access to use the movie or parts of the movie for further production, without seeking prior permission or payment. The ASOA license also allowed the non-commercial screening of the movie, but required an additional license for commercial exploitation (Cassarino and Richter 2008).

ASOA strove to open all dimensions of movie production, including the co-creation of content, the co-funding of the production, and the free distribution of the final products, including work-in-progress. Intentionally, the ASOA production model embodied, according to Hanson, "a valid new alternative, maybe more enlightened" to the Hollywood entertainment world. He didn't want ASOA to be "a massively distributed investment opportunity". Rather, "I'm for ROE (Return On Entertainment) rather than ROI (Return On Investment). Maximising ROI would likely clash with an artistic decision".

To realize his vision, Hanson needed an 'angel' to sustain a groundbreaking movie-making proj-

ect – the answer arrived in the form of gathering a virtual 'Swarm of Angels'. Collaborators paid a small fee (25 GBP) to join the project. The project's members possessed exclusive rights to participate in the decision-making process through a web-based polling system. They were also entitled to participate in the script editing and all other creative processes through an online discussion forum and a wiki platform.

While a number of film projects have attempted to employ a 'many producers/investors route', ASOA represents one of the first projects to tap the wisdom of the producer/investor community to shape and create the actual film.

Governance Structure

ASOA's governance model claimed to be 'open', however, research by our colleagues, (Cassarino and Geuna 2008) found that this does not mean flat or unstructured. Hanson referred to himself as a 'benevolent dictator', borrowing a definition usually applied to leaders of big software projects run using an "open source" approach (Ljungberg 2000).

Hanson's daily responsibilities included keeping the 'Swarm' together. He also was the most active contributor, by an order of magnitude. One ASOA member interviewed acknowledged the importance of Hanson's leadership and did not feel constrained by it. When asked, ASOA angel Marc commented:

"I think strong leadership is needed in any collaborative project. Most decisions made throughout the lifecycle of the project are subjective decisions, there is no right or wrong. The project could never finish unless there is someone at the top with the ability to make the final decisions. In my experience with directing live theatre, it's always been important for me to have a firm vision of the project. Collaboration is always well and good, but when a difference of opinion starts to get out of hand, it's for everyone's benefit the director to be able to say 'that's my decision, let's move on.'"

While the leader had no 'formal' authority, Matt Hanson enjoyed substantial 'real' authority. In this aspect, the governance structure of ASOA embodied that of many other open source projects (Lerner and Tirole 2005). That said, an attempt to decentralize management responsibilities with ASOA appeared in February 2008; when Hanson shared part of his administration tasks with a committee of four 'Archangels'. The appointment of the 'Archangels' helped to create a more rapid decision making process, keep a more consistent drive for the project, and monitor and blog on particular task areas (Cassarino and Richter 2008).

ASOA possessed four distinct levels of contribution. The first level involved leadership of the various tasks. As the project's entrepreneur, Matt Hanson assumed this role as the main leader and coordinator, despite the existence of a meritocratic system similar to that evidence in many open source software communities. The second level included contributions to tasks related to content production. The third level included forum attendance and occasional postings. The fourth level of contribution involved participation in the ASOA voting polls.

With respect to actual levels of participation across the community, the ASOA primarily involved occasional posts by most participants. A core group, which represented 5% of all angels, created 80% of the contributions, as measured by number of posts to the ASOA forums by November 2007 (Cassarino and Geuna 2008).

ASOA Decision-Making

ASOA employed a polling system for the majority of its decisions. Typical polls included critical aspects of project management, such as how to deal with the project's timeline, with rewarding members of the community, or with projecting profits likely from film distribution. Critical points in the development process also employed polls to make decisions, such choosing the trailer, the soundtrack, or the poster for the film. Every Angel could start a voting session about a particular issue.

The electronic platform allowed people to post on the forum and provided a convenient tool for enabling anyone to initiate a poll. Of the 21 polls, Angels initiated 6, with the remainder initiated by Hanson. Hanson accepted the outcome of polls as the final decision, even if it differed from his personal preference. Though Hanson possessed veto power, he had not exercised such power as of February 2009, when our team's study concluded.

ASOA's Model for Collecting and Distributing Resources

The Angels represented the initial and primary source of funding for ASOA. ASOA planned to release its final products under a Creative Commons license, which allowed free sharing for private uses and monetization of commercial use.

The ASOA financial model deviated from the Wikipedia model. With Wikipedia, the Wikimedia Foundation sustained the project based on donations. Contributing funding to a Foundation like Wikimedia to support the good cause represents a different kind of contribution decision, compared to submitting or editing an entry in Wikipedia. With Wikipedia, the two groups, donors and contributors, may or may not be overlapping, but there is no necessary linkage between the two. In contrast, ASOA's donors and contributors are the same individuals.

ASOA also deviated from the traditional model of a feature film crew. Feature film crews often include a small group of actors and the director. Yet in reality, actors and the director represent only the pinnacle of a large group of people working together to create a film, including writers, audio, video, and light technicians, costume designers, editors, lawyers and many others. All these people provide complementary capabilities. In addition, movie production encompasses several small parts and the corresponding small production processes, each one of them requiring different competences. For example, film pre-production involves the selection of the cast, the crew, and the location, the realization of the trailer, the poster, the soundtrack and so on. These steps embody even smaller, elementary steps with the possibility for reuse and remixing of almost all of these smaller steps through a parallel distribution pattern, most notably the soundtrack.

The main feasibility conditions of a peer-production project are 'modularity' of the task and 'granularity' of the process (Benkler 2006; Lerner and Tirole 2002). ASOA aspired to be what Hanson called 'Remixing Cinema'. A preliminary analysis of the outputs released by the ASOA community until December 2007 showed that the community succeeded in defining and allocating elementary parts and smaller subtasks associated with producing a film. Consequentially, ASOA illustrates that the architecture of film products and the structure of the processes associated with film production, is suitable for co-production in a distributed way that would leverage a community of people with different skills and amounts of time to contribute in their hands.

ASOA's Legal Framework

Creating a free space of collaboration, in which material is contributed and shared with a common understanding of what is possible or desired, represents the predominant legal and organizational challenge for communities like ASOA (David and Spence 2003). The common understanding should cover what the individual contribution yielded during the production process as well as to the permissible and desired uses of the final product.

While ASOA did not primarily pursue a profit-maximizing goal, in order to achieve its mission and provide its contributors with the promised 'Return on Entertainment' (ROE), ASOA needed to manage its intellectual property rights. ASOA relied on a well-established licensing model, created and maintained by Creative Commons (CC). Under the CC's "Attribution, Non-commercial, Share alike" license, everybody could remix and share parts or the whole of the ASOA production for free for non-commercial purposes, provided appropriate credit was given to the author and any resulting material was shared under the same Creative Commons license (Cassarino and Richter 2008).

The CC framework provided a flexible and adaptable frame for the complex web of legal relationships between ASOA's contributors. A combination of legal and social norms allowed ASOA to address the issue of distributed control over the creation, based on agreed principles and exceptional arrangements negotiated with individual creators. A community of individuals with different needs and sensibilities, agendas, and motivations to contribute, provided the foundation for this web of legal and organizational relationships.

Although lacking the long-standing social practice of the open source software communities, the discussions in the ASOA forums demonstrated the emergence of a consensus around moving the CC framework into an operational legal and organizational framework for Open Content Movie production.

Matt Hanson seemed capable of keeping the movement ideologically unified, but in the mid-term, a set of codified principles, like those put down in the Free Software definition, seemed to represent the preferred solution to decentralize and broaden the discussion process. The dominance of proprietary standards in the media environment and in particular the lock-in of professionals to proprietary tools and standards through their training, poses a significant challenge to creating an 'Open Content Movie' production process.

Although not the only project in the 'Remixing Cinema' or 'Open Content Movie' space, ASOA embodied one of the most ambitious projects and the only one that addressed all aspects of film production under an 'open' paradigm: the co-creation of content, the co-funding of the production, and the free distribution of the final products.

DISCUSSION OF FINDINGS: CULTIVATING VS. MANAGING

A key theme emerging from analysis of our case studies was the significance of cultivating the wisdom of networked individuals'. The cases indicate that this represents a more significant metaphorical lens than the notion of the 'wisdom of crowds' alone, as the cases did not describe crowd phenomena, nor did they reveal strict management regimes. Specifically, the success of our cases, illustrated by both Sermo and ASOA, depended on how such platforms reconfigured information and communication flows for distributed sharing, generation, or co-creation of content linked in specific contexts, whether the production of an encyclopaedia or a film.

Each platform managed the contributions of individuals and expertise in ways that contributed to pre-determined designs, be they specific goals or more loosely defined meta-goals. The wisdom of these networks therefore seems to be located in the intelligence behind their design and governance. The providers could cultivate the patterns of behaviour and norms of use for their networks in ways that yielded useful outcomes through a variety of levers available to key participants. Table 2 suggests some of the key ways in which CNO platforms can cultivate contributions to encourage constructive contributions.

Approaches to the governance of CNOs also depended on the ways in which they reconfigure accessed to information and people – the type of CNO they defined (sharing, contributing, or co-creating). Because of this, a crucial step that influences the success of a CNO centres with the design or choice of architecture of the platform. This choice defines who participates in the network and the degree of openness adopted. For example, Sermo limited access only to registered physicians and ASOA requested contributors from anywhere to pay a modest fee.

Most networks have created a hierarchy of rights and privileges that determined who could do what within the network, enabling them to configure access to key resources in numerous ways. ASOA demonstrated how the interaction among community members created a sophisticated management hierarchy based on social norms, reputation, and trust. The governance structures of various CNOs varied, but several established more hierarchical than egalitarian arrangements for handling peer production. Even in the several CNOs that represented bottom-up communities (e.g. Sermo), usually a core authority existed responsible either for membership into the community or a core principle governing how the community 'plays the game' and interacts within the network and the larger networked world.

Finally, all the cases we investigated indicated that CNO platforms employ mechanisms to simplify tasks to make them manageable for individual participants with low incentive structures. Given the complex array of personal motives behind individual participation in these networks, a need to keep the cost of participation low exists. One major strategy in this area included modularizing the work in ways that did not overwhelm potential contributors. Table 2 summarizes the different cultivation strategies that were characteristic for CNOs of type 1.0, 2.0, and 3.0 in our cases.

Table 2. Summary of cultivation strategies

Mechanism	1.0 Sharing	2.0 Contributing	3.0 Co-creating
Architecture	One-Many	Many-to-Many	Many-to-One
Openness	Open	Networked	Managed
Control	Low	Moderate (Reputation)	High
Modularization	Low	Moderate (Simple Tasks)	High

The success and continued vitality of the networks explored in the case studies indicated that CNOs are likely to be of growing importance in the future, broadening to address multiple purposes. Understanding the key aspects of their design, structure and use that contributes most to the difference between success and failure represents a critical focus for research of relevance to both practice and theory. That said, despite their apparent potential, these networks do not represent an information Utopia. Many have failed, and even the best networks have faced major management challenges. A CNO approach does not assure success, and thus determinants behind the success vs. failure of CNOs pose critical issues faced by organizational leaders who wish to capture the value of these networks while avoiding unwarranted risks.

The Centrality of Cultivating Networked Individuals

CNOs represent networks of individuals who are free to choose whether and when to enter or exit a network at any point in time; hence, the emphasis on 'cultivating' such a network rather than applying the idea of directed management. CNOs can occur often as accidental associations initially, later defined by a shared group identity. Important activities that could influence the success of CNOs, suggested by our cases, include:

- Creating a critical mass of users; such users help sustain the network. Type 1.0 networks can succeed if open for all on the Internet, but many type 2.0 and 3.0 networks need to restrict participation. In order to limit or enlarge the size of a network, CNOs can regulate participation in a variety of ways, such as introducing formal or material qualifications for membership, introducing staged systems of privileges or opening up for a new cohort of participants at a later stage of development.

- Structuring tasks; akin to individuals structuring their 'to do' list. Incentive structures and information systems need to address issues surrounding the competition for users' limited attention, helping users filter and sort through important tasks. Which pages need editing? Which bugs need fixing? Which e-mails are important to read right now?

The Challenge of Building a Motivated Ecology of Contributors

The case studies focused on a small set of successful CNOs. As technologies for supporting these networks increase in power, confronting the crucial challenge of envisioning and constructing a strategy for developing a viable, value producing CNO *ecology* – i.e., the emergent, "bottom-up" formation of beneficial relationships and shared information within a CNO – represents a difficult challenge. Providing all stakeholders with clear 'wins' for participation represents one critical part of such a strategy; for example, physicians contributing to Sermo value the sense of community or the information and feedback they can obtain through the network, the platform provider values the success of the business model, and third-party sponsors value the early insights they achieve through the community.

People can choose to participate in distributed collaborative networks and can enter and exit at will. However, like organizations, assessing who benefits and who gains from such participation represents an important question to consider. Nicholas Carr argues that users of Web 2.0 platforms may be becoming a 'global pool of cut-rate labour' for the 'digital elite' in the age of the information utilities, such as search engines (Carr 2008). If users perceive themselves as exploited, they are unlikely to sustain their participation. In the cases we studied, the CNOs demonstrated benefits to a wide range of individuals – not simply their developers.

SOLUTIONS LOOKING FOR APPROPRIATE PROBLEMS

Many Internet-based platforms represent solutions for addressing a vast range of problems; however, not all problems appropriately align with such technologies. The legitimacy of problems will influence the alignment (or not) of problems to technologies. For instance, some potential applications may also represent ethically questionable activities (e.g. asking people to predict a human tragedy, such as an assassination). The need to simplify tasks to foster participation (e.g. creating an easily answered questionnaire) can place many practical limits on the quality of information obtained, and therefore the value of a CNO. For example, while Sermo might provide a complement to clinical trials, it is not a substitute for high-quality medical research.

CONCLUSION AND FURTHER RESEARCH

Our case studies underscored the diversity of platforms for distributed problem-solving, leading us to a framework for categorizing 'Collaborative Network Organizations'. A second theme was the degree that the value of CNOs depends on the strength and vibrancy of emergent relationships and useful activities within these networks. Consequentially, we opted to employ the term 'cultivation' instead of 'management' as such efforts often fail if managed too precisely or too restrictively in a "top-down" fashion. For example, the concept of cultivation has been used in similar ways in an analysis of the evolution of communities of practice (Wenger et al 2002), which share some attributes with CNOs, suggesting the generality of this theme beyond the cases examined in the present study. Networked efforts often succeed with the provision of freedoms and loose autonomy to the individuals involved. The

framework we have proposed suggests that the success of such networks depends on how their efforts reconfigure information and communication flows for distributed sharing, generation, or co-creation of content within specific problem-solving contexts.

We have outlined several cultivation strategies evident from our case studies of 1.0, 2.0, and 3.0 CNOs within our framework, which represent different mechanisms of collaboration – sharing, contributing, and co-creating – and which require adequate community architecture as well as adjusted approaches to openness, control, and modularization. With this analytical approach, we have suggested that CNOs represent structured networks of individuals, which can and have to be cultivated to create the valuable output for the range of participants critical to their success.

There are of course many limitations of any set of case studies at a particular point in time. Moreover, the cultivation strategies we found *ex post* merit translation into actionable recommendations to support the design and creation of such networks *ex ante*. Comparative research with traditional forms of knowledge creation, with more familiar sources of expertise and modes of problem solving, could offer one way to take this research forward. We believe the frameworks arrived at through our cases can inform and structure a variety of research on this new approach to Internet-enabled distributed collaboration. Future research might benefit from analyzing attempted CNOs that have failed to attract a critical mass of contributors to validate the identified cultivation strategies against counterexamples. Studies of failures raise different problems, since many failed systems are over-determined, with many rival explanations for the outcome. Nevertheless, it will be important to look beyond the success cases examined in this chapter to develop move the suggested cultivation strategies into blueprints for the design of future CNOs.

ACKNOWLEDGMENT

This research was supported by a joint project with McKinsey & Company's McKinsey Technology Initiative. The fieldwork of the Sermo case study was conducted by David Bray and the fieldwork for the ASOA case study by Irene Cassarino, Polytechnic of Turin. We thank these colleagues for their contributions to these cases and this synthesis paper. The full case studies are available as OII working papers on SSRN (http://www.ssrn.com/link/Oxford-Internet-Institute-RES.html).

REFERENCES

Anderson, P. (1999). Complexity Theory and Organization Science. *Organization Science*, *10*(3), 216–232. doi:10.1287/orsc.10.3.216

Benkler, Y. (2006). *How Social Production transforms Markets and Freedom*. New Haven, CT: Yale University Press.

Bray, D., Croxson, K., Dutton, W., & Konsynski, B. (2008). *Sermo: An Authenticated, Community-Based, Knowledge Ecosystem* (OII DPSN Working Paper No. 7). Oxford, UK: University of Oxford, Oxford Internet Institute. Retrieved from http://ssrn.com/abstract=1016483.

Carr, N. (2008). *The Big Switch: Rewiring the World, From Edison to Google*. London: W. W. Norton and Company.

Cassarino, I., & Geuna, A. (2008). *Distributed Film Production: Artistic Experimentation or Feasible Alternative? The Case of a Swarm of Angels* (OII DPSN Working Paper No. 14). Oxford, UK: University of Oxford, Oxford Internet Institute. Retrieved from http://ssrn.com/abstract=1326510.

Cassarino, I., & Richter, W. (2008). Swarm creativity. The legal and organizational challenges of open content film production (DIME Working Paper No. 45). In Andersen, B. (Ed.), *DIME Working Papers on Intellectual Property Rights*. London: Birkbeck College.

Chui, M., Johnson, B., & Manyika, J. (2009). *Distributed Problem-Solving Networks: An Introduction and Overview* (OII DPSN Working Paper No. 18). Oxford, UK: University of Oxford, Oxford Internet Institute. Retrieved from http://ssrn.com/abstract=1411739.

Daft, R., & Wiginton, J. (1979). Language and Organization. *Academy of Management Review*, *4*(2), 179–191. doi:10.2307/257772

David, P., & Spence, M. (2003). *Towards an institutional infrastructure for e-Science: the scope of the challenge* (Research Report No. 2). Oxford, UK: University of Oxford, Oxford Internet Institute. Retrieved from http://ssrn.com/abstract=1325240.

Dutton, W. H. (2008). The Wisdom of Collaborative Network Organizations: Capturing the Value of Networked Individuals. *Prometheus*, *26*(3), 211–230. doi:10.1080/08109020802270182

Dutton, W. H., & Eynon, R. (2009). Networked Individuals and Institutions: A Cross-Sector Comparative Perspective on Patterns and Strategies in Government and Research. *The Information Society*, *25*(3), 198–207. doi:10.1080/01972240902848914

Eisenhardt, K. (1989). Making Fast Strategic Decisions in High-Velocity Environments. *Academy of Management Journal*, *32*(3), 543–576. doi:10.2307/256434

Galbraith, J. (1982). Designing the Innovating Organization. *Organizational Dynamics*, *10*(3), 4–25. doi:10.1016/0090-2616(82)90033-X

Grudin, J. (1995). Groupware and Social Dynamics, 762-774. In R. M. Baecker, J. Grudin, W. A. S. Buxton & S. Greenberg (Eds.), Readings in Human-Computer Interaction: Toward the Year 2000. San Francisco, CA: Morgan Kaufmann.

Hiltz, R., & Turoff, M. (1978). *The Network Nation*. Reading, MA: Addison-Wesley.

Johansen, R. (1988). *Groupware: Computer Support for Business Teams*. New York: The Free Press.

Kling, R. (1991). Cooperation, Coordination and Control in Computer-Supported Work. *Communications of the ACM, 34*(12), 83–88. doi:10.1145/125319.125396

Lerner, J., & Tirole, J. (2002). Some Simple Economics of Open Source. *The Journal of Industrial Economics, 50*(2), 197–234.

Lerner, J., & Tirole, J. (2005). The Economics of Technology Sharing: Open Source and Beyond. *The Journal of Economic Perspectives, 19*(2), 99–120. doi:10.1257/0895330054048678

Ljungberg, J. (2000). Open Source movements as a model for organizing. *European Journal of Information Systems, 9*(4), 208–216. doi:10.1057/palgrave/ejis/3000373

March, J. (1991). Exploration and Exploitation in Organizational Learning. *Organization Science, 2*(1), 71–87. doi:10.1287/orsc.2.1.71

Sproull, L., & Kiesler, S. (1995). Computer, Networks, and Work. In Baecker, R. M., Grudin, J., Buxton, W. A. S., & Greenberg, S. (Eds.), *Readings in Human-Computer Interaction: Toward the Year 2000* (pp. 755–761). San Francisco, CA: Morgan Kaufmann.

Surowiecki, J. (2004). *The Wisdom of Crowds: Why the Many Are Smarter Than the Few and How Collective Wisdom Shapes Business, Economies, Societies, and Nations*. New York, NY: Doubleday.

Weber, S. (2004). *The Success of Open Source*. Cambridge, MA: Harvard University Press.

Weick, K., & Roberts, K. (1993). Collective Mind in Organizations: Heedful Interrelating on Flight Decks. *Administrative Science Quarterly, 38*(3), 357–381. doi:10.2307/2393372

Wenger, E., McDermott, R., & Snyder, W. M. (2002). *Cultivating Communities of Practice*. Cambridge, MA: Harvard Business School Press.

Chapter 2
Living with New Media Technology:
How the Poor Learn, Share and Experiment on Mobile Phones

Andrew Wong
Telenor Group Business Development and Research, Asia Pacific

ABSTRACT

This chapter considers the collective information behavior of the poor in Bangladesh. It examines the mobile phone as the central node and seeks to understand the construction of collectiveness by examining the collective-mediated learning, sharing and experimenting among the poor. Three brief cases provide the background and illustrate the elements of a Learn, Share and Experiment model. Against this tapestry of multiple perspectives, collective-mediated learning, sharing and experimenting enable the poor to be cost-efficient and socially productive. In conclusion there is an urgent need for all researchers to reexamine and rethink the poor's collective information behavior as new media technology spreads deeper into their lives. Without it, we may miss the opportunity to discover something useful that will eventually lift them out of poverty.

INTRODUCTION

Numerous debates already exist about the impact of new media technology on our everyday lives. The surge in popularity of the Internet in the mid-1990s and its coming of age pushes us to think more creatively in designing new tools for sharing and interacting with each other. The Internet is often touted as a tool for real time or near real time, anytime, anywhere connectivity.

Another new media technology often pronounced as the must-have tool for every common person is the mobile phone. Unlike the Internet or the traditional landline phone, the mobile phone is a space-time compression tool; you can call a person at any time and from any place to arrange a meeting (Ito, 2004; Ito, 2005; Ito, Okabe, & Anderson, 2007). The mobile phone is also often perceived as the more agile tool for connectivity and interaction (Markoff, 2009); and is also more pervasive due to its low cost of ownership and simple functionality (Nokia, 2008 & 2009).

DOI: 10.4018/978-1-61520-797-8.ch002

Discussion of the poor's appropriation and use of the mobile phone often accentuates the impact of the mobile phone as a work and life liberator, and how it enables poor people to enlarge their social network by means of connecting, synthesizing and applying information bits transferred in-between the mobile phones. To put it simply, in an economic and social sense, the mobile phone creates an opportunity space for the poor to lift themselves out of poverty (Hardy, 1980; Marker, McNamara, & Wallace, 2002; Aminuzzaman, Baldersheim, & Jamil, 2003; Abraham, 2007).

This chapter argues that the poor collaborate differently to make sense of this world, and they learn and share information somewhat differently from the more affluent members of society (Wong, 2007). In the developed world, we are drowning with information overload due to a constant flow of voice calls, SMSes, emails, instant messaging and information bits from social network sites (Wei & Kolko, 2005; Kolko, Rose, & Johnson, 2007). This is especially significant for the youth, amid new worlds for communication, friendship, play, and self-expression, known now as the 'digital youth' lifestyle (Ito et al, 2008). In such situations, information collaboration in a group can simply be a matter of managing information seeking, organizing and responding through suitable channels at a particular time (Kuhlthau, 1991; O'Neill, 2003; Hirsh & Dinkelacker, 2004; Javid & Parikh, 2006). In stark contrast, based on what I observed in fieldwork about how the poor learn and share information, they face *uncharted territory* on a daily basis. Not only is information limited; seeking information is problematic since not all information is readily formatted as complete information, or as actionable knowledge. Consequently, the poor need multiple information access points and the time to learn new things that are necessary for them to form the whole information picture (Narayan et al, 2000).

In what follows, a model of collective information behavior is presented, one that has its roots in constructionism and a social-interactional perspective. The collective term denotes the notion of togetherness; the collaborative term denotes the working together for a common purpose. In adopting this model, the process and perspectives of constructionism and a social-interactional perspective are not being rejected or ignored. Rather, a four-step model is introduced that incorporates elements of both constructionism and social-interactional factors and which is intended to act as an aid in explaining how collective information behavior among the poor occurs. The model assumes that collective-mediated learning and sharing (stage 1) initiates creative, synthesis, and cross-pollination activities within the group (stage 2). These activities function as an avenue to greater social interaction within the group. Following this, collective-mediated experimenting will occur primarily because of the confidence and trust in the group (stage 3). At this stage, the condition upon which the previous two stages build provides building blocks that are amenable to group experimenting, such as being willing to take risks and vocalizing opinions. While taking on a new path every time the group experiments, corresponding factors come into play: the creation of localized group knowledge and domestication of this knowledge into their everyday lives. Local ingenuity occurs primarily because the group, in a local setting, comes up with local invention and creativeness that is primarily suited to a local environment (stage 4).

The chapter is organized as follows. First, literature relating to prior work in collective information behavior, constructionism, technology domestication and social-interaction is reviewed. Second, the methodology and methods that inform the study are described. Third, findings from three case studies of the poor's use of the mobile phone are presented. Fourth, the Learn, Share, Experiment (LSE) model is introduced and its importance and applicability to understanding the poor's information needs and their steps to accessing the information via mobile phone discussed. Propositions for further research are also presented; and are developed particularly in relation to whether understanding of the poor's access to and use of mobile phone technology can be transferred to understanding the poor's search and use of information in the new media ecology e.g. their use of social network sites, video-sharing sites and other new worlds of communications such as instant messaging and twittering. Finally, the conclusion addresses how in order to bridge the digital divide it is important to include the perspectives of the poor in current and future debates around collective information and knowledge efforts in the digital age.

LITERATURE REVIEW

In the first section, the literature reviewed examines how the poor construct the world around them. Their information and knowledge construction differs from the rest of us who have the "luxury" of information overload. Here, the meaning-making of the poor through the processes and perspectives of constructionism and a social-interactional perspective is reviewed. Then, we further our discussion on how social constructionism influences collective information behavior. Finally, the case is made that how the poor collaborate for information and knowledge is a world apart. This is a point of departure in order for a case to be made that focuses on mobile phone domestication as a window through which to empathize with the collective information behavior of the poor.

The Poor's Construction of the World around Them: Perspectives from Social-Interactional and New Media Domestication

The poor construct their worldview differently from their richer counterparts. This is mainly due to economic and sociological constraints that impinge on their everyday lives. There are several explanations for this situation. First, the

poor are trapped by infrastructural constraints such as a scarcity of electricity, limited public transportation, restricted communication options, along with limited entertainment options. Second, the poor are restricted by never-ending financial constraints and a set of inter-related challenges such as poor living conditions, low education, poor health, unskilled work and limited education opportunities. Third, the poor are reluctant and wary of trying out or learning new things. This third constraint is a particular point of interest for researchers since by examining the reasons as to why the poor are reluctant to learn new things, some logical reasoning behind their domestication and collective information behavior should be revealed.

Four explanations can be presented that connect the dots about how the poor construct their worldview within a collective information behavior perspective. First, their life is defined by daily survival on limited resources, mainly the struggle to have one or two meals a day. These subsistence conditions dictate the need for immediate gains. There is no reason for the poor person to spend his precious resources of time and money if what he or she has invested does not yield immediate benefits. There is a notion of what-I-see-is-what-I-believe. Second, what the poor learn must be actionable. From their perspective, there is no purpose in learning something new if whatever is learnt cannot be translated into something that can be acted upon. The mantra here is about learning quickly and acting on it so as to get rewarded quickly. Third, the poor have limited resources on their hands; therefore they need to spend their resources wisely. A strategy that is typically employed is to reuse the newly acquired knowledge for many different purposes. Fourth, the newly acquired knowledge must also be easily transferable to others. Ideally, the knowledge should be teachable in that it should be easily digestible by others; this is crucial for the poor as a means to building social capital within the local community through knowledge transfer (Goodman, 2007).

Now, let us apply these four explanations to the mobile phone domestication context and examine how the poor construct their world through the lens of the mobile phone. As evidenced in the earlier literature, the emergent role of the mobile phone in the lives of the poor is a defining moment for them. However, the poor are faced with many barriers to adoption and use e.g. low literacy, availability of sufficiently cheap mobile phones, affordability of per minute usage (Baliamoune-Lutz, 2003; Bell, 2005; Anderson, 2006; Adesope, Olubunmi, & McCracken, 2007; Deepak & Bhamidipaty, 2007). There are already plenty of anecdotes and real data indicating that the impact of mobile use in developing countries is not only pervasive in reaching even the poorest segments of the population; but also deep enough to touch on people's lives in every imaginable way, from alleviating poverty to acting as a source of entertainment during social hours (Castells, Qiu, Fernandez-Ardevol & Sey, 2007; Garbacz & Thompson, 2007). Research has demonstrated that the adoption and domestication of the mobile phone can have many positive socio-economic implications that are crucial to the poor's construction of the world around them (Weilenmann & Catrine, 2002; Taylor & Richard, 2003; Waverman, Meloria, & Melvyn 2005; Ovum, 2006; GSM Association, 2006). Silverstone, Hirsch and Morley (1999) describe how the encounter between human and machine and its domestication is a dialectic process. They distinguish four phases of domestication; namely: appropriation, which relates to practices of ownership and possession; objectification, which focuses on the object and its display in a spatial context; incorporation, which details uses and functions of an object in and over time; and lastly, conversion, which refers to the ways in which the object is employed as a currency for indicating membership in relations with the outside world. This line of thought was further developed by several researchers who have studied the domestication of technology in the home and expanded this to mobile phone and communication study (Silverstone, 1994 & 2005; Silverstone & Haddon, 1998; Lie & Sørensen, 1996). Following a similar line of thought, on the sequential phase of the technology domestication process, the social-interactional perspective informs us about interaction behavior unveiling itself over time. Bakeman and Gottman (1986) argue that through a sequential view, researchers will have the best chance of clarifying the dynamic nature of the social interaction processes that are involved.

A number of researchers have argued that the mobile phone is an extension of self (Cairncross, 1997; Yang, 2005; Vishwanath & Chen, 2008). The mobile phone acts as a communication, interaction and networking tool for most of us, since it acts as an aid in seamlessly performing multiple back-forth actions of communication, interaction and networking. In that sense, the mobile phone has been domesticated as "porous block" within people's everyday lives. The upside is that we are always connected. The downside is that we are supposed or expected to reply or offer feedback almost immediately.

The poor's construction of their worldview through the mobile phone is somewhat different. Their social structuring is defined by "small learning building blocks", constructed through small steps in learning how to make a call, type a SMS, among others. Their efforts of using the mobile phone are purposeful and task-specific, bounded mainly by the need to manage the cost per usage. So, rather than moving through multiple back-forth actions, they will tend to calculate the return on their invested money before making a call or writing an SMS. An important extension to such deliberate and task-specific action is the emergence of a shared mobile phone culture among the poor (Roldan, Wong, & Helmersen, 2007). This has an important implication for social power-geometry among the poor as it affects the need for the poor to stay in a group and conform to the rules of the group.

Social Constructionist Influences on Collective Information Behavior

Papert's constructionism theory focuses on 'learning to learn'. This theory centers on how people learn through engagement in their interaction with their own or other people's artifacts, and how these interactions encourage self-directed learning, and eventually spur the construction of new knowledge. Apart from the influence of media and context, one particular area stressed by the theory is the importance of tools in human development (Papert, 1970 & 1980). The poor have limited access to learning tools mainly due to the fact that in the subsistence environment that the poor exist in, they do not have much monetary resources for such access. In many instances, the poor learn in a shared learning environment and in one way, the social context in which the poor learn heavily influences their social constructions. The term social constructionism was used by Berger and Luckmann (1966) to highlight the importance for society of how individuals and groups interact. Interactions and reciprocal interactions between individuals and groups then become institutionalized and embedded into their everyday lives. Due to this interaction and reciprocal interaction, the poor do not learn in a linear format; rather it is a patchy network of learning: learning from various people from all walks of life, learning in an ad-hoc basis, learning mostly from trial-and-error. Indeed, there is a strong sense of flux and uncertainty whenever the poor are in a learning context.

The crux of the matter here is that the poor always look for common ground in collaboration to minimize uncertainty. It is important for them to find shared values, pay attention and give feedback to each other, and be willing to accept differences in the opinions of others. Durkheim (1893; 1897) also argued that the moral sense of the group is an important element; and that as the collective conscience originates with society he sought to detail the cause and effects of weakening group

ties (and henceforth a weakening of the collective conscience) on the individual.

The goal of this chapter has been to describe some of the specificities of collective information behavior of the poor. Although this section does not make comparisons with other countries, this review is an effort to depict the Bangladeshi case in order that others may make these comparisons against a richer society. Behind this approach is an argument against the debate about what is right and what is not right for the poor. The current debate postulates that new media technology will transform the lives of the poor, and that eventually it will be a factor that lifts them out of poverty.

METHOD

Bangladesh is a country with a population of 159 million; of this population only half is considered literate i.e. definition based on population percentage ages 15 and above. The rural dominate the social structure accounting for 63 percent of the population. There are more mobile subscribers (per 100 people) than landline with 21.7 and 0.7 respectively. This chapter draws from ongoing ethnographic research that integrates findings across all six divisions of Bangladesh and their use of the mobile phone in three different settings. One setting was to understand how the poor youth maximize the cost of using the mobile phone through creative use of SIM card switching and missed calls. Another setting was the study of the poor's early use of the mobile phone, and to a certain extent the Internet, for the purpose of income-earning opportunities. The third setting was the use of the mobile phone by the ultra-poor who are middle aged or elderly for the purpose of developing skills and practices. In these three environments, the objective was to understand the intricacies of individual and group life and to ask this simple question: How can the poor be connected to the world and what are the means for doing this? The central body of data behind this chapter is a set of observations and interviews collected between 2006 and 2008 (see Table 1 below). The definition of the poor is based on income segment: households with less than 7000 Takas (US$102) per month. For this study, the intention was to capture the everyday mobile use and domestication of particular individuals and groups. The adapted data collections methods are based on focus group, quantitative survey and snowballing interviews. All the interviews were conducted by the author with support from two other colleagues who have backgrounds in sociology and psychology. The key here is to understand the social reality of the poor by looking at people in a typical day and everyday setting. As Erickson (1977) posits:

By hanging around and watching people carefully and asking them why they do what they do

... in particular doings of people, qualitative researchers are reluctant to see attributes of the doing abstracted from the scene of social action and counted out of context (pp. 58).

After completion of the data collection in each of the three settings, analysis will begin by comparing these cases as a whole and developing a collective information behavior perspective and model that reflect the poor in their present state. Now we shall turn to the theoretical and conceptual framework.

FINDINGS

A question from a 25 year old Bangladeshi poor youth that I interviewed signals his uneasiness about his and his friends' future: "What in the

Table 1. Description of different case studies: Approach and sample

Setting	Brief description	Approach	Sample
SIM-switching	The study of creative use of SIM-switching and its social and economic implications	Focus group Quantitative survey	SIM-switching * 6 focus groups; ; typically lasted from 1.5 to 2 hours. * 1,600 multi-SIM users (quantitative survey)
Missed calls	The study of creative use of missed calls and its social and economic implications	Focus group	Missed call 8 focus groups; typically lasted from 1.5 to 2 hours.
Non-user and early users of mobile phone and Internet	The study of non-user and early use of mobile phone and Internet in the poor society and its implication towards designing better new service for them	Snowballing interviews of non-users, early users and the local stakeholders	* Interviewed various stakeholders with the local community of 25 villages and semi-urban areas; typically each interviews lasted from 15 minutes to 2 hours. * Observations typically run from 3 to a maximum of 4 hours due to informant's permission.
Ultra poor way of life and its related use of information and communication technology (ICT)	The study of ultra poor (or known as bottom-of-the-pyramid) society and their use and potential use of ICT in the agriculture-based sector	Snowballing interviews of the ultra poor and the local stakeholders namely in the agri-based sector.	* Interviewed various stakeholders with the local community of 15 villages and semi-urban areas; typically each interviews lasted from 15 minutes to 2 hours. * Observations typically run from 3 to a maximum of 4 hours due to informant's permission.

world is going on ... and where are we all heading to? My friends and I always need to find and make sense of everything; every day is so different." Here lies the crux of this chapter, which argues that the poor collaborate differently to make sense of the world. They seem to combine a multitude of information learning, sharing and experimenting activities to form the whole information picture. Thereafter, they use the information gathered to enhance their daily livelihood and productive capacity. As a result, knowledge empowers the poor and provides them with the opportunity to make their own informed choices as to what will work best for them.

This paper also contends that the collective information behavior of the poor is social learning-oriented in nature. Bandura (1977) argued that most human behavior is learned observationally through social learning modeling: from observing others, one forms an idea of how new behaviors are performed, and on subsequent occasions this coded information serves as a guide for action.

The samples of respondents in the three different cases focus more on collective-mediated learning, sharing and experimenting. As a collective unit, the poor gravitate towards collective-mediated learning and sharing in order to create, synthesize and cross-pollinate their recently acquired knowledge and experiences. These three stages are necessary for the poor as a preparation and preconditioning process to try out new experiences and to experiment with new things. This step before the "risk of leaping" forward to experiment with new things is crucial for the development of their own creativity and inventiveness and the advancement of local knowledge. With reference to ethnographic material, this paper explicates how this collective-mediated learning and sharing of the mobile phone operates in the everyday practices of poor people's mobile phone use; and how, more differently, different forms and functions of collective-mediated experimenting persist in different contexts of use, across different media channels and in different cultural ecologies.

By studying the phenomenon of collective-mediated learning, sharing and experimenting, and issues related to the poor's needs and constraints, a model is developed to explain poor people's collective information behavior, known in this research work as the Learn, Share and Experiment (LSE) model. This model, which is influenced by Papert's constructionism and a social-interactional approach, is built from the ground up based on empirical findings from the three specific case environments.

Findings from the Fieldwork

In this section, three case studies based on fieldwork studies are analyzed. The purpose of the analysis is to describe and illuminate the elements that concern the relationship between information collaboration and collective-mediated learning, sharing and experimenting. Ultimately the goal is to offer a set of propositions for consideration that are amenable for further study. A close examination of the case studies' details provides us with insight into phenomena that are often missed in the reliance on quantitative study.

Case 1: The Mobile Phone and Creative Ways of Saving Money

There are peculiarities to the poor Bangladeshi mobile phone use, particularly in the way they maximize minutes per call or per SMS. Most notable are the poor youth, who are the more frequent users of mobile phones. They depend on the mobile phone as their main communication tool. More than ever, they also use the mobile phone as a social tool to expand their network of friends. It used to be that they only communicated with those to whom they were close; however, the situation has changed. The way the poor youth communicate is no longer just a simple and direct call to another party. They have in a sense moved towards creatively manipulating the form and function of a mobile phone, or in a broader context, the mobile services that they subscribe to.

The following quotes illustrate well the homogeneity that exists among the views of interviewees, and their pride towards creative use of mobile services in SIM-switching and missed calls:

A youth talks about his daily switch between different mobile operators to get the best deal: *Tk.1.96 per minute. Again there is Tk.89 call charge. Covers most. Also I used to have Banglalink SIM with 0191 number, but the one I use I get 55 minutes free talk time. I recharge it for Tk300 and still now get 55 minute free. So I use mostly Banglalink.*

A youth talks about his rationale for using different mobile operators: *I use the GP one because most of my friends have GP numbers. I bought Djuice. And one of my cousin calls me from outside, so I use the Banglalink to talk to him. I have one to one with my friends, so I use it to talk to him and I use the Grameen one to talk to my college friends.*

A married female on her perception about the daily needs for missed calls: *After my husband comes back from office at 5:30 pm he gives me a missed call because we live on the 5th floor and when he reaches the ground floor he gives a miss-call to signal me to throw the gate keys down.*

A male on his opportunistic approach towards missed call: *One day I received several missed calls. When I called back, I found it was a girl. I was about to react, but decided against it. Then she asked my name, which I refused to give. For the next 10 minutes we went on arguing but afterwards we became friends.*

This practice was consistent across the youth that were interviewed. The first two quotes describe how they creatively swap their mobile SIM cards in order to benefit from cheaper call rates. SIM-switching refers to the practice of a mobile service subscriber possessing more than one SIM card and alternating the main SIM card with one or more SIM cards. There are cases where a subscriber acquires and possesses multiple SIMs (as many as four to six) to connect to people within his or her social network. Aside from their main

or primary SIM, multiple SIM-switchers possess SIMs from other mobile networks that their contacts use. The last two quotes illustrate the very purpose of a missed call practice. Missed call refers to the practice of calling another and disengaging the call before the other party is able to pick up the call. In a more advanced manner, missed call is a form of coded message. For example, two missed call beeps means "I will be there" or three missed call beeps means "I will be late". These coded missed calls are unique to a particular group, as they form their own way of communicating with each other.

Case 2: The Mobile Phone and Early Use Experiences

The early mobile phone use experiences of the poor are typically not shaped by actual ownership. The poor have some form of user experiences by sharing a mobile phone with another person or through a public calling office (PCO). The shared phone is usually referenced to a group of people who pool their money and share mobile phone usage time. Whenever they need to use the mobile phone, they will insert their own SIM card into the mobile. Financial constraints are the main reason for this. As for the PCO, it has emerged from just being a staffed telephony service to an institution that is valued by people from all walks of life. In rural, semi-urban and urban areas, the PCO is present almost everywhere. Along a street in Cox's Bazaar (a town resort near to the Chittagong city), for example, there are about 300 to 400 PCO operators who have set up their businesses; either just as a standalone desk-and-stool by the roadside or within a shop. The typical customers for the PCOs are those who do not own mobile phones, or those who just need to make a quick call and take advantage of the on-net call rates.

Anchoring their views on early mobile phone experiences, the respondents linked economic and social factors:

A youth accounts his fun experiences in trying out features in the mobile phone that they share together: *Yeah ... most of my friends are pretty much like me. We encourage each other to try out new things.*

A male PCO user explains his reason for going to a PCO - *I can call from my colleagues' mobile and also can go to shops to make calls. So, instead of having no mobile, I am using it.*

A PCO operator rationalizes his service as cost effective:... *in prepaid it takes 2 taka per minute but in case of PCO line, it takes 1.5 taka per minutes.*

Roldan, Helmersen and Wong (2007) affirm that the poor apply different ways to managing their daily expenditure, especially the usage of the mobile phone:

People in the low-income segment are creative in managing ICT (such as mobile) expenditure. They are creative in terms of maximizing their limited financial resources for accessing ICT or owning a device for accessing ICT facilities. Our fieldwork findings reveal several interesting ways as to how they manage their mobile communication and Internet access expenditure. There are two important outcomes from knowing how they manage their ICT expenditures. First, the options available to them can be understood. Second, how they coordinate different options depending on the situation can be also understood (Roldan et al, 2007, p.15).

Case 3: The Mobile Phone and Its Influence on the Ultra Poor

It is a well-researched fact that access to a range of information and communication technologies (ICTs) can give people knowledge that empowers them. ICTs such as the PC, the Internet, radio and television are known to provide access to knowledge and knowledge creation in sectors such as agriculture, trading, education, health and small-scale industry. Moreover, ICTs act as a tool in providing a new realm of choices that enable the poor to improve their quality of life. These choices range from income-generating opportunities such as access to fair market prices to essential lifecycle matters such as telehealthcare for the elderly and sick, remote education via radio, and remote video-conferencing with loved ones who are currently working or residing in a foreign country.

Experience has shown that different economic tiers, gender and age of the society have different priorities and preferences in relation to access, use and domestication of ICTs. This is due to the fact that they are different in terms of disposable income and assets, socially-assigned roles and responsibilities, internal and external influences, and other socio-cultural differences. For example, women are often restricted from using technology due to socio-cultural and religious attitudes and practices. This is manifested in limits a more conservative society can set on the extent to which women and girls can interact with technology, and thereby allow "liberal" communication and interaction with the outside world.

To reiterate, ICTs can serve as a tool to access, disseminate and share information and promote knowledge creation. While they are important drivers of socio-economic growth, they should not be considered as a solution for all the problems and limitations experienced in developing countries (Islam & Gronlund, 2007). It is more of a livable compromise of solution, rather than a cure-all. It is equally essential to assess which type of technology is the most effective and relevant to the developing world. In the context of this study, a particular emphasis is on the base-of-the-pyramid segment and their use of the mobile phone.

Based on the interviews and observations in the field, several notable usages of the mobile phone as a productive tool emerged:

- For the farmer, the mobile acts as a tool for contacting the middlemen about the availability of produce, i.e., timing of harvest, quantity etc. Therefore, the farmer could plan ahead whether he needed to sell more or less for a particular time, bearing in mind the perishable nature of his produce.

Shabul, who is a fresh vegetable seller, illustrates how he uses the mobile to coordinate with his father - *The mobile stays with my father. I use this at night to call my father to ask about what to buy for the next morning.*

- The mobile as a tool for remote communication and coordination. For example, a rice mill trader will coordinate between the farmers, middlemen and transporters to manage the capacity of his rice mill.

Rahman, who is a woodseller, elaborates about his business-sense through using the mobile phone: *Many workers waste time and not on time for work. So, I have to call them and ask them to come immediately. Sometimes I get orders and sometimes I need certain worker immediately to work on machines, etcetera. But, it's mainly regarding my saw mill business.*

As a socializing tool resulting in an increase in social and business networks:

- Mobile as a tool for increasing business network. This is especially crucial for the farmers who have excess produce or would like to expand business regionally and nationwide.

Manoranjan, who is a farmer, on his experiences using the mobile phone for social bonding: *I talk to my relatives, and people living abroad.*

- Mobile as a tool for remote "bonding". Instead of the need to travel physically to meet up with their business partner, which costs time and money, they could instead "just call up" their business partner more frequently, thereby building business relationships (Kavoori & Chadha, 2006).

As an innovation tool:

- In many instances, I noted that the mobile phone empowers the farmers to think differently about the nature of their work. For instance, in the past they did not have people they could discuss the nature of their work with, such as problems encountered with the harvesting. They would just have to rely on local elderly or more experienced farmers. Now it is possible for them to learn from others from other places far away.

A male on his rationale between using the mobile phone and saving money - *I get only 140 taka doing so much hard labor all the day. Is it worth spending the money for 5 minutes talking after working all the day?*

DISCUSSION

This chapter has explored the poor's views regarding an array of issues related to the collective information behavior and the domestication and use of the mobile phone by the poor. How the mobile phone impacts on their everyday lives has been examined. The observation of the informants and analysis of their interview quotes suggest that the poor may strive to experience what they regard as similar to the rich world. Their thoughts and actions reflect a perception of their utmost willingness to learn and share with each other, a demonstration of economic needs due mainly to financial constraints and the perceived risks associated with owning a mobile phone of their own. It is also a social need due mainly to a culture that values sharing with others. Notably, they sense the importance of taking the risk to learn new things through sharing the risk with others. They also exhibit a significant pragmatic perspective: to navigate and acclimatize to different demands of everyday lives in a cost-effective way.

Significantly the poor's theories about the world around them are about the lack of that sense of confidence that what they are doing is right. Will their views alter as a consequence of the path of experiences they walk along? The following section outlines a four-step model of information collaboration among the poor, in which the processes of collective-mediated learning, sharing and experimenting influence the way they navigate information. The first step in the model, collective-mediated learning and sharing, describes how new information and knowledge becomes a collective commodity, such that it provides the basis for the individuals in the group to be more willing to learn and share with each other. The second step, creating, synthesizing and cross-pollinating, is a process based on "information connectedness", a function of taking responsibility and ownership of the information bits. With this "information connectedness" mindset, the poor are more willing to trust each other; therefore they are more willing to create, synthesize and cross-pollinate information for the benefit of others. The third step, collective-mediated experimenting, describes the conditions under which the poor are willing to experiment and take risks to learn new things. The fourth step, local ingenuity, describes the conditions under which the poor contribute to local knowledge creation.

Model Components

In what follows, an illustration of the Learn, Share and Experiment (LSE) model component

is provided. Figure 1 represents the model in diagrammatic form. The elements in solid line boxes refer to the collective states, whereas the dotted line boxes are the results of the collective states. I incorporate some of the previously discussed issues from the cases as a background to the model.

Collective-Mediated Learning and Sharing

The term collective-mediated learning and sharing, as used within the LSE model of information collaboration, refers to group collective effort on a specific issue at hand. As in the case of missed call practices among the poor youth, several groups that were being interviewed talked about "specific coded messages pertaining to meeting up", "coherency and rules of thumb" and "dos and don'ts". There are several dimensions of collective collaboration that were extracted. First, there is the importance of a uniform language. The shared missed calls code or "language" indicates group cohesion and a willingness to make the effort to create a more efficient way of communicating and interacting with each other. Second, there is an unwritten agreement that the members in the group need to adhere to. Consider the case of how the ultra poor use the mobile phone as a productive tool (Case 3). The strategy that the poor exercise here is this: observe, ask, observe with questions, acquire a shared mobile phone and learn with the group; and finally, learn and share new practices within the group. This final step generates a few new insights. New practices reshape and personal-

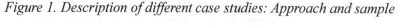

Figure 1. Description of different case studies: Approach and sample

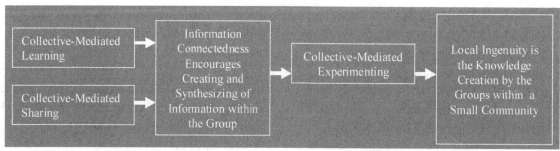

ize the affordances of group space. For example, the mobile phone transforms itself from being a communicator to being a productive tool for checking market prices and seeking advice from others. The new group practices in many senses fill in the uncertainty gaps of the individuals in the group. The logic here is that these new group practices allow the individuals to feel at ease because the new practices are tailor-made for them. Third, in collective collaboration, the purpose of the group practices evolves according to the maturity of the group. From an intra-member perspective, the evolution of group practices will happen eventually due to the fact that given different times and spaces, the individual will have different aspirations and motivations,. This interplay between aspiration-motivation and time-space states provides hints as to how the mobile phone has reshaped the experience of the individuals in the group; and emancipates them to embark on a new venture: the creating, synthesizing and cross-pollinating of information.

Information Connectedness and Its Influence on Creating, Synthesizing and Cross-Pollinating

The preceding section has proposed that collective-mediated learning and sharing creates a shared sense of information, in that information and knowledge belongs to the group rather than to a specific individual. Henceforth, the argument is that the individuals in the group have reached a state of "information connectedness". Thus the information, which has gone through the collective process, is now both an influence on and an outcome of the process by which information and knowledge are produced during a group collective effort. This is represented in Figure 1 by the left-hand box. In the example of early use experiences of the mobile phone among the poor (Case 2), several observations of information being created and synthesized in accordance with their local needs were noted. This information, newly processed by

the individuals within a group, provides the basis for subsequent contributions to inter-group discussion and collaboration. A useful way to think about this is to characterize intra-group collaboration as "closed innovation", and inter-group collaboration as "open innovation". In the intra-group state of "closed innovation", the creation and synthesis of information and knowledge happen as a result of the convergence of similar experiences; and in its developed form shapes the group's characteristics and levels of trust. In the inter-group state of "open innovation", the creation, synthesis and cross-pollination of information and knowledge happen as a result of the convergence of different experiences from different groups. This is due to different group practices and the stage of maturity that domestication of the technology has reached. In its developed form "open innovation" with information and knowledge shapes not only levels of trust within a group but also interaction with outsiders. At this point, cross-pollination of information and knowledge happen; subsequently, it influences the group's willingness to collaborate even more. In addition intra- and inter-group collaboration suggests the presence of specificities of collective style; and of approaches that vary depending on factors such as the prevalence of mobile phones within the group, and the centrality of the mobile phone in their everyday lives.

Collective-Mediated Experimenting

As noted earlier, among the contextual factors that drive collective-mediated learning and sharing, two elements stand out: an appetite for risk and the way in which trust within the group increases over time. These two elements surfaced as the individuals in the group actively made sense of the world around them. Henceforth, interaction within the group is socially constructed; that is, individuals within the group actively participate to uncover their perceived social reality (Pavitt, 1993; Kameda, Ohtsubo, & Takezawa, 1997; Propp, 1999; Knobloch & Solomon, 2002; Larson,

Foster-Fishman, & Schwartz, 2002). Taking up the case of how the poor youth experiment with SIM-switching, it is observed that they continuously expanded their willingness to experiment by linking to the belief that the more you try, the luckier you are. In addition, this willingness to experiment acts as a direct influence on the experience gained from playing with the mobile phone and it is determined by a social-interactional context. In the case of SIM-switching, over time, the poor youth expanded their options to try out different ways of doing SIM-switching. In one example, switching SIM based on a time factor, they are now trying to SIM-switch based on a reciprocal factor (swap SIM cards among themselves to optimize call rates), a price factor and a novelty factor (try out new SIM packages as soon as they are launched).

The term *collective-mediated experimenting* refers then to the active and collective nature of the group working to try out new things. In the context of mobile phone use, the active and collective nature of the group influences both the present perception and the structure of the group's thinking. This in turn is consequential for a subsequent crucial interaction: the creation of local ingenuity.

Local Ingenuity

The discussion of collective-mediated learning, sharing and experimenting extracts and reveals what is rarely obvious to those outside the group: the preparatory step that is taken towards the creation of local ingenuity. Wong (2007) defines local ingenuity or borrowing innovations as a concept about an economy or a group or a person being inventive by adapting and modifying original ideas developed by others, thus creating local ingenuities that better suit the local environment and its needs. The author details four feedback steps as a way to deduce the creation of local ingenuity. The first step is local ingenuity feedback which poses the question: what are the dimensions of

the new technology being modified? The second is preference feedback which focuses on understanding constraints and poses the question: what is being preferred and what not preferred? The third step is consumption feedback which focuses on developing an understanding of the domestication of local ingenuity and which poses the question: what is being consumed and what not consumed? The fourth and final step is local community feedback which focuses on extracting what and how the modification of technology is experienced within the community. Linking the previous three cases with the creation of local ingenuity provides us with new perspectives on how the poor engage in a group. The end goal is about creating a useful solution for the group to use and being a proud creator of it. As a result, the group moves towards a greater sustainable collective behavior. There are three key reasons. First, if the group manages to create a local ingenuity, they reconfirm their group relevancy. This is crucial for group bonding and creates new social disciplines and accountabilities. Second, it reconditions group trust among the members. Trust will solidify group collaboration in many facets of collective group work, such as a uniform degree of participation among the members and greater democracy in voicing one's opinion. Third and more importantly, as the group matures, it will reframe the group identity. This group or collective identity is largely determined by the social-interactional frame of a particular group. As such, it is hard to imagine how a particular group can evolve to be stronger without constitutive role group coherence.

Collective Information Behavior in the LSE Model: Propositions for Further Research

In this section the goal is to offer a set of propositions that are open to further research. A close examination of the three cases offers insight into the poor's collective information behavior (CIB) in terms of their styles and methods. Still, the goal is to highlight the perspectives of the poor, and thus we are better able to inform current and future debates on the future of information and knowledge collective efforts in the new media age. Taken as a whole, the classification of the CIB's style and methods derived from the transcripts of interviews and observations corresponds well with the LSE model. Of course, for any further testing of the CIB style and method, it is necessary for it to be theoretically and contextually relevant. In what follows, two sets of propositions are presented that are relatively concentrated and derived from the particularities of the collective-mediated learning, sharing and experimenting observed. There may be interest in examining perspectives other than the CIB style and methods, but a full treatment of their nuances lies beyond the scope of this chapter. Nevertheless, the discussion here can provide the basis for the examination of other perspectives. As the model treats the CIB of the poor as four inter-related parts of a process, each component will be addressed separately.

CIB Style

The LSE model postulates that the structure of collective-mediated behavior is based on a piecemeal process of learning, sharing and experimenting with new media tools such as the mobile phone. As noted, this piecemeal process occurs as a result of a myriad of constraints experienced by the poor (illiteracy or financial burdens for example). Moreover, the shared culture that is held in high regard by the poor highlights the symbolic value of learning and sharing information collectively.

- **Proposition 1:** Several CIB styles emerged based on specific elements, which were age-specific, task-specific, common value-specific, and risk-specific.
- **Proposition 2:** Different CIB styles are likely to have a direct influence on the composition of the group maturity level in terms of age, purpose and trust.

- **Proposition 3:** Different CIB styles are likely to shape the learning approach and the inherent value of learning shared among the group members.
- **Proposition 4:** Different CIB styles are likely to shape the sharing approach and the inherent value of sharing among the group members, internally and externally.
- **Proposition 5:** Different CIB styles are likely to shape the degree of risk taken in experimenting with new things.

CIB Method

CIB method refers to the inner workings of the group when they collectively collaborate to learn, share and experiment on new things. The degree of information interchange among the members determines the success of any collective effort. Furthermore, as noted earlier, the different CIB styles will reasonably influence and determine which types of CIB methods are engaged in by a particular group. Thus, the centrality of the CIB style should be positively associated, and best understood as co-constructed with the CIB method applied by a particular group.

- **Proposition 1:** Several CIB methods are likely to emerge as a direct result of different CIB styles. The different methods includes the free-flow-approach (links closely with CIB style of common value-specific), the centrality-approach (links closely with CIB style of task-specific), and the external-approach (links closely with CIB style of age-specific and risk-specific).
- **Proposition 2:** The free-flow-approach is likely to influence greatly the degree of risk at the experimenting stage.
- **Proposition 3:** The centrality-approach is likely to influence greatly the degree of willingness to share at the sharing stage.
- **Proposition 4:** The external-approach is likely to influence greatly on the degree of the group learning from external groups.

The propositions set forth here that are based on the LSE model raise several potentially interesting analysis issues. Because trust and social interaction are central to the model, it is crucial for us to understand how the behavioral causes and consequences of trust and social interaction influence the individuals in the group. Also, it is important to further explore collective-mediated learning, sharing and experimenting as an influencing factor on the creation of information connectedness and local ingenuity among the individuals in the group. The implications for the LSE model are potentially profound. For example, researchers in the field of new media studying such things as mobile communication often examine interrelationships between the mobile phone and users (Bayes, 2001; Horst & Miller, 2006; Kavoori & Chanda, 2006; Donner, 2007). Within the LSE model, the model postulates that the mobile phones are mostly a shared commodity for the poor, in contrast to individual own in the richer society. As such, the collective-mediated behavior is common and will have a strong impact on the individuals in a group. It would be interesting to extract similar and dissimilar collective-mediated behavior patterns of other new media tools such as the Internet. It would also be interesting to compare similar and dissimilar collective-mediated behavior patterns between the mobile phone and the Internet. This new information would allow us to advance supporting cases for creating policies and programs to encourage the adoption of new media tools among the poor by leveraging the particularities of collective-mediated behaviors. Moreover, we would be better able to explain the outcome of a new media technology learning program based on our understandings of the collective nature of the poor when learning, sharing and experimenting.

CONCLUSION

The purpose of this chapter was to offer a collective information behavior model of the poor as a complement to constructionist and social-interactional models. The LSE model described above is rooted in the fact that the poor collaborate differently from the rest of society due to lack of information, incomplete information, and barriers to information access. As a consequence, the poor need multiple information access points and the time to learn new things that are necessary for them to form the whole information picture. In most cases the poor learn collectively to domesticate new media technology, and it involves much social interaction among the individuals in the group. In Case 1, the poor collectively created a "local language" in the mobile format of missed calls. Without information sharing and close collaboration, the coded messages of missed calls become irrelevant. In Case 2, the poor collectively shared a mobile phone by pooling money to purchase their first shared ownership of a mobile phone. As far as the poor are concerned, this type of shared ownership is necessary and essential. Without such shared ownership, they would be risking their hard earned money for something they consider a luxury. In Case 3, the mobile phone was credited as a tool for increasing productive capacity and for enlarging a social network.

Against this tapestry of multiple perspectives, the claim is that collective-mediated learning, sharing and experimenting enable the poor to collaborate in a cost-efficient and socially productive manner. In the cost-efficient context, the collective behavior is very much a reflection of the need to save costs and reduce the risk of trying new things. In the socially productive context, the collective behavior is very much a reflection of the need to expand their social network. In a broader perspective, the collective information behavior of the poor in learning, sharing and creating information reflects a sense of urgency on their part to reduce the so-called information divide between them and the richer society. As new media technology slowly enters into the poor's lives, there is an urgent need for researchers to examine their collective behavior in light of their choices. Without a closer examination and rethinking of this behavior, at its initial stages, we may miss the opportunity to truly demonstrate something useful that will eventually lift them out of poverty.

REFERENCES

Abraham, R. (2007). Mobile phones and economic development: Evidence from the fishing industry in India Indian School of Business, Hyderabad, India. *Information Technologies and International Development, 4*(1).

Adesope, O., Olubunmi, S., & McCracken, J. (2007). Implementing mobile learning in developing countries: Prospects and challenges. In Montgomerie, C., & Seale, J. (Eds.), *Proceedings of world conference on educational multimedia, hypermedia and telecommunications 2007* (pp. 1249–1254). Chesapeake, VA: AACE.

Aminuzzaman, S., Baldersheim, H., & Jamil, I. (2003). Talking back: Empowerment and mobile phones in rural Bangladesh: A study of the village pay phone of Grameen Bank. *Contemporary South Asia, 12*(3), 327–348. doi:10.1080/0958493032000175879

Anderson, J. L. (2006). A structured approach for bringing mobile telecommunications to the world's poor. *Electronic Journal of Information Systems in Developing Countries, 27*(2), 1–9.

GSM Association. (2006, June). *Universal access: How mobile can bring communications to all* [Policy Paper 2006023].

Bakeman, R., & Gottman, J. M. (1986). *Observing interaction: An introduction to sequential analysis*. Cambridge, UK: Cambridge University Press.

Baliamoune-Lutz, M. (2003). An analysis of the determinants and effect of ICT diffusion in developing countries. *Information Technology for Development, 10*, 151–169. doi:10.1002/itdj.1590100303

Bandura, A. (1977). *Social learning theory*. New York: General Learning Press.

Bayes, A. (2001). Infrastructure and rural development: Insights from a Grameen bank village phone initiative in Bangladesh. *Agricultural Economics, 25*(2–3), 261–272. doi:10.1111/j.1574-0862.2001.tb00206.x

Bell, G. (2005). The age of the thumb: A cultural reading of mobile technologies from Asia. In Glotz, P., Bertschi, S., & Locke, C. (Eds.), *Thumb culture: The meaning of mobile phones for society* (pp. 67–88). Bielefeld, Germany: Transcript Verlag.

Berger, P. L., & Luckmann, T. (1966). *The social construction of reality: A treatise in the sociology of knowledge*. Garden City, NY: Anchor Books.

Cairncross, F. (1997). *The death of distance: How the communications revolution will change our lives*. Boston, MA: Harvard University Business School Press.

Castells, M., Qiu, J. L., Fernández-Ardévol, M., & Sey, A. (2007). *Mobile communication and society: A global perspective (information revolution and global politics)*. Cambridge, MA: MIT Press.

Deepak, P., & Bhamidipaty, A. (2007). Optimizing on mobile usage cost for the lower income group: Insights and recommendations. In C. Baranauskas, P. Palanque, J. Abascal, S. Diniz, & J. Barbosa, (Eds.), Human–computer interaction—Proceedings of Interact 2007: 11th IFIP TC 13 international conference, Rio de Janeiro, Brazil, September 10–14, 2007 (pp. 339–342). New York: Springer Verlag.

Donner, J. (2007). The rules of beeping: Exchanging messages via intentional missed calls on mobile phones. *Journal of Computer-Mediated Communication, 13*(1), 1–22. doi:10.1111/j.1083-6101.2007.00383.x

Durkheim, E. (1893). *The division of labor in society*. New York: Free Press.

Durkheim, E. (1897). *Suicide: A study in sociology*. New York: Free Press.

Erickson, F. (1977). Some approaches to inquiry in school-community ethnography. *Anthropology & Education Quarterly, 8*(2), 58–69. doi:10.1525/aeq.1977.8.2.05x1396r

Garbacz, C., & Thompson, H. G. (2007). Demand for telecommunication services in developing countries. *Telecommunications Policy, 31*(5), 276–289. doi:10.1016/j.telpol.2007.03.007

Goodman, J. (2007). Linking mobile phone ownership and use to social capital in rural South Africa and Tanzania. *Moving the Debate Forward: The Vodafone Policy Paper Series #3 2005*. Retrieved February 1, 2009, from http://www.vodafone.com/etc/medialib/attachments/cr downloads.Par.78351.File.tmp/GPP. SIM paper 3.pdf

Hardy, A. (1980). The role of the telephone in economic development. *Telecommunications Policy, 4*(4), 278–286. doi:10.1016/0308-5961(80)90044-0

Hirsh, S., & Dinkelacker, J. (2004). Seeking information in order to produce information: An empirical study at Hewlett Packard Labs. *Journal of the American Society for Information Science and Technology, 55*(9), 807–817. doi:10.1002/asi.20024

Horst, H., & Miller, D. (2006). *The cell phone: An anthropology of communication*. Oxford: Berg.

Islam, M. S., & Grönlund, A. (2007). Agriculture market information e-service in Bangladesh: A stakeholder-oriented case analysis. In M. Wimmer (Ed.), Electronic government, proceedings of the 6th international EGOV conference, Regensburg, Germany, September 3–7.

Ito, M. (2004). *Personal portable pedestrian: Lessons from Japanese mobile phone use*. Paper presented at Mobile Communication and Social Change, the 2004 International Conference on Mobile Communication in Seoul, Korea.

Ito, M. (2005). Mobile phones, Japanese youth, and the re-placement of social contact. In Ling, R., & Pedersen, P. E. (Eds.), *Mobile communications: Re-negotiation of the social sphere* (pp. 131–148). London: Springer.

Ito, M., Horst, H., Bittanti, M., Boyd, D., Herr-Stephenson, B., & Lange, P. G. (2008). *Living and learning with new media: Summary of findings from the digital youth project*. The John D. & Catherine T. MacArthur Foundation Reports on Digital Media and Learning.

Ito, M., Okabe, D., & Anderson, K. (2007). Portable objects in three global cities: The personalization of urban places. Forthcoming in L. Rich & C. Scott (Eds.), The mobile communication research annual volume 1: The reconstruction of space & time through mobile communication practices. NJ: Transaction Publishers.

Javid, P. S., & Parikh, T. S. (2006, May). *Augmenting rural supply chains with a location-enhanced mobile information system*. Paper presented at International Conference on Information and Communication Technologies and Development, Berkeley, CA.

Kameda, T., Ohtsubo, Y., & Takezawa, M. (1997). Centrality in socio-cognitive networks and social influence: An illustration in a group decision-making context. *Journal of Personality and Social Psychology, 73*, 296–309. doi:10.1037/0022-3514.73.2.296

Kavoori, A., & Chadha, K. (2006). The cell phone as a cultural technology: Lessons from the Indian case. In Kavoori, A., & Arceneaux, N. (Eds.), *The cell phone reader: Essays in social transformation* (pp. 227–240). New York: Peter Lang.

Knobloch, L. K., & Solomon, D. H. (2002). Information seeking beyond initial interaction: Negotiating relational uncertainty within close relationships. *Human Communication Research, 28*, 243–257. doi:10.1093/hcr/28.2.243

Kolko, B. E., Rose, E. J., & Johnson, E. J. (2007, May). *Communication as information-seeking: The case for mobile social software for developing regions.* Paper presented at 16th international conference on the World Wide Web (WWW), Banff, Alberta, Canada.

Kuhlthau, C. C. (1991). Inside the search process: Information seeking from the user's perspective. *Journal of the American Society for Information Science American Society for Information Science, 42*(5), 361–371. doi:10.1002/(SICI)1097-4571(199106)42:5<361::AID-ASI6>3.0.CO;2-#

Larson, J. R., Foster-Fishman, P. G., & Keys, C. B. (1994). Discussion of shared and unshared information in decision-making groups. *Journal of Personality and Social Psychology, 67*, 446–461. doi:10.1037/0022-3514.67.3.446

Lie, M., & Sørensen, K. H. (1996). Making technology our own? Domesticating technology into everyday life. In Lie, M., & Sørensen, K. H. (Eds.), *Making Technology our Own? Domesticating Technology into Everyday Life* (pp. 1–30). Oslo: Scandinavian University Press.

Marker, P., McNamara, K., & Wallace, L. (2002). *The significance of information and communication technologies for reducing poverty. Development Policy Department, DFID Final Report.* London: DFID.

Markoff, J. (2009, February 17). The cellphone, navigating our lives. *The New York Times*, p. D1.

Narayan, D., Chambers, R., Shah, M. K., & Petesch, P. (2000). *Voices of the poor: Crying out for change.* New York: Oxford University Press. doi:10.1596/0-1952-1602-4

Nokia's Expanding Horizon Magazine (2008, January). *Affordability key in bringing digital inclusion.* 12.

Nokia's Expanding Horizon Magazine (2009, January). *A roadmap to affordable mobility in emerging markets.* 13.

O'Neill, P. D. (2003). The 'poor man's mobile telephone': Access versus possession to control the information gap in India. *Contemporary South Asia, 12*(1), 85–102. doi:10.1080/0958493032000123380

Ovum. (2006). *The economic benefit of mobile services in India.* January. GSM Association Asia Pacific, Oxford: Oxford University Press.

Papert, S. (1970). *Teaching children thinking* (AI Memo No.247 and Logo Memo No. 2). Cambridge, MA: MIT Artificial Intelligence Laboratory.

Papert, S. (1980). *Mindstorms: Children, computers and powerful ideas.* New York: Basic books.

Pavitt, C. (1993). Does communication matter in social influence during small group discussion? Five positions. *Communication Studies, 44*, 216–227.

Propp, K. M. (1999). Collective information processing in groups. In Frey, L. R. (Ed.), *The handbook of group communication theory and research* (pp. 225–250). Thousand Oaks, CA: Sage.

Roldan, G., Helmersen, P., & Wong, A. (2007). *Connecting the Unconnected: Examining Local Needs, Exploring Service Opportunities in Bangladesh.* Telenor research paper.

Silverstone, R. (1994). *Television and everyday life.* London: Routledge.

Silverstone, R. Hirsch, E., & Morley, D. (1999). Information and communication technologies and the moral economy of the household. In R. Silverstone, & E. Hirsch (Eds.). Consuming technologies: Media and information in domestic spaces (pp. 15–31). London: Routledge.

Silverstone, R. (Ed.). (2005). *Media, technology and everyday life in Europe. From information to communication.* Aldershot: Ashgate.

Silverstone, R., & Haddon, L. (1998). Design and the domestication of information and communication technologies: Technical change and everyday life. In Silverstone, R., & Mansell, R. (Eds.), *Communication by design: The politics of information and communication technologies* (pp. 44–74). Oxford: Oxford University Press.

Taylor, A., & Richard, H. (2003). The gift of the gab?: A design oriented sociology of young people's use of mobiles. *Computer Supported Cooperative Work, 12,* 267–296. doi:10.1023/A:1025091532662

Vishwanath, A., & Chen, H. (2008, May). *Personal communication technologies as an extension of the self: A cross-cultural comparison of people's associations with technology and their symbolic proximity with others.* Paper presented at the annual meeting of the International Communication Association, Montreal, Quebec, Canada.

Waverman, L., Meloria, M., & Melvyn, F. (2005, March). The impact of telecoms on economic growth in developing countries. *Vodafone Policy Paper Series,* 2.

Wei, C., & Kolko, B. (2005, July). *Studying mobile phone use in context: Cultural, political, and economic dimensions of mobile phone use.* Paper presented at International Professional Communication Conference, Limerick, Ireland.

Weilenmann, A., & Catrine, L. (2002). Local use and sharing of mobile phones. In B. Brown, N. Green, & R. Harper (Eds.). Wireless world: Social and interactional aspects of the mobile age (pp. 92 107). London: Springer-Verlag.

Wong, A. (2007). The local ingenuity: Maximizing livelihood through improvising current communication access technology. In *Ethnographic Praxis in Industry Conference Proceedings* (Vol. 1, pp.104 – 114). American Anthropological Association.

Yang, B. (2005). *Social networks and individualism: The role of the mobile phone in today's social transformation in urban China.* Presented at the International Conference on Mobile Communication and Asian Modernities II.

APPENDIX

Table of Acronyms

LSE Model	Learn, Share and Experiment model
PCO	Public Calling Office
SIM	Subscriber Identity Module
SMS	Short Messaging System

Chapter 3
Contributors and Lurkers:
Obstacles to Content Creation in a Professional Online Community

Anne Beamish
Massachusetts Institute of Technology, USA

ABSTRACT

The long-term sustainability of online communities depends on the active participation and contribution of its members, but we have limited knowledge about why individuals do not post and how online communities can differ. This chapter presents an exploratory case study of contribution rates and lurking in a professional international online community that focuses on architecture and design in the Islamic world. The purpose of this study was to gain a deeper understanding of the community and the lurking behavior of its members. Using a web-based survey and log files, it asked three primary questions: Who contributes? Where do they contribute? And what reasons do members give for not contributing?

INTRODUCTION

The asynchronous and synchronous communication of Internet technology has facilitated the exchange of information across geographic and cultural boundaries. Groups of people who meet online and whose goal is to share information, ranging from formal work to social to recreational, are variously called communities of practice, networks of practice, learning communities, or simply online communities. Though the desire and enthusiasm for collaboration and sharing of

DOI: 10.4018/978-1-61520-797-8.ch003

knowledge in these communities is high, our understanding about the nature of who contributes, why, and more importantly why not, is much less clear. Our insight is hampered by limited empirical research and detailed data on the activity and participation rates of online communities. Though there has been extensive work done on discussion lists and Usenet newsgroups, most of these have been large-scale surveys aggregating many but often very dissimilar groups. With a few exceptions (Nonnecke & Preece, 2000; Wasco & Faraj, 2005; Schoberth *et al*, 2006), most studies have done little to describe the cultural differences and similarities between topic- or practice-based communities. As

Preece (1999, p. 64) notes, with so many different communities forming, we need to know how they differ in terms of demography, focus or purpose, and the behavior of their members.

Key to the success of online groups is the lively and active participation of their members. We know that group members *should* be contributing, but we know far less about the demographic characteristics of who contributes and who does not, as well as the reasons for their reluctance or resistance to contributing. These are the issues that will be addressed in this chapter.

It is important to understand why group members choose not to contribute because if we can identify the obstacles that community members face, the managers and designers of online environments will be better able to cultivate a culture that encourages members to contribute freely and create the software that enables them to do so. Communities of practice vary in intent and size and because we currently do not know what is typical for particular types, studies such as this can help us begin to understand the range of normal levels of contribution.

The purpose of this study was to investigate ArchNet, a six-year old international professional online community, and to identify who contributes to the site, who does not, and what obstacles prevent them from participating more actively. Using a web-based survey and log activity reports, it is a snapshot of one particular online community at a single point of time.

BACKGROUND

ArchNet

ArchNet's audience is made up of students and professional architects, urban planners, and designers interested in the built environment, with a special focus on the Islamic world. The site is free and open to all; access for viewing is anonymous, but contributing is not. Contributors must be registered and logged on to participate, and first and last names are a visible part of every posting. The site is made up of several areas including a calendar, digital library, personal workspaces, group workspaces, discussion forum, member profiles, and careers. Because of its hybrid nature, the site is difficult to categorize—the digital library with its large collection of images and publications has a different quality and purpose from the discussion forum, which is different again from the collaborative group workspaces.

ArchNet's professional community of practitioners, educators, students, and researchers go to the site because of their work, but there are no work goals, and though it is intended to connect like-minded individuals, it is not meant to serve a social function. It is also somewhat unusual in that its target audience is intentionally more international than many web sites or discussion groups.

The site as a whole could be best described as a not-for-profit, open and regulated community (Plant, 2004), a community of practice (Wenger, 1998), or more specifically a network of practice (Brown & Duguid, 2001). As Henri and Pudelko (2003, p. 483) state, "A community of practice develops among people who, in the real world, are already part of a given community of practice, i.e. practise the same trade or share the same working conditions." "For each individual, the virtual community of practice represents a means of investing themselves in the social or professional definition of their trade, to reinforce their professional identity, to enrich or perfect their daily practice while contributing to the practice of the community." Architects, planners, and designers, like professionals from all disciplines, seek out opportunities for professional development (Sherer *et al*, 2003; Caffarella & Zinn, 1999; Marsick & Watkins, 1990) and for professionals in countries where access to professional journals and funds for international travel is limited, Internet technology offers a tremendous advantage. The aim of ArchNet is to support this community and provide an environment for sharing information.

ArchNet's editorial office provides a great deal of information primarily in the Digital Library where the image and publication collections reside, but the site was also conceived as a place that supported collaboration and local expertise, and as such, there are many opportunities for the members to contribute and share information throughout the site. However, the participation rate has been lower than originally hoped and like many online communities, only a small number of its members contribute or post to the site.

Lurkers

Though there is an extensive literature on communities of practice, learning organizations, and online communities—what they are and their characteristics (Senge, 1990; Wenger, 1998; Wenger *et al*, 2002; Plant, 2004), the literature on lurkers is less abundant but is increasing as our understanding grows.

Lurkers are individuals who read messages or browse a site, but never or rarely contribute. They can be defined as "readers who never post" (Sproull & Faraj, 1997) and their activity as "passive participation" (Schuler, 1996) or "silent participation" (McLaughlin *et al*, 1995). The connotation of the word "lurker" is not especially positive, but as Sproull and Faraj (1997, p. 39) note, it is a "term with more sinister connotations than is perhaps warranted." The pejorative view of lurkers stems from the notion that that they are "free-riders" (Kollock & Smith, 1996), selfish individuals who take from the community and benefit at the expense of others. Their status is ambiguous. Traditionally most groups view lurkers as second-class citizens of the community while only a few are more inclusive and see lurkers' behavior as both legitimate and acceptable (McLaughlin *et al*, 1995).

Because the presence and activity of lurkers is invisible to other users, the extent of lurking or non-contribution has been difficult to assess. There is, however, a general sense that more people read or browse than actively contribute (Smith, 1999), and that small groups of members post proportionally more messages (Baym, 1997). Lurking can range from 1% to 99%, depending on a number of factors including topic and size (Nonnecke & Preece, 2001; Butler, 2001). The rate can also vary with the type of group. For example, lurkers made up 45.5% of health support communities and 82% of software support communities (Preece *et al*, 2004; Nonnecke & Preece, 2000). Since online communities or communities of practice can vary widely in their purpose, structure, and culture, these aspects can have a significant effect on when and why members contribute.

New work is beginning to take a fresh look at lurkers, seeing them in a more positive and nuanced light. Preece et al (2004), for example, sees lurkers not as exploiters, but people who do not contribute for good reasons—sometimes even altruistic ones. Nonnecke and Preece (2001) suggest that rather than being deviant or negative behavior, lurking is a perfectly legitimate form of participation and that group members choose to lurk because it meets both their personal and informational needs. They were still able to feel connected to their groups even though they did not actively post, and in many cases, the information was more important to them than any interaction. In fact, from a pedagogical point of view, lurking may be far more positive than expected because a study done by Dennen (2008) found that students who spent time reading others' messages *and* posting their own felt that they learned more than the students who focused more exclusively on posting messages.

Why do lurkers lurk? A survey by Preece *et al* (2004) of 375 online groups was undertaken. Over half the lurkers said that just reading/browsing is enough, but other reasons included they were shy about posting, they had nothing to offer, and that there was no requirement to post. The list of reasons for not contributing was grouped into five main categories: Didn't need to post; Needed to find out about the group; Thought I was being helpful; Couldn't make the software work; and Didn't like the group dynamics. There are two slightly different ways of thinking about the issue of lurkers. One is to ask why they choose to lurk and the second is to focus on what stops them from contributing. Asking why lurking is the preferred behavior assumes that it an active choice made by the participant and not caused by factors outside their control.

Obstacles

Assuming that group members would participate more if not prevented by a series of obstacles is a more common perspective and there is a myriad of plausible reasons why group members do not contribute or share information (Hall, 2001; Hall & Graham, 2004; Harris, 1999). These obstacles can include: the medium, content, individual, social-cultural environment, physical environment, and economic environment (Beamish, 2008).

Medium

The medium is the "pipe" through which the information flows. If it restricts the flow, for example, if the user is using a dial-up modem instead of broadband, or if the software/hardware is difficult to use, there could be less participation in terms of contribution. Contributing to some areas of ArchNet such as the calendar or discussion forum is unlikely to be a major hurdle because it is text-based. If users can browse through the site, they should have no problem contributing to these areas. However, the bandwidth becomes much more of an issue when downloading and uploading images or files even though the developers of the site have made an effort to minimize this problem. The average speed of ArchNet members has significantly improved over the years, but it is unknown how much the network speed affects contributions.

In addition to bandwidth, ease of use and software functionality plays an important role

that can affect conviviality, efficiency, effectiveness, and satisfaction (de Souza & Preece, 2004, p. 603). If a site is confusing, difficult to use, or unclear, it will inhibit usage and consequently limit contributions and the sharing of information. Preece (2001) bundles these types of issues under the heading of usability, asking questions such as: How long does it take to learn about dialogue and social support? How long does it take to learn to find information? How long does it take to learn to navigate through the communication software and web site or to find something? And can users get access to all the software components that they need and download them in reasonable time?

Content

The flow of information can be impeded if the receiver perceives the content as negative or threatening or if information is irrelevant to the needs of the user (Harris, 1999). As Catherine Marshall *et al* (1995) succinctly noted, members must be aware of each other's contributions, the contributions must be mutually intelligible, and they must be useful. The level of message reciprocity can also affect an individual's willingness to post. A study done by Joyce and Kraut (2006) of initial posts by 2,777 newcomers to six public newsgroups showed that those who received a reply to their first posting were more likely to post again. They were also more likely to receive a response if they asked a question or wrote a longer post. Surprisingly, the tone of the response or whether it answered the original question did not seem to influence the newcomer's enthusiasm to post again.

It was suspected that in ArchNet's case most users saw the content fairly positively because of the number of users and high level of activity, but this might not be true of all individual members—what is beneficial and useful to one may be irrelevant to another. In addition, it is possible that some users are unaware that their input is desired or where. This issue is unlikely to be a problem for a straightforward discussion list—it is clear that the existence of the list depends on postings by members—but it could be less obvious for a more complex site that both provides information and encourages collaboration.

Individual

Even if a site is well designed and easy to use with useful content, individuals may be reluctant to contribute for a number of personal reasons. They may hold a set of beliefs, attitudes, or fears that prevent them from contributing. For example, if an individual believes they do not have the expertise (Wasko & Faraj, 2000), or that that they have nothing to offer, or that the information they provide is not valuable ("Everyone knows that."), or that they do not have the status ("No one would want to hear from a student.") (Hall, 2001), they may be unwilling to share information. In a study of a corporate knowledge-sharing community of practice, Ardichvili *et al* (2003, p. 70) found that employees were often intimidated and hesitated to contribute because of a fear of criticism, afraid that they didn't know enough, and new employees felt that they had not earned the right to post. This fear is not limited to corporate sites and participants in discussion lists also cite the fear of hostile responses as a reason for not posting (Katz, 1998, Preece *et al*, 2004). Bishop (2007) proposes a three-level framework for understanding why members of online communities either participate or do not participate. Level 1 of the framework is made up of an individual's desires, including the desire to become part of the community through socializing and communicating; Level 2 is made up of a person's goals, plans, values, beliefs and interests; and Level 3 of the model is made up of the user's means to interpret and interact with their environment. Or put another way, group members are driven to act by their desires, their desire to act is limited by their goals, plans, values, beliefs

and interests, and a person will act based on how they perceive their environment.

Reasons for individuals to not contribute are not limited to attitude. As Harris (1999) points out, having the requisite skills to navigate, download, upload, and communicate may also be lacking. For example, ArchNet members may feel uncomfortable contributing because even though they may have sophisticated technical skills and be very well educated, they may not be fluent in English, the main language used on the site.

Social-Cultural Environment

The environment—group dynamics and culture—in which users operate will have a major impact on who will and how often they participate and can promote or hinder the exchange of information. For example, if the atmosphere is threatening or hostile, or if individuals feel that sharing information will harm them in some way, there will likely be little or none. And if there is no active encouragement, contribution levels are likely to be lower.

The reasons for not contributing, however, are not always related to a hostile or disinterested atmosphere. The reasons can be more benign and non-contribution can simply be a result of group culture or habit. For example, Nonnecke and Preece (2000) found that health-support discussion lists had significantly fewer lurkers than software-support discussion lists. The size of the group may also influence a member's willingness to share their expertise. Large memberships provide opportunity for individual learning, but knowledge is generated in smaller, less public groups (Hall & Graham, 2004). Butler (2001) found that an increase in membership size posed a dilemma because even though a large membership offers greater resources to its members, it can also cause greater social and logistical problems, making it more difficult to convert the group's resources into benefits.

THE STUDY

The primary aim of this study was to understand who contributes to the site and the obstacles to posting. More specifically three main questions were examined.

1.   Who contributes to ArchNet? What are the demographic characteristics of the contributors compared to the membership as a whole? Are there differences in contribution rates depending on gender, occupational role, or country of residence? Is length of membership a factor?
2.   Where on the site do members contribute (calendar, discussion forum, news, personal workspace, etc.)? Do differences exist in location depending on gender, occupational role, or country of residence?
3.   What reasons do members give for not contributing? What obstacles do they experience? Are members willing to contribute if obstacles are overcome?

The two principle sources of data were the site reporting system and a web-based survey. The site reporting system used the log files to record members' registration dates, recent logins, demographic information, and number of postings to the public, personal, and group workspaces. The web-based survey was made up of seven screens with five sections: demographics, participation, contribution, information seeking, and overall satisfaction. The questions pertaining to the reasons for lurking were derived from two earlier studies (Nonnecke & Preece, 2001, Preece *et al*, 2004) and the survey instrument was designed following as many of the best practice guidelines for conducting a web-based survey (Andrews *et al*, 2004) as possible. Effort was made to create a professional and simple survey with straightforward navigation and the designers strove for consistency and clarity. Questions used radio buttons, check boxes, drop-down menus for multiple-choice selection,

and Likert scales. Open-ended questions were optional with text input boxes for many of the questions.

After the survey was available online for approximately four weeks, the responses were collected electronically and tabulated and analyzed using SAS. Simple frequencies and percentages, cross-tabs, as well as Chi-Square values were calculated. Data from the site reporting system for four months (January–April 2006) were also collected and analyzed, and again, simple frequencies, percentages, and t-tests were calculated.

RESULTS

Respondents and Responses

Email was sent to 1,500 randomly selected members and 225 emails bounced because of non-working accounts or full mailboxes. Because many firms, universities, institutions, and IP providers now implement spam filters, it is very difficult to know how many of the remaining 1,275 members actually received the invitation to participate. Nevertheless, a response rate of 16% was achieved and 204 members completed the survey. Though the sample was relatively small, it gave a confidence level of 95% and a ±7% confidence interval and we felt that it accurately reflected the respondents' perceptions and beliefs.

The response rate of 16% is within the experience of other web-based surveys (Andrews et al, 2003) but was lower than hoped for. It did, however, highlight an important difference between the respondents and the randomly-selected members. Though the respondents and overall randomly selected group were very similar in terms of membership length, their activity on the site was not. The median number of days since the last and second-to-last visit for respondents was 15 and 73 days respectively in contrast to 386 and 455 days of the randomly selected members. Further investigation of the log files showed that

58% of all registered members had not logged in for more than a year and 33% had not logged in for more than two years. Though it might appear that a great many members rarely visit the site, these numbers may still be misleading because it is quite possible for members to visit and view most of the site without logging in. Even so, it does appear that a significant number of members are inactive.

In general the demographics of the 204 survey respondents corresponded with information about the registered members. The largest age group of respondents was 26-35 (35%) with almost sixty percent between the ages of 18 and 35. Forty-one percent of respondents were female. The main occupations of the respondents were architect (34%), student (19%), and educator (12%) and these percentages differed, sometimes substantially, from the general membership. Half of the respondents came from five countries: Egypt, India, Turkey, United Kingdom and the United States. The respondents speak a broad range of languages, but the three largest groups were Arabic (16%), English (26%), and Turkish (9%) native speakers. The respondents were also fluent in other languages, and of those that answered, half were also fluent in English. Respondents said that they visited a few times per month (31%) or one to twelve times per year (46%).

Q1. Who Contributes?

The perceived low contribution rate on the site was one of the reasons that prompted the study, so it came as no surprise when only a quarter of the respondents said that they had ever contributed and even then they were not very specific about where they had posted. Only 9% percent of the female survey respondents reported that they had posted to the site, while 16% of the male members claimed to have contributed. Of all of those who said they contributed, a little over a third were women.

The survey results for contribution levels were not very dependable because of the low number of respondents who had said that they contributed and their uncertainty about how often or where they had posted. As noted in Andrews *et al* (2003, p. 186), surveys are imperfect vehicles for collecting data because they require participants to recall past behavior that is more accurately captured through observation. Though this was not the focus of this study, a quick comparison of the log reports with the survey responses revealed that, as has been found with other studies, respondents significantly overestimated their contributions.

The site activity reports derived from the log files gave a far clearer view of contributors' characteristics. Over a four-month period (January–April), there was a total of 2,047 contributions to the public areas of the site; on average almost 16% were posted by half a dozen ArchNet staff and the remainder was from the members. However, the ratio between staff and member contributions varied considerably with the area. For example, staff contributed 80% of the news items but only 8.8% in the discussion forum.

Over the four-month period, 739 members, representing approximately 2.3% of the total membership, contributed 84.5% of the site's postings in the public areas. Women made up 40% of the contributors but were responsible for 29% of the postings. Students made up 56% of the contributors and were responsible for 44% of the postings (Table 1). The demographic makeup of the contributor group is fairly similar to that of the general membership. Initially it appeared that the percentage of female contributors was considerably higher than the general membership, but this may not be the case. Almost 22% of members do not report their gender and anecdotal evidence suggests that women are more reluctant to report their gender than men. If this was true and most of the undeclared were women, the general membership percentage would be very close to the female contributors. Otherwise, the

Table 1. Number of postings contributed to public areas over a four-month period

	All Public Areas				General Membership
	No. of Individuals		No. of Postings		
SUMMARY					
Staff	6	(0.8%)	317	(15.5%)	
Members	739	(99.2%)	1,730	(84.5%)	
Total	**745**	(100.0%)	**2,047**	(100.0%)	
MEMBER DATA (excluding staff)					
Gender					
Female	297	(40.2%)	209	(29.4%)	(28.4%)
Male	423	(57.2%)	1,179	(68.2%)	(49.7%)
Unknown	19	(2.6%)	42	(2.4%)	(21.9%)
Total	**739**	(100.0%)	**1,730**	(100.0%)	(100.0%)
Occupation					
Educator	38	(5.1%)	60	(3.5%)	(7.9%)
Other	47	(6.4%)	76	(4.4%)	(10.8%)
Professional/Practitioner	187	(25.3%)	455	(26.3%)	(29.5%)
Researcher	53	(7.2%)	379	(21.9%)	(7.8%)
Student	414	(56.0%)	760	(43.9%)	(42.0%)
Unknown	0	(0.0%)			(2.0%)
Total	**739**	(100.0%)	**1,730**	(100.0%)	(100.0%)
Length of Membership (months)					
Mean	11				24
Median	3				21

Note: The public areas included calendar, news, jobs, discussion forum, and portraits.

characteristics of the contributors resemble those of the membership with the exception of students in the contributors group outnumbering those in the general membership.

To verify if contribution rates varied with gender, t-tests were calculated for all contributions in all areas of the site (public, restricted, and private) but gender was not related to the number of contributions ($t = 1.66$, $p = 0.0965$). T-tests were also done for occupation. When all contributions in all areas were analyzed, the difference between students and non-students was statistically significant ($t=3.78$, $p=.0002$) primarily because several classes in the group workspaces had very high contribution levels. When that group was excluded, the difference between students and non-students was not significant and further tests showed that occupation was not systematically related to the rate of contribution.

Of the top 5% contributors, men outnumbered women in both number and postings. Though they represented 54% of this group, men contributed 81% of the postings. In the occupational category researchers made up 11% of this group but were responsible for 39% of the postings, largely because of one "super-contributor" who was a very prolific participant in the discussion forum during this period. When this one individual was removed, the trends remained the same, but the numbers were less extreme. Men were the slight majority (53%) but still contributed 70% of the postings. The occupation categories however shifted significantly with this one individual excluded. Students made up 49% of the contributions followed by professionals at 44%.

Over the four-month period, contributors came from a total of 66 countries with 75% of the contributing individuals coming from the "top ten" countries of Serbia, India, United States, Pakistan, Egypt, United Kingdom, Turkey, Iran, Canada, and Germany. Individuals from these countries contributed 81% of the postings to the public areas. Of this group, Indians contributed in much larger proportion than their numbers—even though they made up only 19% of the contributors, they were responsible for 27% of the postings. Of these countries, Serbia and India were over-represented compared to the general membership while the USA, Egypt, UK, and Turkey were underrepresented.

Contributors to the public areas of the site tend to not post very often. Almost 78% of contributors only posted once, and 10% posted twice. The remaining 12% posted from 3 to 61 times and one "super-contributor" posted an extraordinary 294 times.

The data describing how long the contributors have been members are striking. Contributors to the public areas of the site have been members ranging from 0 months to 6 years, with a mean of 11 months, but over half of the contributors during this period had been members for only 3 months. The data show a sharp spike of participation and contribution for newer members but then a dramatic drop-off by the end of the first year of membership.

Looking at all contributions in all areas of the site (public, restricted, and private), the trend is similar—just over half of all contributors had joined within the past four months and this group was responsible for approximately one third of all postings.

Q2. Where Do They Contribute?

The survey questionnaire was not very informative about the location of postings because of the low number of contributors among the respondents and their uncertainty about how often or where they had contributed. Consequently, the detailed site reports were again much more insightful. During a four-month period during and immediately after the survey, the majority (65%) of the postings in the public areas were to the Discussion Forum.

However, the log files revealed a surprising aspect to contribution rates. In sharp contrast to the belief by site administrators that members were not contributing significantly to the site, the data showed that members *were* contributing to the site, but not necessarily in the public areas. Registered members were making much greater use of the site in more private or restricted spaces such as the group workspaces or individual personal workspaces. For example, over the same four-month time period, members made a total of 33,732 postings. Only 6% of these were visible or accessible in the public spaces. The group workspaces accounted for 83% of the postings and the members' personal workspaces accounted for another 11% (Table 2).

Looking more closely at the location distributions for gender and occupation in all areas of the site, though women provided at least half the postings overall, they were not evenly divided in each area. Men tended to contribute slightly more then women in most areas except for the group workspaces. The uneven distribution was most pronounced in the discussion forum where men posted 75% of the messages. For both women and men, the majority of their contributions were to the restricted group workspaces with 88% and 80% respectively.

Table 2. Location of staff and member postings/contributions over a 4-month period

	Area	No. of Staff Postings	No. of Member Postings		Total Postings	% of Public Postings	% of All Postings
Public Space	News	12	3		15	0.7	0.0
	Calendar	159	47		206	10.1	0.6
	Discussion	118	1,221		1,339	65.4	3.9
	Portraits	0	396		396	19.3	1.2
	Careers	28	63		91	4.4	0.3
	Public Sub-Total	**317**	**1,730**		**2,047**	**100.0**	**6.0**
Re-stricted or Private	Group Workspaces	20	28,213		28,233		82.9
	Personal Workspaces	0	3,789		3,789		11.1
	Restricted Sub-Total	**20**	**32,002**		**32,022**		**94.0**
	TOTAL	**337**	**33,732**		**34,069**		**100.0**

For occupational groups, students contributed 82% of all postings and dominated most of the other areas, especially the group workspaces. Though students were still the largest group of contributors in the discussion forum with 38%, researchers (28%) and professionals/practitioners (27%) were not far behind. Students and educators made greatest use of the group workspaces while professionals and others favored the personal workspaces and researchers tended to contribute most of their postings in the discussion forum followed by the personal workspaces.

Finally, country of residence did not show strong location patterns except for the discussion forum and group workspaces. In the discussion forum, though members representing forty-nine countries took part, Indians dominated with 425 or 35% of all the messages. In the group workspaces, the vast majority of the users were from Serbia reflecting the intensive use of the space for classes at a university in Belgrade. And finally, members from the United States used their personal workspaces most, posting 39% of all files in this area followed by India (9%) and Egypt (7%).

Q3. What Reasons Do Members Give For Not Contributing?

In the survey questionnaire, members were asked why they did not contribute. The top five responses were: Not enough time (52.2%); Only interested in reading/browsing (43.5%); Didn't know I could or was supposed to (30.4%); Nothing to offer (20%); and Don't know how to post (17.4%). Somewhat surprisingly given the international nature of this community, a relatively small number said that their Internet connection was too slow (9.8%) or that they were not comfortable writing in English (7.6%) (Table 3).

In an optional open text field, survey respondents were encouraged to provide any other reasons explaining why they did not post. Of the dozen responses, most simply reiterated reasons on the list, but one mentioned receiving an anonymous sarcastic email in response to a question in the discussion forum, another said that there was not much reaction to his/her first posting, and one respondent said that it was not clear what the benefits of posting would be.

Table 3. Reasons for not contributing

	% of respondents who answered (n=92)
Not enough time.	52.2
Only interested in reading/browsing.	43.5
Didn't know I could or was supposed to.	30.4
Nothing to offer.	20.7
Don't know how to post.	17.4
Shy about posting.	16.3
Had no intention to post from the outset.	14.1
No requirement to post.	13.0
Other	10.9
Internet connection is too slow.	9.8
Too much trouble.	7.6
Not comfortable writing in English.	7.6
If I post, I am making a commitment.	7.6
Concern about critical or hostile responses.	4.3
Long delay in response to postings.	4.3
I want to remain anonymous.	4.3
Poor quality of messages in the discussion forum.	1.1

Interestingly, though the number of members who contributed was relatively low compared to the membership as a whole, the majority of the survey respondents (70.3%) said that they had an expertise and would be willing to share it. Only 21% said that they had nothing to offer. This response is promising for the site because as Wang and Lai (2006) found, simply having the motivation to participate is a necessary but insufficient condition. Individuals must also have the capacity or knowledge to contribute.

The respondents were also asked what could be done to encourage them to contribute more. Their answers could be grouped into four main categories: reminders, interaction, functionality, and content. Several wanted some type of email, newsletter or notification sent to them. Others requested greater interaction and active encour-agement of users to contribute. Some thought making the site easier and clearer to use would help motivate them to contribute, and a number of respondents thought having more content on the site would encourage them to post more.

DISCUSSION

This study was conducted with the purpose of understanding the characteristics and rates of contribution of an international professional community, as well as the obstacles that hindered participation.

Rate of Contribution

The study was motivated by a concern that members were not contributing to the site and indeed, compared to the overall membership (approximately 32,000 at the time of the survey) a relatively small percentage of members (2.3%) contributed to the public areas of the site, though this percentage increases somewhat (4.8%) if the restricted or private areas of the site are included. Still, this proportionally small group was heavily engaged in the production of content for the site, contributing almost 2,000 public postings and another 32,000 to the group and personal workspaces over a four-month period.

Comparing the site to other online communities is not straightforward because ArchNet with its variety of functions is more complex than the frequently-studied discussion forums or Usenet newsgroups. Nevertheless, the site's overall level of contribution is fairly similar to other communities of practice. For example, ArchNet administrative staff was responsible for approximately 16% of postings in the public areas and a small group provided the remainder of the contributions, while Henri and Pudelko (2003) reported that 25% of the messages on a French teachers' community of practice *HFrançais* was provided by the founding members and most of the subscribers remained silent (3.8% of the members sent on average one message per month). In another study, Wasko and Faraj (2005) found that 8.6% of the members of a legal professional network of practice contributed, and still other online communities have had higher contribution and lower lurking rates depending on their topic. For example, Nonnecke and Preece (2000) found that participants were more active on health-related discussion lists and had far fewer lurkers (46%) compared to a software-support discussion list (82%).

The level of participation by ArchNet members is not evenly distributed over the membership and partially reflects the typical level of participation described by Wenger *et al* (2002): intense (by staff), active (by a core group of members) and peripheral by the majority. In ArchNet's case, four levels could better characterize participation. There was intense participation by staff and a group of core members, active contributive participation by new members, active browsing or reading participation by members and non-members, and complete non-participation by lapsed or inactive members.

The data show clearly that staff and a handful of members were responsible for a significant amount of postings during the four-month period. The bulk of the remainder of the contributions was made by a wave of new participants who had joined the site within the past year. Their activity pattern appears to be one of waiting a period of approximately a month before making their first post, posting for the next few months, and then stopping contributions. A third but important category includes the so-called lurkers who in fact actively participated in the site by reading and using the content provided by the staff, core members, and fellow members. Though this group of lurkers is often considered non-participatory, they deserve to be included as active participants (Nonnecke & Preece, 2000; Schultz & Beach, 2004), especially on a site whose mission is education and sharing of expertise, since without an audience of readers and users of the content,

there would be no real purpose to the contributors' participation. Though readers make up a large and important group, they are hard to quantify. We know that during the survey period, the site was visited by over 5,000 individual visitors with unique IP numbers per day, but it is almost impossible to know how many visitors are registered members who have not bothered to log in and how many are non-members. In any case, it is clear by the sheer number of viewers and the heavy traffic on the site that this is a group that cannot be dismissed as non-participatory. The fourth level is made up of lapsed or non-users who are truly non-participants and who neither contribute nor actively use the site. The presence of this group can have both a positive and negative effect on the site. On one hand, as discussed by Butler (2001), a larger number of members can attract new members. On the other, a large membership can be perceived as overwhelmingly large and can suppress communication activity and participation.

In spite of not actively posting to the site, lurkers apparently are fairly satisfied with their participation and benefits of membership. Like the users in a study by Nonnecke and Preece (2001), even though they chose not to contribute, ArchNet survey respondents said that they felt connected and satisfied with the site. Almost 60% said that it had a positive impact on their professional life or education, 51% felt better connected to the international design community, 64% were very satisfied with the site and 72% said it was valuable and beneficial.

Location of Postings

Though this study stemmed from a concern about the perceived low contribution rates, some of the most surprising results were the extent of the members' activity in the more restricted and private parts of the group and private workspaces, contributing over 32,000 postings compared to the 2,000 in the public areas. There are several possible and overlapping explanations for this imbalance. Members may simply feel more comfortable participating in a smaller, more intimate and familiar group setting where they know others and are known by them. This outcome supports the work of others who have found a link between size and participation (Constant *et al*, 1999; Wasko & Faraj, 2000; Butler, 2001; Hall & Graham, 2004). In addition, the most active group workspaces were organized classes where group members mostly knew each other, knew what was expected of them, and there was leadership—usually in the form of professors and teaching assistants—to actively encourage students (and insist when necessary) to participate.

The differences in contribution levels between the large publicly accessible side of the site and the more restricted areas illustrate Brown and Duguid's (2001) differentiation between a community of practice and a network of practice. They propose that a community of practice is a tightly-knit group of members engaged in a shared practice who know each other and work together, and typically meet face-to-face. In contrast, networks of practice consists of a larger loosely-knit geographically distributed group of individuals engaged in shared practice but who may not know each other or necessarily expect to meet face-to-face. Using this useful distinction, ArchNet site looks more like a hybrid with the group workspaces acting as a series of communities of practice and the public side more closely resembling a network of practice.

Obstacles to Participation and Reasons for Lurking

There is a range of obstacles that can prevent group members from contributing but according to the survey results, individual concerns and the social-cultural environment were the most prevalent hurdles.

Somewhat surprisingly, given the wide range of countries represented and the variation in Internet access, limited bandwidth was not a major complaint of survey respondents. In terms of content, very few complained about the relevancy, quality, or timeliness of the information. On an individual level, few claimed to be fearful, though some professed to be shy, but individual circumstances and intention did have a major influence on their posting behavior. Over half said that they did not have the time and another large group said that they never had any intention to post and were only interested in reading. Surprisingly few, again given the international nature of the site, said that they were uncomfortable writing in English. Some felt that they had nothing to offer, but many more said that they had an expertise and were willing to share it. The social-cultural environment also does not appear to have a negative impact on group dynamics. Few claimed to be intimidated and only one mentioned receiving an anonymous sarcastic message after a post. However, a lack of active encouragement does seem to be a significant problem as evidenced by the 30% who said that they did not know they were supposed to contribute. The large size and public nature of the site may also inhibit posting as demonstrated by the much larger number of members who posted in the more restricted or private areas of the site.

The reasons given by ArchNet survey respondents differed from those given by Preece *et al* (2004). In that study of 375 online communities, the most common reasons were not needing to post, needing to find out more about the group before participating, thinking that they were being helpful, not being able to make the software work, and not liking the group dynamics. In another study by Nonnecke *et al* (2006), the main reasons for lurking were just reading is enough, still learning about the group, shy about posting, having nothing to offer, and no requirement to post. In contrast, ArchNet members' top five reasons were a lack of time (52%), never having any intention to post and only being interested in reading (43%), didn't know they were supposed to (30%), had nothing to offer (21%), and didn't know how to post (17%).

The reasons for the difference between the studies are not clear but could be explained by the nature of the group or groups being studied. The studies by Preece *et al* (2004) and Nonnecke *et al* (2006) aggregated responses from a large number of online communities while this looked at only one group, with somewhat special characteristics. It is quite possible that similar results could come from looking at more similar groups.

Implications for Site Management

The survey points to many ways that site managers and designers could help increase contribution levels, but there is also a limit to their influence and control. For example, over half of the respondents said that they did not have time to contribute and clearly there is little to be done by site administrators in this regard, assuming of course that the process is not onerous or time-consuming and there is no reason to suspect that this was the case. Still there is much that could be done in terms of member interaction and site design. The site must have the tools necessary to ensure members have the opportunity to share knowledge and participate (Huysman & Wulf, 2006), but as de Souza and Preece (2004) and many others have pointed out, success—meaning active use and participation—depends on paying as much attention to the social side as to the technical functions such as software functionality and usability of the site.

The survey results suggest several strategies for increasing member participation. For example, site managers could be more active in encouraging members to contribute as well as making it clearer where and when they should post. Here lessons from the Seddon *et al* (2008) longitudinal study on long-term successful online collaboration are helpful. They found that a sense of belonging, positive feedback, and rewards were important contributors to the participants' satisfaction and participation. Site administrators can also play a more active role by providing stimulating and challenging activities (Ruiz-Molina & Cuadrado-

Garcia, 2008). In addition, it is important to make the link between information and the providers transparent because as Raban and Rafaeli (2007) found, people are more inclined to share information when that information is identified with them personally.

The need to encourage members and to specify where their contributions are desired is reinforced by a third of the survey respondents who claimed to be unaware that they could or should post. Fortunately, encouraging members may not be that difficult since the majority claims to have both expertise and a willingness to share it with others. Further proof that the members are willing to contribute is the data on the relationship between the length of membership and number of postings. The initial higher contribution level by new members followed by the dramatic drop in participation after the first six or eight months suggests that new members come to the site with the energy and willingness to contribute but something happens—perhaps discouragement or lack of encouragement, or loss of interest—that causes them to stop contributing. If this group's initial contribution rate could be prolonged over a longer period of time, the number of postings would increase dramatically even without expanding the number of contributors. Of course a balance between posting and lurking must be found (Ridings *et al*, 2006). Some posting is necessary for the long-term survival of the site but care must be taken because the quantity of postings does not equate with quality and an overload can result in disappointment and withdrawal of some users (Cheng & Vassileva, 2005). For example, in the study of a German financial service provider, Schoberth *et al* (2006) found that the size of the membership did not affect the communication activity of the participants, but the number of postings did; participants changed their behavior to cope with the increasing information overload.

Furthermore, the surprisingly large number of people who are apparently willing to use the more private or restricted spaces under the right conditions, as opposed to the more public areas, suggests the importance of finding ways to make a site with a large and relatively anonymous membership more familiar and community-like, including ways of making the presence, interests, and contributions of other members more visible, as well as the importance of supportive and coordinated community activity.

For site managers and designers, the study's results are a reminder that technical infrastructure does not guarantee contributions or participation, and that careful attention needs to be paid to social structure that underlies an online community.

FURTHER RESEARCH

This exploratory study was an initial attempt to assess contribution levels and reasons for lurking in a specific online community, and the results suggest multiple directions for future research concentrating on lurkers, contributors, and visitors.

The survey was limited in its scope and the audience it reached but with the lessons learned from this experience, future surveys should be better able to assess the attitudes and opinions of lurkers, attain a higher response rate, and better reflect the feelings of the members.

The server log files were very useful for gaining a more accurate understanding of the quantity and location of the site contributions, but it was a four-month snapshot of interaction on the site. Though there was no indication that this activity was anything but typical, using the data from a longer period of time such as a year would give better insight into the site's activity and cycles.

Survey respondents stated why they did not post and suggested ways that would encourage them to contribute more. For example, they said that encouragement would prompt them to contribute more and though it makes sense that site promotion such as newsletters and reminders could lead to more posting and less lurking, we do not know for sure if this would be the case.

It is equally possible that many lurkers have no intention of ever posting, but either do not know it or are reluctant to admit it. A time-series analysis monitoring contribution and activity levels before and after an initiative would help provide insight into the effectiveness of interventions and armed with this type of information we would have a much better sense of actions and approaches that are available to site managers.

From the survey questionnaire we learned about the attitudes of lurkers and what prevented members from contributing, but it also highlighted our lack of understanding of the flip side of lurking—why do contributors post? What motivates them to contribute? How much do issues such as trust, status, and reputation play into the process? How do they perceive information and who it belongs to? And what are the practical implications of this knowledge? The majority of the lurkers also said that they had an expertise and would be willing to share it but further investigation is required to find the type of information that members possess and are willing to share. The log files also highlighted the fact that members were much more active in the group and personal workspaces than the more public areas. What is it about these areas that make them more willing to post, or conversely what characteristics of the public side inhibit contribution?

Contributors and their activity are not homogeneous. Within the larger group of contributors, we observed certain contribution patterns and that some nationalities, genders, and occupational groups were more likely to post in a specific area than others. The reasons for this are unclear and warrant a more in-depth investigation.

And finally, the ability to generalize these results may be limited because we examined one specific professional community. To broaden our understanding of the nuances of professional cultures, future studies should examine the similarities and differences of other professional online communities.

CONCLUSION

This study adds to the small but growing research on lurking in online communities and explored the contribution levels and lurking behavior in an international online community. More specifically, it extended the knowledge about lurkers and contributors by looking at who contributed, where they contributed, and reasons for lurking. Several important findings came out of this work. We have seen that a relatively small group of contributors produced the majority of the postings and this group needs to be not only supported, but also expanded to include others who are willing and able. This study also demonstrated that not all online spaces are equal. The public areas of the site operate as a network of practice while the group workspaces are more similar to communities of practice and individuals participated in different ways depending on their demographic characteristics. It not only provided insight into a specific type of community, but showed that there are multiple and complex reasons for lurking and that those reasons can vary with the individual and the type of community. And somewhat surprisingly, given the international nature of the membership, few respondents said that bandwidth or English was an obstacle to their participation. The work also highlighted the importance of site management and design, pointed to practical steps that could be taken to improve contribution levels, and emphasized the need to tailor the technical side to support information sharing and social behavior.

It is important to understand why members do not contribute, but it is also valuable to not lose sight of the fact that lurkers are in fact both participating (Nonnecke & Preece, 2000) and learning (Shultz & Beach, 2004). As noted by the survey respondents, almost sixty percent said that the site had had a positive impact on their professional life or education. In spite of, or perhaps even because of, lurking, the large majority of members were satisfied and thought that the site was valuable and beneficial.

Is the high level of lurking a problem? On one hand, we could argue that browsing or information seeking is a perfectly legitimate form of participation and in many cases it is. However, most professional- or work-oriented sites put a high value on communication and sharing of expertise because without contributions from its members the site becomes a one-way information distribution site. Lurking or browsing may be the norm but for a long-term lively and sustainable site, having a minimal level of contribution is essential, but expecting all participants to contribute equally or act similarly may be impractical. As Wenger *et al* (2002, p. 55) notes, "We used to think that we should encourage all community members to participate equally. But because people have different levels of interest in the community, this expectation is unrealistic." Nevertheless, while still accepting that there will be a range of participation and contribution levels on a site, it remains that a significant resource of knowledge is available within this particular community and the challenge is to find ways of tapping into it.

REFERENCES

Andrews, D., Nonnecke, B., & Preece, J. (2003). Electronic survey methodology: a case study in reaching hard-to-involve Internet users. *International Journal of Human-Computer Interaction, 16*(2), 185–210. doi:10.1207/S15327590IJHC1602_04

Ardichvili, A., Page, V., & Wentling, T. (2003). Motivation and barriers to participation in virtual knowledge-sharing communities of practice. *Journal of Knowledge Management, 7*(1), 64–77. doi:10.1108/13673270310463626

Baym, N. K. (1997). Interpreting soap operas and creating community: inside an electronic fan culture. In Kiesler, S. (Ed.), *Culture of the Internet* (pp. 103–120). Mahwah, NJ: Lawrence Erlbaum Associates.

Beamish, A. (2008). *Learning from work: designing organizations for learning and communication*. Stanford, CA: Stanford University Press.

Bishop, J. (2007). Increasing participation in online communities: A framework for human–computer interaction. *Computers in Human Behavior*, *23*, 1881–1893. doi:10.1016/j.chb.2005.11.004

Brown, J. S., & Duguid, P. (2001). Knowledge and organization: a social-practice perspective. *Organization Science*, *12*(2), 198–213. doi:10.1287/orsc.12.2.198.10116

Butler, B. S. (2001). Membership size, communication activity, and sustainability: a resource-based model of online social structures. *Information Systems Research*, *12*(4), 346–362. doi:10.1287/isre.12.4.346.9703

Caffarella, R. S., & Zinn, L. F. (1999). Professional development for faculty: a conceptual framework of barriers and supports. *Innovative Higher Education*, *23*(4), 241–254. doi:10.1023/A:1022978806131

Cheng, R., & Vassileva, J. (2005). User- and Community-Adaptive Rewards Mechanism for Sustainable Online Community. In Ardissono, L., Brna, P., & Mitrovic, A. (Eds.), *Lecture Notes in Computer Science* (pp. 332–336). Berlin: Springer-Verlag.

Constant, D., Sproull, L., & Kiesler, S. (1999). The kindness of strangers: the usefulness of electronic weak ties for technical advice. In Desanctis, G., & Fulk, J. (Eds.), *Shaping organization form: Communication, connection, and community* (pp. 415–444). Thousand Oaks, CA: Sage Publications, Inc.

de Souza, C. S., & Preece, J. (2004). A framework for analyzing and understanding online communities. *Interacting with Computers*, *16*, 579–610. doi:10.1016/j.intcom.2003.12.006

Dennen, V. P. (2008). Pedagogical lurking: Student engagement in non-posting discussion behavior. *Computers in Human Behavior*, *24*(4), 1624–1633. doi:10.1016/j.chb.2007.06.003

Hall, H. (2001). Input-friendliness: motivating knowledge across intranets. *Journal of Information Science*, *27*(3), 139–146. doi:10.1177/016555150102700303

Hall, H., & Graham, D. (2004). Creation and recreation: motivating collaboration to generate knowledge capital in online communities. *International Journal of Information Management*, *24*, 235–246. doi:10.1016/j.ijinfomgt.2004.02.004

Harris, K. (1999). The online life of communities: nurturing community activity in the information society. In Pantry, S. (Ed.), *Building community information networks: strategies and experiences* (pp. 61–83). London: London Association Publishing.

Henri, F., & Pudelko, B. (2003). Understanding and analysing activity and learning in virtual communities. *Journal of Computer Assisted Learning*, (19): 474–487. doi:10.1046/j.0266-4909.2003.00051.x

Huysman, M., & Wulf, V. (2006). IT to Support Knowledge Sharing in Communities, Towards a Social Capital Analysis. *Journal of Information Technology*, (21): 40–51. doi:10.1057/palgrave.jit.2000053

Joyce, E., & Kraut, R. E. (2006). Predicting Continued Participation in Newsgroups. *Journal of Computer-Mediated Communication*, *11*(3), 723–747. doi:10.1111/j.1083-6101.2006.00033.x

Katz, J. (1998). Luring the lurkers. *Retrieved March 10, 2009 from* http://slashdot.org/features/98/12/28/1745252.shtml.

Kollock, P., & Smith, M. (1996). Managing the virtual commons: Cooperation and conflict in computer communities. In Herring, S. (Ed.), *Computer-mediated communication: Linguistic, social, and cross-cultural perspectives*. Amsterdam: John Benjamins.

Lambropoulos, N. (2005, July). *Paradise Lost? Primary Empathy in Online Communities of Interest and Ways of Use*. Paper presented at the 11th International Conference on Human-Computer Interaction, Las Vegas, NV.

Marshall, C. C., Shipman, F. M. III, & McCall, R. J. (1995). Making large-scale information resources serve communities of practice. *Journal of Management Information Systems: JMIS, 11*(4), 65–86.

Marsick, V. J., & Watkins, K. E. (1990). *Informal and incidental learning in the workplace*. London: Routledge.

McLaughlin, M. L., Osborne, K. K., & Smith, C. B. (1995). Standards of conduct on Usenet. In Jones, S. G. (Ed.), *CyberSociety: Computer-mediated communication and society* (pp. 90–111). Thousand Oaks, CA: Sage Publications.

Nonnecke, B., Andrews, D., & Preece, J. (2006). Non-public and public online community participation: Needs, attitudes and behavior. *Electronic Commerce Research, 6*(1), 7–20. doi:10.1007/s10660-006-5985-x

Nonnecke, B., & Preece, J. (2000). *Lurker demographics: Counting the silent*. Paper presented at the Conference on Human Factors in Computing Systems, The Hague.

Nonnecke, B., & Preece, J. (2001). *Why lurkers lurk*. Paper presented at the Americas Conference on Information Systems, Boston.

Plant, R. (2004). Online communities. *Technology in Society, 26*(1), 51–65. doi:10.1016/j.techsoc.2003.10.005

Preece, J. (1999). Empathic communities: balancing emotional and factual communication. *Interacting with Computers, 12*(1), 63–77. doi:10.1016/S0953-5438(98)00056-3

Preece, J. (2001). Sociability and usability in online communities: Determining and measuring success. *Behaviour & Information Technology, 20*(5), 347–356. doi:10.1080/01449290110084683

Preece, J., Nonnecke, B., & Andrews, D. (2004). The top five reasons for lurking: Improving community experiences for everyone. *Computers in Human Behavior, 20*(2). doi:10.1016/j.chb.2003.10.015

Raban, D. R., & Rafaeli, S. (2007). Investigating ownership and the willingness to share information online. *Computers in Human Behavior, 23*, 2367–2382. doi:10.1016/j.chb.2006.03.013

Ridings, Catherine M., Gefen, D. & Arinze, B. (2006). Psychological Barriers: Lurker and Poster Motivation and Behavior in Online Communities. *Communications of the Association for Information Systems*, (18): 329–354.

Ruiz-Molina, M. E., & Cuadrado-Garcia, M. (2008). E-learning in a university interdisciplinary and bilingual context: Analysis of students' participation, motivation and performance. *Multicultural Education & Technology Journal, 2*(3), 156–169. doi:10.1108/17504970810900450

Schoberth, T., Heinzl, A., & Preece, J. (2006). Exploring Communication Activities in Online Communities: A Longitudinal Analysis in the Financial Services Industry. *Journal of Organizational Computing and Electronic Commerce, 16*(3-4), 247–265. doi:10.1207/s15327744joce1603&4_5

Schuler, D. (1996). *New community networks: Wired for change*. Reading, MA: Addison-Wesley Publishing.

Schultz, N., & Beach, B. (2004). *From lurkers to posters* Australian National Training Authority. Retrieved March 10, 2009, from http://74.125.47.132/custom?q=cache:Vq8ieWkntgUJ:www.flexible-learning.net.au/resources/lurkerstoposters.pdf+From+lurkers+to+posters&cd=2&hl=en&ct=clnk&gl=us&client=google-coop-np.

Seddon, K., Skinner, N., & Postlethwaite, K. (2008). Creating a model to examine motivation for sustained engagement in online communities. *Education and Information Technologies, 13*(1), 17–34. doi:10.1007/s10639-007-9048-2

Senge, P. (1990). *The fifth discipline: The art and practice of the learning organization.* New York: Doubleday/Currency.

Sherer, P. D., Shea, T. P., & Kristensen, E. (2003). Online communities of practice: A catalyst for faculty development. *Innovative Higher Education, 27*(3), 183–194. doi:10.1023/A:1022355226924

Smith, M. A. (1999). Invisible crowds in cyberspace. In Smith, M. A., & Kollock, P. (Eds.), *Communities in cyberspace* (pp. 195–219). New York: Routledge.

Sproull, L., & Faraj, S. (1997). Atheism, sex, and databases: The net as a social technology. In Kiesler, S. (Ed.), *Culture of the internet* (pp. 35–51). Mahwah, NJ: Lawrence Erlbaum Associates.

Wang, C. C., & Lai, C. Y. (2006). Knowledge Contribution in the Online Virtual Community: Capability and Motivation. In by J. Lang, F. Lin and J. Wang (Ed.), Lecture Notes in Computer Science (pp. 442-453). Berlin: Springer-Verlag.

Wasko, M. M., & Faraj, S. (2000). "It is what one does": Why people participate and help others in electronic communities of practice. *The Journal of Strategic Information Systems, 9*(2-3), 155–173. doi:10.1016/S0963-8687(00)00045-7

Wasko, M. M., & Faraj, S. (2005). Why should I share? Examining social capital and knowledge contribution in electronic networks of practice. *Management Information Systems Quarterly, 29*(1), 35–57.

Wenger, E. (1998). *Communities of practice: Learning, meaning, and identity.* New York: Cambridge University Press.

Wenger, E., McDermott, R., & Snyder, W. M. (2002). *Cultivating communities of practice: A guide to managing knowledge.* Boston: Harvard Business School Press.

Chapter 4
On the Challenges of Collaborative Data Processing

Sylvie Noël
Communications Research Centre, Canada

Daniel Lemire
UQAM, Canada

ABSTRACT

The last 30 years have seen the creation of a variety of electronic collaboration tools for science and business. Some of the best-known collaboration tools support text editing (e.g., wikis). Wikipedia's success shows that large-scale collaboration can produce highly valuable content. Meanwhile much structured data is being collected and made publicly available. We have never had access to more powerful databases and statistical packages. Is large-scale collaborative data analysis now possible? Using a quantitative analysis of Web 2.0 data visualization sites, the authors find evidence that at least moderate open collaboration occurs. The authors then explore some of the limiting factors of collaboration over data.

INTRODUCTION

Electronic collaboration tools are widespread. Many of these tools are aimed at supporting either group meetings (brainstorming tools, shared whiteboards, videoconferencing tools) or collaborative writing (wikis). These tools have been studied extensively (Pedersen et al., 1993; Okada et al., 1994; Adler et al., 2006). However, although more and more data is being collected, indexed and made available to all, collaborative data processing has received little attention until recently (Viégas et al., 2007, 2008).

Data analysis is a complex but structured task requiring specialized tools such as spreadsheets or statistical packages, some basic knowledge of statistics and information technology, and the domain knowledge to interpret the results. As opposed to text, scientific or business data is often organized in rigid structures (e.g., tables, lists, networks) and it may be more difficult to interpret without appropriate visualization tools. Regardless

DOI: 10.4018/978-1-61520-797-8.ch004

of these difficulties, people are interested in viewing and understanding this data. Already people have access to and are familiar with financial and meteorological data, which appear regularly on television, in newspapers and on popular news sites. People are also willing to explore other types of data. For example, a website presenting statistics about baby names proved very popular (Wattenberg, 2005). Businesses of all sizes, governments, and academics analyze data for many purposes: financial planning, sales and marketing, stocks analysis, scientific research, and so on.

In companies, work-related data is called business information. The term "Business Intelligence" (BI) refers to the techniques used to improve decisions by collecting and aggregating business information. BI systems typically use a data warehouse: a large collection of historical and current data on business operations. End-user BI tools include static reports, spreadsheets linked to data repositories and interactive web applications. There is a growing business intelligence industry: the BI market grew by 10% in 2007 alone (Gartner Inc., 2007). One example of a collaborative BI business is Salesforce.com, a SaaS (software as a service) company which helps its customers share various types of business information (Dignan, 2007). Salesforce.com charges a monthly fee to customers to be able to share sales information among themselves.

While companies tend to keep their internal data private to keep an advantage over their competitors, governments and funding agencies increasingly require that scientific data repositories be accessible to all. For example, the Canadian Institutes of Health Research have a policy on Access to Research Outputs which requires grant recipients to deposit data into public databases (Canadian Institutes of Health Research, 2007). Several United Kingdom funding agencies have similar policies, including the Biotechnology and Biological Sciences Research Council, the Economic and Social Research Council, and the Engineering and Physical Sciences Research

Council. In 1999, the American Congress passed circular A-110, which extended the Freedom of Information Act (FOIA) to all data produced under a funding award. China plans to make 70% of all scientific data publicly available by 2020 (Niu, 2006). There are a growing number of agencies with Open Access policies, including the U. S. National Institutes of Health, France's Institut National de la Santé et de la Recherche Médicale, Italy's Instituto Superiore di Sanita, Australia's National Health and Medical Research Council, and so on. Some examples of open online scientific databases include the Generic Model Organism Database (Stein et al., 2002), the UK Data Archive for social science data, the Finnish Social Science Data Archive, and Harvard-MIT Data Center. More general open source projects for scientists are also appearing on the web. Examples include OpenWetWare.org (Butler, 2005), Science Commons (Wilbanks & Boyle, 2006), and myExperiment.org. Access to the results of scientific projects has become easier thanks to the proliferation of open access journals; the Directory of Open Access Journals (Lund University Libraries, 2003) lists over 3,000 such journals.

Open database projects also exist outside of the scientific domain, such as Swivel (Swivel Inc., 2007), Freebase (http://www.freebase.com), Numbrary (http://www.numbrary.com), and IBM Many Eyes (IBM, 2007). Amazon makes available large datasets from its web service platform (http://aws.amazon.com/publicdatasets/), including the Human Genome, various US census databases, and various labor statistics. Even the intelligence community, previously focused on secrecy, has been called to focus on information sharing (Jones, 2007). Analysis of the American intelligence efforts to prevent 9/11 has revealed that the lack of information sharing between government agencies left many of them surprised by the attack. There is a call to move from a need-to-know approach to a need-to-share one (Findley & Inge, 2005).

In spite of all this online data, we are not aware of any large-scale collaborative data analysis initiative comparable to those in the fields of software design (open-source software initiatives such as Linux) or documentation (Wikipedia). There might be vast collaborative data-analysis projects, but if there are, they apparently happen behind closed doors or have low visibility.

What is limiting large-scale collaborative data analysis, if anything? Could it be caused by limited accessibility to the data among group members? Is it a lack of collaborative tools or motivation? Or might it be the complexity of the task itself? Is it utopian to think that, one day, experts will collaboratively analyze these data repositories? What conditions must be met, both organizationally and technically, so that collaborative data processing can be fruitful? This chapter presents some of the existing tools that can be used to support collaborative data analysis, explores some of the reasons why people may be refraining from this type of collaboration, and speculates on what we, as researchers and designers, can do to help support this kind of collaboration.

This chapter is divided into the following sections:

- We begin by establishing that the possible lack of collaborative data analysis is not due to the absence of specialized tools. We present and discuss some of these tools, including database tools that store data, and data manipulation tools such as spreadsheets, statistics, and visualization packages. We discuss the recent availability of high quality web-based applications (Descy, 2007), which should make collaborative data analysis more attractive. We also review collaboratories: collaboration tools aimed specifically at scientists.
- We then present the results from an experimental evaluation in which we measured some indicators of how much actual collaboration happens within some of the web-based collaboration tools that are freely available, such as Swivel and IBM

Many Eyes. While limited, the collection of such publicly available data can support basic statistical analysis (Ochoa & Duval, 2008). Our data suggests that some collaboration occurs.

- Finally, we speculate on some of the problems associated with collaborative data analysis that may explain its apparent lack of popularity. For example, data analysis requires a certain level of technical expertise in statistics, mathematics, and information technology that is not necessarily available to everyone. Lack of motivation may also provide an explanation. Other issues may also have harmed people's ability to do collaborative data processing: from human issues such as usability problems or confidentiality, to technical ones such as concurrency, data indexing, or version control.

REVIEW OF EXISTING TOOLS

Data processing requires tools specifically built to handle structured data. There are many ways in which people can interact with structured data, and many different tools available to support these various interaction types. Databases are used to store data. Depending on the type of data, it can be manipulated using tools such as spreadsheets or statistical packages. Data can also be transformed and presented in graphical form using visualization tools. In order for groups to collaboratively access structured data, they must use groupware versions of these various tools. We present a few of the available groupware tools here. We also present collaboratories, which are groupware tools aimed specifically at scientists who need to share data.

Recently, many online tools have become available to help people collaboratively analyze data, not only by storing and accessing data, but also by manipulating, analyzing, and visualizing it. Several of these products are web-based enterprise software, which Göldi (2007) has described as a potentially disruptive new model. Specifically, Göldi suggests that web-based tools create new markets: users who have never adopted groupware or collaboratories may use these online tools because they might be simpler or more convenient.

Database Tools

Collaborative data analysis requires a database. In some instances, it may be preferable to give the users direct access to the database where the data is located. When direct access is not required, web database tools can be used. There are many web databases available including Zoho Creator (http://creator.zoho.com/), Dabble DB (http://dabbledb.com/), Quickbase (http://quickbase.intuit.com/), and Caspio Bridge (http://www.caspio.com/). However, none of these products are fully open. These types of tools are more suited for small groups of people collaborating on a project. Google Base (http://base.google.com/) is an open web database, but it fails to offer much with respect to data analysis.

Apache CouchDB, IBM Lotus Notes, and Amazon SimpleDB are software engines for schema-less document-centric databases. The benefit of such an approach is that the data stored in the database does not need to share an agreed-upon schema. In particular, this allows for open disagreement about the meaning of the data stored. However, these engines do not necessarily offer user front-ends to support collaborative data processing. They also do not specifically support end-users.

Spreadsheet Tools

Collaborative spreadsheet tools let several people work on the same spreadsheet either concurrently or in turn. There are several online collaborative spreadsheet tools available: Google Docs Spreadsheets (http://docs.google.com), EditGrid (http://www.editgrid.com/), SecureSheet (http://www.

securesheet.com/), SocialCalc (formerly known as wikicalc, http://www.socialcalc.org), and Zoho Sheet (http://sheet.zoho.com). There are also both eXpresso (http://www.expressocorp.com/) and Badblue (http://badblue.com/helpxls.htm) for sharing Microsoft Excel spreadsheets over the Internet. Excel itself includes the functionality to allow people to share a spreadsheet over a LAN.

Academic collaborative online spreadsheet tool projects include TellTable and CoExcel. Both of these transpose a familiar single-user spreadsheet program to a web-based environment (in the first case, the open source Open Office calc, in the latter Microsoft Excel). This offers the interesting advantage that the user is not forced to learn a new tool in order to do their work. TellTable (Adler et al., 2006) is a web-based framework that can turn single user software (including spreadsheets) into collaborative software. TellTable was originally built to provide an audit trail for spreadsheets (Nash et al., 2004). By storing the spreadsheet files on a server (in order to reduce the risk of tampering with data or the audit trail), and making people access the file through the web, the developers were able to transform calc into a groupware spreadsheet program. Only one person at a time can modify a file using TellTable. CoExcel (Sun et al., 2006) is a project to transform Microsoft Excel into a collaborative spreadsheet that can be used over the web. Both TellTable and CoExcel are still in development.

We are not aware of the widespread use of spreadsheet documents as collaborative objects. There may be company-wide read/write spreadsheets but we suspect that the structure forced upon the users of such spreadsheets limits collaboration. For example, inserting a row or a column in a read/write spreadsheet may mistakenly break another user' formula.

Statistical Tools

Like spreadsheet tools, collaborative statistical tools allow people to transform shared data. We have found two online collaborative statistical tools. Statcrunch (http://www.statcrunch.com/) offers several statistical analyses, including ANOVAs, T tests, regression analyses, and non-parametric statistics. As well, it can display the data using various types of graphics. Covariable (http://www.covariable.com/) also offers various statistical analyses, including T tests, correlations, and linear regressions. Covariable can also display the data in graph form. Both tools allow data and result sharing.

Visualization Tools

Collaborative visualization tools are tools that let people import datasets, create a graph or other type of visual representation of this data, and then share that visualization with other users. There are many such tools available on the web. We describe a few of these here.

DEVise (Livny et al., 1997) is a system that allows users to develop and share visualizations of large datasets. Users can develop their own visual presentations rather than being forced to rely on a collection of pre-existing presentation types (e.g. piecharts, etc.). Furthermore, a user can drill all the way down into a visual representation to see an individual data record. Users can share visualizations as well as explore them independently or even concurrently. DEVise has been used for financial, medical, meteorological, biological, and soil sciences datasets. DEVise is meant to support groups working together, but it does not support an open source model. This is also the case for Spotfire (http://spotfire.tibco.com/index.cfm), which is aimed at supporting businesses, and Command Post of the Future (Roth, 2004), which is aimed at the military.

IBM Many Eyes (IBM, 2007) has an open web approach. It is meant specifically to let anyone upload any type of database and share the resulting visualization with everyone on the Web (Viégas et al., 2007, 2008). According to its creators, users' most common activities on the site are "to upload

data, construct visualizations, and leave comments on either datasets or visualizations." The authors have included several features specifically to support collaboration, including communication tools such as text comments, annotations, and bookmarks on visualizations. Within the first two months of its life, IBM Many Eyes had gathered over 1,400 users who had uploaded about 2,100 datasets, created 1,700 visualizations and added about 450 comments. These results suggest that people are willing to work together on data analysis.

Swivel (http://www.swivel.com) is somewhat similar to IBM Many Eyes, although the visualization tools it offers are not as powerful (Butler, 2007). Swivel also makes it easy for users to mash datasets together to come up with new and interesting visualizations of their data. Other, similar tools include Data360 (http://www.data360.org) and Trendrr (http://trendrr.com/). Dataplace (http://www.dataplace.org) is aimed more specifically at housing and demographic data from the United States. It lets people quickly create thematic maps by translating data onto maps. Daytum (http://daytum.com) is a social dashboard allowing users to share and visualize data from their daily lives. Finally, Microsoft Research published DataDepot (http://datadepot.msresearch.us), a tool to track and share trend lines generated from data such as precipitation levels or stock prices.

Most of these tools accept standard data formats such as column-separated-values (CSV) files. The results can often be shared as a URI where comments can be added, or new views generated.

Collaboratories

Collaboratories are collaboration tools aimed specifically at scientists. The term 'collaboratory' first appeared in 1993 (Cerf et al., 1993) and describes a virtual research center, in which scientists from various laboratories across the world can cooperate and share data, resources, and information. While early examples of collaboratories were aimed at giving scientists access to expensive instruments such as particle accelerators (Kouzes, Myers & Wulf, 1996), most of the collaboratories we find today are web-based database repositories (Ma, 2007). Collaboratories are very popular. Already in 2004, the Science of Collaboratories website (http://www.scienceofcollaboratories.org/Resources/colisting.php) noted the existence of over 200 different collaboratories. Recent examples of collaboratories include the National Human Neuroimaging Collaboratory (Keator et al., 2008), the Michigan Clinical Research Collaboratory (Schwenk & Green, 2006) and the Center for Behavioral Neuroscience (Powell & Albers, 2006).

There have been several attempts at building true online collaborative tools for scientists (e.g., Reed, Giles & Catlett, 1997; Avery & Foster, 2000; Reed, 2003; Ma, 2007). These collaboratory projects are usually aimed at very specific groups of research labs who are working together on a project and who require tools to support their collaborative needs.

In this section, we have shown that there are several tools available to do collaborative data analysis but are people willing to use them? The following section explores this question by trying to measure the level of collaboration in some web-based data processing tools.

EXPERIMENTAL EVALUATION

Golovchinsky et al. (2008, 2009) uses four dimensions to classify computer-supported information seeking collaboration: intent, depth of mediation, concurrency, and location. Because of the way most collaboration is done with the available open access collaborative data analysis tools, we are more concerned here by the intent dimension. Intent is explicit when people get together and work on a specific topic. For example, if coworkers must produce an annual report or research papers, their collaboration has an explicit intent. An example of collaboration with implicit intent

is certain recommender systems, in which past search behavior is used to suggest other topics (e.g., Amazon's "people who bought this product also bought").

Collaboration is often multimodal: whereas some users may use a chat tool, others will prefer email (Noël & Robert, 2004; Morris, 2008). This may lead to biases in the trace analysis. For example, Grippa et al. (2006) have shown that relying on email traces alone may overestimate the influence of a core group of individuals who dominate a given mode of communication. Thus, one individual might be a prolific email user whereas his peers use the phone. These biases make it difficult to study groups or projects based only on openly available data.

It might be difficult or impossible to evaluate collaboration between any two given individuals by limited traces, but we may compare one social web site with another and derive some quantifiable information. Minimally, posting content for all to see, especially when others can comment, shows an openness to collaboration. Publicly reacting to existing content is also necessarily a form of collaboration. These types of behavior are a form of global (at the scale of the community) collaboration. In the terms of Golovchinsky et al. (2008, 2009), we have collaboration with implicit intent. A large number of people contributing content indicates that more implicit collaboration is occurring.

Using this method of measuring collaboration on a variety of social web sites, Ochoa and Duval (2008) divided the sites into three categories. In the first category (Amazon Reviews, Digg, FanFiction, and SlideShare), 10% of the users contributed 40% to 60% of the content, in the second category (Furl, LibraryThing, and Revver), 10% of the users contributed 60% to 80% of the content, and in the last category, most of the content was contributed by a few users. The first category of tools are built more collaboratively than the other two categories, in the sense that more users contributed to the content.

It might be surprising that having 10% of the users contribute 50% of the content means that these tools foster a (relatively) large amount of collaboration. As a basis for comparison, Lotka's law states that the number of authors making n scientific contributions is about $1/n^a$ of those making one contribution, where a is about two (Lotka, 1926; Chung & Cox, 1990). One consequence of Lotka's law is that given a large enough set of scientists, almost all contributions (say 90%) will be due to the top 10% most prolific authors.

In which of these three categories do open source database projects fit? We began by looking at OpenWetWare. OpenWetWare is a collection of open science notebooks. While not a data processing site per se, we were interested in this site because it still contains a lot of data regarding biological entities and documentation about data processing techniques. We recovered the last 5000 edits from the site (the data was collected on May 16, 2008). We found that 10% of the users contributed 50% of the changes. Hence, by the Ochoa-Duval categorization, there is a significant amount of collaboration. This suggests that scientists are interested in sharing information with others.

Turning to the open data processing sites, we selected three candidates: IBM Many Eyes, Swivel, and StatCrunch. There are no other publicly available sites similar to these three to our knowledge. We were able to retrieve contributions by different users from all three sites. All operate in a similar manner except that StatCrunch is not free: users must pay a small subscription fee to upload new data and do analyses. However, no subscription is required to view work uploaded to the StatCrunch site. Both StatCrunch and IBM Many Eyes require all contributors to have an account. While Swivel requires users to be registered to upload data, anyone can contribute a new plot.

We captured all data by screen scraping: HTML pages were saved to disk and parsed using regular expressions. To ensure that our scripts did not adversely affect these web sites, we limited our queries to one per second, and we chose to retrieve no more than 1,500 pages from each site. Table 1 presents the size of the datasets. Except for Swivel, our datasets cover thousands of users and tens of thousands of items. Ochoa and Duval (2008) had between 2,300 and 82,000 users per dataset. Both our IBM Many Eyes and StatCrunch datasets are similar in size to their samples.

Swivel offers two ways to navigate through recent plot contributions: by dates and by views. Unfortunately, we found that two thirds of all new plots were from unregistered users. So, for Swivel, we limited our investigation to dataset contributions. We found only 536 users had uploaded datasets.

IBM Many Eyes allows users to browse all recent contributions whether they are new datasets, new plots or new comments. Unfortunately, recent plot contributions are not listed together with the contributing users' ID. Retrieving recent plots might have required loading tens of thousands of web pages, one for each plot. To minimize the impact of our data capture, we limited our investigations to datasets and comments. Of the three websites we investigated, IBM Many Eyes has the largest database, with over 37,000 datasets uploaded by over 8,800 users. Only about 7% of all users posted comments.

StatCrunch allows users to navigate through recent datasets, results, and publicly published reports. Whereas the datasets are raw data, results

Table 1. Descriptive statistics of the collected data

		Number of items	Number of users
Swivel	Datasets	1,200	536
IBM Many Eyes	Datasets	37,672	8,843
	Comments	1,223	602
StatCrunch	Datasets	9,351	1,833
	Results	11,403	1,190
	Reports	1,928	358

are the output of some data processing, and the reports are aggregated results. Hence, there is a hierarchy of complexity on StatCrunch, from data to individual results to reports. More users provided datasets than reports. Also, there are far fewer reports than results or datasets. We examined information for datasets, results, and reports from StatCrunch.

For each site, and each chosen type of contribution, we took the 10% most prolific users and counted their contributions. Table 2 presents the results of our analysis. For example, on IBM Many Eyes, the top 10% of users uploaded nearly 19,000 datasets. We did not take into account the volume of each contribution (such as the number of bytes uploaded).

All contributions correspond to the first Ochoa-Duval category: the top 10% of the users contribute 40% to 60% of the content. Hence, at least a moderate amount of collaboration is occurring. The reports in StatCrunch are the only exception. They have an almost flat distribution: the top 10% of all users contribute only 19% of all reports. However, only 358 users published a report compared to 1,833 users who produced at least a dataset (a ratio of 1 to 5).

In summary, data analysis sites such as Swivel, IBM Many Eyes, and StatCrunch are collaborative, in the sense that the most prolific individuals contribute only about half of the content. They are comparable with popular sites such as Amazon Reviews, Digg, FanFiction, and SlideShare.

Table 2. Percentage of contributions by top 10% most prolific users

		Contributions by top 10% of users
Swivel	Datasets	48%
IBM Many Eyes	Datasets	49%
	Comments	55%
StatCrunch	Datasets	57%
	Results	40%
	Reports	19%

We probably underestimate the total number of users of these websites. As we have already mentioned, people can use the systems without leaving a public trace, making them uncounted collaborators. Since these websites let people create private groups, there may be local (at the project-level) collaboration that we are not measuring.

INGREDIENTS FOR A SUCCESSFUL COLLABORATIVE DATA ANALYSIS

We have shown above that people are willing to collaborate on databases, at least on a global community level, and that there exist plenty of groupware tools that could be used to support this collaboration. Yet, our results suggest that contribution may not be as widespread as it could be. For example, while over 8,000 users created graphs on IBM Many Eyes, only about 600 users contributed comments, and 66 of these users contributed 55% of the comments.

Even when people use collaborative tools to work on a project, data analysis may remain a single-user task, at least in our experience. Nor is there any large-scale equivalent to Wikipedia for structured data. Clearly there are stumbling blocks that are limiting the popularity of collaborative data analysis tools. In this section, we examine some of the issues that designers of these tools need to consider if they wish to promote successful collaboration on structured data.

Sharing the Data

The several large repositories listed above show that there is much data being shared. However, data sharing is not always accepted as a requirement, even in science. For example, Reidpath and Allotey (2001) asked 29 corresponding authors of research articles which appeared in the *British Medical Journal* to share their data. Only one author actually shared his data in this survey. In the case of businesses, people may be wary of sharing data with their competitors. Many factors may explain why data sharing is not forthcoming: documenting and packaging data for others requires some work; there can be confidentiality and security issues; there is the fear of ridicule if others find errors in one's work; there may be a competitive edge by having data others do not; and so on. However, there is evidence that sharing detailed research data can be beneficial to authors by increasing their citation rate (Piwowar et al., 2007).

Certainly data sharing, when it occurs, may lead to collaborative efforts in the sense that several distinct teams may successively work on overlapping datasets. However, the processing itself may still be done independently (Shah, 2008).

Task Specialization

Local or internal collaboration occurs within closed teams. It is often customary within teams to delegate specific tasks to specific individuals. While some members may handle data processing, others will write text, contribute ideas, or manage the team. If the team is small and relatively stable, there may not be any reason to share the technical task of analyzing the data. Indeed, specialization may be more effective. Among prolific book writers, dividing up the task into chapters is a common strategy (Hartley & Branthwaite, 1989). Posner and Baecker (1993) provide several reasons to specialize the writing tasks including: access to technology and software, social status, familiarity with the requirements, and uniformity of the final product.

Credit

External or global collaboration occurs more openly. Examples include OpenWetWare where scientists share open notebooks with the world. We believe that external collaboration over data

processing is still an outlier in science. According to Hannay, the biggest barrier to collaboration in science is the credit problem (Waldrop, 2008): individuals need to feel certain that their work will not be scooped by others.

Access

In collaborative writing, Posner and Baecker (1993) have found that access to technology and software sometimes determines the division of labor. Tutt et al. (2007) have presented a generalized concept - local action - wherein some actions can only occur in some locations. With web-based applications we expect this issue to be less significant.

Data is often confidential, making publication and sharing more difficult. This includes personal information and strategic business data. For many users, data privacy remains a necessity and lack of privacy may constitute a barrier to sharing (Descy, 2007). However, a lot of the data being collected is now available freely.

Expertise

Data analysis sometimes requires a technical expertise in statistics, mathematics, and information technology that few people possess. In addition, learning to use spreadsheet or statistical tools requires time and energy that many people may not have. If data analysis can be delegated to a single person who is already familiar with these tools, then the group will waste less time during this phase. While this argument may hold in a closed social network, like a research group, it is less likely to be true for very large groups, where many people have sufficient expertise for data processing. Wikipedia has shown that large-scale collaboration is not only possible on difficult problems, such as crafting a highly technical article, but that it can also be very fruitful.

Concurrency and Asynchronicity

Version control in situations where changes can be reverted or done in parallel remains challenging (Adler et al. 2006). Keeping track of changes can be particularly difficult with databases as compared with text. Furthermore, because the integrity of data can be a very important issue, an audit trail that allows people to track all changes is an essential tool for collaborative databases.

We can distinguish two types of data: collected or raw data, and derived data. Assuming collaborators agree on the meaning of the collected data, they will build upon it by applying various operations. These operations generate views (derived data), which may come to depend on each other. For example, a user may take the raw data, prune some of the outliers (view 1) and then compute statistical measures on the outlier-free data (view 2). If these views are defined only through algorithms, keywords, or formulae it may become difficult for others to follow the flow. Wattenberg (2005) has underlined the importance of letting people access past data states when sharing visualizations. Therefore any system that lets people work on data needs to not only make people aware of the historical modifications and computations made to the data, but also give them easy access to past states and the ability to work on these states (letting people do 'what if' scenarios with ease). Moreover, since interpretation errors are likely to be common, a feedback loop is needed: one should share interpretations in such a way that they can be corrected by others.

As in text processing, users may need to work jointly on the same object. If the tool permits concurrent editing, this can result in conflict (e.g., if people try to modify the same data at the same time). Several methods solve such potential conflicts during synchronous editing (Mitchell, 1996). However, because text tends to convey meaning better than numbers or figures, conflicts of intent may be more difficult to detect and resolve in databases than in text documents. Even if people are only permitted to work on the same data asynchronously, such conflicts can still arise due to the interdependence of data points.

Usability

In large datasets, navigation is difficult and retrieval of data may also prove difficult without proper indexing. Performance issues may plague users who have to work with these very large datasets. The volume of data can make sharing more difficult due to bandwidth limitations. Even though bandwidth and storage are increasing, so is the size of the datasets, eliminating any possible gains.

Reorganizing data on the fly is relatively easy using a wiki, since you can simply copy and paste the data. In a collaborative spreadsheet, the data tends to be more rigidly organized (more structured) making on-the-fly reorganization difficult. In addition, users may be unfamiliar with the existing tools. Exchanging reports prepared by a single individual, and commenting using the familiar email interface is often an attractive proposition.

Preparing a convenient output can be difficult since most data processing tasks are not easily exported in a meaningful format to users, contrary to what is possible with collaborative editing tools such as wikis. One partial solution to that problem is to give people the ability to create and export visualizations, which are outputs that are easy to understand.

Flexible Semantics

Traditional data sharing and data integration approaches require a globally consistent data instance (Taylor & Ives, 2006). Current Business Intelligence techniques tend to define schemas and semantics in a centralized manner (Aouiche et al., 2008). However, people often disagree on the semantics of the collected data. This may be especially challenging in cases where the data was collected by remote groups. Even among the group members who collected the data, there may be disagreement on the meaning of the numbers. Inside businesses, there are commonly disagreements on the exact meaning of simple terms like revenue or profit. Improper or ambiguous documentation may prove problematic.

Meanwhile, schemes for large-scale data sharing have generally failed because database approaches tend to impose strict global constraints: a single global schema, a globally consistent data instance, and central administration (Green et al. 2007). Spotfire, Business Objects, and QlikTech are among the companies providing tools to enable the average user to contribute by relaxing global constraints (Havenstein, 2003).

Motivation

Given access to the right tools, people are willing to engage in social data analysis. For example, Wattenberg (2005) found that people were challenging each other to find trends concerning baby names while using NameVoyager. NameVoyager is a web-based visualization tool (http://www.babynamewizard.com/voyager) that displays the popularity of baby names in the U.S. over time. It covers over 100 years of data. People can drill down to a subset of names by typing in letters; this will display all the names starting with those letters as the letters are typed in. According to Wattenberg, people were building on others' findings, making this an example of group data mining. Wattenberg suggests that if a collaborative tool is to encourage people to share their discoveries it needs to let them easily re-create or access data states previously created by others. The popularity of sites such as IBM Many Eyes and Swivel clearly shows that people are willing to play around with complex data and share their results with the world. Another example of such a site is Mycrocosm, a website published by MIT researchers where users can share the "minutiae of daily life" as simple statistical graphs (http://mycro.media.mit.edu/).

Data analysis may not be perceived as interesting but the ubiquity of statistics in our daily life combined with appealing visualization techniques should alleviate any prejudice. Moreover, programming is also a rather technical task and open source software has shown that open collaboration is a working model for software creation. Prolific contributors to Wikipedia are motivated by increased credibility within the community (Forte & Bruckman, 2005) as well as by altruistic goals such as contributing to the greater good (Wagner & Prasarnphanich, 2007). Participation in open source software is similarly motivated (Wu et al., 2007) by altruistic goals and also by possible career advancement. These same incentives are likely to be present for collaborative data processing. To ensure that individuals get adequate credit for their work, tools should track the authors of various contributions and make this information accessible to users.

CONCLUSION

Ioannidis (2005) claimed that most research results are wrong because most datasets are too small or the investigation is biased. He observed that researchers commonly select the most positive results and discard the negative results prior to publication. These biases may be exacerbated if there are commercial imperatives underlying the work. There is no reason to believe that the same biases are not present in Business Intelligence. If a more diverse set of people could analyze the same data, it seems likely that biases in the analysis would be less frequent. Collaborative data processing tools could help support these multiple analyses. Would open collaborative data processing actually increase the reliability of published results? Given large data repositories, should we set up collaborative data processing initiatives? Should companies rely on a wider range of employees to process their data? While the reliability of open encyclopedias such as Wikipedia is often reported to be good, noise and missing information are concerns (Clauson et al., 2008). However, since open collaborative data processing can contribute to making research reproducible, it might make it easier to detect some types of fraudulent behavior (Laine et al. 2007). We believe that other benefits to open collaborative data analysis are likely to exist, but it remains to identify under which circumstances this type of data analysis is most likely to be beneficial. Ultimately, we need better experimental evaluation of collaborative data analysis, including longitudinal studies.

A distinguishing factor between collaboration over a wiki or software, and collaborative data analysis might be the barrier to entry. Many scientists and business analysts may have a vested interest in controlling not only access to their data, but also the analytical process. A cultural change wherein access to the raw data and to the processing steps would be an essential part of any report or scientific communication, would likely be disruptive in the same way Wikipedia has been disruptive within the encyclopedia industry and open source software disruptive within the software industry. Would collaborative data processing lead us to a new form of highly collaborative science?

There are many good collaborative software packages, and a substantial amount of good collaboration. None of the limitations to collaborative data processing that we have identified are entirely unsolved. Nevertheless, the sophistication of the open data processing tools could be greater. Tools such as IBM Many Eyes or Swivel are appropriate for generating graphics, but they cannot process data. As well, while they permit implicit collaboration, it is not clear how well they support explicit types of collaboration. Shareable spreadsheets are familiar to users, but were designed for single users. Based on our survey and on earlier work (Adler et al., 2006; Aouiche et al., 2008), here are some features that we recommend:

1. Due to the need for flexible semantics, data should be presented in an unstructured manner. We should encourage loose couplings in how data is presented to the users: large structured tables or graphs are probably not appropriate. We expect that it is difficult to scale a spreadsheet to dozens of simultaneous users.

2. In the spirit of tools such as IBM Many Eyes and Swivel, the result of any editing should be immediately shareable in an output easily understood by human readers. Ideally, any result should be shareable as a single URI.

3. Users should be able to go back to past data states and branch out from there to new data analyses.

4. Visualizations can simplify the presentation of complex data. Therefore, some sort of visualization tool should be included.

5. Some type of peer review process may be required to control data quality. Wikipedia offers a working example of group quality control that depends on people, not on complex tools.

6. Any change should be clearly credited to its author.

7. To alleviate the local action problem, we should use open standards to enter data and to publish data analysis.

ACKNOWLEDGMENT

The authors wish to thank Sarah Dumoulin and two anonymous reviewers for their suggestions and comments. The second author is supported by NSERC grant 261437.

REFERENCES

Adler, A., Nash, J. C., & Noël, S. (2006). Evaluating and implementing a collaborative office document system. *Interacting with Computers, 18*(4), 665–682. doi:10.1016/j.intcom.2005.10.001

Aouiche, K., Lemire, D., & Godin, R. (2008). Collaborative OLAP with tag clouds: Web 2.0 OLAP formalism and experimental evaluation. In *Proceedings of the 4th International Conference on Web Information Systems and Technologies (WEBIST 2008)*, Funchal, Madeira, Portugal (pp. 5-12).

Avery, P., & Foster, I. (2000). The GriPhyN Project: Towards petascale virtual-data grids. *GryPhyn Report 2000-1*. Retrieved February 9, 2009, from http://www.griphyn.org/documents/document_server/uploaded_documents/doc--501--proposal_all.doc

Butler, D. (2005). Science in the web age: Joint efforts. *Nature, 438,* 548–549. doi:10.1038/438548a

Butler, D. (2007). Data sharing: The next generation. *Nature, 446,* 10–11. doi:10.1038/446010b

Canadian Institutes of Health Research. (2007). *Access to research outputs.* Retrieved February 9, 2009, from http://www.cihr-irsc.gc.ca/e/34846.html

Cerf, V. G., Cameron, A., Lederberg, J., Russel, C., Schatz, B., & Shames, P. (1993). *National Collaboratories: Applying Information Technologies for Scientific Research.* Washington, DC: National Academy Press.

Chung, K. H., & Cox, R. A. K. (1990). Patterns of productivity in the finance literature: A study of the bibliometric distributions. *The Journal of Finance, 45*(1), 301–309. doi:10.2307/2328824

Clauson, K. A., Polen, H. H., Boulos, M. N. K., & Dzenowagis, J. H. (2008). Scope, completeness, and accuracy of drug information in Wikipedia. *The Annals of Pharmacotherapy, 42*(12), 1814. doi:10.1345/aph.1L474

Descy, D. E. (2007). Browser-based online applications: Something for everyone! *TechTrends: Linking Research and Practice to Improve Learning, 51*(2), 3–5.

Dignan, L. (2007). Salesforce.com rolls out customer data sharing; eyes 1 million subscribers. *ZDNet.* Retrieved February 9, 2009, from http://blogs.zdnet.com/BTL/?p=7239

Findley, L. G. R., & Inge, L. G. J. (2005). North American defence and security in the aftermath of 9/11. *Canadian Military Journal, 6*(1), 9–16.

Forte, A., & Bruckman, A. (2005). *Why do people write for Wikipedia? Incentives to contribute to open-content publishing.* Paper presented at the *GROUP* workshop "Sustaining community: The role and design of incentive mechanisms in online systems", Sanibel Island, FL. Retrieved February 9, 2009, from http://www.cc.gatech.edu/~aforte/ForteBruckmanWhyPeopleWrite.pdf

Gartner Inc. (2007, January 30). *Business intelligence market will grow 10 percent in EMEA in 2007 according to Gartner* [Press release]. Retrieved February 9, 2009, from http://www.gartner.com/it/page.jsp?id=500680

Göldi, A. (2007). *The Emerging Market for Web-based Enterprise Software.* Unpublished master's thesis, Massachusetts Institute of Technology, Boston, MA.

Golovchinsky, G., Pickens, J., & Back, M. (2008). A taxonomy of collaboration in online information seeking. In *11th International Workshop on Collaborative Information Retrieval, JCDL 2008*, June 20, 2008.

Golovchinsky, G., Qvarfordt, P., & Pickens, J. (2009, March). Collaborative information seeking. *Computer*, 47–51. doi:10.1109/MC.2009.73

Green, T. J., Karvounarakis, G., Taylor, N. E., Biton, O., Ives, Z. G., & Tannen, V. (2007). ORCHESTRA: Facilitating collaborative data sharing. In *Proceedings of the ACM International Conference on Management of Data (SIGMOD'07)*, Beijing, China (pp. 1131-1133).

Grippa, F., Zilli, A., Laubacher, R., & Gloor, P. (2006). E-mail may not reflect the social network. In *Proceedings of the 2006 International Sunbelt Social Network Conference*, Vancouver, BC, Canada.

Hartley, J., & Branthwaite, A. (1989). The psychologist as wordsmith: A questionnaire study of the writing strategies of productive British psychologists. *Higher Education, 18*(4), 423–452. doi:10.1007/BF00140748

Havenstein, H. (2003). BI vendors seek to tap end-user power. *InfoWorld, 25*(22).

IBM, Inc. (2007). *Many Eyes*. Retrieved February 9, 2009, from http://manyeyes.alphaworks.ibm.com/manyeyes/

Ioannidis, J. P. (2005). Why most published research findings are false. *PLoS Medicine, 2*(8), e124. doi:10.1371/journal.pmed.0020124

Jones, C. (2007). Intelligence reform: The logic of information sharing. *Intelligence and National Security, 22*(3), 384–401. doi:10.1080/02684520701415214

Keator, D. B., Grethe, J. S., Marcus, D., Ozyurt, B., Gadde, S., & Murphy, S. (2008). A national human neuroimaging collaboratory enabled by the Biomedical Informatics Research Network (BIRN). *IEEE Transactions on Information Technology in Biomedicine, 12*(2), 162–172. doi:10.1109/TITB.2008.917893

Kouzes, R. T., Myers, J. D., & Wulf, W. A. (1996). Collaboratories: Doing science on the Internet. *Computer, 29*(8), 40–46. doi:10.1109/2.532044

Laine, C., Goodman, S. N., Griswold, M. E., & Sox, H. C. (2007). Reproducible research: Moving toward research the public can really trust. *Annals of Internal Medicine, 146*(6), 450–453.

Livny, M., Ramakrishnan, R., Beyer, K., Chen, G., Donjerkovic, D., Lawande, S., et al. (1997). DEVise: Integrated querying and visual exploration of large datasets. In *Proceedings of the ACM International Conference on Management of Data (SIGMOD'97)* (301-312).

Lotka, A. J. (1926). The frequency distribution of scientific productivity. *Journal of the Washington Academy of Sciences, 16*(12), 317–324.

Lund University Libraries. (2003). *Directory of open access journals*. Retrieved February 9, 2009, from http://www.doaj.org/

Ma, K.-L. (2007). Creating a collaborative space to share data, visualization and knowledge. *ACM SIGGRAPH Computer Graphics Quarterly, 41*(4).

Mitchell, A. (1996). *Communication and Shared Understanding in Collaborative Writing*. Unpublished Master's Thesis, Computer Science Department, University of Toronto.

Morris, M. R. (2008). A survey of collaborative web search practices. In *Proceedings of the ACM Conference on Computer-Human Interaction (CHI'08)* (pp. 1657-1660).

Nash, J., Adler, A., & Smith, N. (2004). TellTable spreadsheet audit: From technical possibility to operating prototype. In *Proceedings 2004 Conference European Spreadsheet Interest Group* (pp. 45-56).

Niu, J. (2006). *Incentive study for research data sharing*. Retrieved February 9, 2009, from http://icd.si.umich.edu/twiki/pub/ICD/LabGroup/fieldpaper_6_25.pdf

Noël, S., & Robert, J.-M. (2004). Empirical study on collaborative writing: What do co-authors do, use and like? *Computer Supported Cooperative Work*, *13*(1), 63–89. doi:10.1023/B:COSU.0000014876.96003.be

Ochoa, X., & Duval, E. (2008). *Quantitative analysis of user-generated content on the Web.* Web Science Workshop WebEvolve.

Okada, K. I., Maeda, F., Ichikawaa, Y., & Matsushita, Y. (1994). Multiparty videoconferencing at virtual social distance: MAJIC design. In *Proceedings 1994 ACM conference on Computer supported cooperative work* (pp. 385-393).

Pedersen, E. R., McCall, K., Moran, T. P., & Halasz, F. G. (1993). Tivoli: An electronic whiteboard for informal workgroup meetings. In *Proceedings SIGCHI conference on Human factors in computing systems* (pp. 391-398).

Piwowar, H. A., Day, R. S., & Fridsma, D. B. (2007). Sharing Detailed Research Data Is Associated with Increased Citation Rate. *PLoS ONE*, *2*(3). doi:10.1371/journal.pone.0000308

Posner, I., & Baecker, R. M. (1993). How people write together. In Baecker, R. M. (Ed.), *Readings in Groupware and Computer-Supported Cooperative Work: Assisting Human-Human Collaboration* (pp. 239–250). San Mateo, CA: Morgan Kaufman.

Powell, K. R., & Albers, H. E. (2006). Center for Behavioral Neuroscience: A prototype multi-institutional collaborative research center. *Journal of Biomedical Discovery and Collaboration*, *1*(1), 9. doi:10.1186/1747-5333-1-9

Reed, D. A. (2003). Grids, the TeraGrid, and Beyond. *Computer*, *36*(1), 62–68. doi:10.1109/MC.2003.1160057

Reed, D. A., Giles, R. C., & Catlett, C. E. (1997). Distributed data and immersive collaboration. *Communications of the ACM*, *40*(11), 38–48. doi:10.1145/265684.265691

Reidpath, D. D., & Allotey, P. A. (2001). Data Sharing in Medical Research: An Empirical Investigation. *Bioethics*, *15*(2), 125–134. doi:10.1111/1467-8519.00220

Roth, S. (2004). Capstone Address: Visualization as a medium for capturing and sharing thoughts. In *Proceedings IEEE InfoVis 2004* (pp. 8).

Schwenk, T. L., & Green, L. A. (2006). The Michigan Clinical Research Collaboratory: Following the NIH roadmap to the community. *Annals of Family Medicine*, *4*(1), 49–54. doi:10.1370/afm.538

Shah, C. (2008). Toward Collaborative Information Seeking (CIS). *Proceedings of the Collaborative Exploratory Search Workshop*.

Stein, L. D., Mungall, C., Shu, S. Q., Caudy, M., Mangone, M., & Day, A. (2002). The Generic Genome Browser: A building block for a model organism system database. *Genome Research*, *12*, 1599–1610. doi:10.1101/gr.403602

Sun, C., Xia, S., Sun, D., Chen, D., Shen, H., & Cai, W. (2006). Transparent adaptation of single-user applications for multi-user real-time collaboration. *ACM Transactions on Computer-Human Interaction*, *13*(4), 531–582. doi:10.1145/1188816.1188821

Swivel, Inc. (2007). *Swivel*. Retrieved February 9, 2009, from http://www.swivel.com

Taylor, N. E., & Ives, Z. G. (2006). Reconciling while tolerating disagreement in collaborative data sharing. In *Proceedings of the ACM Conference on Management of Data (SIGMOD '06)* (pp. 13-24).

Tutt, D., Hindmarsh, J., & Fraser, M. (2007). The distributed work of local action: Interaction amongst virtually collocated research teams. In *Proceedings of the European Conference on Computer-Supported Cooperative Work (ECSCW 2007)* (pp. 199-218).

Viégas, F. B., Wattenberg, M., McKeon, M., van Ham, F., & Kriss, J. (2008). Harry Potter and the meat-filled freezer: A case study of spontaneous usage of visualization tools. In *Proceedings HICSS 2008* (pp. 159).

Viégas, F. B., Wattenberg, M., van Ham, F., Kriss, J., & McKeon, M. (2007). A site for visualization at internet scale. In *Proceedings Infovis 2007* (pp. 1121–1128). Many Eyes.

Wagner, C., & Prasarnphanich, P. (2007). Innovating collaborative content creation: The role of altruism and wiki technology. In *Proceedings HICSS 2007, 40*(1), 278.

Waldrop, M. M. (2008). Science 2.0 - Is Open Access Science the Future? *Scientific American*. Retrieved February 9, 2009, from http://www.sciam.com/article.cfm?id=science-2-point-0

Wattenberg, M. (2005). Baby names, visualization, and social data analysis. In Proceedings Infovis 2005 (pp. 1-7).

Wilbanks, J., & Boyle, J. (2006). *Introduction to Science Commons*. Retrieved February 23, 2009, from http://sciencecommons.org/wp-content/uploads/ScienceCommons_Concept_Paper.pdf

Wu, C. G., Gerlach, J. H., & Young, C. E. (2007). An empirical analysis of open source software developers' motivations and continuance intentions. *Information & Management, 44*(3), 253–262. doi:10.1016/j.im.2006.12.006

ADDITIONAL READING

Adler, A., & Nash, J. C. (2004). Knowing what was done: uses of a spreadsheet log file. *Spreadsheets in Education, 1*(2), 118–130.

Arita, M., & Suwa, K. (2008). Search extension transforms wiki into a relational system: A case for flavonoid metabolite database. *BioData Mining, 1*(7).

Bentley, R., Horstmann, T., & Trevor, J. (1997). The World Wide Web as enabling technology for CSCW: The case of BSCW. *Computer Supported Cooperative Work, 6*(2-3), 111–134. doi:10.1023/A:1008631823217

Cederqvist, P. (2002). *Version management with CVS*. Bristol, UK: Network Theory.

Cole, P., & Nast-Cole, J. (1992). A primer on group dynamics for groupware developers. In Marca, D., & Bock, G. (Eds.), *Groupware: Software for Computer-Supported Cooperative Work* (pp. 44–57). Los Alamitos, CA: IEEE Computer Society Press.

Dillon, A., & Maynard, S. (1995). 'Don't forget to put the cat out' - Or why collaborative authoring software and everyday writing pass one another by! *New Review of Hypermedia and Multimedia, 1*, 135–153. doi:10.1080/13614569508914663

Dix, A. (1997). Challenges for Cooperative Work on the Web: An Analytical Approach. *Computer Supported Cooperative Work, 6*(2), 135–156. doi:10.1023/A:1008635907287

Elbashir, M. Z., Collier, P. A., & Lee, S.-F. (2008). Measuring the effects of business intelligence systems: The relationship between business process and organizational performance. *International Journal of Accounting Information Systems, 9*(3), 135–153. doi:10.1016/j.accinf.2008.03.001

Grigori, D., Casati, F., Castellanos, M., Dayal, U., Sayal, M., & Shan, M. C. (2004). Business Process Intelligence. *Computers in Industry, 53*(3), 321–343. doi:10.1016/j.compind.2003.10.007

Grudin, J. (1992). Why CSCW applications fail: Problems in the design and evaluation of organisational interfaces. In Marca, D., & Bock, G. (Eds.), *Groupware: Software for Computer-Supported Cooperative Work* (pp. 552–560). Los Alamitos, CA: IEEE Computer Society Press.

Grudin, J. (1994). Groupware and social dynamics: Eight challenges for developers. *Communications of the ACM, 37*(1), 92–105. doi:10.1145/175222.175230

Grudin, J., & Palen, L. (1995). Why Groupware Succeeds: Discretion or Mandate? *Proceedings of the European Conference on Computer-Supported Cooperative Work (ECSCW'95)*, 263-278.

Hodis, E., Prilusky, J., Martz, E., Silman, I., Moult, J., & Sussman, J. L. (2008). Proteopedia - A scientific 'wiki' bridging the rift between three-dimensional strucutre and function of biomacromolecules. *Genome Biology, 9*, R121. doi:10.1186/gb-2008-9-8-r121

Hoffmann, R. (2008). A wiki for the life sciences where authorship matters. *Nature Genetics, 40*, 1047–1051. doi:10.1038/ng.f.217

Kaser, O., & Lemire, D. (2007). *Tag-Cloud Drawing: Algorithms for Cloud Visualization.* Paper presented at the WWW2007 Workshop: Tagging and Metadata for Social Information Organization.

Leuf, B., & Cunningham, W. (2001). *The Wiki Way: Quick Collaboration.* Reading, MA: Addison-Wesley.

Noël, S., & Robert, J.-M. (2003). How the Web is used to support collaborative writing. *Behaviour & Information Technology, 22*(4), 245–262. doi:10.1080/0144929031000120860

Powel, S. G., Baker, K. R., & Lawson, B. (2007). An auditing protocol for spreadsheet models. *Information & Management, 45*(5), 312–320. doi:10.1016/j.im.2008.03.004

Powel, S. G., Baker, K. R., & Lawson, B. (2008). A critical review of the literature on spreadsheet errors. *Decision Support Systems, 46*(1), 128–138. doi:10.1016/j.dss.2008.06.001

Rao, V. S., McLeod, P. L., & Beard, K. M. (1996). Adoption patterns of lowstructure groupware: Experiences with collaborative writing software. *Proceedings HICSS, 96*, 41–50.

Rivadeneira, A. W., Gruen, D. M., Muller, M. J., & Millen, D. R. (2007). Getting our head in the clouds: toward evaluation studies of tagclouds. *Proceedings of the ACM Conference on Computer-Human Interaction (CHI'07)*, 995–998.

Russell, T. (2006). Cloudalicious: folksonomy over time. *Proceedings of the Joint Conference on Digital Libraries (JCDL'06)*, 364–364.

Wang, X. (2008). miRDB: A microRNA target prediction and functional database with a wiki interface. *RNA (New York, N.Y.), 14*(6), 1012–1017. doi:10.1261/rna.965408

Wattenberg, M., & Kriss, J. (2006). Designing for social data analysis. *IEEE Transactions on Visualization and Computer Graphics, 12*(4), 549–557. doi:10.1109/TVCG.2006.65

Wu, P., Sismanis, Y., & Reinwald, B. (2007). Towards keyword-driven analytical processing. *Proceedings of the ACM Conference on Management of Data (SIGMOD'07)*, 617–628.

Section 2
Collaborative Information Behavior in Small Groups

Chapter 5

Collaborative Information Behavior:
Exploring Collaboration and Coordination during Information Seeking and Retrieval Activities

Madhu C. Reddy
The Pennsylvania State University, USA

Bernard J. Jansen
The Pennsylvania State University, USA

Patricia R. Spence
The Pennsylvania State University, USA

ABSTRACT

Collaborative information behavior is an important and growing area of research in the field of information behavior. Although collaboration is a key component of work in organizational and other settings, most research has primarily focused on individual information behavior and not the collaborative aspects of information behavior. Consequently, there is a pressing need to understand both the conceptual features of this type of behavior and the technical approaches to support these collaborative activities. In this chapter, the authors describe current research in this area and what we are learning about collaboration and coordination during these activities. In particular, the authors present details of ethnographic field studies that are starting to uncover the characteristics of collaborative information behavior. They also discuss a preliminary collaborative information behavior model and some technical explorations that they are conducting in this space.

INTRODUCTION

Most information retrieval systems and underlying conceptualizations of information behavior are still viewed primarily from an individual user's perspective, despite the mounting evidence that collaborative information behavior (CIB) plays an important role in organizational work. Focusing solely on individual information behavior

DOI: 10.4018/978-1-61520-797-8.ch005

(IIB) has lead to processes and technologies that support individual information seeking but often constrains collaborative information behavior. However, many models and studies of information seeking behavior have focused on individual needs and behavior. For example,

- Kuhlthau's studies (1989; 1991) of high school students examined individual information seeking behavior; therefore, her model conceptualized information seeking as an individual activity.
- Ellis' model reflects his studies' (1993; 1997) emphasis on information seeking as an individual activity.
- Wilson (1981) developed his model after examining information needs and seeking studies. The model is his conception of the information needs and seeking process but also reflects the individual nature of the information seeking typified in earlier user studies.
- Leckie et al.'s model (1996) was developed from a literature survey of studies examining the largely individual information seeking behavior of engineers, physicians, and lawyers.

These studies and models focused on IIB primarily because information seeking was viewed as being embedded in individual not collaborative work. Furthermore, the focus was on the conventional pattern of interaction between a single user and technology. However, this is acutely problematic in settings where teams and team work are important. Consequently, this perspective of focusing primarily on IIB is now being challenged by a number of studies examining information seeking in a wide variety of collaborative settings (Fidel, Bruce et al. 2000; Foster 2006). These studies are starting to pave the way for both a conceptual understanding of collaborative information seeking and the improved design of collaborative information retrieval (CIR) systems.

Our research team has been exploring collaborative information seeking practices in a variety of organizational settings such intensive care units (Reddy and Dourish 2002), emergency departments (Reddy and Spence 2006), and academic research (Spence, Reddy et al. 2005) for the last ten years. We have used the term *collaborative information behavior* (CIB) in our research studies to describe these broad range of activities (Reddy and Jansen 2008). Our team's research goals have been two-fold: First, to develop a conceptual understanding of CIB and second, to gather requirements for the design of organizational CIR systems.

In this chapter, we focus our attention on some of the empirical and technical aspects of our team's research. We synthesize findings from our earlier studies and describe what we are learning about collaboration and coordination during CIB activities. In the rest of the chapter, we provide some background in this area, describe our methodology for collecting data on CIB, present a general overview of our research, discuss lessons that we are learning about CIB, and highlight future directions that we need to further explore in the CIB research space.

BACKGROUND

Even though information seeking is an important part of collaborative work (Cicourel 1990; Paepcke 1996; Hansen and Jarvelin 2005; Foster 2006), researchers have only recently begun to examine the particulars of CIB (Foster 2006). For instance, Talja and Hansen (2005) describe the important role that collaborative information seeking play in everyday work. Much of this research has been influenced by Dervin's (1992) work on sense-making and Kling's (1980) research on the role of technology in organizations. Dervin's sense-making research highlights the sense-making "gaps" and addresses how people try to bridge these gaps. Kling focuses our attention on the importance of understanding the context in which technology will be implemented and the social interactions that impact the use of the technology.

Conceptual Perspective

Researchers are starting to lay a conceptual foundation for understanding CIB. Karamuftuoglu (1998) outlined the beginnings of a theoretical framework for understanding the collaborative nature of information seeking. The core of this framework is that information seeking is just as much about producing new knowledge, a creative and inventive activity, as it is about finding extant information. Karamuftuoglu addresses two knowledge functions of information retrieval (IR) systems. These IR systems should support transferring and creating new knowledge, where new knowledge creation is dependent on social networks. This ties in with work on social intelligence (Cronin and Davenport 1993) and with attempts to subsume support for information seeking in the broader area of group support (Romano, Roussinov et al. 1999; Hyldegard 2006). Cross et al. (2003) point to five categories of benefits of collaboration during information retrieval. These benefits range from people turning to each other to get specific information to people validating each other's search plans.

The collaborative information retrieval (CIR) project undertaken by the researchers at the University of Washington (Fidel, Bruce et al. 2000; Bruce, Fidel et al. 2003; Poltrock, Dumais et al. 2003; Fidel, Pejtersen et al. 2004) has helped lay an important foundation for understanding CIB. Their cognitive work analysis approach highlighted the important interactions that took place between team members as they sought, retrieved, and used information. They examined the collaborative information retrieval activities of design teams in Boeing and Microsoft. The researchers found that team members collaborated when developing information seeking and retrieval strategies to address an information problem

within the team. Their research revealed factors such as communication patterns and work activities that influence the need for information and for collaboration during information searching. Similarly, Hansen and Jarvelin (2005) discuss CIR practices of information workers in patent offices. They found that awareness workers have of each other's work activities plays an important role in the success of the CIR activities. They also state that there has been very little empirical work on collaborative information seeking and retrieval.

Sonnenwald and Pierce's (2000) study of information behavior in a hierarchical work environment (i.e., a military command and control) highlights the collaborative nature of the activity. They described collaborative information seeking (CIS) as a dynamic activity in which "individuals must work together to seek, synthesize and disseminate information". They placed collaborative information seeking within the wider context of the group communication process. Sonnenwald and Pierce examined how team members maintained awareness of each other's information activities and how this awareness influenced their information sharing with each other.

In educational settings, Hyldegard (2006; Hyldegard 2009) looked at collaborative information seeking from the perspective of extending Kuhlthau's (1989) Information Search Process model. She was interested in examining how well the model explained CIB activities in students. Hyldegard (Hyldegard 2006) found that the model needed to be extended to support collaboration. In a survey of CIB activities among academic researchers, Spence, Reddy, and Hall (2005) found that researchers used a variety of tools ranging from e-mail to video-conferencing to support their collaboration during information seeking activities.

In the medical domain, Reddy and Dourish (2002) described the role that work rhythms played in team members' collaborative information seeking practices in an intensive care unit. The rhythms provided team members with information about each other, which allowed them to plan their search for information accordingly. Therefore, when team members understood the rhythms of the unit, they also knew when information was needed. Team members could then collaborate for needed information in a "just in time" fashion (not too soon and not too late) based on the rhythms of the unit. In a study of a patient care team, Forsythe et al. (1992) examined information needs of the team. Their focus was on the questions that these members asked to satisfy their needs. In another study of an intensive care team, Gorman et al. (2000) looked at how team members worked together to find and share needed information. They discussed the importance of tying different sources of information together to answer team members' questions.

Researchers in the computer-supported co-operative work (CSCW) community have also provided useful insights into collaborative aspects of information and work. For instance, CSCW researchers have highlighted the importance of people maintaining "awareness" of each other's activities to coordinate their work (Dourish and Belotti 1992a; Symon, Long et al. 1996). Clearly, this concept of awareness applies to CIB. Similarly, CSCW researchers have also discussed the impact of distance and time on collaboration (Ackerman 2000; Olson and Olson 2000; Mark, Abrams et al. 2003). Through these and other studies (Ackerman 2000), CSCW research has informed our under-standing of collaborative information behavior.

Technical Perspective

Researchers are also beginning to explore CIB from a technical perspective. Twidale and Nichols (1998), in their study focused on designing interfaces to support CIR, suggested that support tools must provide a visualization of the search process which can be changed and talked about by the users. Furthermore, they believe that collaboration can improve the users understanding of the search process. Based on their observations in conventional and electronic libraries, they developed ARIADNE, one of the earliest collaborative retrieval tools. The system provides features for saving and sharing the search process and visualization of the search. ARIADNE highlights the significance of supporting collaboration by allowing users to share views and knowledge with each other during the search process. Similarly, Blackwell et al. (2004) describe the design of a tangible interface that allows multiple users to collaborate to refine a query. They found that it can improve relevance rankings when compared to single-user interfaces.

Another system that supports collaborative information retrieval is FoRSIC (Ertzscheid 2001). This system attempts to address the issue of information overload by devising a dynamic means of supporting connections between information seekers, information trainers, information tools, and information sources. The research team looked at neglected social factors such as communication and collaboration in information retrieval systems. A research team at Microsoft has explored supporting collaboration in general Web searching and have developed SearchTogether (Morris and Horvitz 2007). This tool is designed to support collaborative Web-based searching. It allows remote users to share searches and results with each other.

A few commercial systems have implemented functionality which supports some aspects of CIB. For example, IBM offers many products which allow collaborations among colleagues, customers, business partners and suppliers. These products offer presence awareness, instant messaging, and Web conferencing. In addition, the latest Netscape browser allows a team leader to share their Web page with multiple users. Although not specifically focused on CIB, there are several project team environments, such as Microsoft's Groove. Lastly, Enlista's Chat in Context allows users to browse and share information while chatting.

RESEARCH METHODS

In our field research examining CIB, we have primarily been utilizing qualitative methods (Reddy and Spence 2008). Although we have also utilized quantitative methods such as surveys to examine CIB (Spence, Reddy et al. 2005), our primary empirical approach is ethnographic fieldwork. Ethnographic observation is designed to provide a deep understanding and support rich analytical description of a phenomenon, as part of an iterative cycle of observation and analysis (Strauss and Corbin 1990). It seeks not just to document actions, but to examine what is experienced in the course of these actions.

Studying CIB requires careful observation and questioning. Multiple people need to be interviewed, and only with sufficient observation can we identify different CIB practices and their effects on daily work activities. Since people often cannot tell a researcher what they actually do in practice (rather than what they are supposed to do), it has been found more useful to both interview and observe study participants. For instance, in an example of tacit understandings, people may tell a researcher that they "officially" ask the unit pharmacist when seeking information about a particular medication. However, in practice, they may be observed to bypass the unit pharmacist and directly ask a pharmacist outside the unit about the medication. It is probable that many other tacit understandings about how people collaborate when seeking information exist (e.g., assumptions about the quality of the information, background of individuals, individual's knowledge); only a field study can reveal them. Indeed, only a field study can uncover CIB practices, can tell us what issues are important for which groups of people, and most importantly, can tell us *why* these issues are important.

To analyze data, we have used grounded theory (GT) (Strauss and Corbin 1990). The underlying assumption of GT is that a deep understanding of social phenomena can only occur from real-world observations. It is a set of methods for analyzing qualitative data such as interviews and observations. GT foregrounds this data and helps create an evolving hypothesis through systematic data coding. In the course of this coding, patterns become visible giving rise to hypotheses that in turn are strengthened or dismissed through further coding of the data and, in some cases, additional data collection. The strength of GT lies in the interaction between the data collection and the coding. The coding is a continual process that occurs not at the end of the data collection but during it; categories (e.g. themes) *emerge* from the data and are strengthened, modified, or discarded as more data is collected. We are using a qualitative data analysis software, NVivo7 (QSR International), to assist in this analysis. All the data is imported into the software as documents. Artifacts (e.g., forms) can be captured as "external" documents with a rich description of their use and contents. Then, as data is reviewed and compared, categories will emerge and nodes are created. The text will be "coded" on the respective node(s). This allowed for easy comparisons of text coded on the same node and across nodes. As analysis progresses, memos of emerging hypotheses will be documented by the software at both the document and node level. As these hypotheses were tested and strengthened, nodes were modified (e.g. ordered, combined, and collapsed). The software provides this functionality without any loss of coding ability. GT will help us identify categories of team information seeking interactions and practices as they emerge from the data.

RESEARCH FINDINGS

We have been investigating CIB through empirical fieldwork using the methods described in the last section. The early results have been both enlightening and promising. In this section, we highlight our important findings from our team's prior work.

Fieldwork: CIB in Medical Work

We have been investigating how team members collaborate when seeking, retrieving and using information in the healthcare domain. In particular, we have examined patient care teams in the surgical intensive care unit (SICU) of a large urban teaching hospital and the emergency department (ED) in a small rural non-teaching hospital (Reddy and Dourish 2002; Reddy and Spence 2006).

Previous studies of information seeking in medical settings have focused primarily on individual information behavior (Dee and Blazek 1993; Detlefsen 1998). However, as our fieldwork highlights, medical care is a highly collaborative endeavor (Reddy, Dourish et al. 2001). In information-intensive environments such as the SICU and ED, information is available from a variety of different resources. The goal of providing all these resources is to allow people to easily find needed information. Yet, at the same time, the increasing number of information resources and systems has created a problem of *information fragmentation*. Therefore, patient care team members in both settings have to gather information from different sources to make appropriate patient care decisions (Spence and Reddy 2007). What our fieldwork shows is that team members in the course of their work collaborate when seeking and retrieving information to ensure that they get the right information. The focus of our analysis has been on how this happens.

We found that CIB often occurs when there is a breakdown in the information flow. We have identified three reasons for information flow breakdowns in the two units. First, the information was not available when anticipated. For instance, a lab result was not ready when the physician expected it and he had to ask another team member about the results. Second, the information was either incorrect or incomplete. Therefore, team members had to ask questions to find the correct or complete information. Finally, the information was delivered to the wrong person. These

breakdowns lead to team members collaborating to find needed information.

To understand why team members collaborate during information seeking and retrieval activities, we utilized the analytical concept of *triggers - an event or situation within the environment that initiates CIB amongst a formal or informal group of people* (Reddy and Spence 2008). Triggers are key events or situations in initiating a shift from individual information behavior to CIB. In particular, we have identified four triggers for CIB.

- **Complexity of information need:** Complex information problems often with multiple components lead to the need for collaboration.
- **Lack of immediately accessible information:** When information is not easily accessible, people often had to collaborate to find the information.
- **Lack of domain expertise:** When an individual does not have the prerequisite knowledge she will turn to people with the necessary knowledge to help him or her find the needed information.
- **Fragmented information resources:** Work environments where information resources reside in multiple and dispersed systems can often necessitate collaboration.

When these triggers occurred, team members turned to each other for help in seeking information.

A key element of CIB is communication. During information seeking activities, team members followed an iterative pattern of information seeking-sharing-seeking. This pattern highlights two important aspects of communication during CIB activities. First, when team members were verbally communicating, turn-taking was involved. One team member would present some information followed by another team member's presenting what she found. Second, sharing information was an essential part of CIB. The turn-taking and information sharing allowed team members to collect pieces of information that they put together to resolve their information need.

We also found information retrieval technologies played a different role in IIB than in CIB. In the two units, there are a number of such technologies ranging from the electronic patient record to Web-based systems. Team members used them constantly to find needed information. However, unlike in IIB where interacting with the IR technologies is the last step in the process of the information seeking, it was often the *first* step in a CIB activity. Team members often used the information found in the systems as a starting point for their collaborative activities. The fieldwork in the SICU and ED reveal the complex nature of collaborative information behavior and lead to the development of a preliminary CIB model.

Collaborative Information Behavior Model

Based on the fieldwork, we have been developing a preliminary CIB model (Figure 1) (Reddy and Jansen 2008). One can view information environments along two axes: (1) Behavior axis: ranging on a spectrum from information searching to information seeking and use and (2) Context axis: ranging on a spectrum from IIB to CIB. Both axes affect the environmental characteristics of interactions (at the information searching level), agents (at the information seeking level), and problems (at the information behavior level). Naturally, these levels are not precisely bordered; there is a degree of overlap among the three. These two factors (behavior and context) interplay simultaneously across problems, agents, and interactions. The interplay of the complexity of the problem, the number of agents interacting, and the nature of these interactions initiates a trigger that transforms the context from IIB to CIB. At the individual level, the information problem is relatively simple when compared to the collaborative level. As the information problem

becomes more complex and nuanced, the need to seek out other information sources becomes more pronounced. This is especially true in domains where multiple areas of expertise are needed to address the information problem. In these domains, several agents must interact. Problem complexity occurs at many dimensions, including number of sources to be consulted, closed or open problem, non-routine/unusualness of the information need, etc. Interactions include those involving systems and people. At IIB, these interactions are direct, even when interacting with people. With CIB, the interactions are much more conversational such as "query/question – response from agent – refinement of query/question", with shifts in the information need at each iteration. This model points to *triggers* (discussed earlier) as a key event that separates IIB from CIB. However, the model is still very preliminary and requires a great deal more fieldwork to further develop it. For instance, we need to investigate issues affecting CIB such as trust, rhythms, oral versus written sources, and coupling of work tasks.

Technology Prototyping

One characteristic of our research is that it involves not just the collection and analysis of ethnographic field data but also the development of prototype collaborative information retrieval (CIR) system. The development of information systems can benefit from ethnography's detailed, open-ended style of investigation. However, despite the broad recognition of both the value of ethnographic techniques as a basis for understanding working settings and the critical need to ground system development efforts in empirical detail, the question of just *how* ethnographic findings can be turned into design recommendations is still a challenge. Although no one systematic method has been developed, CSCW and HCI researchers have developed effective methods for developing recommendations and designing systems (Ackerman and McDonald 1996; Moran and Carroll

Figure 1. Individual vs. collaborative information behavior

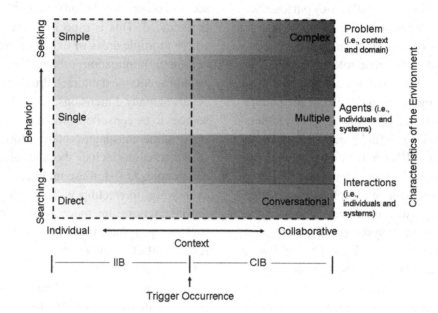

1996; Twidale, Nichols et al. 1997; McDonald and Ackerman 1998). Our intention, in this research, is to use ethnographic analysis as a means to systematically question the assumptions behind traditional technology designs of conventional IR systems, and through this questioning, generate design recommendations for CIR systems.

Consequently, drawing on our ethnographic fieldwork, we developed a CIR prototype. Along with our fieldwork, the CIR prototype helped us examine collaborative information behavior. We explored how features identified through the fieldwork are utilized by users. For instance, our preliminary fieldwork has begun to uncover the central role that collaboration plays in information seeking and retrieval activities. However, issues such as communication amongst collaborators has largely been ignored in current information retrieval tools (Reddy, Jansen et al. 2008). Developing a CIR prototype allowed us to explore whether incorporating features such as peer-to-peer and group communication along with other collaborative features can better support multi-user collaboration during information seeking and retrieval.

The CIR prototype allowed us to examine how team members who may not be physically co-present interact while collaboratively searching for information. The development of the CIR prototype builds on and extends our ethnographic fieldwork and provides us with another venue to investigate CIB. To initially explore technical approaches to supporting collaborative information behavior, we focused on communication and searching through the development of a simple CIR tool – Multi-User Search Engine (MUSE) (Figure 2).

MUSE (Reddy, Jansen et al. 2008) allows two users to search independently for information while sharing that information at the same time communicate with each other through a built-in chat feature. MUSE is a fully functional prototype developed using JAVA and JAVA Swing. An Apache server was used to enable networking between different computers. MUSE has features to support communication and sharing of the search results between two users. The front-end interface consists of three distinct features: search, share, and chat.

Figure 2. MUSE interface with three windows: (a) chat, (b) share, and (c) search

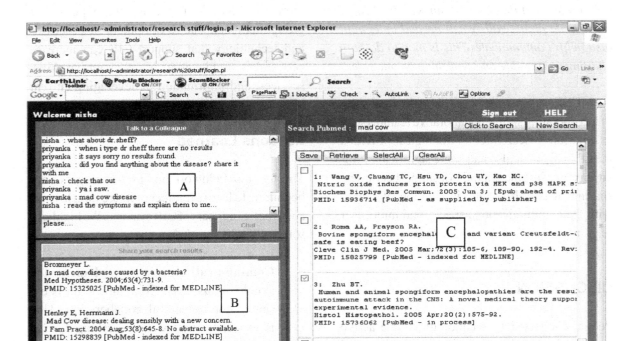

- **Chat:** MUSE supports text based messaging between two users. (Figure 2a)
- **Share:** Users can share the search results with each other in the share window. The users selects the results they want to share from the results in the search window and then clicks the 'share the search results' button. The results will appear in the share window of the other user. (Figure 2b)
- **Search:** Users type in a keyword to search for information. The search engine retrieves the available results from the database and displays the first twenty results. (Figure 2c)

To evaluate MUSE, we conducted a user study with ten teams (two participants per team) (Reddy, Jansen et al. 2008). We asked the participants to use MUSE to find information about *mad cow disease*. For this search, MUSE was connected to the National Institute of Health's Pubmed

database. We observed the teams in a controlled environment. We provided the participants with two computers at opposite ends of the room. The participants were unable to see each other, and were instructed to communicate with each other only through the chat feature. We captured data through chat logs, query logs, observations, and interviews. We found that the chat feature played a prominent role in supporting the collaboration between team members during their information seeking and retrieval activities. For instance, participants used the chat feature to consult with each other during the search process. The participant would then ask the other team member for information that she could use in her own search. One participant noted that

"I have never used a system that allowed me to chat with others when looking for information and I have used forums that support topic specific discussion, where there are a lot of people

who post their ideas and views, lot of consulting goes on too, but that is again not synchronous. I have made phone calls when needed and email also helps communicate. This is nice to do both chatting on one side and searching on one side."

MUSE was intended to explore the feasibility of incorporating simple collaborative features such as chat into a search tool. Although it provided useful insights, it also had some significant limitations. For instance, it did not support complete sharing of search results, integration of search with the communication aspects, and multi-user (e.g. more than 2 users) interaction.

DISCUSSION

People connected by technology enable active examination of data, information sharing, and the creation of new knowledge, permitting teams, groups, and organizations to make more informed decisions. Many of these needed information processes are collaborative in nature. However, prior work has shown that these collaborative information seeking processes are extremely nuanced. At the individual level, there are a variety of factors that influence information seeking (e.g., domain expertise, temporality, technological expertise). At levels above the individual, these factors also affect the collaborative information seeking process. In addition, in collaborative information seeking, group and organizational factors also come into play of which we currently have little understanding.

Researchers have examined aspects of collaboration (e.g., CSCW), decision-making (e.g., business), and problem-solving (e.g., cognitive science). However, in each of these domains, we are just starting to examine information seeking within collaborative processes in any great detail. Previously, information seeking has been subsumed into larger issues of collaboration, decision-making, and problem-solving. Therefore,

an understanding of CIB is needed to sustain the 'network effect' and leverage the expertise of group members. The development of processes and technology that support CIB can increase cooperation and leverage of collaborative skills, services, and information by leveraging current lessons learned.

Lessons Learned

Through our fieldwork and prototyping, we are beginning to learn a number of interesting lessons about potential users of CIR systems. We highlight some of the lessons below.

- **Communication is a key element for synchronous CIB:** Communication is essential for successful collaboration. This is especially true when searching for information. Team members continuously exchanged information about the *search process* as they collaborated during information seeking and retrieval activities. Exchanging information about the search process allowed team members to stay on track and alerted other team members when they may be taking a wrong search path.

- **Targeted vs. general information search:** Team members most often collaborated to find information in order to answer specific questions. The information seeking was targeted and specific. This is not to say that team members knew what they were looking for (or where to look for it). This highlights the issue that the collaboration in these settings was not for general knowledge acquisition but rather for specific purposes.

- **Formal and informal sources:** Information in these organizational settings (especially in the healthcare domain) is scattered across a number of different resources including electronic, paper, and human. Therefore, it was not the simple task to find the source of information.

- **Simultaneous levels of information engagement:** People engage simultaneously in tactic and strategic information searching at both the individual and collaborative level. The results are that collaborative tasks and actions are interwoven with individual information seeking.

- **Contextual aspects:** There are some information tasks, even in team environments that are individual; however, as information problems become more complex, people begin to collaborate with others in order to address these complex issues. As the information problem becomes more complex and nuanced, the need to seek out other information sources becomes more pronounced, especially domains where multiple areas of expertise are teamed.

- **Interaction characteristics:** Commonly, in domains where CIB is common, both people and technology must interact. In these CIB situations, interactions are conversational with aspects of give and take between group members as they find, share, exchange, and process information. This highlights the aspects of *triggers* and *common ground* as key events in CIB. Consequently, we need to understand these events when designing technologies to support CIB.

Future Research Directions

Through our team's and other's research, we know that CIB is composed of a complex set of interactions involving people and technology. Yet, there are still some important questions that must be answered to strengthen our understanding of this area.

1. How does CIB differ from individual information behavior?

   a. What are the characteristics of CIB?
   b. Why do people collaborate when seeking information?
   c. What techniques/methods do people use to collaborate when seeking and retrieving information?

2. What role do current information retrieval technologies play in supporting CIB?

   a. What are the limitations of the current information retrieval technologies?

3. What are the design requirements for collaborative information retrieval (CIR) systems?

4. In what ways does the introduction of a CIR tool impact CIB?

   a. What combination of technical features best support CIB?

To answer these questions, we plan on using a variety of research methods including ethnographic fieldwork, survey research, technology prototyping, and technology evaluation. Our aim is that this work will lead to both a better conceptual understanding of CIB and the development of enhanced technologies to support CIB.

From a prototyping perspective, there are at least six areas of particular technical interest based on our research (Reddy, Dourish et al. 2001; Reddy and Jansen 2008).

- **Asynchronous collaboration:** There has been a great deal of focus on supporting synchronous collaboration during information seeking and retrieval activities (Twidale, Nichols et al. 1997; Morris and Horvitz 2007). Yet, supporting asynchronous collaboration is also vital in CIB (Edwards, Mynatt et al. 1997). Therefore, we need to incorporate features that best support this type of collaboration during these activities.

- **Awareness:** Knowing what other people are doing is an important during CIB activities. Therefore, the system should provide presence awareness information for the group members (e.g., letting the user know if the person she wants to collaborate with is or is not busy).

- **Chat:** Clearly, one of the most important functions that CIR systems need to support is communication. A chat function allows collaborators to interact with each other and will play an important role in enhancing the information-seeking and retrieval process.
- **Conferencing**: Chatting is typically viewed as a mechanism for communication between two users; the system should provide mechanisms for communication amongst many users. This would be especially useful for members of geographically dispersed groups.
- **Privacy:** With any kind of system that supports awareness, communication, and information sharing, there is concern about user privacy. This issue raises the questions about what information users may or may not want to share. The system should support the user's ability to control how much information that she wants to share.
- **Visualization:** Users need a robust visualization of not only their search process and results but also of their collaborators' search processes and results. Providing this feature will help facilitate users discussion of each other's searches and how to improve these searches. In order to provide the appropriate visualizations, we need to explore what and how much information to present.

The challenge in designing these and other features identified through the fieldwork lies in not only developing the individual components but also effectively *integrating* them together in order to ensure that the system seamlessly supports CIB.

CONCLUSION

Through our team's research, we are starting to understand CIB in different settings. We have, for instance, identified some work features that trigger CIB (Reddy and Spence 2008). We have also identified features through the fieldwork that we believe are essential for effective CIR systems; in particular, awareness and communication. We are exploring these features in our CIR prototypes (Reddy and Jansen 2008). While this preliminary work has promise, what researchers and practitioners critically need are more granular models of CIB to form the basis of investigations of information behavior in collaborative contexts and to help design processes, organization structures, and technologies to support these contexts. This is the aim of our continued work in this area.

ACKNOWLEDGMENT

We would like to thank the participants from our various field studies. This research has been supported in part by National Science Foundation grants IIS 0832428 and IIS 0844947.

REFERENCES

Ackerman, M. S. (2000). The Intellectual Challenge of CSCW: The Gap Between Social Requirements and Technical Feasibility. *Human-Computer Interaction, 15*(2-3), 181–205.

Ackerman, M. S., & McDonald, D. W. (1996). Answer Garden 2: Merging Organizational Memory with Collaborative Help. In *Proc of ACM Conf. on Computer Supported Cooperative Work* (CSCW '96) (pp. 97-105). Boston, MA: ACM Press.

Blackwell, A., Stringer, M., Toye, E. F., & Rode, J. A. (2004). Tangible interface for collaborative information retrieval. In *Proc. of ACM Conference on Human Factors in Computing Systems* (CHI'04), Vienna, Austria (pp. 1473-1476).

Bruce, H., Fidel, R., Pejtersen, A., Dumais, S., Grudin, J., & Poltrock, S. (2003). A comparison of the collaborative information retrieval behaviors of two design teams. *New Review of Information Behaviour Research: Studies of Information Seeking in Context*, *4*(1), 139–153. doi:10.1080/1471 6310310001631499

Cicourel, A. V. (1990). The Integration of Distributed Knowledge in Collaborative Medical Diagnosis. In Galegher, J., Kraut, R. E., & Egido, C. (Eds.), *Intellectual Teamwork* (pp. 221–242). Hillsdale, NJ: Lawrence Erlbaum Associates.

Cronin, B., & Davenport, E. (1993). Social intelligence. [ARIST]. *Annual Review of Information Science & Technology*, *29*, 3–44.

Cross, R., Davenport, T., & Cantrell, S. (2003). The Social Side of High Performance. *Sloan Management Review*, *45*(1), 20–24.

Dee, C., & Blazek, R. (1993). Information needs of the rural physician: a descriptive study. *Bulletin of the Medical Library Association*, *81*(3), 259–264.

Dervin, B. (1992). From the Mind's Eye of the User: The Sense-Making Qualitative-Quantitative Methodology. In Glazer, J. D., & Powell, R. R. (Eds.), *Qualitative Research in Information Management* (pp. 61–82). Englewood, CO: Libraries Unlimited, Inc.

Detlefsen, E. G. (1998). The information behaviors of life and health scientists and health care providers: characteristics of the research literature. *Bulletin of the Medical Library Association*, *86*(3), 385–390.

Dourish, P., & Belotti, V. (1992a). Awareness and coordination in shared workspaces. In *Proc of the 1992 ACM Conference on Computer Supported Cooperative Work* (CSCW'92) (pp: 107-115). New York: ACM.

Edwards, K., Mynatt, E., Petersen, K., Spreitzer, M., Terry, D., & Theimer, M. (1997). Designing and Implementing asynchronous collaborative applications with Bayou. In P*roc. of 10th Annual ACM Symp. on User Interface Software and Technology* (UIST'97), Banff, Alberta, Canada (pp. 119-128).

Ellis, D., Cox, D., & Hall, K. (1993). A comparison of the information seeking patterns of researchers in the physical and social sciences. *The Journal of Documentation*, *49*(4), 356–369. doi:10.1108/eb026919

Ellis, D., & Haugan, M. (1997). Modeling the Information Seeking Patterns of Engineers and Research Scientists in an Industrial Environment. *The Journal of Documentation*, *53*(4), 384–403. doi:10.1108/EUM0000000007204

Ertzscheid, O. (2001). An attempt to identify and manage collective practices involved in information retrieval. In *Proc of 5th World Multi conference on Systemics, Cybernetics and Informatics* (SCI / ISAS 2001), Orlando, FL.

Fidel, R., Bruce, H., Pejtersen, A. M., Dumais, S., Grudin, J., & Poltrock, S. (2000). Collaborative Information Retrieval (CIR). *New Review of Information Behaviour Research: Studies of Information Seeking in Context*, *1*(1), 235–247.

Fidel, R., Pejtersen, A., Cleal, B., & Bruce, H. (2004). A Multidimensional Approach to the Study of Human-Information Interaction: A Case Study of Collaborative Information Retrieval. *Journal of the American Society for Information Science American Society for Information Science*, *55*(11), 939–953.

Forsythe, D. E., Buchanan, B. G., Osheroff, J. A., & Miller, R. A. (1992). Expanding the concept of medical information: An observational study of physicians' information needs. *Computers and Biomedical Research, an International Journal, 25*(2), 181–200. doi:10.1016/0010-4809(92)90020-B

Foster, J. (2006). Collaborative Information Seeking and Retrieval. *Annual Review of Information Science & Technology, 40,* 329–356. doi:10.1002/aris.1440400115

Gorman, P. N., Ash, J., Lavelle, M., Lyman, J., Delcambre, L., & Maier, D. (2000). Bundles in the Wild: Managing Information to Solve Problems and Maintain Situation Awareness. *Library Trends, 49*(2), 266–289.

Hansen, P., & Jarvelin, K. (2005). Collaborative Information Retrieval in an information-intensive domain. *Information Processing & Management, 41,* 1101–1119. doi:10.1016/j.ipm.2004.04.016

Hyldegard, J. (2006). Collaborative information behavior - exploring Kuhlthau's Information Search Process model in a group-based educational setting. *Information Processing & Management, 42*(1), 276–298. doi:10.1016/j.ipm.2004.06.013

Hyldegard, J. (2009). Beyond the search process – Exploring group members' information behavior in context. *Information Processing & Management, 45*(1), 142–158. doi:10.1016/j.ipm.2008.05.007

International, Q. S. R. (n.d.). *N6 Software.* Retrieved July 19, 2008, from http://www.qsrinternational.com/products_previous-products_n6.aspx

Karamuftuoglu, M. (1998). Collaborative Information Retrieval: Towards a Social Informatics View of IR interaction. *Journal of the American Society for Information Science American Society for Information Science, 49*(12), 1070–1080. doi:10.1002/(SICI)1097-4571(1998)49:12<1070::AID-ASI3>3.0.CO;2-S

Kling, R. (1980). Social Analyses of Computing: Theoretical Perspectives in Recent Empirical Research. *Computing Surveys, 12*(1), 61–110. doi:10.1145/356802.356806

Kuhlthau, C. C. (1989). The information search process of high-middle-low achieving high school seniors. *School Library Media Quarterly, 17,* 224–228.

Kuhlthau, C. C. (1991). Inside the Search Process: Information Seeking from the User's Perspective. *Journal of the American Society for Information Science American Society for Information Science, 42*(5), 361–371. doi:10.1002/(SICI)1097-4571(199106)42:5<361::AID-ASI6>3.0.CO;2-#

Leckie, G. J., Pettigrew, K. E., & Sylvain, C. (1996). Modeling the Information Seeking of Professionals: A General Model Derived from Research on Engineers, Health Care Professionals, and Lawyers. *The Library Quarterly, 66*(2), 161–193. doi:10.1086/602864

Mark, G., Abrams, S., & Nassif, N. (2003). Group-to-Group Distance Collaboration: Examining the Space Between. In *Proc. of the 8th European Conference of Computer-Supported Cooperative Work* (*ECSCW'03*), Helsinki, Finland (pp. 99-118).

McDonald, D. W., & Ackerman, M. S. (1998). Just Talk to Me: A Field Study of Expertise Location. In *Proc. of the ACM Conference on Computer-Supported Cooperative Work* (CSCW'98), Seattle, WA (pp. 315-324).

Moran, T. P., & Carroll, J. M. (Eds.). (1996). *Design Rationale: Concepts, Techniques, and Use.* Mahwah, NJ: Lawrence Erlbaum Associates, Inc.

Morris, M. R., & Horvitz, E. (2007). SearchTogether: An Interface for Collaborative Web Search. In *Proc. of ACM Conf on User Interface Software and Technology* (UIST'07) Newport, RI (pp. 3-12).

Olson, G., & Olson, J. (2000). Distance Matters. *Human-Computer Interaction, 15,* 139–179. doi:10.1207/S15327051HCI1523_4

Paepcke, A. (1996). Information Needs in Technical Work Settings and Their Implications for the Design of Computer Tools. *Computer Supported Cooperative Work: The Journal of Collaborative Computing, 5,* 63–92. doi:10.1007/BF00141936

Poltrock, S., Dumais, S., Fidel, R., Bruce, H., & Pejtersen, A. M. (2003). Information Seeking and Sharing in Design Teams. In *the ACM Conf. on Supporting Group Work* (GROUP'03), Sanibal Island, FL (pp. 239-247).

Reddy, M., & Dourish, P. (2002). A Finger on the Pulse: Temporal Rhythms and Information Seeking in Medical Care. In *Proc. of ACM Conf. on Computer Supported Cooperative Work* (CSCW'02), New Orleans, LA (pp. 344-353).

Reddy, M., Dourish, P., & Pratt, W. (2001). Coordinating Heterogeneous Work: Information and Representation in Medical Care. In *European Conference on Computer Supported Cooperative Work (ECSCW'01)*, Bonn, Germany (pp. 239-258).

Reddy, M., Jansen, B. J., & Krishnappa, R. (2008). The Role of Communication in Collaborative Information Searching. In Proc. of American Society of Information Sciences and Technology (ASIST'08), Columbus, OH.

Reddy, M., & Jansen, J. (2008). A Model for Understanding Collaborative Information Behavior in Context: A Study of Two Healthcare Teams. *Information Processing & Management, 44*(1), 256–273. doi:10.1016/j.ipm.2006.12.010

Reddy, M., & Spence, P. R. (2006). Finding Answers: Information Needs of a Multidisciplinary Patient Care Team in an Emergency Department. In *Proc. of American Medical Informatics Association Fall Symposium* (AMIA'06), Washington, DC (pp. 649-653).

Reddy, M., & Spence, P. R. (2008). Collaborative Information Seeking: A field study of a multidisciplinary patient care team. *Information Processing & Management, 44*(1), 242–255. doi:10.1016/j.ipm.2006.12.003

Romano, N., Roussinov, D., Nunamaker, J., & Chen, H. (1999). Collaborative Information Retrieval Environment: Integration of Information Retrieval with Group Support Systems. In *Proc of the 32nd Hawaii International Conference on System Sciences* (HICCS'99), Hawaii (pp. 1-10).

Sonnenwald, D. H., & Pierce, L. G. (2000). Information behavior in dynamic group work contexts: interwoven situational awareness, dense social networks and contested collaboration in command and control. *Information Processing & Management, 36,* 461–479. doi:10.1016/S0306-4573(99)00039-4

Spence, P., & Reddy, M. (2007). The Active Gatekeeper in Collaborative Information Seeking Activities. In *Proc. of ACM Conf. on Supporting Group Work* (GROUP'07), Sanibel Island, FL (pp. 277-280).

Spence, P. R., Reddy, M., & Hall, R. (2005). A Survey of Collaborative Information Seeking of Academic Researchers. In *Proc. of ACM Conf. on Supporting Group Work* (*GROUP'05*), Sanibel Island, FL (pp. 85-88).

Strauss, A., & Corbin, J. (1990). *Basics of Qualitative Research: Grounded Theory Procedures and Techniques.* Newbury Park, CA: Sage Publications.

Symon, G., Long, K., & Ellis, J. (1996). The Coordination of Work Activities: Cooperation and Conflict in a Hospital Context. *Computer Supported Cooperative Work, 5*(1), 1–31. doi:10.1007/BF00141934

Talja, S., & Hansen, P. (2005). Information Sharing. In Spink, A., & Cole, C. (Eds.), *New Directions in Human Information Behavior* (pp. 113–134). Dordrect, Netherlands: Springer.

Twidale, M., & Nichols, D. M. (1998). Designing Interfaces to Support Collaboration in Information Retrieval. *Interacting with Computers, 10*(2), 177–193. doi:10.1016/S0953-5438(97)00022-2

Twidale, M., Nichols, D. M., & Paice, C. D. (1997). Browsing is a Collaborative Activity. *Information Processing & Management, 33*(6), 761–783. doi:10.1016/S0306-4573(97)00040-X

Wilson, T. D. (1981). On User Studies and Information Needs. *The Journal of Documentation, 37*(1), 3–15. doi:10.1108/eb026702

Chapter 6
Why Do We Need to Share Information?
Analysis of Collaborative Task Management Meetings

Nozomi Ikeya
Palo Alto Research Center, USA

Norihisa Awamur
Keio University and Research Fellow of the Japan Society for the Promotion of Science, Japan

Shinichiro Sakai
Rikkyo University, Japan

ABSTRACT

In order to study collaborative information behaviour (e.g. information search, creation, and sharing) in the work environment, it is important that we take into consideration its embedded nature in collaborative work, however not many studies have actually taken this into consideration. In conducting fieldwork, we studied group task management in the work of IT product hardware designers. The study shows how understanding the details of information activities embedded in task management allowed us to generate some ideas for transforming task management into a more collaborative activity, and for reembedding task management more thoroughly into their work practices together with the practitioners. The paper discusses how taking an ethnomethodological approach can be fruitful for researchers who want to gain a close understanding of actual collaborative information activities and their embedded nature in work, and how understandings of this kind can be important for developing ideas for transforming practice, both with or without the introduction of technology.

INTRODUCTION

When management introduces new policies for their personnel to carry out an activity where information sharing is involved, it is often assumed that it is a good thing to do so. However, members of personnel often do not know how they can actually make use of such occasions and some feel that will involve extra work for them. The policy of information sharing or visualisation itself may be treated as a goal until people come to realise

DOI: 10.4018/978-1-61520-797-8.ch006

that it is a means for accomplishing something. In such cases, members' involvement in the activity can vary and their motivation for the activity is not necessarily high[1]. Some studies have been carried out in CSCW examining why people do not want to invest their time in using new collaborative systems that encourage information sharing (Grudin, 1988; Orlikowski, 1992). First of all, it has been found that management often fails to convey to the employees the intention and goals that will be achieved by introducing a new system. Such communication is necessary for the employees to see the reason for using the new system, and then decide to invest the time to learn the new technology, adjust their work practice around it, and so on. But it has been recognised that management is not necessarily aware of the efforts and consequent work necessary to adopt a new policy or technology (Huysman & de Wit 2003). However, there have been few studies that examine the problem of 'information and knowledge sharing activities' as embedded in peoples' everyday work (Mengis & Eppler, 2005). Specifically, there have not been many studies which look in detail at how people actually deal with a new technology or policy for information sharing as part of their work by studying the ways in which they organise their work in a natural setting through interactions, focusing on understanding their practice.

Our aim in this chapter is to show how much information sharing is *embedded* in the work; and thus how important it is to take into consideration this embedded nature when introducing new technologies or new policies in relation to information sharing. This is especially true as the new technology or policy is bound to affect the existing work practices and therefore may just be seen as additional work if employees cannot see the point in using it. The second point we want to demonstrate is how much information sharing is collaboratively achieved in the work; and thus how important it is to take into consideration this collaborative nature, again, when introducing new technologies or new policies related to information sharing.

We conducted a fieldwork study of IT product designers of a large company in Japan[2]. Our focus was mainly on a particular group; following members as they attended various meetings, worked with computers, and did other tasks. This chapter focuses on one kind of regular meeting introduced by the management for enhancing collaboration. They call this weekly task management meeting 'Tanaoroshi-kai', which literally means 'stock taking meeting'. In this meeting, the team members were expected to share with each other what tasks they were planning to do. The management provided a task schedule format to be used for task management and the rest was up to the members regarding how they carried out task management in the meeting.

What we found was that the newly introduced meeting was not yet fully embedded in the team members' daily work. The meeting was not yet ingrained in the ways of organising their work and thus, they were treating it as an extra task on top of what they already had to do. The meeting itself was not yet part of the rhythm of how their work was organised (Reddy & Dourish, 2002). Based on a detailed analysis of the meeting, we provided some ideas for *re*designing activities related to the meeting, and implemented these ideas with the members.

This chapter first describes how a group of IT product designers actually try to carry out information sharing activites through the meeting. Through ethnomethodological analysis of ethnographic data including actual interactions, it will be demonstrated how members experience difficulties in getting engaged in the activity and in achieving what is supposed to be achieved. In other words, it will be shown how the new meeting was not actually embedded in their work (i.e., the members were making as little effort as possible for the new meeting as it meant 'extra work' to them). Further, sharing information in the meeting was carried out on an individual basis (between a member and the group leader), so it appeared to the members that this was an activity solely for the group leader. In other words, sharing information was not yet collaboratively carried out, and thus, it was not contributing to the work, which needs to be collaboratively achieved.

Secondly, this chapter argues that because information sharing is embedded and collaborative in the current work, any change to this can inevitably affect the existing work practice. Thus, one should allow ample for the necessary time and effort needed to work on designing the practice transformation, if they are serious about the introduction of technology and policy to achieve the goals of information sharing. By doing so, we are going to show that by demonstrating to practitioners (as well as researchers and system designers) an analysis of how members' activities are organised as part of their practice, we can create a space for considering the *re*design of practices or systems (Randall et al., 2007). Such an analysis is often successful in allowing the practitioners to reflect on their own practice. The detailed analysis of how problems get organised often also enables practitioners and researchers to come up with alternative ideas for *re*designing their practices[3].

Thus, this study focuses on collaborative information behaviour as embedded in work practice and how this particular way of approaching practice can lead to informing the *re*design of practices and systems. In the next section, the development of studies of collaborative information behaviour is reviewed in terms of how the collaborative and embedded nature of information activities including information sharing is approached.

STUDYING COLLABORATIVE INFORMATION BEHAVIOUR

There is much interest in conducting studies of information seeking in various social settings, as has been reviewed in ARIST by Pettigrew et al. (2001), Vakkari (2003), Case (2006), Courtright (2007), Wilson (2008), and Fisher and Julien (2009) to name a few. Moves for locating information seeking studies in a broader context of 'human information behaviour' have also taken place (Wilson, 2000; Spink & Cole, 2006). At the same time, calls for shedding light on the collaborative nature of information behaviour has also arisen as has been reviewed by Foster (2006) and Talja & Hansen (2006), and more recently by Reddy and Jansen (2008) as part of their study. However, as will be demonstrated, the research focus remains on information seeking and retrieval, and which is often treated as a discrete unit of activity. While it is clear that this focus is continuous with the traditional interest in designing information sources and services where people come to seek information with more or less clear-cut intentions, it is not very clear whether this choice still fits with burgeoning interest in studying information behaviour in a broader context.

Recently, the research focus has been extended as far as 'human information behaviour', and it has become necessary to reconsider some theoretical choices to make in conducting studies. This is reflected in some definitions of the concepts. For example, Wilson (2000) defined 'human information behaviour' to mean 'the totality of human behaviour in relation to sources and channels of information, including both active and passive information seeking, and information use'. He then defined 'information seeking behaviour' as 'the purposive seeking of information as a consequence of a need to satisfy some goal'. Information behaviour includes both active and passive information seeking while information seeking behaviour involves purposeful information behaviour.

In spite of the move to extend the research scope as far as 'human information behavior', some researchers view that the actual scope of research has not been changed much. Järvelin and Ingwersen (2004) pointed out that information seeking is still studied in isolation from other tasks that people are engaged in.

...information seeking research, as such, still seems to be the study of the behaviour that takes place between tasks and information sources and cannot be theoretically justified as an isolated area. Why? From the actors' point-of-view, seeking does not always constitute an independent system, or meaningful system of activities as a focus of attention. At least for many actors engaged in information seeking, it may be an activity that is not considered – if recognised at all – in isolation. They are just doing their work and might welcome better ways of doing it, but are not used to notice or discuss the seeking component in which the information seeking and retrieval community is interested.

Many researchers in the field recognize that information behaviour is deeply embedded in the activity where it takes place. How information is sought, searched, accessed, exchanged, acquired, and used is closely related to the activity. If we try to take this fact seriously, it means that we need to reconsider how we approach the embedded nature of information behaviour. In order to understand this nature of information behaviour, one needs to be faithful to the ways in which members experience reality; that is to say, we should reconsider treating information seeking as a predefined discrete unit of analysis.

Moreover, information behaviour is often embedded in collaborative work as many researchers have pointed out (Foster, 2006; Talja & Hansen, 2006). Foster (2006), for instance, argues that 'all information tasks (e.g., seeking, querying, filtering, and navigating) and their subtasks (e.g., evaluation) can be performed in collaboration with others' (p.350). Until recently, however, both collective and collaborative aspects of information behaviour have not received much attention (Hansen & Järvelin, 2000, 2004; Talja & Hansen, 2006). The focus of research has been mostly on information seeking of individuals in terms of one-way activity, rather than 'collaborative' activity.

The collective aspects of human information behaviour (HIB) have only been conceptualised as consulting, information seeking, use of personal sources, and peer influence. Such conceptualisations suggest a one-way process in which an individual consults another individual. Group seeking, the more or less systematic collaboration in information acquisition, has received less attention (Talja & Hansen, 2006, p.113).

Recently, we see a growing number of studies which look at the qualitative aspect of collaborative information behaviour (CIB) (Foster, 2006; Talja & Hansen, 2006). The concept of 'collaborative information behaviour' itself is defined rather broadly. For example, Reddy and Jansen (2008) defined it as "activities that a group or team of people undertakes to identify and resolve a shared information need" (p.257) and Talja and Hansen (2006) define it as "an activity where two or more actors communicate to identify information for accomplishing a task or solving a problem" (p.114).

However, 'collaborative information behaviour' itself has never been the focus of research; instead, 'collaborative information seeking and retrieval' has been. 'Collaborative information seeking and retrieval' is often contrasted with 'information sharing', where the former is active and explicit and the latter is less goal oriented and implicit (Hansen & Järvelin, 2004). Poltrock et al. (2004) for example define 'information sharing' as exchanges of already acquired information, and collaborative information retrieval as actors' acquiring information from the external source. Having clearly separated the two, they decide to place their research focus only on collaborative information retrieval. Thus, in studies of CIB, the above two aspects of information behaviour, i.e., what is defined as 'information sharing' and 'information seeking and retrieval', have rarely been studied together. Research tends to focus on the information seeking and retrieval aspect by separating it out from the rest. However, both often occur simultaneously in settings where work needs to be coordinated among members. Also, creation of information should be involved as a result of information seeking and retrieval, which can be examined at the same time.

How then is the collaborative nature of information seeking and retrieval treated in studies of CIB? As the focus has been narrowed down to collaborative information seeking and retrieval, the focus on collaboration has also been narrowed down to the information seeking part of collaboration taking place during the process.

CIS&R research [collaborative information seeking and retrieval] is not interested in collaboration per se. It is not interested in the dynamics of group work, the emergence and sustenance of collaborations, or human relationships within collaborative work processes. Rather, CIB research looks at collaboration in the processes of information seeking, retrieval, filtering, and synthesis. However, it views these processes as taking place and being deeply embedded in work and other kinds of everyday life practices. CIB investigates manifestations of collaboration in information seeking and retrieval to better understand and support work and knowledge processes (Talja and Hansen, 2006, p.116).

In this way, a set of theoretical decisions have been made as to how to approach CIB so that researchers can strategically concentrate on issues directly connected with information seeking and retrieval.

What one is left to wonder is whether the approach formulated by predefining the concept of CIB is relevant to how practitioners experience the activity, as has been pointed out by Järvelin and Ingwersen (2004) about the approach to human information behaviour. In the context of collaborative work, information is interactionally made available constantly throughout the course of activity, whether or not people are engaged in 'collaborative information seeking and retrieval',

and whether or not they seek and use 'information' newly acquired from an external resource. In fact, some studies indicate the need for approaching CIB without deciding the research focus in advance. For example, Sonnenwald and Pierce (2000) take into account 'situated awareness' of team members working in a command and control context in the military, as a concept to characterise team members' information behaviour. Further, by paying attention to the situated aspects of information in the course of activity, they manage to get close to what team members treat as 'information'. By studying how doctors, nurses, and other professionals seek, formulate, and share information through their collaborative work in the ICU, Reddy and colleagues manage to capture what practitioners try to do to work collaboratively in order to manage the information they need to do the work (Reddy & Dourish, 2002). These studies seem to indicate the need to approach the phenomenon of CIB as a whole without narrowing down the focus in advance to certain aspects of phenomenon such as 'information seeking and retrieval' or 'information sharing'.

Similarly, Foster (2006) points out that there are different modes of collaboration involved in CIB:

Collaboration on an information task can be direct (e.g., when members of a team share a common work task) or indirect (e.g., when individuals draw on the explicit or implicit informational activity of others while performing their own information tasks). Collaboration on an information task may be invisible. For example, it may be subsumed within a more clearly identifiable work task (p.350).

By pointing out that there are 'direct' and 'indirect' modes of collaboration on information task, Foster implies there is a need to attend to not only purposive CIB (i.e. collaborative information and retrieval), but also to the embedded nature of CIB, when he points out that there is an 'invisible' information task.

Now we should turn to the issue of providing ideas for *re*designing practices and systems which support practices, for this issue is connected with the issue of how to approach the embedded and collaborative nature of information behaviour. If we want to contribute to informing *re*design of practices and systems, first of all, it is necessary for us to understand practitioners' problems from within the activity. Good design ideas need to be derived from a good understanding of what it is to solve their problems in terms of their logic-in-use in the activity, not in terms of some criteria external to their logic (Anderson, 1994). In order to understand how practitioners experience the activity and their problems as they encounter them, it is necessary to put any theoretical preconceptions aside, and to try to understand how the activity is socially organised in relation to the practitioners' assumptions, and how they encounter problems.

In summary, there is a need to reconsider how to approach the embedded nature as well as the collaborative nature of information behaviour in terms of informing the design of practices and systems. As we have reviewed, the issue of how to approach the embedded nature of CIB remains up till now one in which information seeking and retrieval is treated as a discrete unit of activity. Similarly, how we approach the collaborative nature of information behaviour still remains an issue as long as we treat the collaboration during information seeking and retrieval as a discrete unit of analysis. Furthermore, in order for studies to be able to inform the *re*design of practices and systems, it is important that we take an approach that enables us to understand how practitioners experience reality.

Taking the above issues into consideration, we decided to study CIB without pre-deciding which part we should focus on. In other words, instead of separating out different kinds and parts of behaviour such as those concerning purposive and passive information behaviour or others concerning information already known or newly acquired from an external source, we decided to study collaborative work more broadly where CIB is a part, in other words, to study work practice. First we conducted fieldwork where a group of IT product designers were working in collaboration with other groups, and in this way, found actual instances of difficulties they were struggling with as part of their work activity. We then analysed what we found in terms of how they actually organised their collaborative work, and how problems were actually organised as part of accomplishing their work. To put it differently, we took an ethnomethodological approach to deal with the issues of the embedded and the collaborative nature of information behaviour by paying careful attention to the people's work in its natural setting, looking at interactions among them during the work, including at meetings. In this way, we tried to understand the ways in which their activities are practically organised with reliance on practical knowledge on how to progress various kinds of work, relying on information exchanged and certain tools. We took this naturalistic approach because this would allow us to understand the ways in which the phenomena are organised; in other words, the approach would allow us to understand the phenomenon of information sharing by taking into consideration its embedded and collaborative nature.

In the following, we first provide an analysis of how the IT product designers we studied found difficulties in fitting the newly introduced information sharing activity into their work and how the analysis informed the *re*design of that activity. By also presenting the process of design implementation, we hope to bring to light some considerations to be taken into account when researchers attempt to inform design by studying CIB.

FINDINGS FROM THE INITIAL FIELDWORK

As part of our fieldwork in the department which designs and develops IT product hardware, we had a chance to focus on a group in charge of designing the chassis itself. They also mount different components and wirings within the chassis, determine what kind of parts are to be used, and put all the design specifications together before handing them over to the factory. At the time we started fieldwork, the group was in the middle of the development of a new machine. The group had to handle a variety of tasks simultaneously: not only designing and developing new machines, but also they had to respond to various requests with regards to machines they had developed earlier, such as responding to fault reports or specification changes. These requests come from different organisations, e.g., the planning office, the quality assurance office, various producers of different parts and factories assembling parts, the service engineering department, and so forth. Responding to such requests often involves coordinating with different organisations; thus it can take multiple steps, and may not be recognised as a 'task-in-process' as sometimes it takes some time for a group to respond to requests for various reasons (e.g., it is assumed that another group or another person will take up the task, a group is busy with other tasks, etc.). On the other hand, due to serious consequences such as the whole production line being put on hold, some requests may require an immediate response.

Thus, individuals keep getting bombarded with new tasks through emails and phone-calls, as well as through their managers, their group leaders, and from external departments with whom they interact at meetings, etc. These items constantly change task priority and interrupt the current tasks. Readjustment of delivery date often becomes necessary. However, not all delivery dates have the same weight. They vary from 'utmost priority' to 'can be delayed', depending on the kind of task and in what context the task is assigned. Accordingly, some dates are officially negotiated for rescheduling by the manager or by the individual member, and others get delayed without any specific negotiation. At the time we

conducted the initial fieldwork, it was mainly left to an individual member as to how to handle the delivery dates, while it was one of the group leaders' tasks to try to keep to the delivery dates for all the tasks the group was assigned to do.

In these circumstances, the erroneous omission of tasks is bound to occur, and some tasks remain untouched until they get 'rediscovered,' often through being chased up by other organisations. As an erroneous omission can affect the progress of other tasks, the people who made the request often try to remind and chase the other person who is responsible for it. During the peak development periods for a new machine, members of the group were constantly getting chased by different organisations and at one point, some members were in a state where they were responding to one request after another from the organisation in charge. In other words, at that time, the rhythms of work for these members were being created mostly by the other organisations that made the requests through reminders and pressure on the group (Reddy & Dourish, 2002).

When we started the fieldwork, the Group Leader (GL) was struggling with task management, especially in terms of information sharing. The GL was initially trying to carry out task management by creating a list of the group's task statuses and by having a task management meeting every Friday morning with all members. The introduction of the task management meeting was initiated by the management. Groups were expected to hold this meeting every week, and a task schedule format had been provided for this purpose, but the rest was up to the groups as to how they organised the meeting. Thus, the GL was trying to conduct task management by creating a comprehensive list of information on his group's tasks statuses based on the lists of information submitted by the individuals; in such a way that the GL was hoping to keep to delivery dates and prevent erroneous omissions. The GL's 'model' can be termed a 'document based individual task management model' as he insisted on individuals keeping record of their tasks in the form of document independent of other members and task management meetings (Figure 1).

This model can be contrasted with a model we proposed to them later where task coordination across the group can be carried out as part of the meeting.

At first, the GL asked individual members to help him update the task status list he created based on the format the management provided and shared on the server. However, only a few people responded to his request. Three weeks later, the GL told members that it had been hard for him to keep track of individual tasks, and he asked individuals to create a list of tasks without a specific format. However, in the following week, the GL found that only one out of eight members had responded to the request. So, the GL had to keep asking the same request. The GL was obviously suffering from lack of members' participation and cooperation in updating the task status list. Members did not see the immediate benefit of creating a list of tasks to share with the GL. In other words, the ways in which the GL was trying to do task management was not yet embedded in their practice. We were told that similar practices

had been introduced in the past, but apparently did not last very long. On the other hand, we observed that another group had been holding a weekly meeting where the GL was discussing the status with his group members and at the same time, updating the status task document in Word© format while projecting it on the wall.

In fact, the actual process of collecting the information of the group's task status affected the way the weekly task management meeting was organised. In each meeting, the GL had to ask each member to report his/her plan of the day as well as the plan of the coming week. No particular documents were used for the report. The GL selected the next speaker, and the member selected started to report. Often, the GL spent much time collecting information on each task one by one, e.g., its delivery date and whether tasks were handled properly or not.

[Excerpt 1: Weekly meeting, June 06][5]

01 GL Is there anything you need to finish this week?

Figure 1. Document bases individual task management model: Information sharing is directed to the leader

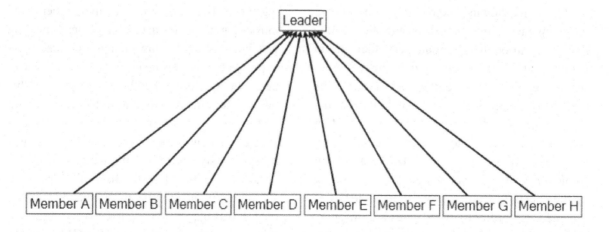

* Arrows show information flow.

02 FU Yes, things to do with boards

03 [...]

04 FU and I was to finish them by Monday, but I asked to move it to

05 Tuesday, and probably I can finish it by coming in on Sunday

06 (laugh) that is about it

By asking, "Is there anything you need to finish this week?," the GL is checking whether Fujimoto (FU) still has any remaining tasks due today, as it is Friday, the last day of the week. The GL tries to detect tasks that may be potentially delayed. It is important for him to be aware of what has been delayed and whether a rescheduled date has been negotiated.

Erroneous omissions are another thing the GL was concerned about.

[Excerpt 2: Weekly meeting June 27]

01 GL What we need to finish quickly at present with regards to

02 design is cable management. And labels. So please

03 concentrate on these tasks. And try to put down items on the

04 server so that we can prevent erroneous omissions

The GL is prioritizing the work by identifying specifically two tasks: cable management and labels. Then the GL again asks group members to make a list of task items and put it on the server. The GL wants members to keep the list and make it public by putting the task status on the server so that he can keep track of tasks so that erroneous omissions can be prevented.

In the interaction described above, the GL also takes notes during the meeting to keep track of the members' tasks. At the individual level, they had different ways of keeping track of their tasks. Many put sticky notes both in paper and digital form over their computer displays, and were taking notes in their notebooks. One member had kept a list of tasks and schedules on his computer for a while, but did not share it with others. When he became extremely busy, he stopped updating the list. In short, they were keeping track of their action items in one way or another, but never as a group.

Also, some members had too many tasks to keep a list. It made more sense for them to complete each task one by one by responding to each reminder rather than spending a long time creating a list. For example, Itao had to prioritise incoming tasks before he asked the two colleagues to help him. Since so many tasks were delayed, in the end, Itao was asked to spend time during the weekend creating a 'comprehensive task status list' by the GL. Since he had been at the center of new development work, it turned out that Itao carried out over 100 task items. However, making the list alone did not help him much to prioritise the tasks.

In addition, not all group members were able to attend due to individuals' work schedules e.g. some had other engagements such as other meetings. This conflict between each member's schedules made task management even harder.

Thus, the GL was trying to accomplish two things: eliminating the erroneous omission of tasks, and keeping to delivery dates. Two of the central means the GL was trying to use for this purpose was the idea of creating and maintaining the task status list to be as comprehensive as possible, as well as the idea of holding the weekly meeting, both newly asked for by the management. From our analysis of a series of the weekly meetings, the meeting was organised as an occasion to ask individuals to create a tasks status list, as well as to actually obtain details of task items from individuals. As most members were clearly reluctant to respond to his request of updating and sharing the list as a group, the GL had to learn about each individual's task status as exhaustively as possible by inquiring one member at a time, while the rest of the participants sat in silence for an hour in the weekly meetings. It appeared that the GL interpreted the model introduced by the management as something that can be called the 'document based individual task management model'. However, since members were never enthusiastic about his request to keep the task status list as comprehensive as possible, the GL struggled with how to put this model into practice.

CO-DESIGN OF TASK MANAGEMENT

Reconsidering the Work Practice

When we presented our findings to the group, we were requested to reconsider how the group carried out their task management. Our analysis showed that the GL aimed to create a complete list of task status whereby he was hoping to keep track of what had been completed, what had fallen through the cracks, and what had been behind schedule. However, the GL was not able to get the lists from the members. So, in the weekly meeting, he asked individuals what tasks they were completing, and what they had on for the next week. Because the GL was asking each member directly, interaction was mostly on a one-on-one basis and other members were there but did not have much of an opportunity to interact with each

other. Often, the GL could do little more than ask group members about their task status; he did not go as far as managing the tasks across the team, reallocating some tasks to other members, or rescheduling the delivery dates by negotiating with other organisations. They were reporting to the GL, often relying on each individual's memory rather than on written documents.

The tasks were falling behind quite often and other departments were constantly pressing the group for them. At the peak of the new product development, the requests coming from different departments became the "cues" that were defining the rhythm of their work. We were aware that this activity was affecting the members psychologically.

It was clear to us that the GL's effort in carrying out task management by centralizing the information about tasks on an individual basis through the creation of a comprehensive list, what we call the 'document based individual task management model,' was difficult for both members and the GL. Hence, we developed an alternative model, the model we can call 'collaborative task management'. In this model, not only can all group members share their plan for the day with each other, but also they can coordinate with each other to prioritise their work and decide which tasks to do when and how. Thus, we tried to *re*embed the task management into their work practice.

Generating Ideas for Reembedding Task Management

However, with two months left before the delivery deadline, it was the peak of the development of the new machine. Thus, we needed some concrete and feasible ideas for redesigning their task management practice, which were easy to implement, and would allow them to immediately experience and quickly realise that it was worth doing.

We still thought that some kind of regular meeting could be a good vehicle for putting the model of 'collaborative task management' into work. We chose a 'morning meeting', which would be held daily. Given constant changes occurring in the priority of tasks, more frequent meeting would enable members to share information more often, and best of all, in a timely manner. Additionally, by holding the meeting in the morning, we thought members would be able to use this as an occasion for organising their work collaboratively at the beginning of the day. This would give them a chance to plan before leaving their desks to perform their own tasks, such as attending a meeting, conducting experiments in a laboratory located in a different building, or even trips outside the company. Once members departed to different places, members of this organisation had very little chance to talk to each other during the day.

As for the meeting style, we decided to make a transition from the reporting-to-the-leader style under the document based individual task management model to sharing-and-coordinating-the-plan-of-the-day under the collaborative task management model (Figure 2). To make this transition smooth for the members, we felt that a few more details needed to be worked out. New ideas were suggested: one was that individuals would share their plan for the day as well as make requests and suggestions to other members in order to coordinate with one another. For this, individual members needed to manage their own tasks and prepare a plan before the meeting. It was also suggested that an individual could leave work when their plan for the day was completed. We thought this would ensure that some autonomy remained in the hands of individuals even while they made their plan of the day open to other members.

In order to make it easier for members to share individuals' tasks with each other, we also suggested using some kind of 'public display' where individuals write down their plan of the day. We learned from fieldwork that members had a difficult time looking for the files on the server and updating it each time there was a change. Thus,

Figure 2. Collaborative task management: Sharing-and-coordinating-the-plan-of-the-day

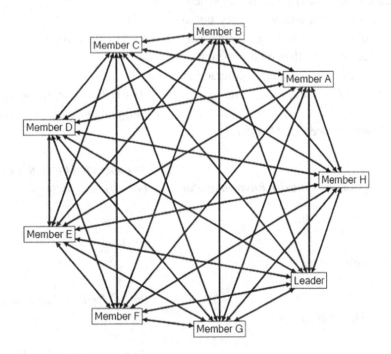

* Arrows show information flow.

we suggested "analog" tools such as whiteboards and self-adhesive paper sheets of different sizes to be used. However, we left it open as to which specific type of 'media' they would use for this purpose.

We held a mini workshop with the group to show our fieldwork findings and share ideas and agree upon a set of suggestions we explained above. We also decided that we would continue fieldwork as members tried to implement some of the ideas we agreed to in the workshop and offer our feedback later.

Collaborative Task Management in Action

Coordinating Work with Other Members by Seeking Information

The first obvious change we observed was that members started coordinating amongst themselves for example, seeking information from each other during the morning meeting about the delivery date of specific tasks, as to how they had scheduled to do specific tasks, and when they could get together to discuss a specific task. What was especially noticeable was that members across different teams in the group started interacting with each other to coordinate their work.

[Excerpt 3: Morning meeting, October 1]

01 IT ((pointing at the board)) Environmental assessment

02 NO Registration?

03 IT Not yet up to registration

04 NO Can you register tomorrow?

05 IT I have to make an arrangement with the Quality Assessment

06 and others, so I want to set it up by then.

In excerpt 3 (above), Nosaka starts asking questions (line 2) as to how Itao was planning to do the task as soon as Itao mentioned the word "environmental assessment". Nosaka was supposed to coordinate with Itao to work with the Department of Quality Assessment to complete this task. It is also to be noted that they were now using the handwritten board to talk about and share the task with each other.

Deciding on What to do Next Based on the Shared Information

[Excerpt 4: Morning meeting, October 7]

01 FU I have finished

02 NO Have you?

03 FU There are no action items for the machine that you and I are working on, as I

04 completed them all last week. ((pointing at the board)) See, there is

05 none

06 NO None of those that are most pressing

07 FU Specification document for the machine A

08 NO Specifications for bar code?

09 FU I need to revise them, and I have not submitted the document for

10 the machine L, either

In excerpt 4 (above), Fujimoto is telling Nosaka that she has finished the most pressing items for the new development project, machine A. Then she points at the task plan they share for confirmation. Nosaka finally admits that there are none of the highest priority tasks for the project, and then they start listing items they need to do for other machines. An obvious, but important point would be that by using a written list of task status, they are able to quickly confirm with each other that the items of the highest priority are now completed. This enables them to move onto other tasks which have been set aside while Fujimoto was occupied with the pressing tasks from other project. In this excerpt, once Fujimoto draws Nosaka's attention to the sheet (line 3-5), she manages to get his confirmation and agreement (line 6). This continues as they start talking about what tasks are now of high priority. This is a change from the way they used to manage their tasks by only talking from personal memory.

Avoiding Redoing Tasks by Sharing Information in a Timely Manner

[Excerpt 5: Morning meeting, September 30]

01 NO You know what, you may not know this, about the electronic

02 rating

03 ((Every member turns attention to Nosaka))

04 FU Oh, right on. The rating has changed, right?

05 NO Yes. It is from the Department E, and they are trying to change the

06 voltage from 120V to 100V. It may officially come out today

07 from the department. We may have to change data.

08 [...]

09 FU I shall not start working on the label data and wait for the information to come by

10 then. For I need to include them all in the label data

In excerpt 5 (above), Nosaka makes an announcement that there may be a change in the electronic rating (line 1-2), and it becomes apparent to Fujimoto that the change can affect her work; if she creates documents for manuals and rating labels now, she will have to redo the task later with the new rates. She then announces that she will wait for the data to come and work on manuals and rating labels (line 9-10). Note that Nosaka's announcement is made to attract everybody's attention. His information sharing is apparently delivered in a timely manner for Fujimoto. His piece of information saved her from redoing the same task; and at the same time allowed Fujimoto to let others, especially the GL, know that she will not work on this particular task for the legitimate reason now shared among them.

Development of the Trials

In the course of members' trials of the new way of conducting task management, one thing that became apparent in our fieldwork that the GL started treating the task board as a means of realising what he initially wanted to do: creating a complete list of task status of the group. One day the GL asked a member who was in charge of the development of the new system to list the tasks he had, as comprehensively as possible on a big board. It was obviously a little different from our idea of creating a plan of the day on each board. It was clear that the GL wished to obtain information as comprehensively as possible, so he could keep track of the group's work and keep the delivery time and prevent tasks from falling through the cracks. Eventually, the GL extended the list by adding a few more boards so that items for other machines could also be listed. In this way, at the start, some boards were owned and managed by individuals and at the same time, were publicly available displayed on the desk close to the group. But once the GL started working on the board, the individuals were no longer owners of the board, and the boards turned into tools for the leader and the manager. Thus, displaying the plan of the day was being replaced by a long list of task statuses. The GL saw the board could be used as a space for displaying comprehensive information of his group's tasks. Based on the information on the boards, the GL started creating a task status list in "digital" form, saving it on the server. When we interviewed one member, he wondered what the point of the GL's 'visualisation' of information was. To him, it was just a time consuming task[4].

Also, the GL quickly went back to the style of individually based task management as he started taking more time on inquiring about each individual. When the group finally completed the

process of delivering the whole set of manufacturing specifications and parts of the new machine to the factory, the frequency of the morning meeting dropped to as low as twice a week. On the other hand, the GL told the group and the manager that he would like to continue the meeting. We were also aware that members had started talking about creating a small board for each member to plan their work. We considered this a good idea to be welcomed and supported. First of all, it was obvious that our initial idea of collaborative task management was underlying their ideas. It was probably fair to say that they saw some sense in our idea of collaborative management by experimenting with a different way of doing task management. However, we wanted make sure that we could help them to realize their idea in a way all members could see sense. For this, we first decided to interview members to ask them to reflect on their practice., e.g., what they liked about the meeting, what changes they wanted to see, and their ideas for improvement. Based on what we gathered from the interviews, we talked with their manager and team leader to see why members' ideas for task management made sense for them, and what kind of change the manager and team leader made in their leadership.

Dimensions of Task Management from Members' Point of View

It turned out that members expected task management to be carried out in two dimensions. One was coordination of work among members through collaborative task management. That is to say, by sharing the information of plans of the day with each other, they want to coordinate their work so that each member can complete their tasks smoothly. When we asked a member of the team in charge of integrating design information if it was of any benefit to have the morning meeting another team in charge of structural design, she replied as follows:

" We need to do it [the morning meeting]. Why? For example, right now I am doing this task for tomorrow and I will not be able to complete it without the input from the structural designers. So I need to ask them to do it by tomorrow, I need them to create work 'backups'."

This member was in charge of integrating all design information ready for the production work. In order for her to complete her work on time, she needed to inform the structural designer to get a specific piece of design ready. She saw the morning meetings as a good occasion for doing this kind of coordination. This is only possible when tasks are planned in such a way that one can remind others in advance. What she had started trying to do was to organise her tasks for today, tomorrow, and the day after tomorrow by using self-adhesive pads. She thought that by keeping the board beside her on her desk this would allow her to organise her tasks easily whenever she remembered things; at the same time people could see and discuss it if she kept it on her desk.

Another dimension of task management that members wanted to see was related to reassignment, rescheduling or even declining tasks. They wanted their manager and the GL to take up this role more. This dimension often involved negotiating with other organisations. They especially wanted to see some measures taken to alleviate the situation when it looked obvious that they were overloaded with work.

In fact, one member told us how she viewed the way tasks were managed:

"...even if I tell the leader that 'I cannot do them all,' because he does not see what tasks others have, he would not take it away [meaning reallocating and/or dispatching], but he simply tells me 'I guess you just need to work harder'."

She is pointing out that it is not currently visible to the GL how busy each member is on the day. And later, she proposes that they use handy

individual task boards to help him to see how much they are already occupied. It is hoped that this will lead him to think of alternatives.

Timing: Tuning and Creating Rhythms of Work

One member described the morning meeting as an occasion for confirming the delivery dates of different tasks.

"I thought I knew what I was doing, but it was good to be able to check what were the tasks that needed to be finished today. When you become busy, you tend to think according to your priorities, and decide on your own, 'this can be done later' or 'just one day delay will be fine', and I have experienced this. But if 'we decide to deliver this by this date', then you will aim for it, which is good."

This member says that the morning meeting was a good occasion to tune his mind into rhythms of the work in the group, as well as collaboratively creating rhythms of work in the group by deciding when to finish which tasks.

Further, a novice member who joined in the middle of the development told us that he liked the fact that they had set the meeting in the morning, as he could get enough information prior to starting work on the tasks of the day.

"When I report to the leader in the evening, since it is not a meeting before the work starts, and it is the time we are about to go home, it is not very intense, and we can often end up saying 'let's think about this tomorrow'. And in the morning, since he [the leader] is busy, I cannot ask. It was good to have the regular time, especially in the morning, so I wish we could somehow continue this."

He also told us that part of the reason why the meetings became less frequent was that a sub-leader who used to start the meeting when the GL was out busy or had been transferred to another team. When the GL was otherwise occupied in the morning, the morning meeting was called off. He then told us if other people could start the meeting, it would be more frequent.

Reviving Collaborative Task Management

We could see that they wanted to revive the morning meeting by introducing the small individual boards. We could also confirm that what they were looking for was a way to coordinate with others in the busy environment where they could easily loose the opportunity to exchange information. Hence, we decided to reorganise our set of design ideas for collaborative task management in the morning meeting by incorporating the use of individual boards. We had another mini workshop, and the group agreed to hold the meeting every morning, with the GL or the new sub-leader taking the initiative, and we also suggested keeping it to about a half-an-hour at most. Individuals were to present the plan of the day with requests and suggestions made as to how the work would be coordinated; the GL would be responsible

for reassignment, rescheduling, and so forth. We asked Fujimoto, who had now become the sub-leader, to take the initiative and share her method of using the board as a starting point. It was also agreed that the GL would make use of the individual board to maintain the list of task statuses. It was also agreed to revive the weekly meeting so that their group manager could keep track of what his team was doing and take care of issues they could not solve in the morning meetings. Because of limited space, we have not gone in detail on how the morning meetings have proceeded since then, but it has been observed that members are so far enthusiastically participating in the meetings in the way they all agreed. Also, we have been informed that other groups have also started morning meetings following our group's practice. The development of the whole process is illustrated in Figure 3.

CONCLUSION

We have shown that embeddedness and collaboration are important aspects of information sharing activities; but that despite strong interest in these

Figure 3. From fieldwork to co-design of task management

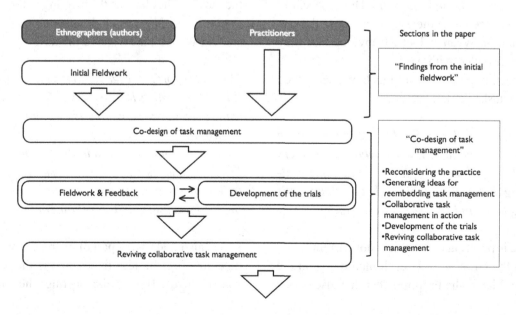

aspects in CIB studies, it is often not easy for researchers to actually take them into account in the empirical studies. We decided to take a naturalistic approach called ethnomethodology when looking at the actual work, so that we could begin to understand how practitioners' work is practically organised and where information sharing is organised as a part of this. As a consequence, it became possible for us to observe and examine various kinds of information sharing activities embedded in collaborative work. For example, as we demonstrated, that in order for the group leader to achieve task management, various information sharing activities were carried out by different parties: individual members creating status lists, the leader compiling an integrated status list, members announcing that they need specific work items done for them to complete a task, finding out the delivery date of a task, informing others that one has to change the previously announced priority of work because one has a more pressing task to do, to name a few. This allowed us to understand and capture task management as collaborative work more holistically, in relation to different forms of information sharing activities. Thus, we were able to present to the practitioners how information sharing activities are organised as part of task management, how their difficulties in participating in the activities are actually organised. However, we did not stop there.

We organised further mini-workshops where we presented a set of ideas for redesigning their practice, elicited practitioners' ideas, and agreed upon a set of ideas to try. This was an iterative process that we repeated several times. There were two things we paid specific attention to. One was to explicate what was taken for granted by the manager in introducing a new policy, by the group leader when trying to follow the policy, and the group members in participating in new activities introduced by the group leader. Another point we paid great attention to was to create a consensus

around what they were going to do and why they were going to do it, not only among group members but also the leader and the managers. In order to accomplish this, attempts were made not to impose researchers' ideas based on the fieldwork findings unless the members as well as the manager and the leader could see some sense in the idea, whilst eliciting their views about our ideas and those of others. Thus the transformation of practice that came about as a result of the process involved reinventing the manager's idea with integration of members' ideas.

Once Grudin (1988:p.86) analysed why CSCW applications fail in organisational settings:

- The application fails because it requires that some people do additional work, while those people are not the ones who perceive a direct benefit from the use of the application.
- The design process fails because our intuitions are poor for multi-user applications – decision-makers see the potential benefits for people similar to themselves, but don't see the implications of the fact that extra work will be required of others.

The whole process we reported here to some degrees affirms Grudin's findings, yet in a situation where no new technology is involved. This implies that any attempt to change practice, with or without the introduction of technology, requires some kind of transformation of practice in one way or another. A key feature for the transformation of practice to be successfully achieved from the perspective of all levels of practitioners is both the perceived and actual utility of the attempted change, for all, which in turn is directly implicated in the level of group buy-in and participation. For this, this chapter has shown at least a good understanding of practice where information-sharing activities are a part can play a crucial role.

ACKNOWLEDGMENT

We thank members of the IT Company for letting us to work with them. Our great appreciation also goes first to our editor Jonathan Foster, and to Shunsaku Tamura, Paul Luff, Dave Martin and Rachael Luck who carefully read our paper and gave us insightful and useful comments.

REFERENCES

Anderson, R. J. (1994). Representations and requirements: The value of ethnography in system design. *Human-Computer Interaction, 9*(2), 151–182. doi:10.1207/s15327051hci0902_1

Bobrow, D. G., & Whalen, J. (2002). Community Knowledge Sharing in Practice: The Eureka Story. *Reflections-Society for Organizational Learning, 4*(2), 47–59.

Case, D. (2006). Information seeking. *Annual Review of Information Science & Technology, 40,* 293–327. doi:10.1002/aris.1440400114

Courtright, C. (2007). Context in information behavior research. *Annual Review of Information Science & Technology, 41,* 273–306. doi:10.1002/aris.2007.1440410113

Fisher, K., & Julien, H. (2009). Information behavior. *Annual Review of Information Science & Technology, 43,* 317–358.

Foster, J. (2006). Collaborative information seeking and retrieval. *Annual Review of Information Science & Technology, 40,* 329–356. doi:10.1002/aris.1440400115

Garcia, A., Dawes, M. E., Kohne, M. L., Miller, F. M., & Groschwitz, S. F. (2006). Workplace studies and technological change. *Annual Review of Information Science & Technology, 40,* 393–437. doi:10.1002/aris.1440400117

Grudin, J. (1988). Problems in the Design and Evaluation of Organisational Interfaces. In *CSCW '88* (pp. 85–93). Portland, Oregon: Why CSCW Applications Fail.

Huysman, M., & de Wit, D. (2004). A critical evaluation of knowledge management practices. In Ackerman, M., Pipek, V., & Wulf, V. (Eds.), *Sharing Expertise: Beyond Knowledge Management* (pp. 27–55). Cambridge: MIT Press.

Ikeya, N., & Okada, M. (2007) Doctors' Practical Management of Knowledge in the Daily Case Conference. In S. Hester & D. Francis (Eds.), *Orders of Ordinary Action: Respecifying Sociological Knowledge* (pp. 69-89). Aldershot, UK: Ashgate.

Ikeya, N., & Vinkhuyzen, E. (in press). Designing beyond the meeting: accommodating collaborative problem solving and risk management. In Szymanski, P. (Ed.), *Making Work Visible: Ethnographically grounded case studies of work practice.* Cambridge, UK: Cambridge University Press.

Järvelin, K., & Ingwersen, P. (2004). Information seeking research needs extension towards tasks and technology. Information Research, 10(1), paper 212 [Available at http://InformationR.net/ir/10-1/paper212.html].

Mengis, J., & Eppler, M. (2005). *Understanding and enabling knowledge sharing in conversations: a literature review and management framework.* 2nd Annual Conference on Knowledge Management in the Asian Pacific (KMAP), Wellington (New Zealand).

Orlikowski, W. J. (1992). Learning from Notes: Organizational Issues in Groupware Implementation. In *CSCW 92* (pp. 362–369). Toronto: ACM Press.

Orr, J. E. (1996). *Talking about machines: An ethnography of a modern job.* Ithaca, NY: ILR Press/ Cornell University Press.

Pettigrew, K. a. (2001). Conceptual frameworks in information behavior. *Annual Review of Information Science & Technology, 35*, 43–78.

Poltrock, S., Grudin, J., Dumais, S., Fidel, R., Bruce, H., & Pejtersen, A. (2003). Information seeking and sharing in design teams. In *Proceedings of the 2003 international ACM SIGGROUP conference on Supporting group work* (pp. 239-247). New York: ACM.

Randall, D., Harper, R., & Rouncefield, M. (2007). *Fieldwork for design: theory and practice*. London: Springer-Verlag.

Reddy, M., & Dourish, P. (2002). A finger on the pulse: temporal rhythms and information seeking in medical work. In *CSCW '02: Proceedings of the 2002 ACM conference on Computer supported cooperative work* (pp. 344-353). New York: ACM.

Reddy, M. C., & Jansen, B. J. (2008). A model for understanding collaborative information behavior in context: A study of two healthcare teams. *Information Processing & Management, 44*(1), 256–273. doi:10.1016/j.ipm.2006.12.010

Savolainen, R. (2009). Epistemic work and knowing in practice as conceptualizations of information use. Information Research, 14(1), paper 392. [Available at http://InformationR.net/ir/14-1/paper392.html]

Sonnenwald, D., & Pierce, L. (2000). Information behavior in dynamic group work contexts: interwoven situational awareness, dense social networks and contested collaboration in command and control. *Information Processing & Management, 36*(3), 461–479. doi:10.1016/S0306-4573(99)00039-4

Spink, A., & Cole, C. (2006). Human information behavior: Integrating diverse approaches and information use. *Journal of the American Society for Information Science and Technology, 57*(1), 25–35. doi:10.1002/asi.20249

Suchman, L. A. (1987). *Plans and situated actions: The problem of human-machine communication*. Cambridge, UK: Cambridge University Press.

Talja, S., & Hansen, P. (2006). Information sharing. In Spink, A., & Cole, C. (Eds.), *New Directions in Human Information Behavior* (pp. 113–134). Dordrecht, The Netherlands: Springer. doi:10.1007/1-4020-3670-1_7

Vakkari, P. (2003). Task-based information searching. *Annual Review of Information Science & Technology, 37*, 413–464. doi:10.1002/aris.1440370110

von Krogh, G., Ichijo, K., & Nonaka, I. (2000). *Enabling knowledge creation: How to unlock the mystery of tacit knowledge and release the power of innovation*. Oxford, UK: Oxford University Press.

Whalen, M., Whalen, J., Moore, R. J., Raymond, G. T., Szymanski, M. H., & Vinkhuyzen, E. (2004). Studying workscapes. In *Discourse & technology: multimodal discourse analysis* (pp. 208–229). Washington, DC: Georgetown University Press.

Wilson, T. (2000). Human information behavior. *Informing Science, 3*(2), 49–56.

Wilson, T. (2008). Activity Theory and Information Seeking. *Annual Review of Information Science & Technology, 37*, 119–161. doi:10.1002/aris.2008.1440420111

ENDNOTES

[1] Practitioners' hostility towards knowledge sharing is reported in some cases (von Krogh et al., 2000).

[2] While our study took place in Japan, to what extent our findings are unique to 'Japanese culture' as such is beyond the scope of our paper.

[3] This approach was taken by L. Suchman (1987) who studied the ways in which people

use photocopy machines. This became the first successful case that demonstrated that taking the embedded nature of activities seriously came to have practical implications for design. Similar studies are found in Orr (1996), Bobrow & Whalen (2004), Whalen et al (2004), Ikeya & Vinkhuyzen (forthcoming).

4   His comment made us even more aware of the importance of assuring the benefit of 'visualizing' implicit information or knowledge, and also of creating a balance between the benefit for the persons who are asked to do the work of visualisation and the benefit for others.

5   The list following includes abbreviations used in all excerpts; GL=the group leader, FU=Fujimoto, NO=Nosaka, IT=Itao, [...]=omitted conversation. All names in this chapter are anonymised.

6   While it is in a different setting, a study of morning meetings at an emergency hospital can be found in Ikeya & Okada (2007).

Chapter 7
Collaborative Information Behavior in Completely Online Groups

Sean Goggins
Drexel University, USA

Sanda Erdelez
University of Missouri, USA

ABSTRACT

This chapter situates collaborative information behavior in completely online groups as a phenomenon distinct from prior work understanding collaborative information behavior in face-to-face groups, free and open source software groups and Wikipedia groups. The unexpected diversity of information resources utilized by completely online group members is analyzed through Sonnenwald's Information Horizons theory. Information practices of completely online group members are described, and the key themes of groups as information resources, the influence of tool change on collaborative information behavior online, and the focusing potential of collaborative information tools for completely online group work are explicated. Future research directions that explore the potential of COGs for distributed innovation; new types of collaborative information behavior and breaking down the digital divide are reviewed.

INTRODUCTION

Information and communication technologies designed for computer supported collaborative learning (CSCL) have enabled new collaboration phenomena, including groups who come together online without ever meeting face-to-face. In these settings, people from diverse backgrounds come together for eight to sixteen weeks to perform group activities using only online course

management systems like Blackboard, Sakai or Moodle. Research to understand the collaborative information behavior of Completely Online Groups (COGs) is sometimes conflated with studies of free and open source software (FOSS) and Wikipedia groups. Like these other types of technology-centered groups, COGs exchange information and maintain awareness primarily through shared artifacts and asynchronous communication. However, COGs differ from these types of groups in three significant ways. First, their members have a common organizational af-

DOI: 10.4018/978-1-61520-797-8.ch007

filiation, similar to work groups or student groups in face-to-face settings. Second, also like members of face-to-face groups, COG members are often assigned to their groups by an organizational leader or instructor. Finally, like many but not all FOSS and Wikipedia groups, COG members do not meet face-to-face.

Collaborative information behavior in COGs is challenging because members share some information resources in common, such as those contained within the collaborative tools they use, but also rely on information resources unique to each individual's physical location and internet use habits. Sonnenwald (1999) first identified these different arrays of available information resources as Information Horizons, suggesting that information resources are used to a greater and lesser extent depending how near on ones horizon they are. How the Information Horizons of COG members influence collaborative information behavior within these groups is illustrative of phenomena emerging from the use of technology to establish and maintain online groups. Collaboration around information in COGs is influenced by the specific information in the group's field of view, and member information horizons similarly influence the group's collaborative information practices.

This chapter looks at the special case of collaborative information behavior among completely online groups from three perspectives. First, COGs are distinguished from other types of groups whose information behavior is examined in the literature. Second, Information Horizons theory is presented as a framework for examining the collaborative information behavior of COGs. Third, four collaborative information behavior themes, identified in one study of COGs, are used to frame our current understanding of COG information behavior, and the next steps in explicating collaborative information behavior in COGs. We explore collaborative information behavior using Sonnenwald's (2000) critical incident interview technique. Our methods included in depth inter-

views with three informants, whom we asked to describe incidents of information retrieval and the resources they understood to be available to them during those incidents. Subsequently we conducted a qualitative survey based on the findings from the interviews with 21 informants.

BACKGROUND

Patterns of collaborative information behavior emerge as COGs perform tasks, maintain social relations and coordinate member responsibilities. Similar technology-mediated collaborative information behavior has been explored through the free and open source software (FOSS) movement, Wikipedia and through ethnographically informed work studies of technology use in mixed mode (face-to-face and technology-mediated) groups.

The case of work groups composed of strangers that are brought together exclusively through technology to collaborate on a set of activities without ever meeting face-to-face is not addressed in this prior work, though the practices associated with building and maintaining community in face-to-face settings has been widely studied and theorized about. Wenger (1998) described communities of practice (COPS) who work together on information intensive problems in face-to-face settings and, through a process of negotiation, develop reified practices supporting the consistent performance of work. Discussing partially online groups, Gloor (2006) noted that the perfect example of a collaborative innovation network (COIN) is one comprised of people who know each other from some prior face-to-face work setting, and subsequently adapt technology to support collaboration over distance. Completely online groups (COGs) are distinct from Wenger's COPS and Gloor's COINS. COGs are groups whose members may have occasionally encountered each other face-to-face, may have occasionally encountered each other as members of different COGs in online courses, but have never worked together in a face-to-face setting on a project. COG members are at most acquaintances, and more typically they are strangers who have never met face-to-face.

FOSS, Wikipedia & Face-To-Face Groups

COG research exists somewhere between COGS & COINS and research detailing Free and Open Source Software teams (FOSS) and Wikipedia groups. In addition the work performed by COGs is usually not technical in nature; while FOSS work is highly technical and the work of Wikipedia editing groups typically include some shared expertise. Compared with FOSS groups, COGs are organized to meet a less negotiable set of goals and objectives. In COGs, membership and activities are defined *a priori* by an instructor or manager. FOSS groups, in contrast, maintain agency and direct their own goals and objectives, and their activities emerge and evolve around shared values, technical skills and aspirations. Crowston and Howison (2005) describe the information sharing and communication structure of FOSS projects during the bug fixing process. They show that projects with larger code bases tend to have more decentralized communication networks while smaller projects are inclined toward more centralized communication networks. In other words, there are a few people in the center of small projects with critical roles, and these roles tend to become more distributed within the community as projects grow larger. Bird, Pattison, D'Souza, Filkov, and Davanbu, (2008) found that code structure on FOSS projects mirrored social relations between individuals. They found these individual relations reflected in the code on individual FOSS projects, but also across FOSS projects which shared software developer groups. In these cases, both social relations and code crossed between projects. Scacchi (2007) describes the role that linchpin developers on FOSS projects play in the knitting together of multiple projects, showing that individuals in the

center of code networks are also in the center of communication networks on FOSS projects. Research on technology-mediated distributed group work in FOSS includes themes of common values, common interests, and the desire to demonstrate superior technical skill. These studies examine amorphous networks of technologists. COGs, in contrast, are studied as *a priori* groups, whose membership does not shift. In this way, COGs are more like the groups that Wenger (1998) and Gloor (2005) study, than FOSS networks.

The contrast between FOSS groups and Wikipedia participation is helpful for situating COG research in the literature. Collaborative information behavior in Wikipedia is similar to open source projects, in that a distributed collective of experts is responsible for the admission of thought work products into a commons. Occasionally, disagreement about accuracy of information surfaces in Wikipedia. Kittur, Suh, Pendleton and Chi (2007) noted that Wikipedia takes the form of a collaborative information environment where conflicts in information accuracy are resolved through both direct and indirect mediation. Wikipedia's gating of information contrasts with FOSS discussions where bug fix implementation is negotiated by project leaders, prior to the implementation of a published code change. The identification of a bug and the fixing of a bug often include two different people. In Wikipedia, the system allows each member to make a change to the information resource without public negotiation. In conflict situations, Wikipedia has an established set of cultural practices for resolving issues. While FOSS projects maintain collaborative information cultures that may be distinct by project, Wikipedia has a consistent set of cultural practices for mediation across all knowledge areas. COGs show some of the task focus of a FOSS group, directed in a manner similar to face-to-face groups, combined with the openness of Wikipedia.

The similarity of COG practices and organization to face-to-face teams suggests that COGs might be more common than they are. There is a

111

preponderance of research that demonstrates work teams are more effective when periodic face-to-face meetings are part of the team organization (Nardi & Whittaker, 2002; Hinds & Weisband, 2003). Some of the work conducted in FOSS and Wikipedia groups hints at the possibility that this established constraint might be softening. Kittur and Kraut (2008) noted that implicit coordination in Wikipedia is more effective than explicit coordination. In other words, successful collaborative information mediation practices are dependent on the culture of Wikipedia, and not hierarchy. Like FOSS groups, Wikipedia groups have core members, but membership changes and the activities are not tightly time bound. COGs, in contrast, focus on work that is deadline driven and directed at a specific set of outcomes. When the outcomes are achieved, the group disbands. In this way, COGs are similar to project teams described by Wenger and Gloor, but use collaborative information practices that have common ground with FOSS and Wikipedia groups.

As indicated above, it is important to position COG research in the context of other online group research. COGs, like other types of online groups are also informed by extensive research in collaborative information seeking. Reddy and Spence (2008) examine collaborative information seeking in a hospital emergency room, suggesting that face-to-face interaction is essential for collaborative information behavior in that particular context. Sonnenwald and Pierce (2000) identify three themes present in high intensity battlefield information sharing situations, two of which have saliency in a completely online context. First, similar to Reddy and Spence, they observe that individual, intergroup and intragroup situational awareness of information is essential for high intensity collaboration. Second, they identify the need for frequent communication between participants in these intense situations in order to maintain a common understanding of events. Maintaining both intergroup awareness and frequent communication is especially difficult.

in COGs, due to the nature of the collaboration environment.

Pulling COGs Together

COG collaborations are distinguished from their physically situated and partially distributed counterparts in three significant ways. First, opportunities to exchange social information online are constrained in different and challenging ways when compared with groups in the physical world. The social orientation of participants in an online setting is reflected through constructs like social presence, social navigation and social awareness. Swan and Shih (2005) describe social presence as the degree to which participants in an electronically mediated forum feel emotionally connected to one another. Social navigation is the capacity for members to see and follow the work trails of their group mates in an online forum (Story, Cheng, Bull, & Rigby, 2006). Social awareness is the ability of COG members to coordinate with each other by maintaining awareness of each other's participation and online presence (Erickson & Kellogg, 2000). Together, these dimensions of social information aid group collaboration in a completely online context like the course management systems described later in this chapter.

The second significant distinction between COGs and other collaborative groups are the differences in what coordination information is used and how it influences collaboration trajectories in groups. In face-to-face groups, awareness of roles and progress is readily available through co-presence, which sustains social awareness of deadlines, group accomplishments and critical next steps. Physically co-located groups benefit from feedback that is rich and visible across a myriad of communication channels in each group interaction. Open source teams benefit from a common set of ethics that serve to build trust, and often include core members who have worked together in a physically co-located setting. Wikipedia groups are similarly aware of the actions of others vis-à-vis common tools and established practices for communicating within those tools. The co-presence of face-to-face groups and the established practices of FOSS and Wikipedia cultures are not available to COGs. However, like to face-to-face groups, the framework of a common purpose derived from organizational affiliation is the ground upon which COGs build collaborative practices.

Third, COGs are composed of people who are likely to be in different geographical locations, different organizational units (or different organizations), and consequently have access to different social networks and different information resources. Savolainen (2006) contrasted these types of differences in individual information resources using three categories of spatial information behavior theory: Objectifying, Realistic-Pragmatic and Perspectivist. Objectivist theories are those that address the distance between information resources as objective, physical distances. Realistic-Pragmatic theories acknowledge differences in physical distance, but evaluate the importance of these differences in context. Perspectivist theories view distance between information resources and the consumer of information resources as subjectively interpreted. The user and the context play a role in determining the significance in these situations. For COGs, geographic distance is not as significant as the information practices and preferred information resources of members. The perspectivist theories, lacking a ground truth (truth grounded?) in the physical world, are the most salient. According to Savolainen, Information Horizons is the central theory reflecting the perspectivist view.

Information horizons theory (Sonnenwald & Wildemuth, 2001) builds on the concepts of context, situations and social networks to explore human information behavior. Sonnenwald's information horizons theory describes five propositions related to human information behavior (Sonnenwald, 1999; Sonnenwald, 2003):

1. Human information behavior is shaped by and shapes individuals, social networks and situations and contexts.

2. Individuals or systems within a particular situation and context may perceive, reflect and/or evaluate change in others, self and/ or their environment. Information behavior is constructed amidst the flow of such reflections.

3. Within a context or situation is an "information horizon", within which we can act. When an individual decides to seek information, there is an information horizon in which they may seek information. Information horizons, and subsequently information resources, are determined socially and individually and may be different for different contexts, even for the same individual.

4. Human information seeking behavior may be viewed as collaboration between an individual and their information resources. Some resources lead to others.

5. Information horizons consist of a variety of information resources, many of which have knowledge of each other. They may be conceptualized as densely populated spaces. In a densely populated solution space, many solutions are assumed and the information retrieval problem expands.

Sonnenwald (1999, 2000) characterized the constraining and enabling forces experienced by individual information seekers as information horizons. Information horizons theory suggests a collaborative relationship between the information seeking behavior of an individual and their information resources. These resources are defined for each individual based on the particular context within which they describe themselves. The diversity of social network connections in a completely online collaboration suggests that COGs will likely have information horizons that are distinct from groups formed in the same locale. The COG information horizon is centered on the member but will influence trajectories of collaborative information behavior for the whole group.

Examining the collaborative information behavior of COGs through the lens of Information Horizons theory allows the researcher to recognize that COGs are different from physically situated groups. At the same time, Information Horizons theory encompasses the situational awareness and frequent communication needs of collaborative groups, identified as significant by both Reddy and Spence (2008) and Sonnenwald and Pierce (2000). The diversity of Information Horizons among COG members is a source of difference in the collaborative information behavior observed in COGs.

Information Horizons and COGs

Information Horizon differences in COGs drive their unique collaborative information behavior practices. While much collaborative information behavior research focuses on groups who collaborate around common information resources, COGs collaborate in a common tool, but they bring diverse information (resource) horizons with them to the collaboration. For example, in a physically situated group, the most central and influential information horizon for group members is the location and organizational context for the collaboration. In an online group, each participant is likely to have a distinct context, a distinct personal situation and distinct social networks. The online tool where the group meets represents one of many information resources, readily available to members, which will influence the contributions of those members to group work. In COGs, the boundaries of the information space are diffuse.

Extending Sonnenwald's work, Savolainen and Kari (2004) developed a taxonomy of information horizon zones in their analysis of the information seeking behavior of 18 Internet users. Zones represent the relative importance of information sources, with Zone 1 indicating the most significant sources, Zone 2 representing interme-

diate sources and Zone 3 representing peripheral sources. They then placed 21 specific information source types into five defined categories and one miscellaneous category. Their study concluded that human sources of information remained most significant among their informants, followed by print media and the internet. The primacy of interpersonal relations for information implies that the social connections people have still play a significant role in scoping the information available to them in day-to-day life.

Completely online groups are an emerging phenomenon whose collaborative information behavior is naturally understood through the lens of Information Horizons theory. The goal of this chapter is to build the information science research and design community's understanding of how socio-technical systems influence—and may be designed to support—collaborative information generation and sharing among people working on discrete activities in a priori defined groups who never meet face-to-face. Groups we call COGs. We will work toward this goal by surfacing key themes from a case study of 25 individuals divided into eight groups in a completely online, eight week graduate level course. Group membership was randomly assigned, and groups ranged in size from three to four people. All names in this chapter are pseudonyms. Our case study is framed using the above discussed Sonnenwald's Information Horizons theory.

In the remainder of this chapter we will describe the context of the study, identify collaborative information behavior themes observed in COGs, identify key issues in this research and frame an agenda for future studies.

AN EXPLORATION OF COLLABORATIVE INFORMATION BEHAVIOR IN COGS

The data presented in this section is a subset of data gathered in a larger study that was conducted in the context of an online graduate student course on Computer Support for Collaborative Learning (CSCL) offered in the summer of 2008 at a large US university. All students were invited to participate in critical incident information horizons interviews similar to those conducted by Sonnenwald (2001), with an incentive of an online gift certificate of $10 for completing a series of three interviews. We obtained university approval for human subjects research. All course participants consented to be part of the study. Fourteen students volunteered to be interviewed three times using the telephone. Each of the 42 interview sessions lasted between 40 minutes and one hour and 40 minutes. All interviews were transcribed. Three individuals of the 14 were interviewed in depth using Sonnenwald's (2000) Information Horizons critical incident technique, and all informants were asked to describe their main sources of information. Individuals were selected for in depth information horizons interviews based on observed contrasts in their post quality and frequency in the course during the first two weeks. The information horizons interviews took place at the end of the third week of the course, and the serial interviews took place in the second, fifth and eighth weeks of the course. In the information horizons interviews informants described experiences of finding information for their group within and outside the course management system. Diagrams presented in the chapter were constructed with informants using desktop sharing software and a tablet PC or, in one case, the exchange of scanned images. Following Savolainen and Kari (2004), we developed a taxonomy of information resources used by the three informants. We then converted that taxonomy to a survey of information resource use that 21 of 25 course members completed. In these surveys, the members ranked information resources from 1 (being the most significant) to 28 (being the least significant).

The socio-technical system that facilitated the CSCL course was Sakai, with activity awareness provided by CANS and discussion forums pro-vided by JForum. The CANS system was used to provide activity notification and awareness information to course members, in the form of daily email activity digests, and visual feedback of relative participation of students in the course over varying periods of time. When a student logged into Sakai and posted or read a message, CANS made a note of it and presented summary data in the digest and the activity visualization page CANS provides in Sakai. All assignments and discussion to support group collaboration in the course were facilitated through Sakai, using a JForum discussion board. JForum is integrated with both CANS and Sakai. Some groups elected to use other technologies in addition to Sakai for collaborating, including external wikis. So long as they granted access to the instructor and the first author this was allowed. Access to external tools was also requested for the researcher, and granted by all group members in all cases. The work conducted in those tools is included in this analysis.

The course work after the first week was completed in groups, making this an ideal context for gathering of data to explicate collaborative information behavior within COGs. At several points in the course, data were gathered in correspondence with course activities. The structure of the course was as follows:

1. Week 1 – Module 1 – Explore what CSCL is (Individual Activity)
2. Week 2 – Module 2 – Each group was assigned a position related to a research paper read by the class, and engaged in a debate with another group assigned an opposing position.
3. Week 3 – Module 3 – A Group activity to construct a coherent story of past online learning. First, students described individual experiences. Then, as a group they were asked to design an online experience that is improved, using available 2D and 3D collaboration technologies

4. Week 4 – Continue module 3
5. Week 5 – Module 4 – A Group activity to design a 2 day online learning module to be delivered to 2 other teams in Module 5. This module involved the most intense period of creative collaboration among the groups.
6. Week 6 – Continue Module 4
7. Week 7 – Module 5 – Groups delivered modules designed in Module 4 to two other student groups. The groups also participated in the module designed by a different group. During this period, each group of three to four students had three different, unrelated work tasks to attend to.
8. Week 8 – Module 6 – Group and individual reflections.

Our analysis was both qualitative and quantitative. Our qualitative data analysis included the importing of interview transcripts, discussion boards, course reflections, chat transcripts and wiki data into nVivo 8, and the performance of ethnographically informed open coding (Charmaz, 2003) for information resource utilization. The researchers developed more than 500 interview codes, with 17% of the codes addressing collaborative information behavior among the eight COGs. All of these artifacts and the resulting codes were then refined through constant comparison to arrive at a set of core collaborative information behavior themes within this course.

Our analysis uncovered a set of themes in the collaborative information behavior of the eight COGs in this study. The meta theme that emerges from these discrete themes is the centrality of shared information resources, embodied in technology as collaborative grounds in COGs. This centrality of technology diverges from prior findings regarding technology use in the physical world, which showed that other people remained (retained?) dominant information resources following the introduction of technology (Savolainen, 2006). In COGs, information resources themselves are the center of collaborative information behavior. The four themes under this meta theme are:

- Groups as information resources in COGs
- Tools to control collaboration
- Rapid tool changes diffuse collaborative information behavior
- Tools to constrain and focus collaboration

In the next sections we report on each of these four themes and draw contrasts between the collaborative information behaviors observed in each of the eight COGs.

Collaborative Information Behavior Theme: Groups as Information Resources

The COGs who relied on each other and shared information resources described fewer incidences of collaborative frustration. Group Six and Group One members had little alignment of preferred information resources, while Group Eight's members shared many of the same information resources. Group Eight was cohesive, collaborative and successful in completing their work. Group Six's members had two of the lowest three scores in the class, and Group One member Alan had the very lowest overall score. These performance differences could imply that information horizons play a role in the development of group identity and especially group cohesion. It is also possible that COGs composed of members with diverse information horizons have difficulty building common information grounds to collaborate around.

Diversity in information horizons within a group influenced group development, but across groups there were patterns of information resource utilization which emerged. Most notably, the information resources used by COG members often centered on group coordination. Table 1 displays the rankings of each of the 21 members of the course who responded to our information horizons survey. We see a diversity of information resources, and differences in information resource use by the members of different groups. Group Two, for example, is concentrated on the use of other people in their group, the instructor and the group wiki. Group Five members show some contrast, with two members concentrating the information resources on the group centric resources like discussion boards and other people in their group, while a third member, Agnes, has very different information horizons that include children, and rate the use of group information resources at the bottom.

Table 1 has shading for the top five information resources for each individual to provide a visual indication of how each group and each information resource clusters. The rankings are raw rankings provided by each group member. In a few cases, "0" is displayed, indicating the respondent did not provide a rank at all. The 28 resources listed in the survey are condensed into the 15 that provide the most interesting contrasts in Table 1. While some of the resources may appear to not be mutually exclusive – for example, types of people and modes of communication could overlap – this is consistent with prior studies examining information horizons (Savolainen, 2006).

The influence of information (resource) horizons on group development is most vivid in the experiences of Group Six. Two of Group Six's members participated in Information Horizons interviews near the beginning of their collaboration as a group. As a result, we have deeper information regarding the members of Group Six than other groups, but we lack complete information, since Steven did not respond to the survey. There is a pronounced contrast between the information resources that Malakai references and those that Yoda references. For example, Malakai is one of two people in the course who listed their spouse as one of their top five sources of information. Though we did not ask explicitly, we know from interview discussions and call logistics that ten of the fourteen informants we spoke with are married.

In our analysis of interview transcripts and survey data we noticed a strong contrast between the information horizons of Yoda and Malakai: Yoda's information resources are dominated by

tools while Malakai's are dominated by people. Malakai lists "other people in their group" as a top resource, which is common (16 out of 20 information horizons respondents) in the course, while Yoda listed this resource as 20th out of 28. Yoda's top information resources were tool focused. Some of Yoda's descriptions in the interview are inconsistent with her observed behavior in the course. For example, Yoda lists the group's wiki as her third most relied upon resource when completing course work, although her group's utilization of the wiki is limited. Given the fundamentally collaborative nature of a wiki, it could be that the dearth of truly collaborative information behavior in Yoda's group is either discoverable through tool utilization or predicted by interest in collaborative editing tools. This may be another example of Yoda's technology utilization not being in sync with Malakai or Steven. The common resource between them, the instructor, is an expected point of common ground in an online course.

The interviews for information horizons, conducted with both Yoda and Malakai, make the differences in how they use information even more striking. Figure 1 shows Malakai's information horizons, which include references to individuals at one level, and electronic resources in general at the same level. Then, Malakai references specific electronic resources.

Figure 2 shows Yoda's information horizons. Yoda does not distinguish between different types of electronic or human information resources using categorization, as Malakai does. Yoda also includes more of the fine grained dimensions of the course management system than Malakai does. Given their distinct information horizons, it is easy to imagine that these two members would have a difficult time agreeing on an information based premise for completing group work.

Group members bring diverse information experiences to COG participation, and these diverse experiences and expectations are not easy to reconcile in a completely online environment. Further, when it comes to group problem solving,

Table 1. Most used information resources by course members, by group

Member	Spouse or Significant 'other'	Children	The Instructor	Other people in your small group	Other people in the course	Sakai Discussion Board for your group	Sakai Discussion Board for another group	Sakai Discussion Board for everyone	course	Google.com	email	Your group's wiki	Sakai Private Messages	Sakai Assignments	Sakai Announcements
Group 1															
Andrea	15	28	2	13	12	3	14	11	1	10	7	21	6	5	4
Alan	10	25	6	1	11	2	13	12	9	8	4	7	3	5	15
Jessica	16	15	8	1	9	10	11	12	13	4	18	3	5	6	7
Group 2															
Alice	27	28	6	1	7	5	14	8	9	10	17	2	11	20	13
Dora	16	25	2	1	11	5	14	13	6	17	8	4	15	7	9
Kylie	21	28	3	5	6	2	4	1	17	18	20	7	10	9	16
Liz	0	0	12	1	15	3	0	11	6	17	0	5	13	14	16
Group 3															
John	1	2	4	3	8	5	17	9	7	15	19	6	10	12	11
Jessica	0	0	5	0	7	1	0	6	0	0	13	2	12	3	4
Winston	26	27	20	1	8	3	11	4	5	7	9	6	10	2	22
Group 4															
Genny	14	3	4	2	11	20	26	9	12	5	7	1	16	8	6
Group 5															
Agnes	14	1	26	28	5	27	13	24	25	17	20	8	22	23	15
Lolly	10	25	2	1	3	5	7	6	4	9	8	11	12	14	13
Poncho	27	28	2	1	3	4	13	6	5	24	17	18	10	9	11
Group 6															
Malakai	4	28	1	20	14	9	10	8	2	16	22	27	7	5	6
Yoda	12	28	5	1	6	2	4	13	15	16	10	3	11	8	9
Group 7															
Colina	19	20	5	1	3	2	14	4	21	7	17	26	9	8	10
Sandy	16	11	2	13	14	4	5	6	7	3	24	25	8	1	9
Group 8															
Dawn	28	27	3	1	5	2	10	6	11	23	4	2	8	7	9
Jesslyn	19	20	5	3	16	1	17	6	7	11	4	2	8	9	10
Scott	26	27	2	1	3	4	6	5	7	14	13	8	10	11	12
Mean	16.9	20.8	6.0	5.0	8.4	5.7	11.7	8.6	9.5	12.6	13.1	9.2	10.3	8.9	10.8
Standard Deviation	8.9	11.1	6.3	7.5	4.2	6.5	6.2	4.8	6.4	6.5	6.9	8.7	4.1	5.5	4.4

Figure 1. Malakai's information horizons

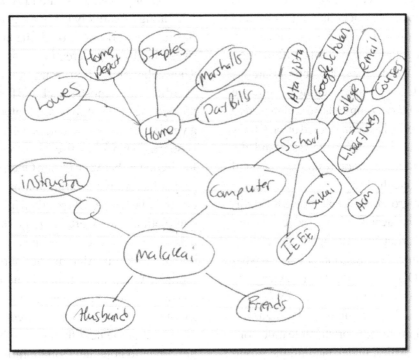

Figure 2. Yoda's information horizons

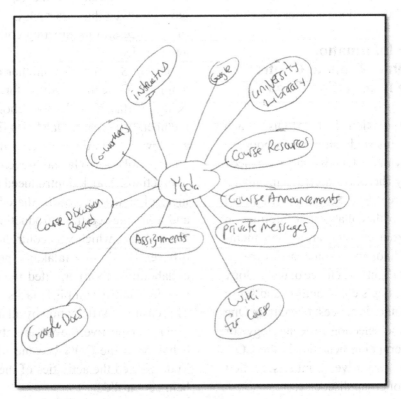

members clearly bring diverse resources to the table. In a COG, members are not collaborating around shared information and negotiating its meaning. They are first negotiating about what information resources, tools and practices are appropriate for the task at hand. Unlike hospital settings, insurance companies or military groups whose collaborative information behavior has been studied prior, COGs first negotiate the meaning of the tasks and the technological and information resources that will be used to complete the task.

The theme of groups as collaborative information resources, influencing both trajectory and outcome of the group's work, opens three main avenues for future investigation. First, to what extent might COGs be scaffolded to emerge as innovation networks like Gloor's COINS? Second, what information sharing or tool designs aid COGs in developing a more predictable trajectory of development? Third, understanding the group as the central information resource for many COG members, what effect does the deliberate injection of social activities into planned COG work have on the collaborative information behavior of COGs?

Collaborative Information Behavior Theme: Tools to Control Collaborative Information Behavior

The selection and adoption of online tools by each of the groups in this study shows collaborative information behavior in COGs is easily influenced by the technology choices of assertive members. Groups One, Three, Six, Seven and Eight all provide examples of the collaborative information practices of the group evolving around one member's choice of technology. In some cases, (groups Three, Seven and Eight) the choice of technology is benign to the group's collaboration and sense of groupness. In other instances, like Group One and Group Six, the selection of technology for collaborative information behavior in the COG emerges out of an assertive member's explicit attempts to control group discourse.

In Group One, Jessica and Andrea were collaborating effectively using discussion boards in Sakai, and working through the tasks of module two, which was the creation of an online debate. They collaborated first around a shared Microsoft Word document, posted back and forth as an attachment in the discussion board. Later, they emailed a version of the document. When complete, they posted their work in a discussion board designated for the debate between Group One and Group Two. The collaborative information behavior of these two members in a COG resulted in successful task completion (they were judged to have won their debate) because there was one channel, and they both agreed to it. Alan did not participate in this module. When he returned in module three, he drove the group to use synchronous collaboration technology – Skype – The effects of which are discussed in the next theme. For this theme, it is important to note that Collaborative Information Behavior in COGs is easily influenced by members' choices and practices. An assertion of power, such as Alan's, can upset that equilibrium, and we have observed that assertive COG members are often successful in directing collaboration tools and practices.

Group Six provides another compelling example of COG collaborative information behavior being overtaken by the tool choices of a single member. In this case, Malakai at first participated at a low level in the course, as did Group Six's other members, Yoda and Steven. In subsequent interactions, Malakai introduced a desktop sharing tool called Microsoft SharedView. Malakai and Yoda viewed the introduction of Microsoft SharedView, which was controlled by Malakai, differently. From Malakai's perspective, the collaborative tool permitted the group to work together and accomplish tasks synchronously. This ensured participation by all members. From Yoda's perspective, the collaborative information behavior in the COG became Malakai-centric. Yoda viewed the activities of the group as now being controlled.

If one member controls the collaborative information tools in a COG they in effect also control collaborative information behavior terms and conditions for the group. This contrasts with face-to-face groups, where controlling strategies may be averted or argued against directly through conversation or indirectly through body language and arrangement of collaborative space. Ultimately, the shared space modulates attempts to aggressively direct collaborative information behavior in the physical world. In a completely online setting, discourse rules may be set out by a member and the tendency toward politeness in online groups (Goggins, Laffey & Tsai, 2007) mutes what might become rebellion in face-to-face groups.

Further examination of this COG-centered collaborative information behavior theme should include questions about the types of tasks that may be effectively managed through highly controlled COG organizations, the types of activities that will not be effectively managed this way, and whether or not experience using a particular set of tools mutes the likelihood of these types of controlling behaviors over time.

Collaborative Information Behavior Theme: Rapid Tool Changes Diffuse Collaboration

As noted before, Group One developed a fluid practice between two members who utilized a discussion board and the exchange of Microsoft Word documents to create an argument in a structured debate. When Alan, who was missing from the first two modules of the course, but reappeared in module three, began participating in the group, the technology used for collaboration changed. Alan asserted the benefits of Skype, and although it was inconvenient for Andrea and Jessica, who both live in rural areas with dial-up internet connections, Alan drove the team toward Skype. Skype provided asynchronous awareness when a person is on the internet, while the discus-

sion board and course chat tool available in Sakai required the user to navigate to a specific page in order to participate.

Jessica is not frequently online, and found the emerging use of Skype, which notably followed her sharp decline in participation, stressful. Jessica notes:

Finding times to chat on Skype sometimes proved to be difficult (work, personal schedules) and the final assignments issued by the other groups (module 5) caused our group a lot of confusion and stress.

Alan, as the introducer of Skype, found it to be especially useful in collaboration with his team mates:

Posting to the discussion boards was fine and all, but in order to communicate with one partner in California and one in Philadelphia, I would first have to log on…then see if they were online… then figure out how to talk with them. (Saying to myself…Should I go into the chat room and wait to see if they realize I'm in the chat room hoping they come in because I have a question. Or… should I send them a private message…hoping they check their messages to say I have a question and I am in the chat room.) WOW. Using Skype I able to see if they were online immediately, and chat with them immediately.

This excerpt from a module reflection identifies the limitations of the chat tool in the course management system: *Many steps are required to reach synchronous awareness of the other students in the CMS. In contrast, there is no explicit work required to establish a feed of awareness information in Skype. If people are online and you notice it, you can instant message or call them.*

Andrea's views on the use of Skype evolve through use, and her initial reticence to take advantage of Skype is transformed by the end of the collaboration. Andrea notes in the last of three interviews:

Well once we got everybody, I mean, everybody was on Skype, once we got everyone's names so we could add them to our contact list on Skype—cuz we all Skype—um, it was a matter of, you know, waiting for someone to be on there at the same time and saying, aha! You know, we have this part of the assignment due. Or, you know, we have this portion. And we broke things out so that, um, and divided them out so that they weren't last minute.

The effect of Skype's rapid introduction in this group was to diffuse collaboration from one dyad – Jessica and Andrea – to a second dyad – Andrea and Alan. Jessica remained a participant, but her participation continued to center on asynchronous discussion board posts. Andrea dialed up to contact Alan on Skype whenever coordination or collaboration around course deadlines was required. The collaborative information behavior, notably the exchange of information to coordinate work, shifted from asynchronous to synchronous, and was then diffused into the discussion boards so that Jessica would remain in the loop.

Skype came about on the insistence of Alan, rejoining the collaboration at around the same time as Jessica's participation declined. Once implemented, Andrea found that mode of collaboration preferable to the previously established asynchronous practices of the group. When Jessica returned, the shift in technology was not supportive of her participation on a dial up line, but the practices built up by the other members in her absence were either too powerful, or too late in the collaboration to permit a shift back to prior work practices.

The influence of tool changes on collaborative information behavior in COGs is likely to be fertile ground for continued research. Future questions include: Do collaborative outcomes change when new tools are introduced? How do tools influence the effectiveness of collaboration? How can collaborative information tools be developed to level and make consistent COG member information horizons, driving the possibility of COGs in health care, science and technology?

Collaborative Information Behavior Theme: Tools to Constrain and Focus Collaboration

Practices supporting fluid collaboration and cooperation online were developed along a wide spectrum among the COGs in the study. Some groups built a simple rhythm that they followed. Group One and Group Six demonstrated difficulty getting into a rhythm, struggling to develop common ground and common practices. Group Eight reified the practice of opening each new module by structuring work using discussion boards focused on the major activities of a module. This practice was central to the work that Group Eight did, and acted as a scaffold for most of their collaboration. The members viewed the structured discussion boards as a key component of their success as a group, although it sometimes slowed Group Eight's adaptation to new task types.

The practice of structuring new modules with discussion board topics was the principle factor in Group Eight's struggle at the beginning of module four. Module four was composed of unstructured collaboration and required task enumeration prior to task completion. Creating information resources to structure their collaboration was not possible in this scenario. The members eventually developed a new practice, the use of a wiki, to work on these kinds of open-ended design tasks. A researcher's field notes reflect this quick adaptation to wikis:

This wiki goes through 57 different iterations... which is the most I've seen so far.... The work represents mostly Scott and Jesslyn; Dawn's contributions seem less significant in this activity, and mostly confined to the correction of grammatical errors and things like that.

Scott described the group's practices around the wiki in greater detail:

Well we kind of actually, what we did is we went to, obviously went to the discussion board just to kind of post the assignment and in general just saying ok this is what we have to do, and the majority of our work was done through the wiki for that process. We updated things, we each, when we make a change to the wiki we select a color, so I may do green and somebody else may do blue and somebody else may use orange, so what we'll do is if we make a change to the wiki or something like that we will do it in our assigned, or chosen colors not so much assigned as, it's a chosen thing

The discussion board practice is noted, but the use of the wiki and the integration of the discussion board with the wiki becomes a defining characteristic of Group Eight's collaboration practices after module four. Making the work of the members visible is accomplished through this theme of structured work practices that incorporate discrete awareness, coordination and leadership practices.

In this case and others, we see that COGs who develop a set of reified practices for collaborating in their group are effective until a change is required, and then face an adjustment period. The adaptation of these new practices, while common in face-to-face groups encountering new phenomena, are more difficult to accomplish exclusively through tools as tools must be both the subject and the object of discussion. Tools are used to negotiate change in COGs, and changes in tools drive the collaborative information behavior of COGs.

Future research questions related to tools focusing and constraining the online work of COGs include the possibility that collaborative information behavior in COGs takes a special, tool dependent, form. Questions about structuring the practice of COG members identifying tools of preference, and the possibility of the digital divide limiting COG participation in some populations also warrant investigation.

INFORMATION HORIZON MACRO TRENDS ACROSS COGS

Finally, it is informative to look across all eight groups and describe the information resources used most commonly. The information resources used by group members showed some variability across the eight groups and individuals. Table 2 shows the mean ranks of the information resources used by members of the course, using the 1 to 28 ranking previously noted. Each information resource in the list of 28 was derived from information horizons interviews with three members of the course.

The top two resources across all respondents are related directly to the member's assigned small groups. Given the group work focus of this context, future studies should inquire about how information horizons are perceived differently in a setting that is not centered on small groups work.

In addition to the collaborative information behavior themes identified within the groups, we also note that, in this group work intensive course, member information horizons center on information resources that are used for activity coordination. The survey of all course participants showed that the information resources that are prominent are those that members use to coordinate their work within their group. Exceptions exist, such as Malakai, who relies heavily on resources outside of group coordination. Sixteen of the 21 people who responded to the survey had "Other people in my small group" in the top five information resources used. Twelve of those had that information resource at number one. Seventeen of 21 also had their small group discussion board in the top five information resources used. In a course with diverse tasks and diverse group experiences, the dominance of small group focused information resources is somewhat surprising. These results indicate that, for members of these COGs, the information resources about their group are primary; coordination work takes precedence over information used to solve problems.

Table 2. Mean rank of information resources by 21 members, organized by group

Mean Rank	Information Resource
5	Other people in your small group
5.7	Sakai discussion board for your group
6	Instructor
8.4	Other people in the course
8.6	Sakai discussion board for everyone
8.9	Sakai assignments
9.2	Your group's wiki
9.5	Course
10.3	Sakai private messages
10.8	Sakai announcements
11.7	Sakai discussion board for another group
12.6	Google
13.1	Email
15	University library's web site
16.4	Other library
16.9	Spouse or significant other
17.3	Friends
17.7	People at work
17.8	University libraries
18.1	Google docs
18.3	Scholar.google.com
18.8	Another group's wiki
18.9	ISLS
20.1	IEEE.org
20.7	ACM.org
20.8	Children
21.2	University intranet
22.5	Alta Vista

FUTURE RESEARCH TRENDS

Collaborative information behavior in COGs is little studied, especially compared with Wikipedia and FOSS groups. We believe Information Horizons theory provides a compelling framework for understanding the individual experiences of group members in COGs, and the influence of differing information resources on collaborative information behavior in COGs. Four key areas for collaborative information behavior research in COGs could be identified from our themes:

1. COGs may emerge as a principal construct for distributed creative work, advancing Gloor's notion of collaborative innovation networks (COINs) to fully distributed models where collaborators never meet
2. Designing activities to support collaborative information behavior within COGs
3. Designing tools to support collaborative information behavior within and between COGs, possibly recognizing that differences in members' Information Horizons play a central role in COG success
4. Explore how increasing use of social software like Facebook, Twitter and others is influencing the Information Horizons of technology-enabled collaborators. Consider the likely isolating effect on those who are on the other side of the digital divide.

CONCLUSION

Collaborative information behavior in COGs is little studied and often conflated with Wikipedia and FOSS collaborative information behavior. COGs are emerging through online graduate school courses and will likely find their way into mainstream collaboration environments in the near future. We believe collaborative information behavior in COGs is partially understood through an analysis of the varying information (resource) horizons among COG members.

There are distinguishing characteristics of COG collaborative information behavior. First, COGs whose members rely on each other as shared information resources appear to have fewer collaborative challenges. This observation suggests that information horizons may play a role in supporting effective group development trajectories in completely online settings.

Second, the manner in which COGs adapt the tools used as the instruments of their collaboration has a significant effect on collaborative information behavior. COGs whose tool choices change rapidly experience challenges collaborating around shared information. COGs that develop a set of collaborative information practices around tools are able to build a rhythm and work effectively together.

Finally, COG information horizons are distinct from those of physically situated groups studied in the past. While those groups showed other people as the information resources closest on the horizon, COG members place information and communication technology resources that are unique to their group on their near horizon. Perhaps out of necessity or the structure of the experience, COGs demonstrate innovative new types of collaborative information behavior that warrant future study.

REFERENCES

Bird, C., Pattison, D., D'Souza, R., Filkov, V., & Davanbu, P. (2008). *Latent Social Structure in Open Source Projects*. Paper presented at the SIGSOFT 2008, Atlanta, GA.

Charmaz, K. (2003). Qualitative Interviewing and Grounded Theory Analysis. In Holstein, J. A., & Gubrium, J. F. (Eds.), *Inside Interviewing: New Lenses, New Concerns* (pp. 311–330). Thousand Oaks, CA: Sage Publications.

Crowston, K., & Howison, J. (2005). The Social Structure of Free and Open Source Software Development. *First Monday, 10*(2).

Erickson, T., & Kellogg, W. A. (2000). Social Translucence: An Approach to Designing Systems that Support Social Processes. *ACM Transactions on Computer-Human Interaction, 7*, 59–83. doi:10.1145/344949.345004

Gibson, C., & Cohen, S. (Eds.). (2003). *Knowledge Sharing and Shared Understanding in Virtual Teams*. San Francisco, CA: Jossey-Bass.

Gloor, P. (2005). *Swarm Creativity, COIN*. Boston, MA: MIT Press.

Kittur, A., & Kraut, R. (2008). *Harnessing the Wisdom of Crowds in Wikipedia: Quality Through Coordination*. Paper presented at the CSCW 2008, San Diego, CA.

Kittur, A., Suh, B., Pendleton, B. A., & Chi, E. H. (2007). *He Says, She Says: Conflict and Co-ordination in Wikipedia*. Paper presented at the CHI 2007, San Jose, CA.

Nardi, B., Whittaker, S., & Schwarz, H. (2002). NetWORKers and their Activity in Intentional Networks. *Computer Supported Cooperative Work, 11*, 205–242. doi:10.1023/A:1015241914483

Reddy, M., & Ruma Spence, P. (2008). Collaborative Information Seeking: A Field Study of a Multidisciplinary Patient Care Team. *Information Processing & Management, 44*, 242–255. doi:10.1016/j.ipm.2006.12.003

Savolainen, R., & Kari, J. (2004). Placing the Internet in Information Source Horizons. A Study of Information Seeking by Internet Users in the Context of Self Development. *Library and Information Research, 26*, 415–433. doi:10.1016/j.lisr.2004.04.004

Scacchi, W. (2007). *Free/Open Source Software Development: Recent Research Results and Emerging Opportunities*. Paper presented at the ESEC/FSE 2007, Cvtat, Croatia.

Sonnenwald, D. I. H. (1999). Evolving Perspectives of Human Information Behavior: Contexts, Situations, Social Networks and Information Horizons. In Wilson, T., & Allen, D. (Eds.), *Exploring the Contexts of Information Behavior* (pp. 176–190). London: Taylor Graham.

Sonnenwald, D. I. H. (2005). Information Horizons. In K. Fischer, S. Erdelez, & L. E. F. McKechnie (Eds.), Theories of Information Behavior (pp. 191-197). Medford, NJ: Asis&t.

Sonnenwald, D. I. H., & Pierce, L. G. (2000). Information Behavior in Dynamic Group Work Contexts: Interwoven Situational Awareness, Dense Social Networks and Contested Collaboration in Command and Control. *Information Processing & Management, 36*, 461–479. doi:10.1016/S0306-4573(99)00039-4

Sonnenwald, D. I. H., Whitton, M. C., & Maglaughlin, K. L. (2003). Evaluating a Scientific Collaboratory: Results of a Controlled Experiment. *ACM Transactions on Computer-Human Interaction, 10*(2), 150–176. doi:10.1145/772047.772051

Sonnenwald, D. I. H., & Wildemuth, B. M. (2001). *Investigating Information Seeking Behavior Using the Concept of Information Horizons.* Paper presented at the ALISE Methodology Paper Competition.

Story, M.-A., Cheng, L.-T., Bull, I., & Rigby, P. (2006). *Shared Waypoints and Social Tagging to Support Collaboration in Software Development.* Paper presented at the CSCW '06, Banff, Alberta Canada.

Swan, K., & Shih, L. F. (2006). On the nature and Development of Social Presence in Online Course Discussions. *Journal of Asynchronous Learning Networks.*

Wenger, E. (1998). *Communities of Practice: Learning, Meaning and Identity.* New York: Cambridge University Press.

Chapter 8
Building a Learning Community:
Students Teaching Students Using Video Podcasts

Philip Scown
Manchester Metropolitan University Business School, UK

ABSTRACT

Typically education is a process that is done to students. The work reported here relates to students who collaborate in the education process so that they become educators of later students. This collaboration takes the form of development of re-usable learning objects (RLOs) that are firstly used to assess each student's understanding, but which are then to be used for the education of subsequent cohorts. This approach is based on a range of pedagogic concerns with motivational and social aspects of teaching. Students are given the options of producing a written or a video assignment. They make this decision in the knowledge that their work will be used to instruct students who will come after them. The video is relatively short at 5 – 10 minutes in length. Once assessed the video is added to a library for later use. Students report that they enjoy these assessments and that it is valuable to see the work of previous students.

INTRODUCTION

This chapter relates the practice of one part of Manchester Metropolitan University in using student made podcasts to assess at undergraduate level. The podcasts produced by students are then used to teach subsequent cohorts of students. This is explicit in the assignment, so that those students who take this route know that they are collaborat-

ing with the teaching staff in the development of a library of teaching resources. This collaboration is asynchronous.

Podcasting

In the Business School of Manchester Metropolitan University we are making use of podcasts in a number of ways. These can be broadly categorized as mainstream and innovative. The mainstream approach will be briefly discussed to put the in-

DOI: 10.4018/978-1-61520-797-8.ch008

novative approach into context both pedagogically, and from the point of view of collaboration. The innovative approach is the subject of this chapter. The innovation is that students produce their podcasts as part of their assessment regime. However, following assessment, the work is used for the education of subsequent cohorts of students. This transforms those students who take part, which is not all possible students, from just being receivers of education into agents who also collaborate with the teaching staff to be providers of teaching.

An understanding of the mainstream approach is useful to put the new approach into context. In the mainstream approach lecturers produce podcasts for use by students. Typically a podcast can be from a few minutes in length, up to approximately an hour. The podcasts make use of video and are uploaded to a multi-media server. Links to the podcasts relevant to each group of students are posted to their course areas on the respective pages of the institutional intranet. This mainstream approach can be further sub-divided into two. The first is based on an edited recording of a live lecture, using a specially set-up lecture theatre. The theatre is equipped with cameras to capture both the activities of the lecturer and the images displayed on the lecture theatre screen. Audio is recorded simultaneously and is synchronized with the video. At the end of the lecture a multi-media file is automatically made available to the lecturer for editing. This enables glitches and interruptions to be edited out prior to release by the lecturer to students via a multi-media server. The benefit of this technical approach is that the overhead of podcast production is relatively low: no pedagogic planning and design is required above what would normally take place for a standard lecture, and the technology is easily managed.

The second mainstream approach is based on the production of short videos, by the lecturer, in a non-theatre environment. Typically these are much shorter than lectures, and are intended to provide clear focus on one academic issue. These may provide a short demonstration of a technique, or a brief overview of an academic author, or similar focused piece. These *do* require pedagogic planning both in terms of the topic area and the content. The subject of the podcasts has to be recognized as needing this treatment, and the content needs to be designed, executed and simultaneously recorded (typically using screen capture software). Not only is there a pedagogic overhead but there is also a technical overhead, as the production process is entirely the responsibility of the lecturer.

Mainstream podcasts are not collaborative, but are examples of students' passive receipt of learning resources. The lecturer produces them and the students individually make use of them or not. The mainstream approach is an example of education being "done" to students. The use of automated technologies for managing uploading makes for a semi-industrial approach of re-usable learning objects (RLOs). The production is efficient, and their availability is appreciated by students, particularly as revision aids on the approach to exams (Scott, 2008). An aspect of this approach that is particularly useful relates to the benefits gained from blended-learning (Stubbs & Martin, 2003). This is where a mix of approaches and media are used to bring a range of benefits. In a business school, these benefits include: using a mix of media to reduce the monotony that can occur if there is over-reliance on printed media; making use of dynamic demonstrations to illustrate the building up of an equation in a spreadsheet, or the development of a database. Video podcasts can also be used to present real-time situations, such as interview techniques or process control. Within the Business School there have been particular benefits in the area of Finance and Accountancy (Scott, 2008). Students have found podcasts particularly useful as a part of their preparation for exams. Benefits are gained from both conceptual and skill-based RLOs.

Podcasting in education is used under the broader technical umbrella of blended-learning. Though *blended-learning* is not rigidly defined

(Sharpe, Benfield, Roberts & Francis, 2006) it is useful to consider the benefits of it here. It can be considered to be the integrated use of technology in synchronous and asynchronous learning situations. The Sharpe et al. (2006) literature review considers materials produced by lecturers, not by students (apart from discussion board comments). Blended-learning may include, for example, multi-media in lectures, lectures podcast for later use, and discussion boards. Students, particularly those with disabilities find blended-learning useful. It enables them to review material again. Multi-media blended-learning is particularly useful for students with dyslexia and related conditions. Blended-learning approaches work best when used explicitly and in an integrated way. That is, blended-learning resources are more effective if properly integrated, and not provided as a "bolt-on" afterthought.

The approach described in the main part of this chapter, is about collaboration between students and staff to develop podcasts as re-usable learning objects. As such it is an extension of the usual blended-learning paradigm, in that students are part of the creative team. Though the overt, functional, aim of the innovation is to assist with assessment, there is a more complex rationale behind this. A surface level analysis shows students being offered a choice of either written assignments, or video production, that demonstrates their understanding of key concepts. The assignment takes place near the end of their undergraduate course, and so video production provides some relief from written work. Deeper analysis reveals deeper social and collaborative benefits from this approach. The strategy has students collaborating asynchronously to develop a library of re-usable learning objects that is used to instruct subsequent cohorts of students. This approach is aimed at improving the learning experience and transforming the degree process from something that is *done to students* to something that is done *with* them. In addition this collaboration has two main benefits for the lecturer facilitating the process. The first of

these is to make assessment more interesting by adding variety and from the entertainment value of the video. The second benefit is from the help gained in building the library of RLOs.

Collaboration

There are a number of ways that collaboration is used within undergraduate teaching in HE. The most common form is for lecturers and students to collaborate in the making of a successful lecture. The lecture explains points and students collaborate by taking notes and asking pertinent questions. Both are working to a common goal – knowledge transference from lecturer, as knowledge repository, to student, as learner. While this may not be true for all students, or all lectures, this behaviour is commonly exhibited. This is synchronous, real-time collaboration towards the goal of moving knowledge from the head of the lecturer to the head of each student. When it occurs, this form of collaboration has some similarities with team activities seen in sports or complex domains such as aviation, though with less dramatic outcomes. The collaboration works only when sufficient participants agree with the goal. Collaboration can break down when the flow of information is disrupted by the behaviour of non-cooperating students (for example mobile phone use, or talking with another student), or when a student chooses to opt out and disengages from the lecture. It can also break-down if the lecturer is disinterested or insufficiently skilled.

Viewing learning from a collaborative perspective allows us to examine the range of collaborative activities across the range of teaching and learning in a university. Lectures alone are not enough to constitute a course of Higher Education. Universities will also make use of tutorials, seminars, assessments (both formative and summative), guided learning, multi-media materials, laboratory sessions, field-trips, etc. All of these require collaboration between a range of individuals. Whilst mainly involving the lecturers and the students, there will also be support from administrators, lab technicians, librarians, and others. In the context of this work we are concerned with the change in collaborative practices of lecturers and students; the role of supporting staff is not considered, though it is not something that can be done without. In all cases there is the over-arching goal that "each student should reach their potential"; though there will be sub-goals *en route*, such as "passing an assignment (at each student's potential)", attending special events, downloading podcasts. In all cases each student must collaborate with University staff by playing a role that is actively participative. Such participation may be in the form of arranging and attending group meetings, asking appropriate questions – even when these are awkward for either the lecturer or for the student, and requesting additional reading. In addition, in all conventional teaching, the materials are decided and/or designed by the lecturer for use by students. Collaboration is necessary to facilitate the efficient and effective flow of knowledge. In subsequent years the process is repeated. The knowledge being transferred may be the same, or it may be updated to reflect changes in the field of study. However, such changes are typically independent of whatever work previous students have done.

It is not true that all student learning is collaborative. This is something educators aim for; and it is explicit when we consider learners to be motivated and autonomous. However, there are students who may be considered to be cooperative rather than collaborative. Cooperative students are not disruptive, but neither do they contribute actively to classes or to their own learning. Rather, they are passive receivers of the flow of information presented to them.

Asynchronous collaboration takes place when students access learning materials made available by the academic staff in order to complete an assignment. A podcast or a reference may be made available on-line, which students may choose to download, at some later point in time, to learn from and incorporate into their work. In the work

at MMU students collaborate with the lecturing staff in the provision of learning materials, whilst later cohorts collaborate by making use of those resources. A non-educational parallel can be drawn with systems development work where stages of activity follow in sequence, with the output of each stage being evaluated prior to being signed-off and becoming the input to the next stage.

BACKGROUND

Two of the recent changes in the environment of higher education (HE) are relevant to the work described here. The first of these relates to the nature of students, the second relates to the technologies available to both students and to educators. These respectively represent changes in demands and needs of the educational system, and improvements in the range of tools available to meet the new demands.

Educational Background

The educational context of this work is a final level undergraduate elective within a business school. The students are mostly from an IT related course (Business Information Technology), though there are some students who are from areas such as business administration or marketing. The academic leading this unit became aware that at the point of the second assignment, in the Spring term, the students were jaded, suffering from an excess of written assignments, including their final dissertations and projects. A new approach was required to increase levels of student engagement and reduce levels of *instrumentalism*. In this context instrumentalism is a reference to a student attitude of mind in which the only thing that matters about an assignment is the mark gained, and only work directly related to assignments is considered (Torrance, 2007). This may seem to be an efficient approach, but it takes the focus from learning and moves it to getting graded.

This is a fundamental shift in approach that means students display less interest in the subject and learning and more in getting marks and proper administration. A more sinister possibility is that an instrumental approach may be responsible for increased cheating in assessment. This appears to be an international phenomenon, rather than just a problem for the United Kingdom or even Europe (Lindsay, 2008). However, there is little hard evidence for this. An approach is needed that is more likely to have intrinsic interest for students. The aim is to increase engagement with the learning process, rather than with the assessment process. Though these overlap they are not synonymous.

It was thought that by introducing a new form of assignment it might be possible to reduce students' perceptions of overload (Chambers, 1992). Video is a medium in vogue. It supports creativity, and allows for less formal and threatening forms of interaction. While traditional students brought up on formal essays and exams may be comfortable with writing, the non-traditional entrant may be less so. Though students may not write for pleasure there is evidence that they will use digital still and video cameras as a part of their leisure activities. The basis for these assumptions is the growth in the use of media such as youTube and FaceBook for distribution of a variety of home and amateur produced still images and digital video. There are parallels with theatre, where expression of current and possible selves allows new ways of thinking to be explored and demonstrated (Yang, 2003). The advantage of digital technologies, in this context, is that the performance can be viewed, edited and viewed again by the producer(s) and by others such as fellow students and lecturers. This may be done through public forums, such as FaceBook, or through more private organisational intranets. While much public video may be considered as merely narcissism, some content is intended as collaboration for the public good. For example, it is possible to find video on how to build a wood-burning stove from scrap materials. In this situation the producers of the video are collaborating with unknown others to produce artifacts with the common good of saving the planet.

The increase in diversity of students in recent years also means that the development of similarly diverse teaching and learning resources is now more appropriate (Rhodes & Nevill, 2004). The range of prior experiences of students is wider now than before. In addition the expansion of higher education has meant that students with a different set of intellectual tools are now on undergraduate courses. This is evidenced by the wider range of entry qualifications now used to indicate readiness for study at university level. More practical and applied qualifications now exist, with a lower reliance on examinations for assessment of student performance at secondary level.

Finally, for consideration here, is the course context. The students, being near the end of their undergraduate studies, are immersed in writing – assignments, dissertations, and note taking for exams. Some students are jaded by this, coming as it does at the end of three years of study. An alternate approach is needed, so that students can take a break from writing, yet still be engaged in useful formative and summative work.

Available Technologies

Recently podcasting has come into use in higher education. This involves the production of sound or video digital multi-media files that can be distributed by automatic-push (sent to subscribers) or user-pull (user requests podcasts of potential interest). These multi-media files can be viewed as many times as the user wants. This enables a range of materials, from introductory to advanced, to be used at each learner's convenience, and as many times as they require. The overall effect can be to improve engagement and achievement (Bongey, Cizadlo & Kalnbach, 2006). The advent of portable technologies, such as laptops, PDAs (personal digital assistants), iPods, and mobile phones, enables podcasts to be experienced in any location.

In the specific context of this work, the unit leader had produced a small number of podcasts to improve the effectiveness and experience of the learning within the final level elective (Human Factors for Business Information Systems – HFBIS). Podcasts were useful, but the limited resources of a single academic meant that only a small number could be produced. A way was needed to make the process more efficient – more podcasts needed to be produced, but with little more effort from the lecturer. At this point a solution was not identified, just the problem.

In the course of discussing assignments with students the question often came up – "what did last year's students do, can we see what they did?" A lack of confidence in their own abilities often leads students to look for examples of past work. From a negative perspective, this can lead to a lack of originality and a tendency to "play safe". However, it revealed the notion that this year's students perceive themselves to have a relationship with last year's students – they believe that they have something to learn from them.

THE CONTEXT OF ASSESSMENT IN UK HIGHER EDUCATION

In recent years the nature of higher education (HE) in the UK has changed dramatically. The number of institutions termed "University" has more than doubled, Government policy being that half of the population should be able to experience Higher Education through universities and institutions of similar standing. This has meant that the demographic of HE students has changed dramatically. For previous generations students were drawn from a relatively narrow social group, typically from families with professional backgrounds and a family history of university attendance. This has now been changed so that students from a wider range of backgrounds, socially and educationally, now study in HE.

This change has a number of consequences, including the following areas:

- macro-level national funding, down to micro-level family finances,
- HE institutions having to adapt to rapidly changing environment,
- the need for a greater range and volume of accommodation for teaching and for student living,
- a broader range of student competences socially and academically,
- an increasing number of students with some form of special educational need,
- pedagogic issues resulting from a change in the external environment and the nature of the student body.

In this chapter the focus is on the last three issues: student competencies, special educational needs, and the pedagogy of assessment.

Student Competencies

The change in the student demographic has coincided with the early stages of the information revolution. Many more technologies are available relating to the processing of text, audio and video. Students are able to create their own video using their mobile phones, digital cameras (with video capability) and with digital video cameras. The resultant files can be edited with software bundled in with operating systems such as Apple OS X, and Windows Vista. In addition, there has been a considerable uptake of social networking sites, such as Bebo and Facebook, plus YouTube, that all allow easy distribution of video and other material. Students have acquired a range of technological skills that enable them to manipulate information in a variety of forms.

The increase in technological competence of students is counter-balanced by the shift away from exam based qualifications gained at school as the main measure of applicant suitability for HE, towards a broader range of qualifications that are less reliant on essays produced under examination conditions. As a whole, students are gaining technical skills and losing more traditional academic skills. In addition, the ethnic profile has also changed, with an increase in the number of students from families where English is not the first language. Students, as a body, appear to have more difficulty producing written exams and assignments at undergraduate level than was previously the case. A consequence of this is that there are groups of students who are disadvantaged by an assessment system that is heavily reliant on essays; whether or not these are produced under examination conditions.

Special Educational Needs

The number of cases of dyslexia, and other language-based problems, is anecdotally reported to have risen considerably in recent years. Student support staff report having to create more learning needs plans than previously. Many HE institutions now have assessment regulations that provide additional support for students with this type of educational special need. These include additional time and human readers for support in exams. The argument is made that subject knowledge is not an issue for these students, but that written assessment to determine the level of understanding is. The spirit of the law in relation to disability is that those with a disability should not be unnecessarily disadvantaged. Extra areas of support with exams go someway to remove disadvantage, but cannot resolve it completely.

Assessment

The previous reliance on secondary school exam results, as a determinant of student suitability for study at HE level, has been replaced by a much broader spectrum of acceptable prior qualifications. While exams are still part of that spectrum, it now also includes work-based experience, a wide range of sub-degree, skills based, vocational qualifications, and qualifications awarded by overseas examination boards. This has a number of consequences. It can no longer be assumed that undergraduate students have the particular skill sets required to be successful in taking exams or in submitting extended essays or written reports. This requires that new forms of assessment be put in place if HE is not to accept this new type of student only onto undergraduate courses to fail them not because they have not acquired knowledge, but because they have not been able to articulate that knowledge in a particular abstract way through the written word.

A range of assessment techniques is now available to HE lecturers. A non-exclusive list includes the following:

- Exams (for example: unseen, seen, and open book),
- Written reports (including essays, experimental write-ups, reviews, reflective diary, and dissertations),
- Demonstrations (demonstration of surgical skills; musical, dancing or acting performances),
- Video production (skill demonstrations, product reviews and advertisements, video diary), and
- Viva voce examination (including interview and presentation).

An examination of this list will show that some forms of assessment rely heavily on the written word, which would be disadvantageous to students with dyslexia, or with the language of the university as a second language, which, in our case, is English. If our focus is to be on the acquisition and application of knowledge then HE lecturers need to consciously develop a portfolio of assessment techniques that allows students to acquire and demonstrate all the skills needed to have a rounded education and to be employable.

Summary of Issues Relating to the Context of Assessment in UK HE

The areas of competencies, special educational needs, and assessment all pull in one direction. The net effect of these issues is that the essay, as examination component or assignment, presents particular difficulties for a considerable number of students. In turn this presents problems for teachers in HE. It is necessary to assess students' knowledge of their subject, but traditional methods may not reveal a true and accurate description of competence. The traditional examination explores subject knowledge, but then attenuates this knowledge as it passes through the essay writing process. The more difficult the student finds language to be the greater will be the level of attenuation. This suggests alternate approaches are needed, so that knowledge can be more directly, and thus reliably, revealed.

In additional to these group trends, there are pressures felt by individuals who are near the end of their undergraduate studies. These students will have completed a considerable number of written assignments, and are simultaneously expected to be immersed in their final dissertation or project, often the biggest piece of work they have written. Students often feel pressured and overburdened at this stage, increasing their levels of stress.

THE SOLUTION

From the combination of educational and technological factors it became clear that altering the second assessment, to enable students to produce an assignment using video, could be useful. By making it explicit from the outset, that the work produced for assignments be used by future students to aid their learning, there could be a shift in the relationship of students to their education. By making students part of the educational process *as producers,* rather than consumers, it might be pos-

sible to reduce alienation and increase engagement (Mann 2001; Lucas, 2000). This solution would also help to develop a form of learning community. Each cohort of students would potentially see their place in a "tradition" of learning from previous students, whilst also developing learning resources for future cohorts. Those students so choosing could feel that they were recipients benefiting from previous students, and would also be able to act in a spirit of enlightened self-interest to pass something on themselves.

Further consideration indicated a number of possible benefits:

- Increased engagement with the subject:
  ◦ As a result of the different form of assessment
  ◦ As a result of their involvement with future teaching
  ◦ Feeling part of a learning community with continuity
- Higher achievement:
  ◦ Making video can more engaging than writing
  ◦ Learning from video can be more engaging than reading
- A library of teaching and learning resources that grows more quickly than if developed by lecturers alone.

The rapid growth in popularity of YouTube was perceived as supporting evidence for this approach: demonstrating a culture of making and sharing video. In this context it was also noted that more emphasis was placed on the quality of the *content* - semantics, rather than on the quality of *production*. This lead to the expectation that students would not feel intimidated by a perceived gap in production values between their efforts and those of others in the public domain. The work was never going to be of "broadcast quality", but this wouldn't matter to producers, viewers or assessors.

Practice

The assignment process provided some useful constraints:

- The video was limited to five to ten minutes duration (achievable),
- Students had to appear in it at some point (original),
- The subject of the video was from a limited list of options (focussed).

However, the format of the video was not constrained, in that students were encouraged to be creative. Though they had to appear in the video they were made aware that this didn't mean they were restricted to a "talking head" approach. During the tutorial sessions students were able to discuss possibilities with the lecturer and with other students. This was useful for maintaining focus and building enthusiasm.

Students, both as creators and users of video enjoy the process. Those that participate in the collaboration report benefits. These are usually reported as (1) being able to see the mistakes of previous students and so avoid them, (2) learning useful subject material from the video, (3) getting ideas and a feel for what is possible. Mistake avoidance relates to issues such as poor lighting, and avoiding background clutter "in-shot". Subject learning is an obvious benefit. Learning what is possible helps those students who lack the confidence to be original. Seeing the work of students who have been able to present an academic concept in an original way demonstrates that lecturers are not the only people capable of a useful, educational, performance.

Collaboration is optional. The decisions to make participation through video production optional was to support those students lacking the confidence to tackle a video project. Making video optional also supports those students who feel that they have a working method for producing assignments that they are comfort-

able with, particularly at this stressful time in their academic careers. In addition, there was an ethical consideration. From a student perspective the video approach may be seen as experimental. As such students should have the option not to take part in an experimental procedure that could have either a positive or negative impact on their degree results and classification.

Outcomes

During the execution of the assignment students were given the usual support regarding questions of content: tutorial discussion, clarification of concepts, etc. In addition some technical support was available. This was provided in order to allow students a reasonable chance of overcoming technical issues that they had not previously encountered. The main issue here was file conversion. The assignment brief required students to put the finished work into a number of formats. However, this was not a trivial task for some (a result of incompatibility between the hardware and software on their own PCs and cameras and those of the University). The provision of QuickTimePro licences, and guidance on use of other software resolved the problems.

Findings

The marks students received for the assignment and student feedback on the unit as a whole were analysed. A student with a late submission has been excluded from the analysis to assist with parity of comparison. Two markers were involved, each taking a set of assignments, both written and podcast. Following the marking phase was the moderation phase. The mean marks of the two markers were found to be within two percent of each other. Some further commentary is needed to explain some of the differences between the groups. Within the podcast group there were no failures, and there were no detected cases of plagiarism. Since the student is required to appear in their podcast there is reduced opportunity for plagiarism. In addition, it was the experience of the lecturer in tutorials that students attempting the podcast had higher levels of engagement. This was demonstrated in the questions asked during tutorials and in the creative input to the finished product. It is to be expected that higher levels of engagement would lead to higher marks – one of the objectives of the approach; and students with higher levels of engagement may well be more likely to try podcast production. However, this hypothesis has yet to be tested.

Results for the first, written only, assignment are included in table one for comparison purposes. For the purposes of comparison, those found with zero scores in the first assignment have been excluded from the statistics (two cases). For the second assignment there were two non-submissions, so that the count of students is the same for both assignments. The non-submissions of assignment two were not the same students as the plagiarists of assignment one.

A student, who had a formal statement of educational needs with respect to dyslexia, demonstrated a higher level of achievement with the podcast. The first, written assignment was marked at 51. The podcast assignment achieved 62. However, had the podcast assignment brief not required supporting written documentation then the mark would have been higher – there was clear evidence that problems completing the written component cost the student up to eight marks. Thus a brief that was based completely on video submission

could, potentially, have raised the achievement of the student from borderline 3rd-2ii (around 50%) up to borderline 2i-1st (around 70%). No cases of plagiarism were detected during the assessment of either the video or written alternatives of the second assignment.

Student Feedback

Student feedback, elicited by a standard unit questionnaire, was variable; indicating that podcasting worked well for at least some of the students. One student wrote:

"The assignments! Fantastic! Fun!" (sic.)

A balancing comment from another student indicated that they would have liked more support – a not uncommon request (though other students commented that support was good: "superb feedback with support when needed"). Informally, students did comment that they enjoyed the assignment, but still found it challenging. These challenges were in getting a sufficient grip on the content, working out how to present the content in an appropriate way, and learning the new technology. This last point related to video editing. While many students have experience of taking video few have had to edit with an objective in mind. Editing difficulties related to: special effects (credits, fade, adding a background track, controlling sound levels), and getting to the time limit while maintaining the content.

Table 1. Summary of marks for written and podcast assignment groups

	Assignment 1:	**Assignment 2:**		
	Written first assignment	**Whole group**	**Podcasts only**	**Written only**
Mean	53.76	56.64	63.15	55.20
Standard deviation	15.48	13.43	11.70	13.44
Minimum	19	11	45	11
Maximum	85	86	85	86

Recent students have provided some qualitative feedback. These indicate a range of benefits to both students and their teachers:

- *"...seeing previous student assignments ... helped put the assignment into perspective."* and *"I found the videos very helpful. I was not sure where to start with the first assignment... I then watched the videos and... understood more what you were looking for !"* suggest that being able to see the work of peers, albeit from previous cohorts, enabled students to tackle assignment work with more confidence, and with a more positive attitude. This suggests higher levels of engagement with their work, and may be responsible for higher achievement – though this would need to be confirmed by further study.

- *"...it was good to put the video in the lectures as it got your point across better compared (sic) to some lectures (sic) who actually wanted to create a version of "death by powerpoint"!!!"* Providing a variety of presentation formats increases engagement during teaching sessions, with benefits to the learning of students and the classroom experience of the lecturer.

- *"...the two tasks were much more interesting because they weren't simply essays!"* This is taken as an indication that enabling the production of video as a component to assignments increases student engagement. The assignments become something that students positively want to do, rather than just being another one of a series of essays or reports; thus their motivation appears to be for intrinsic motivations rather than extrinsic rewards found in other student group situations (Shapira et al, 2001). From a lecturing perspective this also means that interactions with students, regarding the assignments, are more about the knowledge and the work; and less

about the instrumental minimum to get a particular grade.

Building a Learning Community

One aim of this project was to use the developed video to teach later cohorts of students. In this way we get learning benefit from the development of the video, and subsequent learning benefit from those using the video. A comment from a (dyslexic) student of the 2007-2008 cohort is as follows:

"I found the content very useful. The videos I looked at explained the [usability] heuristics in a way that I was able to understand. I also found it useful to be able to look back at the content. Being able to pause and continue playing the content was also very useful. Having the content explained in a verity (sic) of ways was helpful. Also having the visual and sound element helped a grate (sic) deal."

The collaborative assessment regime of the elective contributes to the positive regard in which students hold the elective. The elective has been formally recognised as one of a few that are exceptionally well regarded by its students. That is, by enabling collaboration through the medium of video, students feel that they gain, both as producers of video this year, and as users of the video produced by students last year.

A statistical view of the assessment data shows that those making the video tend to be better students. This was determined by an examination of the marks for written first assignment for the elective. The average score on the first assignment was about 5% higher for those choosing to make a video for the second assignment compared with those who didn't. The reason for this is not known. However, from a collaboration perspective, it seems that those most likely to collaborate are the better students. This has benefits for all of the students, as the video materials produced are of a higher standard than would be the case if collaboration volunteers were more evenly distributed across the cohort. Those that do not choose the video option are still able to benefit from the efforts of the actively collaborating students by making use of the video that they produce to assist their learning.

Recommendations

There appear to be benefits from this approach, though they are not startlingly great for non-dyslexic students. Better students appear to do slightly better, and report that they enjoyed the experience. Though how much of this was due to the novelty of the assessment method and how much was due to expectations management by the lecturer is unclear. Throughout the assessment process it was stressed to students that if they found the assignment boring that it would be their own fault: they choose the method of illustrating their understanding and are responsible for the video production. Within the tutorial session the possibilities for making the work interesting were discussed. Consequently students have, amongst other things, put cameras onto shopping trolleys, worn bizarre sets of clothes, explored the workings of on-line gambling, and pretended to be Don Corleone or broadcast news journalists. The lesson from this is that some students will respond if encouraged to try something different and if their creative ideas are discussed in a positive, "can do", environment.

From a technical perspective, students were allowed to make their video using whatever technologies were available to them. This is in contrast to the option of rigorously enforced regime of standardised file formats. The reason for this was that it would be more encouraging to students if they were allowed to use the technology that they were most comfortable with and that was most readily available to them. In a different economic environment the University would be able to provide a video camera and editing suit to any student needing one. This may be the case in the future, when video production by students is more mainstream, but for the moment a workaround is required. A consequence of this approach is that the lecturing staff, and their technical support, are required to do some minor file management and post production to enable other students to view the material. With the current generation of personal computers this is not a significant problem.

FUTURE RESEARCH DIRECTIONS

One disappointing outcome of this research has been that some students do not take up the option of podcast production. These tend to be weaker students, those for whom written work does not yield excellent marks. This suggests two further areas of work. Firstly, to identify those factors that have the most influence on the choice between written assignment or video. Secondly, to test the hypothesis that students who don't perform well with written work would be more successful with video. These two areas of work present a number of methodological difficulties.

In examining the factors affecting choice there is the problem that reported reasons, gained from interview or questionnaire, may not be the actual and underlying reasons. Whether the questions are being asked by a lecturer, or by a fellow student, there is always the possibility of a socially determined "experimenter effect". That is, the responses given may be heavily influence by social norms and anticipated expectations in relation to the specific individual collecting the data or conducting the experiment. Students have been asked about the reasons behind their choices. Those choosing video expressed a willingness to try something new, and to get a break from writing. Those who chose not to make video gave reasons linked to familiarity with written work and not wanting to appear in a video. Apart from this last reason, it is not clear why these "reasons" are distributed the way that they are. There is an additional difficulty that cohorts are different to each other, making comparison of data difficult and unreliable. For example, within a recession students in their final year may have a different perspective to students who are about to graduate in an economic boom. Job-hunting (un)certainty may influence their willingness to try the unfamiliar, to experiment on themselves by submitting video rather than written assignments.

Testing the hypothesis that students who are weaker with written work would benefit from video presents an ethical challenge. The current work offers students a choice. There are two main reasons behind offering a choice. The first recognises that assessment by video is not yet mainstream – so the students have little or no prior experience of it, and may be uncertain and anxious about how to proceed. Thus forcing video onto them, not offering a choice, could add to their anxieties, and so disadvantage them. The second reason is much more positive. Student engagement and buy-in to assessment is much more positive when they have some choice in it. By allowing students to choose between video production or written work it is hoped that levels of instrumentalism will reduce and that students will consciously, or unconsciously, use the assignment more as a potential learning experience than as an opportunity for a box-ticking, instrumental approach to getting their degree certificate.

CONCLUSION

As each student cohorts progresses they learn from the mistakes of those that went before. For example, the early video contains basic errors such a poor control or lighting, forgetting to control shot background, clarity of explanation. As a result the work of new students improves both conceptually and in terms of production. This isn't a result of altruism, but an explicit reward for collaboration: tangibly in terms of marks awarded for the assignment, and intangibly through experiencing a more interesting assignment and an increased

sense of community. That said, the alteration of the social relationship between each student and the educational process in this way suggests an increase in student engagement and self-perceptions of autonomy (McFadden & Munns, 2002).

The collaboration we have encouraged, and that is described here, is of an asynchronous nature and has considerable temporal dislocation. That is, last year's students communicate with this year's, but not the other way around. One analogy might be a relay race. The "baton of knowledge" is passed from cohort to cohort though their hands never touch. What makes this different from making the work of past students available to current students is that the process is made explicit. Students know that their work will be seen and that they will be seen in it. The students seeing the work this year know that the students producing *knew* that their work would be viewed by others. This should alter their perceptions of past students, and of themselves, as active participants in the creation and dissemination of knowledge. The lecturer takes on the additional roles of moderator and facilitator. In the role of moderator there is an obligation to maintain standards of quality. As facilitator there is a requirement to provide the intellectual and technical frameworks within which the learning collaboration can take place. By making work more personal, for example by including a voice or video, and making collaboration more explicit, it is hoped that a feeling of community can be strengthened with consequent improvement in educational outcomes.

Since undertaking this work in mainstream Higher Education, other uses for this collaborative use of video have been considered, though without additional work being undertaken. Those uses include:

- Dissemination of knowledge – those with a skill share it by creating video to be made public (in-house or unlimited circulation). This can demonstrate physical skills (e.g. sport, manufacturing) or clerical tasks (correct use and completion of a form),

- Multi-speaker lectures: asynchronous production of a single video podcast lecture, with components provided by different speakers at different times, before editing into a coherent resource.

REFERENCES

Bongey, S. B., Cizadlo, G., & Kalnbach, L. (2006). Explorations in course-casting: podcasts in higher education. *Campus-Wide Information Systems, 23*(5), 350–367. doi:10.1108/10650740610714107

Chambers, E. (1992). Work load and the quality of student learning. *Studies in Higher Education, 17*(2), 141–153. doi:10.1080/03075079212331382627

Lindsay, B. (2008). Breaking university rules. *Australian Universities Review, 50*(1), 37–39.

Lucas, U. (2000). Worlds apart: students' experiences of learning introductory accounting. *Critical Perspectives on Accounting, 11*(4), 479–504. doi:10.1006/cpac.1999.0390

Mann, S. J. (2001). Alternative perspectives on the student experience: alienation and engagement. *Studies in Higher Education, 26*(1), 7–19. doi:10.1080/03075070020030689

McFadden, M., & Munns, G. (2002). Student engagement and the social relations of pedagogy. *British Journal of Sociology of Education, 23*(3), 357–366. doi:10.1080/0142569022000015409

Pheiffer, G., Holley, D., & Andrew, D. (2006). Developing thoughtful students: using learning styles in an HE context. *Education + Training, 47*(6), 422–431. doi:10.1108/00400910510617042

Rhodes, C., & Nevill, A. (2004). Academic and social integration in higher education: a survey of satisfaction and dissatisfaction within a first-year education studies cohort at a new university. *Journal of Further and Higher Education, 28*(2), 179–193. doi:10.1080/0309877042000206741

Scott, N. (2008). An evaluation of enhanced student support (including podcasting) on assessed course work achievement and student satisfaction. *Learning and Teaching in Action, 7*(1). Retrieved September 16, 2009, from http://www.celt.mmu.ac.uk/ltia/issue15/scott.php

Shapira, B., Kantor, P. B., & Melamed, B. The effect of extrinsic motivation on user behaviour in a collaborative information finding system. *Journal of the American Society for Information Science and Technology, 52*(11), 879–887. doi:10.1002/asi.1148

Sharpe, R., Benfield, G., Roberts, G., & Francis, R. (2006, October). *The undergraduate experience of blended e-learning: a review of UK literature and practice*. Retrieved September 16, 2009, from http://www.heacademy.ac.uk/assets/York/documents/ourwork/research/literature_reviews/blended_elearning_full_review.pdf

Stubbs, M., & Martin, I. (2003). Blended learning: one small step. *Learning and Teaching in Action, 2*(3). Retrieved September 16, 2009, from http://www.celt.mmu.ac.uk/ltia/issue6/stubbsmartin.shtml

Torrance, H. (2007). Assessment as learning? How the use of explicit learning objectives, assessment criteria and feedback in post-secondary education and training can come to dominate learning. *Assessment in Education, 14*(3), 281–294. doi:10.1080/09695940701591867

Yang, S. C. (2003). Creating an Internet theatre in gender education. *Journal of Computer Assisted Learning, 19*(1), 249–251. doi:10.1046/j.1365-2729.2003.00251.x

Chapter 9
Designs for Systems to Support Collaborative Information Behavior

Chirag Shah
Rutgers, The State University of New Jersey, USA

ABSTRACT

Designing systems that support collaborative information behavior (CIB) pose many unique challenges that single-user systems typically do not face. This chapter attempts to take the reader through a variety of notions, design principles, and instantiations of CIB systems. Requirements and guidelines for a good CIB system are provided based on various research studies and projects done in different domains. It is pointed out that in the information seeking field, control, communication, and awareness are some of the most critical aspects of a CIB system that caters to multi-user and multi-session collaborative projects. Several actual implementations of CIB systems are described, and suggestions for designing a successful CIB system are presented.

INTRODUCTION

There are several reasons for humans to work together. For one, sometimes a problem is just too complex for a single individual to tackle. Denning & Yaholkovsky (2008) regard such problems as "messy" or "wicked" and argue that collaboration is essential for resolving such messes. When it comes to accessing or processing some information, it seems that in many situations, multiple people working together will be able to do a *better*

job than any one of them individually, given that they have appropriate tools. For instance, Olson et al. (1993) developed *ShrEdit*, a shared text editor. To their surprise, they discovered that the groups working with *ShrEdit* generated fewer design ideas, but apparently better ones. They believed their tool helped the supported groups keep more focused on the core issues in the emerging design, to waste less time on less important topics, and to capture what was said as they went.

Despite the importance of collaboration in many situations, there is a lack of support for people working to collaborate on information

DOI: 10.4018/978-1-61520-797-8.ch009

seeking. Morris (2008) showed from a survey of 204 knowledge workers that the majority of them wanted to collaborate, but often found it difficult due to the lack of specialized tools to support their natural behavior for working in collaboration. Twidale & Nichols (1996) pointed out that *"The use of library resources is often stereotyped as a solitary activity, with hardly any mention in the substantial library science and information retrieval literature of the social aspects of information systems."* They argued that introducing support for collaboration into information retrieval systems would help users to learn and use the systems more effectively. In general, for solving complex problems, inducing better learning, and catering to the social aspect of information seeking, a new paradigm of systems design is needed that goes beyond supporting individual activities in information seeking. The present chapter aims to provide an overview of such design practices and implementations to support collaborative information behavior (CIB).

The rest of the chapter is organized as follows. The exploration of the CIB design paradigm begins with a review of some of the definitions, challenges, and design principles reported in the literature. This background section will take the reader from various concepts and theories about CIB system designs to their practical instantiations. This review is followed by detailed descriptions of three systems that support CIB. Pointers to future research directions are then provided, and the chapter concludes with some remarks on the lessons learned from past and current CIB systems designs, and the implications for designers and researchers in this field.

BACKGROUND

In this section, the reader will be introduced to a number of definitions, concepts, and principles for designing and developing systems that support CIB. A good design follows a thorough understand-ing of user needs, requirements of the problems, and carefully derived principles. An insight into these aspects will be provided through a number of studies reported in the literature.

Definitions and Terminology

Let us begin by looking at the concept of collaboration. As its Latin roots 'com' and 'laborate' suggest *collaboration* indicates "to work together". London (1995) interpreted this meaning as *working together synergistically*. Gray (1989) defined collaboration as *"a process of joint decision-making among key stakeholders of a problem domain about the future of that domain."* Roberts & Bradley (1991) called collaboration *"an interactive process having a shared transmutational purpose."* What all these definitions inform us is that collaboration is an active, interactive, and usually a mutually beneficial process. It is often used interchangeably with *coordination* and *cooperation*. However, for the purpose of our discussion here, we need to clarify the distinction among these seemingly similar terms. Austin & Baldwin (1991, p.4) noted that while there are obvious similarities between cooperation and collaboration, the former involves pre-established interests, while the latter involves collectively defined goals. Malone (1988) defined coordination as *"the additional information processing performed when multiple, connected actors pursue goals that a single actor pursuing the same goals would not perform."* Note that this definition of coordination says nothing about working or creating solutions together, thus distinguishing it from collaboration. Denning & Yaholkovsky (2008) suggested that coordination and cooperation are weaker forms of working together, while collaboration indicates a stronger, more focused tie among the participants. Similarly, Chrislip & Larson (1994, p.5) defined collaboration as *"...a mutually beneficial relationship between two or more parties [agents] who work toward common goals by sharing responsibility, authority, and accountability for achieving results."*

Such understanding and clarification are important to designing and instantiating a CIB system in order to make decisions regarding the support that the system is intended to provide - merely coordination, exchange of information, or full-fledged collaboration that allows people not only to communicate and coordinate, but also to facilitate formation of a stronger tie leading to a mutually beneficial outcome.

Let us turn our attention to collaboration in information seeking domain. There are several definitions of collaborative information seeking or retrieval in the literature. For instance, Foster (2006) defined collaborative information retrieval (IR) as *"the study of the systems and practices that enable individuals to collaborate during the seeking, searching, and retrieval of information."* Hansen & Jarvelin (2005) defined collaborative IR as *"an information access activity related to a specific problem solving activity that, implicitly or explicitly, involves human beings interacting with other human(s) directly and/or through texts (e.g., documents, notes, figures) as information sources in an work task related information seeking and retrieval process either in a specific workplace setting or in a more open community or environment"*. Shah (2009) referred to collaborative information seeking as a process of information seeking *"that is defined explicitly among the participants, interactive, and mutually beneficial."*

The literature is filled with studies that use terms such as *collaborative IR* (Fidel et al., 2000), *social searching* (Evans & Chi, 2008), *concurrent search* (Baecker, 1995), *collaborative exploratory search* (Pickens & Golovchinsky, 2007), *co-browsing* (Gerosa et al., 2004), *collaborative information behavior* (Reddy & Jansen, 2008; Talja & Hansen, 2006), *collaborative information synthesis* (Blake & Pratt, 1957), and *collaborative information seeking* (Hertzum, 2008; Shah, 2008), which are often used interchangeably. What we observe from all these studies is that they reflect a notion of collaboration that is active, interactive,

and geared toward solving a mutual problem of information seeking.

To this point, we would like to point out the major difference between the above studies and the ones on collaborative filtering. In the case of collaborative filtering, one benefits from other people's past actions; however, these people may not be actively working on a joint project in an interactive fashion. Some researchers classify this as passive collaboration. Recommendations provided on Amazon and Netflix are examples of such collaborative filtering.

In contrast to such passive collaboration, our emphasis in this chapter will be on active and explicitly defined collaboration. Thus, for the purpose of our discussion here, we will focus on the systems that provide support for multiple people working together with a common and mutually beneficial goal in an active and interactive manner.

Design Considerations for a Collaborative Information Seeking System

Space and Time Aspects

The classical way of organizing collaborative activities is based on two factors: location and time (Rodden, 1991). Recently Hansen & Jarvelin (2005) and Golovchinsky, Pickens, & Back (2008) also classified approaches to collaborative IR using these two dimensions of space and time. Inspired by a similar illustration by Twidale & Nichols (1996) incorporating several library-related activities, we present a depiction of various CIB tools in Figure 1. The figure depicts the systems that support active or passive collaboration to put them in proper perspective. Examples of active collaboration include Ariadne and SearchTogether (described in detail later). Examples of passive collaboration include Amazon and Netflix. The figure shows a range of the systems from the early days of CIB projects such as Ariadne to recent tools such as TeamSearch. Interfaces such as

OPAC are still used widely, while systems such as I-Spy have been discontinued.[1]

The placement of a CIB system on this figure has implications for its implementation, functionalities, and evaluation. For instance, Adobe Connect[2] facilitates online meetings where the participants can share and discuss information. Such an environment will fall under Synchronous-Remote collaboration in Figure 1. Thus, this environment needs to have a way to connect remote participants in real-time, and a shared space for exchanging and processing information.

Control, Communication, and Awareness

Three components specific to group-work or collaboration that are highly predominant in the CIB or Computer Supported Cooperative Work (CSCW) literature are control, communication, and awareness. In this subsection we will look at some of the definitions and related studies for these components. Understanding their roles can also help us address various design issues with CIB systems.

Control

Rodden (1991) identified the value of control in CSCW systems and listed a number of projects with their corresponding schemes for implementing control. For instance, the COSMOS project (Wilbur & Young, 1988) had a formal structure to represent control in the system. They used roles to represent people or automatons, and rules to represent the flow and processes. People's roles included supervisor, processor, analyst, etc. Rules could be a condition that a process needs to satisfy in order to start or finish. Rodden classified these types of control systems as procedural based systems.

To express control and pass it from one entity to another, early CSCW systems used various forms of messages. These messages were often referred to as Structured Definition Language (SDL) messages. In the most basic sense, these were email messages that were sent back and forth among the participants of a collaborative project. However, for a collaborative project, an organization often needs more support than simply passing the information in messages. SDL provides this support by imposing a structure to these messages,

Figure 1. CIB systems, supporting active or passive collaboration, organized according to time and space aspects

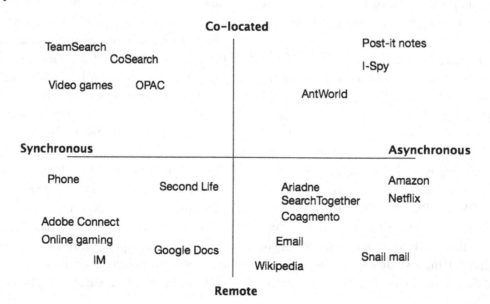

and incorporating additional fields of information that can be used to filter and distribute messages appropriately.

For instance, Malone et al. (1987) proposed the Information Lens framework, in which the messages carried additional information (some of which was automatically generated) that can later be used to filter and classify the messages to suit an individual's need in a group.

Here is how it worked. Sam sends a message to circulate in the group that he belongs to, asking for an opinion. At the time of sending this, Sam was not clear about who might be the right person in the group to inquire about that question, but since the system has additional information, such as user profiles and preferences, it can use this information to redirect and distribute the message to appropriate individuals. This way, Sam does not have to worry about looking for the right people, and the receivers do not have to worry about getting the messages that are not intended for them, even though they are useful for the group as a whole.

Looking at the above scheme with a different perspective, we are distributing the control between humans and automatons involved in the whole group process. Instead of explicitly deciding by himself who should receive the message, Sam is letting the system take charge of this process, thus relinquishing control to the system. The system is driven by the rules that guide its decision-making. It is important to note that such a system is different than a traditional collaborative filtering system, where the system filters information based on similarities among the users. Here, the messages are filtered based on the sender's intention (Sam chose to distribute his message this way), and the receiver's intention to receive such messages that are relevant to them. Malone referred to such kind of filtering as *cognitive filtering*.

Some of the recent projects have reintroduced control with the notion of user roles., For instance, Pickens et al. (2008) demonstrated a collaborative video search system where one of the participants was responsible for issuing queries (prospector), and the other participant was responsible for going through the results looking for relevant information (miner), thus, distributing control of different aspects. In its most basic version, this system had pre-defined roles and these roles followed a fixed set of rules. However, with the ability to have structured messages with appropriate information, we can have more flexible roles with dynamic distribution of control among the participants and the system.

Communication

This is one of the most critical components of any collaboration. In fact, Rodden (1991) identified message or communication systems as the class of systems in CSCW that is most mature and most widely used.

Since we are interested in CIB systems that allow its participants to engage in an intentional and interactive collaboration, there must be a way for the participants to communicate with each other. What is interesting to note is that often, collaboration could begin by simply letting a group of users communicate with each other without any pre-conceived notion or intention for collaboration. For instance, Donath & Robertson (1994) presented a system that allows a user to know that others were currently viewing the same webpage and communicate with those people to initiate a possible collaboration or at least a co-browsing experience. Providing communication capabilities even in an environment that was not originally designed for carrying out collaboration is an interesting way of encouraging collaboration.

Using four multidisciplinary design situations in the USA and Europe, Sonnenwald (1996) came up with 13 communication roles. The author showed how these roles can support collaboration, among other aspects of the information seeking process. These aspects included knowledge exploration and integration, and task and project completion, by filtering and providing information and negotiating differences across organizational, task, discipline and personal boundaries.

Awareness

Awareness, in the context of CSCW, has been defined as *"an understanding of the activities of others, which provides a context for your own activity."* (Dourish & Bellotti, 1992) The following four kinds of awareness are often discussed and addressed in CSCW literature (Liechti & Sumi, 2002):

1. *Group awareness.* This kind of awareness includes providing information to each group member about the status and activities of the other collaborators at a given time.
2. *Workspace awareness.* This refers to a common workspace that the group has where they can bring and discuss their findings, and create a common product.
3. *Contextual awareness.* This type of awareness relates to the application domain, rather than the users. Here, we want to identify what content is useful for the group, and what the goals are for the current project.
4. *Peripheral awareness.* This relates to the kind of information that has resulted from personal and the group's collective history, and should be kept separate from what a participant is currently viewing or doing.

Design Implications

The findings from empirical observations and other studies of usability testing relating to control, communication, and awareness inform us that an effective CIB system should have the following attributes.

1. A flexible mechanism to incorporate structured message passing.
2. A way of facilitating control among the participants as well as by automaton components.
3. Ways to present awareness of various objects, processes, and people at any given time to everyone in the group.

While these attributes are derived from general collaborative systems, they apply to CIB systems too. Let us explore how such attributes have been adopted and implemented in various CIB systems.

Several CIB systems, such as *SearchTogether* (Morris & Horvitz, 2007) incorporate support for chat or IM (discussed later at length). Such a support is crucial as the group members need a way to communicate with each other. The support for communication can also be provided as audio chat, videoconference, or bulletin boards.

While chat is an obvious choice for synchronous communication, email still prevails when it comes to providing asynchronous communication. Recently, Morris (2008) found from a survey of knowledge workers that email is still one of the most used methods of communicating while working on a collaborative project. Given the importance of email, and the level of familiarity and comfort that most people have with it, an effective CIB system should provide support for passing such messages among the participants during collaboration, either through an already familiar tool (e.g., Microsoft Exchange), or with an integrated messaging interface. In addition to this, we need to have some kind of structure imposed on the messages passed to incorporate additional information, such as timestamps, tags, and associated processes. Such structure and information can be helpful in distributing the messages, according to various filters, and passing the control from one entity to another.

Finally, providing awareness is highly important for a CIB system. Since the users of a CIB system will be working with different sources, documents, queries, snippets, and annotations of varying kind, we need to keep everyone in the group aware of all such objects as they are collected and modified. In addition to this, it is important to show various attributes associated with an object. For instance, it is useful to indicate on the interface that a document has already been viewed, and who viewed that document.

Several systems supporting collaboration have identified the above issues (control, communication, and awareness) as critical to their design. For instance, Farooq et al. (2009) presented a collaborative design for CiteCeer, a search engine and digital library of research literature in the computer and information science disciplines. Based on a survey and follow-up interviews with CiteCeer users, the authors presented four novel implications for designing the CiteCeer collaboratory: (1) visualize query-based social networks to identify scholarly communities of interest, (2) provide online collaborative tool support for upstream stages of scientific collaboration, (3) support activity awareness for staying cognizant of online scientific activities, and (4) use notification systems to convey scientific activity awareness.

Costs and Challenges of CIB Systems, and Their Implications for the Designers

There are several costs associated with using a system that supports collaborative information behavior, some of which are listed below. Understanding these costs is vital for a good system design, and it is possible that each system designer may have to address these costs in different ways.

1. *Cost of learning.* This is the cost associated with learning a new system. A CIB system is likely to be complex and one may need to be educated about the functionalities and scope of each of its components.
2. *Adaptation/adoption cost.* Knowing how to use a system does not necessarily mean the users will adopt it in the long run. One of the findings from the pilot runs of *Coagmento* (discussed later in detail) and reported in Shah (2009), is that the subjects failed to see why someone would use such a system instead of using Google, IM, and email. The subjects successfully learned the system, but they did not see how they could adopt it, leaving more

familiar and already adopted systems such as Google, IM, and email. There is a cost associated with such adoption or adapting to such a new system.

3. *Cognitive load.* Many projects have attempted to address the issue of cognitive load induced by a system. Part of the cognitive load is in learning and then adapting to the system, which are presented before. The other aspect of cognitive load for a CIB system will be induced during the actual usage of it. As presented in the guidelines of a successful CIB system, four kinds of awareness are essential to provide. While such awareness is useful, it can also be overwhelming.
4. *Collaborative cost.* Often referred to as the *collaborative load*, this is a kind of cognitive load that is unique to the CIB environment, and comes from being a part of a group. For instance a participant in a collaborative project may have to pay attention to the group's history in addition to the personal history, inducing additional cognitive load.

In addition to dealing with these costs, a CIB system designer faces several challenges. Grudin (1994) recognized eight challenges for designing groupware systems.

1. *Bringing a balance in work and benefit.* More than often, the users of a groupware system do not all get the same benefits for the amount of work they have to do. The designer has to address the needs and the work distribution for all the users.
2. *Building a critical mass.* If a groupware cannot achieve "critical mass" of users to be useful, it can fail as it is never to any one individual's advantage to use it.
3. *Entertaining to normal social processes.* A groupware system may sometimes hinder the social and political norms that its users have. A good system design adapts to an existing social structure rather than imposing one.

4. *Handling the errors*. A system needs to be prepared to handle a wide range of exceptions and support improvisations that characterize much of the group activities.

5. *Providing unobtrusive accessibility*. Features that support group processes may be used relatively infrequently, and one needs to design a system that provides unobtrusive accessibility and integration of them with more heavily used features.

6. *Evaluation*. Due to its often-complex design, multi-faceted and multi-user interface, and a variety of user and system interactions, evaluating a groupware system can be a huge challenge.

7. *Addressing the intuition*. Decision makers in a production environment rely heavily on informed intuition. Most product development experience is based on single-user applications, and transferring it to a multi-user groupware application can be a challenge.

8. *Adaptation*. Groupware systems require more careful implementation and introduction in the workplace than product developers usually confront.

Based on the costs and challenges presented above the following five design guidelines can be useful for the CIB system designers.

1. *Understand the real needs*. Just because some software has the supportive tools for CIB, does not mean it will actually be used to help a user's CIB. The designers need to understand various aspects of the target domain, educate the users and managers, and design the system that can provide a good balance of costs and benefits to each user.

2. *Keep it simple*. The design of the interface needs to be very intuitive and easy to use. As we saw before, there are costs associated with learning a new system as well as adopting it. The users may feel more comfortable if the system appears very user friendly. This will help in lowering the costs for learning and continual usage of the system.

3. *Make it accessible*. Similar to Grudin (1994), the CIR group of University of Washington (Fidel et al., 2004) recommended that instead of designing a collaborative system that the users have to get used to, one should design a system that fits the way the users are used to working. While several of the components of a CIB system may be new to a typical user, we should try to minimize imposing a rigidly structured system on a new user. Instead, the system should have many components that the user is already familiar with and know how to use, and allow the user to explore other innovative tools provided.

4. *Provide the right tools*. As we discussed earlier, support for control, communication, and awareness (group, workspace, contextual, and peripheral) are very crucial to a good CIB system. It is important to provide the tools that implement these features in an unobtrusive manner. Often, it may be useful to extend a single-user application that is already adopted and add collaboration features to it.

5. *Allow private working*. One of the requirements of a successful collaboration is independence (Surowiecki, 2004). The participants should be able to work by themselves without the pressure of being "watched" or requiring anyone's opinions. Eventually, of course, we expect the participants to share their findings and have interactions that can lead to better solutions, but one should have the ability to work on his/her own at times. This can help in reducing the cost of cognitive load induced by the system as well as the collaboration, and bring in the benefit of individual contributions.

Turning Design into Realization

There are several ways in which collaboration can be achieved. People can use familiar tools such as telephones and email for doing collaboration with remotely located users asynchronously or synchronously. However, these tools are not specifically designed to do collaboration. If we take a step back and analyze what we really need for an effective collaboration, we may come up with a different set of tools. To understand the issues in implementing a collaborative system, we identify these important aspects: processes, content, and devices. A brief description of each of these aspects follows along with related projects.

Processes

In its most basic form, a collaborative environment lets the collaborators to divide up the workload and/or combine their inputs in some way. Several examples of a collaborative environment have primarily focused on the system side. These projects typically present some algorithmic way of combining multiple instances of search request, result lists, or other interactions from different users to perform implicit "collaboration". For instance, a good deal of work in implementing a collaborative search system has been done around reformulating search requests of a user based on other users' search requests on the same/similar search goals. This is reflected in a study by Fu, Kelly, & Shah (2007), who showed how different queries from a set of users for the same information goal can be combined, calling them "collaborative queries", for better retrieval performance.

Content

A simple way of taking advantage of collaboration is dividing the content among the users for viewing, judging, or manipulating. With *WebSplitter*, Han, Perret, & Naghshineh (2000) demonstrated how a unified XML framework can support multi-device

and multi-user web browsing. *WebSplitter* splits a requested web page and delivers the appropriate partial view of each page to each user, or more accurately to each user's set of devices. Multiple users can participate in the same browsing session, as in traditional conferencing groupware. Similarly, Maekawa, Hara, & Nishio (2006) developed a page partitioning method for collaborative browsing, which divides a webpage into multiple components. They also designed and implemented a collaborative web browsing system in which users can search and browse their target information by discussing and watching partial pages displayed on multiple devices. As a part of their *SearchTogether* system, Morris & Horvitz (2007) incorporated a feature that lets users dynamically distribute the web pages among themselves. The authors identified such a division of labor as one of the appeals of their collaborative IR system.

Devices

Typically, in a CIB environment, systems refer to computers, but several projects have tried to extend information access and distribution to other forms of devices to enable collaboration among the users in a variety of work places. For instance, Maekawa, Hara, & Nishio (2006) presented a collaborative web browsing system in a mobile computing environment. Their motivation for using collaboration in the mobile device environment was to overcome the issue of low functionality that restricts the services provided for mobile users. Rutger's DISCIPLE (DIstributed System for Collaborative Information Processing and LEarning) project (Rutgers, 2009) is another example of introducing collaborative processes to mobile users. The key objective of the DISCIPLE project has been to develop an advanced groupware design that enables interactive collaboration in the context of the task at hand. Amershi & Morris (2008) presented *CoSearch* - a collaborative browsing interface to be used on computers, and introduced *CoSearchMobile*, designed to provide similar functionalities on mobile devices. The *CoSearch* system leverages readily available devices such as mobile phones and extra mice to facilitate collaborative browsing among co-located users.

Blackwell, Stringer, Toye, & Rode (2004) described a tangible interface for collaborative IR. The purpose of this interface was to allow multiple users to interact simultaneously to refine a query. Morris, Paepcke, & Winograd (2006) presented the *TeamSearch* system, which used an interactive table for a small group of co-located participants in searching for digital images to use in a report. Mitsubishi Electric Research Lab (MERL) has developed *DiamondTouch* (Smeaton et al., 2006), an interface device that supports direct user collaboration on a tabletop. Such an interactive tabletop is ideal for multimedia searches in collaboration. Among other things, the authors found about a 10% increase in the level of user-interaction as the users moved from their first search to the last one with *DiamondTouch*.

SYSTEMS

Let us now look at some of the systems implemented to support CIB. While these systems offer slightly different functionalities, they all have in common many of the design principles presented in the previous section..

Ariadne

Twidale et al. (1995) developed *Ariadne* to support the collaborative learning of database browsing skills. In addition to enhancing the opportunities and effectiveness of the collaborative learning that already occurred, *Ariadne* was designed to provide the facilities that would allow collaborations to persist as people increasingly searched information remotely and had less opportunity for spontaneous face-to-face collaboration.

Ariadne was developed in the days when Telnet-based access to library catalogues was a common practice. Building on top of this command-line interface, *Ariadne* could capture the users' input and the database's output, and form them into a search history that consisted of a series of *command-output* pairs. Such a separation of capture and display allowed *Ariadne* to work with various forms of data capture methods.

To support complex browsing processes in collaboration, *Ariadne* presented a visualization of the search process (Figure 2). This visualization consisted of thumbnails of screens, looking like playing cards, which represented *command-output* pairs. Any such card can be expanded to reveal its details. The horizontal axis on *Ariadne*'s display represented time, and the vertical axis showed information on the semantics of the action it represented: the top row for the top level menus, the middle row for specifying a search, and the bottom row for looking at particular book details.

This visualization of the search process in *Ariadne* makes it possible to annotate, discuss with colleagues around the screen, and distribute to remote collaborators for asynchronous commenting easily and effectively. As we saw in the previous section, having access to one's history as well as the history of one's collaborators are very crucial to effective collaboration. *Ariadne* implements these requirements with the features that let one visualize, save, and share a search process. In fact, the authors found one of the advantages of search visualization was the ability to recap previous searching sessions easily in a multi-session exploratory searching.

SearchTogether

More recently, one of the collaborative information seeking tools that have caught a lot of attention is *SearchTogether*, developed by Morris and Horvitz (2007). The design of this tool was motivated by a survey that the researchers did with 204 knowledge workers (Morris, 2008), in which they discovered the following.

Figure 2. A search visualization in Ariadne. © 1995, Michael B. Twidale. Used with permission

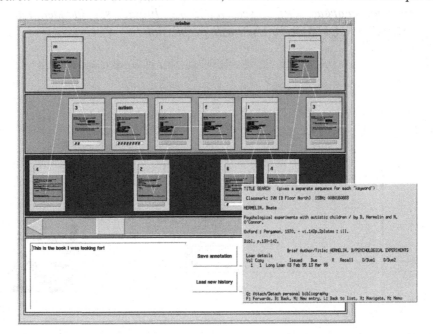

- A majority of respondents wanted to collaborate while searching on the Web.
- The most common ways of collaborating in information seeking tasks are sending emails back and forth, using IM to exchange links and query terms, and using phone calls while looking at a Web browser.
- Some of the most popular Web searching tasks on which people like to collaborate are planning travels or social events, making expensive purchases, researching medical conditions, and looking for information related to a common project.

Based on the survey responses, and the current and desired practices for collaborative search, the authors of *SearchTogether* identified three key features for supporting people's collaborative information behavior while searching on the Web: awareness, division of labor, and persistence. Let us look at how these three features are implemented. A snapshot of the *SearchTogether* client is shown in Figure 3.

As we saw before, awareness is one of the most critical elements of a collaborative system. *SearchTogether* instantiates awareness in several ways, one of which is per-user query histories. This is done by showing each group member's screen name, his/her photo and queries in the "Query Awareness" region (Figure 3b). The access to the query histories is immediate and interactive, as clicking on a query brings back the results of that query from when it was executed. The authors identified query awareness as a very important feature in collaborative searching, which allows group members to not only share their query terms, but also learn better query formulation techniques from one another.

Another component of *SearchTogether* that facilitates awareness is the display of page-specific metadata (Figure 3h). This region includes several pieces of information about the displayed page, including group members who viewed the given page, and their comments and ratings. The authors claim that such visitation information can help one either choose to avoid a page already visited by someone in the group to reduce the duplication of

Figure 3. Screenshot of SearchTogether. (a) integrated messaging, (b) query awareness, (c) current results, (d) recommendation queue, (e)(f)(g) search buttons, (h) page-specific metadata, (i) toolbar, (j) browser. © 2007 Meredith Ringel Morris. Used with permission

efforts, or perhaps choose to visit such pages, as they provide a sign of promising leads as indicated by the presence of comments and/or ratings.

Division of labor in *SearchTogether* is implemented in three ways: (1) "Split Search" allows one to split the search results among all online group members in a round-robin fashion, (2) "Multi-Engine Search" takes a query and runs it on *n* different search engines, where *n* is the number of online group members, (3) manual division of labor can be facilitated using integrated IM.

Despite the anticipated benefits that the authors anticipated, the automatic division of labor features, implemented using split search and multi-engine search were not heavily used during their user studies. The lack of usage of these features does not indicate their failure; it shows their misfit for the given situation. Performing automatic split implies that the person doing the

split is the group leader. While such a scenario is possible in many business and management situations, it did not come up during the lab studies.

Finally, the persistence feature in *SearchTogether* is instantiated by storing all the objects and actions, including IM conversations, query histories, recommendation queues, and page-specific metadata. Such data about all the group members are available to each member when he/she logs in. This allows one to easily carry a multi-session collaborative project.

Coagmento

Coagmento,[3] another tool developed recently for providing collaborative information seeking, builds on the framework of other tools such as *SearchTogether*, and extends them in certain ways. The current implementation of *Coagmento* is search focused, with emphasis on keeping things as simple and familiar to a novice user as possible. Based on this design guideline, *Coagmento*'s display incorporates a well-known search box and rank-list interface occupying a majority of the screen, with a collection of tools on one side that support communication and certain aspects of awareness that are essential for collaboration.

Using *Coagmento*, collaborators can work synchronously or asynchronously, and they may be co-located or remotely connected. The main screen of *Coagmento* is shown in Figure 4a. As we can see, *Coagmento* includes a search interface, chat, and document space (the same space where the results are displayed in the figure), as well as various marking facilities (discussed later) - all in one place. *Coagmento* displays the partnership information and provides visual feedback based on one's partner's as well as one's own actions. For instance, if a document is already viewed by anyone in the group, it will be highlighted anywhere it appears in a rank-list. *Coagmento* keeps a log of all the queries used during a search session. The list of these queries is presented on the interface. (Unlike *SearchTogether*, clicking on a query executes fresh results, and not its history.) Users of *Coagmento* can save any document that they find useful or flag it to be discussed with their partners. Once again, these two lists are readily available on the interface and clicking on the name of a document displays it. If users are working alone, they may not see much use in writing notes about everything that they save if they have a good understanding about the relevance of those results. While working in a group, on the other hand, the user may need to specify which aspects of a document are useful and why. *Coagmento* allows users to add notes to any document (Figure 4b). Morris & Horvitz (2007) found such a feature useful, but they also realized that they needed a way for users to simply highlight and save portions of pages. *Coagmento* provides a way for users to 'snip' passages of

documents (Figure 4b). *Coagmento* saves the state information. This means a user can leave a session and when he comes back, he will find the session as it was, with some possible updates in case his collaborators kept working while he was gone. This allows the users to collaborate in either synchronous or asynchronous mode. There is an indication on the interface to let a user know if his partners are online or not.

One aspect of *SearchTogether* that *Coagmento* does not implement fully is the division of labor. There are three ways in which this feature is realized in *SearchTogether* (Morris & Horvitz, 2007): (1) chat, (2) recommendations, and (3) split search. Coagmento has a chat feature, which can be used to talk about the distribution of the work. As far as the recommendations feature is concerned, the authors of *SearchTogether* found it underutilized. They concluded that rather than providing a "recommend" option, providing a "share this" option would allow a better way of sending pages back and forth. *Coagmento* does this through its "discuss this document" feature. For the *SearchTogether* system, it was found that the automatic division of labor features such as split search was not heavily used. The usefulness of such a feature needs further investigation.

FUTURE RESEARCH DIRECTIONS

From the early days of groupware systems to Web 2.0 based online collaborations, the systems to support CIB have come a long way. Several challenges, however, remain to be addressed. The most important of these challenges are not about the technology, but about their right implementation, usage, and sustainability. As Grudin (1994) noted, *"Many expensive failures in developing and marketing software that is designed to support groups are not due to technical problems. They result from not understanding the unique demands this class of software imposes on developers and users."*

Figure 4. Screenshots of Coagmento. (a) main screen, (b) toolbar while viewing a document

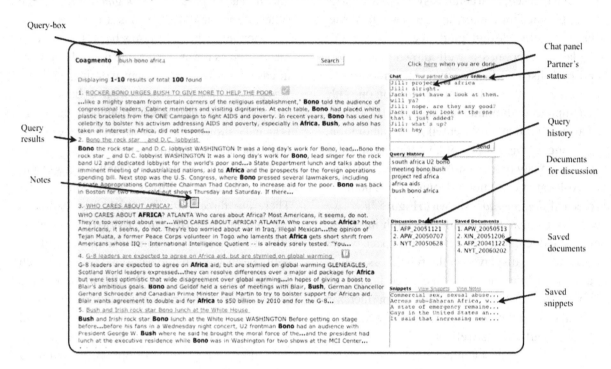

Thus, the researchers and developers interested in designing, implementing, and studying the systems to support CIB will have to go beyond understanding the technology; they will need to understand certain fundamental aspects about the target domain, such as decision-making processes, existing practices, and user expectations and interactions in group/social settings. Many studies in the past used empirical observation method (e.g., Olson et al., 1992) to study these aspects and design their systems. While several of their findings are still relevant, new studies with emerging information sources and recent technologies are needed.

One of the biggest challenges that most CIB systems face is the issue of adoption. Before designing or implementing a CIB system, one will need to study the bigger context and see how collaborative features of a CIB system can fit in an existing environment, instead of imposing a rigid structure on the user.

Finally, there is something to be said about the value of innovations. Often, as Steve Jobs said, *"People don't know what they want until you show it to them."* There is plenty of room in the field of CIB to bring in new and innovative design ideas that can inspire the users and the researchers.

CONCLUSION

Many studies confirm the fact that collaborating on complex problems is a natural tendency for humans, and numerous research works have attempted to address several of the challenges in this field. However, there is still much to be learned about building good systems that support people's natural behavior of working in collaboration. The present chapter provided an overview of the past and the current notions, practices, and systems to support collaborative information behavior (CIB). The focus of our discussion here was the design aspect of CIB systems. The lessons from various design principles and system implementations can be summarized as the following.

1. It is very critical to understand certain fundamental issues of the target domain for designing a CIB system. Often, a successful CIB system is built around already existing systems and practices, providing additional features to support group-work.
2. A good CIB system design should aim for a simple, intuitive, and flexible interface. It should enable the developers to implement a system that works around the way its users work, rather than imposing a rigid structure onto them.
3. Control, communication, and awareness are essential to any good CIB system.
4. CIB systems induce additional cognitive load, sometimes referred to as the collaborative load, and system designers should try to minimize it. One way of doing this is by designing the system interface that is very familiar to the users and letting them gradually adopt the new features.
5. As Grudin (1994) noted, certain issues of working in collaboration are beyond the reach of a developer. For instance, a system cannot make two users cooperate with each other if they do not want to. However, a well-designed system should encourage and support any possible collaboration – planned or impromptu – among its users.

ACKNOWLEDGMENT

The work reported here is supported by NSF grant # IIS 0812363.

REFERENCES

Amershi, S., & Morris, M. R. (2008, April 5-10). CoSearch: a system for co-located collaborative Web search. In *Proceedings of SIGCHI Conference on Human Factors in Computing Systems* (pp. 1647-1656). Florence, Italy.

Austin, A. E., & Baldwin, R. G. (1991). *Faculty collaboration: Enhancing the quality of scholarship and teaching*. San Francisco: Jossey-Bass.

Baecker, R. M. (1995). *Readings in Human-Computer Interaction: Towards the Year 2000*. San Francisco: Morgan Kaufmann.

Blackwell, A. F., Stringer, M., Toye, E. F., & Rode, J. A. (2004). Tangible interface for collaborative information retrieval. In *Proceedings of SIGCHI Conference on Human Factors in Computing Systems* Vienna, Austria (pp. 1473-1476).

Blake, C., & Pratt, W. (2006). Collaborative information synthesis: a model of information behaviors of scientists in medicine and public health. *Journal of the American Society for Information Science and Technology, 57*(13), 1740–1749. doi:10.1002/asi.20487

Chrislip, D. D., & Larson, C. E. (1994). *Collaborative leadership: How citizens and civic leaders can make a difference*. San Francisco: Jossey-Bass.

Denning, P. J., & Yaholkovsky, P. (2008, April). Getting to We. *Communications of the ACM, 51*(4), 19–24. doi:10.1145/1330311.1330316

Donath, J. S., & Robertson, N. (1994, May 25-27). The sociable web. In *Proceedings of WWW Conference*. Geneva, Switzerland: CERN.

Dourish, P., & Bellotti, V. (1992). Awareness and coordination in shared workspaces. In *Proceedings of ACM Computer-Supported Cooperative Work (CSCW)* (pp. 107-114). Toronto, Ontario.

Evans, B. M., & Chi, E. H. (2008, June 20). Towards a model of understanding social search. In *Proceedings of IEEE/ACM JCDL 2008 Collaborative Exploratory Search*, Pittsburgh, PA. Retrieved from http://workshops.fxpal.com/jcdl2008/submissions/tmpDE.pdf

Farooq, U., Ganoe, C. H., Carroll, J. M., & Giles, C. L. (2009). Designing for e-science: Requirements gathering for collaboration in CiteSeer. *International Journal of Human-Computer Studies*, *67*, 297–312. doi:10.1016/j.ijhcs.2007.10.005

Fidel, R., Bruce, H., Pejtersen, A. M., Dumais, S. T., Grudin, J., & Poltrock, S. (2000). Collaborative Information Retrieval (CIR). *The New Review of Information Behaviour Research*, *1*, 235–247.

Fidel, R., Pejtersen, A. M., Cleal, B., & Bruce, H. (2004). A multidimensional approach to the study of human-information interaction: A case study of collaborative information retrieval. *Journal of the American Society for Information Science and Technology*, *55*(11), 939–953. doi:10.1002/asi.20041

Foster, J. (2006). Collaborative information seeking and retrieval. [ARIST]. *Annual Review of Information Science & Technology*, *40*, 329–356. doi:10.1002/aris.1440400115

Fu, X., Kelly, D., & Shah, C. (2007, July 23-27,). Using collaborative queries to improve retrieval for difficult topics. In *Proceedings of ACM SIGIR*, Amsterdam, The Netherlands (pp. 879-880).

Gerosa, L., Giordani, A., Ronchetti, M., Soller, A., & Stevens, R. (2004, October 6-9). Symmetric synchronous collaborative navigation. In *Proceedings of the 2004 IADIS International WWW/Internet Conference*, Madrid, Spain (pp. 1-7).

Golovchinsky, G., Pickens, J., & Back, M. (2008, June 20). A taxonomy of collaboration in online information seeking. In *Proceedings of IEEE/ACM JCDL 2008 Collaborative Exploratory Search*, Pittsburgh, PA.

Gray, B. (1989). *Collaborating: Finding common ground for multiparty problems*. San Francisco: Jossey-Bass.

Grudin, J. (1994, January). Groupware and social dynamics: eight challenges for developers. *Communications of the ACM*, *37*(1), 92–105. doi:10.1145/175222.175230

Han, R., Perret, V., & Naghshineh, M. (2000). WebSplitter: A Unified XML Framework for Multi-Device Collaborative Web Browsing. In *Proceedings of ACM Computer-Supported Cooperative Work (CSCW)*, Philadelphia, Pennsylvania, USA (pp. 221-230).

Hansen, P., & Jarvelin, K. (2005). Collaborative information retrieval in an information-intensive domain. *Information Processing & Management*, *41*, 1101–1119. doi:10.1016/j.ipm.2004.04.016

Hertzum, M. (2008). Collaborative information seeking: The combined activity of information seeking and collaborative grounding. *Information Processing & Management*, *44*, 957–962. doi:10.1016/j.ipm.2007.03.007

Liechti, O., & Sumi, Y. (2002). Awareness and the WWW. *International Journal of Human-Computer Studies*, *56*(1), 1–5. doi:10.1006/ijhc.2001.0512

London, S. (1995, November). *Collaboration and community*. Retrieved April 9, 2008, from http://scottlondon.com/reports/ppcc.html

Maekawa, T., Hara, T., & Nishio, S. (2006). A collaborative web browsing system for multiple mobile users. In *Proceedings of IEEE Conference on Pervasive Computing and Communications (PERCOM)*, Pisa, Italy.

Malone, T. W. (1988, February). *What is coordination theory?* (Tech. Rep. No. SSM WP # 2051-88). Boston, MA: Massachusetts Institute of Technology.

Malone, T. W., Grant, K. R., Turbak, F. A., Brobst, S. S., & Cohen, M. D. (1987). Intelligent information sharing systems. *Communications of the ACM, 30*(5), 390–402. doi:10.1145/22899.22903

Morris, M. R. (2008, April 5-10,). A survey of collaborative web search practices. In *Proceedings of ACM SIGCHI Conference on Human Factors in Computing Systems,* Florence, Italy (pp. 1657-1660).

Morris, M. R., & Horvitz, E. (2007, October 7-10). SearchTogether: An Interface for Collaborative Web Search. In *ACM Symposium on User Interface Software and Technology (UIST),* Newport, RI (pp. 3-12).

Morris, M. R., Paepcke, A., & Winograd, T. (2006). TeamSearch: Comparing Techniques for Co-Present Collaborative Search of Digital Media. In *First IEEE International Workshop on Horizontal Interactive Human-Computer Systems (TABLETOP '06),* Adelaide, South Australia (pp. 97-104).

Olson, G. M., Olson, J. S., Carter, M. R., & Storrosten, M. (1992, February). Small group design meetings: An analysis of collaboration. *Human-Computer Interaction, 7*(4), 347–374. doi:10.1207/s15327051hci0704_1

Olson, J. S., Olson, G. M., Storrøsten, M., & Carter, M. (1993, October). Groupwork close up: a comparison of the group design process with and without a simple group editor. *ACM Transactions on Information Systems, 11*(4), 321–348. doi:10.1145/159764.159763

Pickens, J., & Golovchinsky, G. (2007, October 23). Collaborative Exploratory Search. In *Proceedings of Workshop on Human-Computer Interaction and Information Retrieval* (pp. 21-22). Cambridge, MA: MIT CSAIL.

Reddy, M. C., & Jansen, B. J. (2008). A model for understanding collaborative information behavior in context: a study of two healthcare teams. *Information Processing & Management, 44*(1), 256–273. doi:10.1016/j.ipm.2006.12.010

Roberts, N. C., & Bradley, R. T. (1991, June). Stakeholder collaboration and innovation: a study of public policy initiation at the state level. *The Journal of Applied Behavioral Science, 27*(2), 209. doi:10.1177/0021886391272004

Rodden, T. (1991). A Survey of CSCW Systems. *Interacting with Computers, 3*(3), 319–353. doi:10.1016/0953-5438(91)90020-3

Rodden, T., & Blair, G. (1991, September 25-27). CSCW and distributed systems: the problem of control. In *Proceedings of ECSCW,* Amsterdam, The Netherlands (pp. 49—64).

Rutgers. (2009). *Rutgers DISCIPLE project.* Retrieved March 7, 2009, from http://www.caip.rutgers.edu/disciple

Shah, C. (2008, June 20). Toward Collaborative Information Seeking (CIS). In *Proceedings of JCDL 2008 Collaborative Exploratory Search,* Pittsburgh, PA. Available from http://workshops.fxpal.com/jcdl2008/submissions/tmpE1.pdf

Shah, C. (2009, May 10). Lessons and Challenges for Collaborative Information Seeking (CIS) Systems Developers. In *GROUP 2009 Workshop on Collaborative Information Behavior,* Sanibel Island, Florida. Available from http://www.personal.psu.edu/sap246/Shah_CIB_Workshop.pdf.

Shah, C., Marchionini, G., & Kelly, D. (2009, April 4-9). Learning design principles for a collaborative information seeking system. In *Proceedings of ACM SIGCHI Conference on Human Factors in Computing Systems,* Boston, MA.

Smeaton, A. F., Lee, H., Foley, C., & Givney, S. M. (2006). Collaborative video searching on a tabletop. *Multimedia Systems Journal, 12*(4), 375–391. doi:10.1007/s00530-006-0064-7

Sonnenwald, D. H. (1996, July). Communication roles that support collaboration during the design process. *Design Studies, 17*(3), 277–301. doi:10.1016/0142-694X(96)00002-6

Surowiecki, J. (2004). *Wisdom of crowds: Why the many are smarter than the few and how collective wisdom shapes business, economies, societies and nations*. New York: Doubleday Publishing.

Talja, S., & Hansen, P. (2006). Information sharing. In Spink, A., & Cole, C. (Eds.), *New Directions in Human Information Behavior* (pp. 113–134). New York: Springer. doi:10.1007/1-4020-3670-1_7

Twidale, M. B., & Nichols, D. M. (1996). Collaborative browsing and visualisation of the search process. In *Proceedings of Aslib* (Vol. 48, p. 177-182). Available from http://www.comp.lancs.ac.uk/computing/research/cseg/projects/ariadne/docs/elvira96.html

Twidale, M. B., Nichols, D. M., & Paice, C. D. (1995). Supporting collaborative learning during information searching. In *Proceedings of Computer Supported Collaborative Learning* (pp. 367–374). Bloomington, Indiana: CSCL.

Wilbur, S. B., & Young, R. E. (1988, April 20-22). The COSMOS project: a multi-disciplinary approach to design of computer supported group working. In R. Speth (Ed.), *EUTECO 88: Research into Networks and Distributed Applications*. Vienna, Austria.

ENDNOTES

[1] I-Spy is now converted to HeyStaks project (http://www.heystaks.com)

[2] http://www.adobe.com/products/acrobat-connect/

[3] In Latin, *Coagmento* means working or joining together. It is available from http://www.coagmento.org

Section 3
Language and Communication in Collaborative Information Behavior

Chapter 10

It Was Only Natural:
A Cross–Disciplinary Approach to a CMC Study

Elizabeth Meyers Hendrickson
The University of Tennessee – Knoxville, USA

ABSTRACT

This chapter describes the cross-disciplinary conceptual frameworks used to examine a popular American entertainment website that employs a virtual newsroom utilizing instant messaging as its primary means of communication. This computer-mediated communication reconfigures the standard place-based newsroom arrangements and significantly influences the group's organizational dynamics and culture. Because of the distinctive content and unconventional organizational structure of this site, no single theoretical perspective can be applied to its organizational context and content. Therefore a combination of organization theory (Schein, 2004), and newsroom sociology theoretical frameworks articulates an emerging dynamic represented by such a medium's evolution from hierarchical to networked organization. This chapter exemplifies the potential for new media researchers to adopt a cross-disciplinary approach to their analysis. As old models for understanding media cease to support the complex structures of new organizations we must look to other frameworks for additional guidance.

INTRODUCTION

This chapter describes the cross-disciplinary conceptual frameworks used to examine a popular American entertainment website that employs a virtual newsroom and instant messaging as its primary means of communication. This research is derived from a case study of the website *Je-zebel.com* which considered how organizational structure and routines shaped the site's media product. This case study initially posed three central questions. What effect do personal values and professional roles and ethical norms play at the individual level? What news values, sources of routines and routine channels are utilized within the organization?, How does instant messaging affect communication and organization dynamics? In addition, this research presented

DOI: 10.4018/978-1-61520-797-8.ch010

three assumptions. Despite employing new technology, many conventional elements of media production routines, such as accountability and deadlines, remain intact; a virtual newsroom will utilize a more lateral power configuration, rather than a hierarchical organizational structure, and; because instant messaging is a more informal mode of communication than face-to-face, email or telephone interaction, the culture will promote a sense of creativity and community.

As background to *Jezebel*'s operations, the site's content is written by five editors and helmed by a managing editor (also called a site lead), and consists of original content that links to stories culled from the online versions of conventional news sources, such as *The New York Times, The New York Post,* and *Glamour* magazine.

Each editor is responsible for six to ten posts per day and the site lead, Anna, assigns and edits each post and controls the site activity (by making content "live"). The site's parent corporation, Gawker Media, monitors the site's traffic by tracking the page views for each linked post and rewards editors who exceed an individual page view goal with quarterly bonuses to their salary.

What makes this site exemplary is its use of instant messaging (IM) as the primary method of communication. Taken as a whole, the instant messages exchanged between Anna and the different editors are inconspicuously extremely nuanced, not because of their exceptional prose or complex writing style, but because they contain so many dialogues. Informal chitchats folded into editing directions, gossip about other sites coupled with story assignments: all of it together, exchanged rapidly and without florid elaboration. These instant messages are a crucial part of the culture, in that they are the main dialogue of the workers. The exchanges are processed in syncopation with editors while they cultivate information, write and edit. The following excerpts from their IM conversations illustrate this multi-faceted dialogue. These excerpts are categorized here utilizing four thematic concepts: friendly banter, editing copy, assigning stories, and complaints about other editors:

Figure 1. A glimpse of the Jezebel homepage (6/12/09)

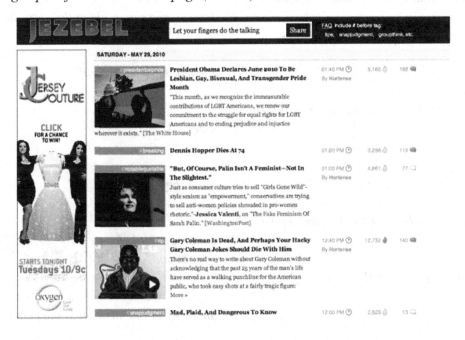

Figure 2. Gawker Media's sitetracker illustrating Jezebel's pageviews (6/12/09)

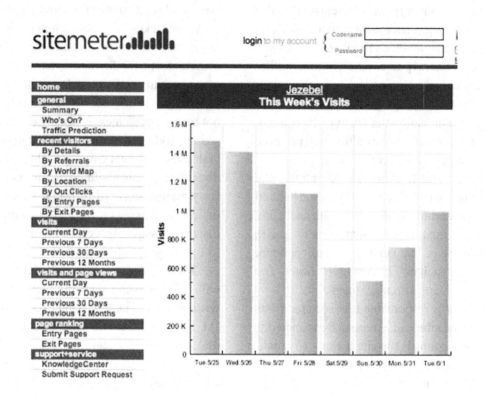

Friendly Banter

Jennifer: pencil sharpener ql [Quick Link] is done

Anna: ok

Jessica: btw, if you know anyone who wants a kitten

Anna: aw

Jessica: mike's brother's gf has four free kitties

Jessica: looking for a home!

Anna: what do they look like?

Jessica: she sent a pic of the mom, hold on

Jessica: kitty pic is sent!

Anna: ok!

Anna: hey btw

Anna: go look for a post we did on an axe "mousepad"

Anna: we could mention in the pencil QL

Jessica: oh cool

Anna: i just tweaked the item

Anna: if you can't find the axe thing let me know

Anna: i'll look too

Anna: i found it

9:20 AM

Jessica: ok, ql is fixed

Anna: ok

Anna: dude

Anna: those kittens!

Jessica: i know

Anna: so cute!·

Editing Copy

Anna: lets say we'll do best/worst comments at 4:45

Dodai: cool

Anna: is your Celebritease done?

Dodai: yep

Anna: ok thanks

Dodai: ok

Anna: i want you to look at what i did to celeb-riteasequick preview it

Dodai: sure

Anna: where do you get the little dot from?

Dodai: just a bullet

Anna: option 8

Dodai: word

Anna: and then just put all links at end in one big bracket

Dodai: ok cool

Assigning Stories

Jennifer: hey there –

Anna: hi

Jennifer: i don't know if you would want something like this in Morning Crap? if not, as a ql? marie osmond is doing a line of dolls for her collection based on herself and her costumes from dancing with the stars. there are images. they scare me.

Anna: yeah lets do that as a QL later

Jennifer: 'ok great

Anna: i think suri cruise should be lead CD item maybe, folllowed by WWD memo pad quotes from marc Jacobs

Jennifer: yes yes!!!

Jennifer: i cannot believe that child has louboutins

Jennifer: that is so unacceptable

Complaints About Other Editors

*Jennifer: Mo is b****ing to me about faran*

Jennifer: faran is INSANE

*Anna: what do u mean "b****ing"*

Jennifer: and i don't think any of us need to hear it from her

Jennifer: like, that faran emails Mo all the time with "notes" on CD

Jennifer: and says that whenever i leak to sassy-bella faran emails Mo telling her

Jennifer: its a bad source

Jennifer: and so Mo was like, when you link to them, i hear about it from faran...

Jennifer: and i was like, faran ain't our boss

Anna: just ignore her

Anna: ill have a talk with her later about it

Jennifer: and i just don't think faran's whims should be dictacting how we run our site

Both the interviews with *Jezebel*'s editors, and the communication literature (citations?) often refer to computer-mediated communication (CMC) as being a double-edged sword. While methods such as IM boast benefits such as efficiency and directedness, they also possess more challenging characteristics, such as the misinterpretation of information. Anna articulated this dichotomy in her interview, saying:

The pros are that it's instantaneous and it's in writing. The cons are they misinterpret what I say. So on the one hand, they can misconstrue tone and intent, but they're not going to misconstrue the content of what you're saying. So if you say, 'I want you to do this,' they can't say "I didn't understand what you meant,' because you said, 'I want you to…' They might think that I said it in a bitchy way when I just said it in a busy way. But it just really depends on how busy I am, because if I have something difficult to say, like, 'I'm not going to put this post up,' or like, 'I have a problem with it and will you please redo it,' if I have the time I might massage it by saying, 'You know, I love this idea,' and I'll qualify it and I'll be nice and then I'll get into the good news/bad news. If I'm too busy I'll just be the bad news though.

While most editors claim that they try not to take terse instant messages personally, all admit this can be difficult to do. Dodai provides a scenario that illustrates the situation from the editor's perspective:

If I mess something up and she was like, 'You have to fix that,' or something, and then none of us said anything and it was just like silence, so I was under the impression that she was pissed at me. It may or may not have been true, but because you don't see their face and there's no emotion in the thing, just like, 'You have to fix that.' So then I try to fix it. And I'm like, 'I wonder if she's mad.' And then I'm like, 'she's probably moved on to something else.' I try to convince myself. But yeah, I don't know…it's hard to tell.

Although I am a mass communication researcher this, by media standards, unconventional communication system inspired me to extend my theoretical schema beyond conventional mass communication constructs which have primarily studied place-based organizations use of CMC (Singer, 1996; Singer, Tharp & Haruta, 2001). It was my opinion that different times called for different measures. In this case, a cross-disciplinary approach seemed most suitable. Because of the diverse content and unconventional organizational structure of the site, no single theoretical perspective offered a way of understanding its organizational context and content. Therefore, this study employed a combination of organizational theory, specifically Schein (2004), and newsroom sociology frameworks. This theoretical arrangement, while unconventional from a mass com-

munication approach, permitted a more holistic perspective of the organization. Organizational theory encouraged a nuanced view of the site's workplace culture and helped unveil the basic assumptions that drive these dynamics to emerge. In addition, this framework provided the tools to individually examine the collaborative layers of media workers. The newsroom sociology frameworks, culled from mass communication literature, were compared with findings derived from an organizational analysis. The union of this information created a fertile ground for understanding additional ramifications, such as adaptability, economics and personal economy. The objective of this chapter is to thus illustrate how a cross-disciplinary approach of an emerging collaborative environment might be examined utilizing diverse theory-in-practice.

CONVERGENCE OF THEORETICAL FRAMEWORKS

Organization Theory

This initial research referred to two established dimensions of organization theory, the clinical and interpretive paradigms, to examine the organizational culture and leadership roles in an organization (Denison, 1996). This model, examined by Schein (2004), contextualizes occupational cultures from the individual and social levels that shape an organization and its decision-making processes. The framework places importance on both subjective and objective data so that observers can understand how a culture performs in its environment. The validity can be located within the narrative data.

Culture, as defined by Schein (2004) is a dynamic and evolving phenomenon that is continually created by our communications with other people. In the case of this research, we can comprehend an organization as a network, composed of many parts unified under a governing culture.

Our behavior is limited by a set of rules, norms, routines and structure. Leadership plays an integral role in both organizational culture formation and maintenance (Schein, 2004). The culture of any group is difficult to change because people prefer stability to instability, and a stable culture offers predictability and coherence (Schein, 2004). This consistency offers group members self-esteem and connectedness with others, thus helping to satisfy their ego ideal, or feeling of self at their future best (Stapley, 1996; Diamond & Allcorn, 2003). In addition, culture is omnipresent in that every facet of an organization is influenced by how the group/individual behaves towards the organization's internal operations, different environments and primary tasks (Schein, 2004). Individuals cultivate internalized knowledge that is then contrasted with data in their environment. Consequently we employ beneath-the-surface processes such as conflict, boundaries, defense mechanisms, and creativity to help us cope with our feelings and thoughts (Stapley, 1996). Similarly, when we come into relationships with other individuals, we may experience inner dynamics involving power and authority, relatedness and trust (Stapley, 2006). When considering the group or organization, we might not perceive it as a separate entity, but as an organism utilizing a group mind, where the group-as-a-whole exhibits defenses against anxiety as well as basic assumption behavior (Stacey, 1996; Stapley, 1996).

An organization's culture is disseminated through a process of socialization, whereby a new member interprets the operating norms and assumptions of the group (Schein, 2004). While an organization's stated mission or operating espoused values might be the initial method in which a new employee can gauge how to act, the group's operating basic assumptions, or tacit behavior, drives the culture. Therefore, one learns the organizational culture's assumptions when old members of the group provide feedback to new members as the new members experiment with various types of behavior (Schein, 2004).

This study also examined the evolution of culture within a new organization and utilized the idea of a group as a microcosm of an organizational system. Significant to this research is Schein's (2004) description of the four stages of shared underlying assumptions that exist within group evolution: group formation, group building, group work and group maturity. These stages are dynamic, in that groups can move from one to another as appropriate. Each stage is divided into a set of dominant assumptions and socioemotional focus. The socioemotional focus, or group purpose, is shaped by the predominant assumptions. With group formation, the dominant assumption is that of dependence on the leader and the socioemotional focus is one of self-orientation, or issues of power and influence, inclusion, identity and role, and acceptance and intimacy (Schein, 2004). Considering group building, the dominant assumption emphasizes fusion between group member and the socioemotional focus is that of the group as idealized object, such as conformity and harmony. Group work's dominant assumption is that of their job, where individuals feel acceptance toward one another, and the socioemotional focus on the group mission and tasks, such as teamwork and accomplishment. With group maturity, the dominant assumption is experience, where the group feels employees are correct if they have been successful. The socioemotional focus is thus one of group survival and comfort, where the culture and group are defended and individual difference are perceived as dangerous (Schein, 2004).

The role of the leader is one of the most significant aspects of workplace culture. Schein (2004) writes that leaders differ from administrators and managers in that leaders exhibit a concern for the organization's culture. Furthermore, a leader's impact on the formation of an organization's culture in a new group is considerable in the beginning, in that they impress their values, beliefs and assumptions on the group in the beginning (Schein, 2004). If the leader of a new organization is also the founder, they might also decide the fundamental mission and context of the group, in addition to hiring the group members (Schein, 2004). While the leaders certainly have an impact on the initial group culture, their experience dealing with internal integration issues and external adaptation also affects the evolving ethos. Kets de Vries' (2001) research into leadership suggests that the most successful leaders are able to reconceptualize complex situations. As such, by adjusting what they see, an effective leader can alter how they perceive a situation (Kets de Vries, 2001). Much of this depends on the "emotional intelligence" (Kets de Vries, 2001, p. 5) of leaders or their ability to comprehend their own motivational drive as well as those of others. This intelligence might be learned by understanding the clinical paradigm, which holds that: 1) What you see isn't always what you get, 2) No matter how irrational human behavior seems, it has a rationale, and 3) We're all results of our past (Kets de Vries, 2001). Persons possessing emotional intelligence, which is learned through experience, will usually be more effective leaders (Kets de Vries, 2001). In addition to leaders, Kets de Vries (2001) examines the "clusters" (p. 144) of behavior patterns within key organization members. While these clusters may or may not mirror those of the organization's leader, they have a profound effect on the organizational culture. These behavioral patterns may be referred to as a "neurotic style" (p. 143), and include the suspicious (or paranoid), dramatic (want for grandiosity), detached (noninvolvement), compulsive (desire for control) and depressive (hopelessness and helplessness) styles. While some organizations display only elements of these styles, others may excessively adopt elements of particular behaviors, thus creating an organizational pathology (Kets de Vries, 2001).

The clinical and interpretive paradigms both utilize a psychological approach to understanding the individual and group notions of culture. However, it is also essential to employ multiple lenses to ensure a holistic understanding of this new media. Accordingly, a sociological perspective culled from mass communication adds to this analysis.

Newsroom Sociology and Routines

Shoemaker & Reese (1996) describe the interplay of routines and organizational structure with their model of the influences of hierarchical organization of news work; including five components ranging from micro to macro levels: individual, routines, organizational, extramedia and ideology. These components unify to form a complete interrelated media system. Much of the supporting mass communication literature is embedded within this illustration, and therefore it is imperative to recognize the different levels of the hierarchy from a theoretical perspective. The key components of the individual level include the newsroom socialization process, personal values, a journalist's personal background and their professional roles and ethics. Breed (1955) wrote about the socialization process, which includes both technical and ethical socialization. In interviewing legions of journalists about this process, he found that many of them ascribed socialization to "learning by osmosis," (p. 182) or something that is not specifically stated within the organization's text, but acquired through watching and learning. Personal values have an indirect affect on the news process and many scholars claim that their impact is greatly diminished by routines and organizational constraints (Shoemaker & Reese, 1996; Tuchman, 1978). Regardless, Gans (1978) found that the prevalence of "motherhood values" (ie: family, love, friendship, economic prosperity) that are often found within society are also held by journalists. Factors that play a more significant role are professional roles and codes of ethics. These elements are inherent to most conventional media professions and are often acquired via the socialization process. Specifically the code of ethics, which is usually a written set of regulations (many journalists utilize the Society of Professional Journalists' code), gives journalists guidelines for their actions both inside and outside the newsroom.

Routines are an established and defined set of procedures that one follows within an organization that together make up the mechanics of news work. Some of the key components found within this body of literature are gatekeeping, objectivity, sources of routines and routine channels. White (1950) initially defined gatekeeping as a person's in and out decisions in terms of what is news. However, his study must be recognized as an individual operating within a formal structure, in that he ("Mr. Gates") made decisions based on the stories that had already passed through numerous gates before arriving at his desk (White, 1950). As such, Shoemaker & Reese (1996) cite that a gatekeeper's decisions are quite limited within an organizational structure.

Organizational level components consist of the hiring and firing of individuals, the tensions between levels of the organization and the established roles of journalists within the media system. The hiring and firing system allows an organization to exercise a sense of control within newsroom dynamics. By hiring persons who fit in with the already-established culture of the workplace environment, they are able to perpetuate a stable culture (Breed, 1955). Similarly by firing those who do not assimilate to the culture they can keep a cohesive environment. Within this layer one must also consider the inevitable tensions between different levels of the organization. A significant example is the relationship between the economic goals and the editorial goals of a news organization, both of which can positively and negatively influence the workplace environment (Steinem, 1994). When a media organization depends on advertisers to pay its bills, the editorial staff may feel its news values become threatened, which can create conflict between departments (Shoemaker & Reese, 1996). Progressive organizational leaders might utilize such tensions as an opportunity to foster editorial creativity, by opening the organization to potential learning and

change. For example, the editorial group might find ways to better understand and provide for their audience's wants and needs. However, less insightful leaders could react defensively to such organizational tensions by disregarding possible changes and further distancing staff members from new organizational possibilities.

Extramedia pertains to those dynamics that occur between the news workers and outside factors. Some of the most important extramedia interactions include those between the news worker and their sources, their advertisers and their competition. Sources can refer to anyone providing the journalist with valuable information. Oftentimes, sources include public relations workers, or what Schudson (2003) refers to as "para-journalists." These are individuals versed in the news process who offer information to journalists that will benefit that agent's client. Gandy (1982) refers to the interaction between journalist and source as an "information subsidy" where one party often the journalist wishes to gain the information from the source but must pay a price, referred to as the subsidy, for that information. That price might pertain to how and where that information is used. For example in the realm of celebrity journalism Gamson (1994) describes this exchange as the "consciousness industry," whereby the system of cultural controls consists of a give-and-take between suppliers (para-journalists) and journalists.

Finally, the ideological level pertains to journalists' power to define a situation. Gans (1979) writes that journalists share the ideological values of responsible journalism, private ownership and liberal democracy. Accordingly, these values are filtered down through symbolic content to society. Cultural studies of hegemony and Marxist theories of economy often criticize the ideological implications of mass media, saying it in effect perpetuates the status quo. Similarly, scholars studying celebrity media claim that another ideological function of celebrity journalism is to perpetuate a belief in the democracy of fame or that anyone can be famous (Marshall, 1997; Giles, 2002).

These notions herald back to the individualism embedded within our society as well as to our capitalistic ambitions and therefore support a Marxist critique.

The utilization of these two diverse theoretical frameworks, organization theory and newsroom sociology, allowed for both a psychological and sociological perspective on the virtual organization and its communication processes. Previous studies relating to separate conceptual spheres assisted in understanding the application of these frameworks to CMC technology.

STUDIES OF TECHNOLOGY AND NEWSROOM SOCIOLOGY

New Media Organizations

Media work can be considered as one of society's most adaptable industries in that media producers have the ability to immediately respond to consumer demands (Deuze, 2007). Theoretically this flexibility allows media organizations to adopt new ways of media production and content formats to increase audience size. While some of the more conventional media systems still find themselves mired in bureaucratic constraints, other more contemporary organizations are discovering virtually endless production options. Many of these alternatives involve a less formal structuring and a reconfiguration of the conventional hierarchical system which often results in a complex seemingly disconnected system. As a result the most significant consideration for these innovative organizations becomes how to unite all the parts into a cohesive adaptable whole. Many businesses decide to adopt unconventional communication methods in an effort to connect these components. When paired with alternative workplace structures this technology creates unique new media interpersonal communications. This research considers elements of a new workplace structure that employs IM and virtual teamwork

and examines what happens to communication when the two components are linked.

Instant Messaging

Presence and instant messaging applications (PIM) can be described as text-based near-synchronous communication that is computer-mediated (Ter Hofte, Multer & Verwijs, 2006). This technology is utilized in over 70 percent of all companies today (Computer Bulletin, 2005). The various PIM vehicles, which include AOL instant messenger (AIM), Yahoo! Messenger and MSN Messenger, operate to link groups of individual Internet users to virtual chat rooms, so that they may have a computer-mediated conversation in real time (Ter Hofte, Multer & Verwijs, 2006). Because IM communication is computer-mediated no verbal-cues are present although emoticons are often utilized (Ter Hofte, Multer & Verwijs, 2006). In addition, the technology is transparent in that presence information of IM group members is shared. Kim, Kim, Park & Rice (2005) examined the use of CMC in a Korean high-tech organization and established that CMC serves a different communication goal than that of telephone or face-to-face contact. Their study illustrates that IM is used to monitor the accessibility of others, discuss issues, schedule a face-to-face meeting and "check in" without the obligation of urgent response (Kim, Kim, Park & Rice, 2005). The researchers (Kim, Kim, Park & Rice, 2005) also found that unlike mobile phones or face-to-face contact IM users do not use the technology to foster relationships but use the technology as a group-talking tool (Kim, Kim, Park & Rice, 2005). In addition they claim that younger people tend to adopt IM more readily than adults who often chose to communicate via email instead (Kim, Kim, Park & Rice, 2005). Correspondingly, Zack (1994) cites that electronic communication aids in organizing tasks, while face-to-face communication allows for more problem-solving needs. Other research (Strom, 2006) maintains that more companies are choosing to implement IM as a way of improving response times between employees (Strom, 2006) and some, such as IBM, have virtually phased out voice mails entirely (citation?). As such, many companies are choosing to implement the messaging software to enhance collaboration through faster communication.

Virtual Teams

The concept of virtual teamwork considers a group of individuals who collaborate with each other despite being separated by time space and organizational obstacles (Johnson, Heimann & O'Neill, 2001). This research considers the telecommuters who become part of a virtual team working with others on a collaborative project outside a shared office environment. The US Census Bureau calculates the number of individuals with this arrangement to be 4.5 million in 2003 (Blanton, 2005). The most suitable jobs for telecommuting are those in the white-collar sector that can be accomplished outside of the traditional office environment; such as consulting research analysis and writing (Ahmadi, Helms & Ross, 2000). Telecommunicating benefits include those at the employee level (they can spend more time with their family), the organizational level (the company can cut costs and also retain employees who might otherwise leave the organization) and the community level (telecommuting reduces traffic congestion and pollution) (Ahmadi, Helms & Ross, 2000). Research into the employee level is the most common. Studies illustrate that despite the espoused benefits of a virtual arrangement, one of the most frequent risks is an overlapping of work and private life which often results in a telecommuter working more hours than their coworkers (Vos & van der Voordt, 2001). In order to be productive the telecommuter must receive pointed feedback, guidance, and instruction, in the form of supervision (Ahmadi, Helms and Ross, 2000). Research shows that for those involved in a virtual team, it is essential that the

individual exercise self-discipline, is accountable, is flexible and is able to trust other virtual team members (Johnson, Heimann & O'Neill, 2001). When virtual team members are able to demonstrate these four qualities their alliance increases a sense of organizational achievement and thus workplace fulfillment. A study of virtual workplace employees in Germany found that these workers exhibit a higher level of work satisfaction than those of their traditional workplace counterparts (Akkirman, Harris & Drew, 2005). The authors concluded that this satisfaction runs parallel to a well-organized virtual office plan, where organizational climate and integration is sufficiently communicated. By offering culture training, technical training and social support to employees, a company employing virtual team members might better equip itself to take on this new workplace configuration (Akkirman and Harris, 2005).

New Media Interpersonal Communication

As previously stated virtual teamwork while often heralded as a logical step for corporations is not without its drawbacks. Most of these criticisms involve the issue of collaborative communication. Some of the most prevalent grievances include difficulties getting in touch with team members, a lack of mutual project visibility, and the constraints of CMC; much of it due to an inability to accurately determine the meaning of text-based messages (Johnson, Heimann & O'Neill, 2001). Because virtual teams often employ persons living in different time zones, individual accessibility can certainly pose problems. Time lapses between computer-mediated communications can negatively affect collaborative endeavors and thus perpetuate inter-organizational stress. In addition, the element of ineffectual project visibility can pose great detriments to joint efforts, as previously examined. But perhaps the most fundamental challenge involves the potential constraints of

CMC, considering all other inter-organizational dynamics are derived from this interaction.

The challenges to the virtual workplace often involve building trust among employees, which is difficult without effective communication. Because interpersonal communications in virtual teams lack conventional communication methods such as head nodding, informal openings and closings to conversations and turn taking, mediated communication may at times be problematic (Nardi, 2005). Accordingly, instant messaging utilizes what Clark (1992) describes as the theory of common ground. This concept refers to the established shared knowledge that group members communicate through each other's discourse, which conceivably improves through time as members increase their communication (Clark, 1992). Instant messaging implies a shared space and the sensation of affinity that accompanies it (Nardi, 2005). As such, virtual team members using IM may improve their social bonding by embedding informal conversations within formal discourse (Nardi, 2005). Quan-Haase, Cothrel and Wellman (2005) established the term "local virtualities" to explain physically restricted places where computer-mediated communication allows for the formation of intense collaborative networks. The researchers (Quan-Haase, Cothrel & Wellman, 2005) found that for organizations that perform work primarily online, IM is often carried out while multitasking other jobs. This, in addition to other factors, contributes to the formation of higher connectivity as well as to an increased sense of community within the organization (Quan-Haase, Cothrel & Wellman, 2005). But once more, trust remains a significant factor within this mediated communication. While Nardi (2005) concludes that such trust takes time and frequent contact between members, research demonstrates that online interpersonal trust between communication members increases when the partners establish both a supportive relationship and empathic accuracy with one another (Fen, Lazar & Preece, 2004). With empathetic accuracy, communication

partners are able to correctly infer the particular content of each other's feelings and thoughts (Fen, Lazar & Preece, 2004).

The last component of new media interpersonal communication to be addressed concerns that of leadership. Farmer (2005) refers to situational leadership to describe telecommuting, or in this case, virtual leadership. Leadership and management might be explained differently; as leadership refers to the influence a person has on employees to inspire or motivate them to accomplish organizational goals (Gibson, Blackwell, Dominicus & Demerath, 2002), while management deals with leadership and routine events (Farmer, 2005). Situational leadership forms when a leader pairs the developmental stage of the employee with a particular leadership style (Farmer, 2005). Consequently, the situational leader does not apply one leadership style to all employees, but different leadership approaches according to the competence, performance and dedication of the employee. For example, an employee exhibiting high supporting behavior and high directive might only need coaching from the leader, while an employee showing low supporting behavior and high directive might warrant more direction from the leader (Farmer, 2005). In the case of online organizations, a leader can monitor these levels by both interpersonal communication within the group and individual output.

Newsroom Sociology

Studies in newsroom sociology often follow the research of Breed (1955), Gans (1979) and Tuchman (1978). In addition, much of this literature examines one or more of the different levels of hierarchical news work (individual, routines, organization, extramedia and ideology) as established by Shoemaker and Reese (1996). Research considering the individual level encompasses studies of both magazine and newspaper organizations. Dellinger's (2004) comparative case study of the organizational cultures of a pornographic magazine's and a feminist magazine's accounting departments examined how male employees combine personal values and professional roles when negotiating masculinity. The researcher concluded these individual level components are in tension depending on how "safe" or "embattled" a workplace is (2004, p. 545). It follows therefore that, regardless of personal values, a successfully socialized employee will adjust their behavior according to the workplace environment. Shoemaker and Reese (1996) wrote about background considerations of journalists in newsrooms and found that the majority of these journalists were white men with a college education, either in journalism or liberal arts. In addition, Shoemaker and Reese (1996) cite that burnout rates are high among journalists because of low salaries, poor benefits and high stress. The researchers (Shoemaker & Reese, 1996) found that many journalists opt out of the news work by their mid-30s, with a majority of these numbers being women. In addition, the numbers of journalists who claim job satisfaction have been decreasing steadily since the mid-1970s. A more recent study, the 2002 American Journalist survey, found these statistics to have changed minimally, with 41 now being the median age of a journalist and the level of job satisfaction slightly higher (Poynteronline, 2003). Sigelman (1973) looked at the organizational processes of a newspaper to examine how an individual character's may affect bias in news. Similar to Breed (1950), Sigelman (1973) cites the socialization process and recruitment of employees who complement the professional roles and values of the organization as the backbone of any media organization's perception of objectivity. In other words, news management will often choose people who possess similar values (personal and professional) to those of the current employees so the newly-hired journalists can better mesh with their new organization culture.

Most research examining routines comes from studying newspaper and television organizations. Reisner (1992) analyzed conferences between newspaper editors who were deciding story newsworthiness and concluded that ongoing stories usually merit newspaper prominence. However, the researcher noted that oftentimes the editors also utilized this traditional news value rationalization as a means to mask their own ideologies. Similarly Sumpter (2000) conducted a case study of a large daily newspaper to examine the utilization of budget meetings as a vehicle for constructing newsworthiness. He found that editors often use these meetings to construct audience reactions to various story selections. Berkowitz (1992) observed a network television station and concluded that well-established routines such as story typification allow newsworkers to handle non-routine events, also dubbed a "what-a-story." Gaziano and Coulson (1988) considered organizational components such as newsroom management styles, to determine whether a democratic or authoritarian style influences a news employee's opinion of their jobs, newspapers, supervisors and readers. After surveying two newspapers, each operating under a different style, the researchers (Gaziano & Coulson, 1988) determined a democratic style improved the work environment because journalists' prefer participating in decision-making. However, regardless of leadership style, journalists reported a deficiency in communication between editors and reporters to be a larger organizational detriment (Gaziano & Coulson, 1988).

Ryan (2005) studied the extramedia level issue of editorial content and advertising by conducting a case study of MAMM magazine, a publication covering women's cancers. MAMM struggled to obtain advertising from companies without bowing to the advertisers' editorial demands, and ultimately the magazine folded. While many magazines participate in such negotiations with advertisers, other media vehicles resist. While Ryan's research primarily involves extramedia level decisions, ideological factors are certainly applicable as well.

Perhaps a more overt example of the ideological level is Martinez's (2004) case study of *Latina* magazine, which examined the role of marketing of ethnicity and popular culture. In her analysis,

Martinez (2004) interviewed the editorial staff of *Latina* and conducting a textual analysis of six years of *Latina* articles. The researcher concluded the magazine provides the Latina consumer "more ethnically relevant material than does the main-stream media" (Martinez, 2004). The publication thus functions to define a situation that might normally exist outside the realm of conventional media vehicles.

SIGNIFICANCE OF STUDY: ANALYSIS AND FINDINGS

The case study of *Jezebel* consisted of five weeks of 12-hour day observations of editors, each in their own apartment. While the intrusiveness of my approach could act as a limitation, it was my hope that my ten years experience working in enter-tainment journalism (and by proxy, non-academic observation/participation), might increase the trust of the editors and allow them to view me as a former journalist who is now interested in the workings of a new genre, rather than some strange interloper. In addition to observation, I collected data via in-depth interviews, company memos and copies of instant messages between editors. This material was analyzed and considered from the cross disciplinary approach. This study located four assumptions within the workplace culture of *Jezebel*: editors believed in the site's mission, they believed working from home was a positive aspect of work, they believed IM was the most effective way to communicate and they believed the page view bonus system did not influence the quality of their posts. In addition, the fieldwork illustrated the nature of the organization to reside within both formal and informal relationships between editors, relationships between editors and company, and relationships between editors and audience. These elements all contributed to a subsequent discus-sion of technology and place, and how authority, adaptability, business economics and personal economy entwine within a networked organization

such as this collaborative environment. It is my belief that these findings were achievable only by merging mass communication frameworks with other conceptual systems.

Mass communication theories pertaining to newsroom organizational behaviors have his-torically grounded their concepts in place-based settings. Scholars such as Breed, Tuchman and Shoemaker have undoubtedly influenced the way we understand media. However many of their constructs, conceptualized decades ago, are less applicable to the changing environment of today's media. While some of the more traditional news structures continue to employ a linear, hierarchi-cal organizational system with a well-preserved culture, those situations are becoming atypical as newsrooms adapt to the shifting marketplace by adopting convergent platforms. New media scholars such as Deuze (2007) recognize such an incompatibility of mass communication theory and convergence culture when noting, "Even though Tuchman's research has been repeated in other media institutions with similar results, it seems to fit rather awkwardly with the current dogma of flexible production, increasing precariousness of employment arrangements, a globally emerging convergence culture, and an all-consuming shift of responsibility toward the individual," (p. 86). Accordingly, the media's existing transforma-tion requires certain scholarly innovation. This research reflects such a theoretical shift. While I initially believed that organization theory and mass communications might hold equal explanatory power, the fieldwork and first phase of analysis indicated that an organization theory application more effectively examined the media system as a whole. By utilizing this approach, this study examined essential elements of culture produc-tion, such as content, connectivity, creativity and commerce (Deuze, 2007). The latter portion of analysis illustrated how these elements are embedded within the organizational dynamics and structure. However, there is still some value in locating components of this research within newsroom sociology despite the awkwardness of fit. By comparing aspects of this study to those found in previous mass communication research, we might gain insights that help us further distinguish this medium from its predecessors.

This study initially posed three central questions: What effect do personal values and professional roles and ethical norms play at the individual level? What news values, sources of routines and routine channels are utilized within the organization? And how does instant messaging affect communication and organization dynamics? Conventional newsroom sociology research (Shoemaker & Reese, 1996; Tuchman, 1978) holds that personal values indirectly affect the news process, but the influence is greatly reduced by routines and organizational constraints. In contrast, this research indicated that personal values are significant factors for media organizations such as Jezebel, which intentionally employs people who fit in with the already-established culture of the workplace environment and thus promotes a stable culture. Additionally, while mass communication literature supports mostly structured professional roles and clear ethical norms within conventional media industries, this research illustrated an organization that employs flexible professional roles and assumed ethical norms that are carried over from previous media experience.

This study also located the site's news values within standard representational media values, such as individualism, free enterprise, competition and materialism. While the website indeed emphasized these values, the context often employed an ironic manifestation. Instead of perpetuating the status quo, the content frequently utilized subjects such as celebrity or consumerism to question cultural assumptions perpetuated by other media outlets. In this way, the ideological function of the site presumably differed from most other mainstream media outlets. Another twist to conventional theory was the site's utilization of sources of routines and routine channels.

While mass communication research hold that news workers usually gather raw news via human channels, this is rarely the case with media such as *Jezebel*. Although the site occasionally employed a "tip" from a source, the main means of information gathering was RSS feeds, which provided a significant increase of incoming information when compared to conventional media using human sources and standard wire feeds. Indeed, this research represents a different notion of what might connote "sources" to begin with. The final portion of the analysis examined how instant messaging affected communication and organizational dynamics. While journalism literature has often studied face-to-face and even telephone interactions in the newsroom, very little has been done on an organization solely using CMC such as IM.

This research also presented three assumptions. Despite employing new technology, many conventional elements of media production routines, such as accountability and deadlines, remain intact; a virtual newsroom will utilize a more lateral power configuration, rather than a hierarchical organizational structure; and because instant messaging is a more informal mode of communication than face-to-face, email or telephone interaction, the culture will promote a sense of creativity and community. All these assumptions proved to be accurate to some degree. Jennifer's explanation of her workday personifies much of what encompasses these assumptions, saying:

This is probably the hardest I've ever worked, because you're always working when you have this kind of job. There's no walking away from it. And if you're not even technically working, you're still thinking, like, 'What is a story idea and how am I going to do it?' Or 'Why haven't I thought of another story? What am I going to do tomorrow?' The interesting thing about what we do is you wake up every morning and you're not really sure what you'll be doing. You get up and you pray and say, 'Okay, let there be something for me to write about today,' and you hold your breath and you go.

The issue of leadership proved to be the ultimate force driving the site, although it is somewhat veiled by informal communication structures. In such a flexible organizational structure, the leader is ultimately accountable for the site's operations. She chooses the employees according to fit and thus wagers that the worker will both adapt to the more flexible organizational structure and thrive creatively. Deuze (2007) writes that managers hiring new media workers should consider three elements, all previously examined within this research: prior trust of the manager (often done through networked association), the likely trust amongst employees (attuning chemistry), and the employee's reputation for minimal group conflict. In this case, Anna carefully hired editors who appeared to fit within the organizational culture. Comparable to Deuze's (2007) suggestions, this fit considered writing ability, personal dynamics and attitude. Her choices have proven to be judicious.

In addition, within the elements of *Jezebel*'s mission, organizational culture and virtual workplace, certain core characteristics remain unwavering under the site lead's direction. The component of mission is represented by the site's dominant assumption that editors are sincere with their work and duties. The overlapping elements of culture and virtual workplace are exemplified by the assumptions that editors can efficiently work from home using IM and that they, with one exception, abide by company policy. Consequently, the editors demonstrate an ability to negotiate the informal and formal systems to their advantage, which in turn perpetuates a feeling of both individual and group satisfaction. It is also a particular fit between employee and organizational culture that allows the site to successfully adapt to its environment. *Jezebel*'s cohesion as a group encourages the editors to collectively adjust to factors such as the evolving market, shifting audience and the site's strategic alliance with other organizational groups. Their unity allows them a sense of comfort within sometimes-unstable situations. For example, the editors can minimize their uncertainty with a shifting audience demographic by cultivating social capital with their commentators, which may promote a sense of confidence within group members. This workplace design could make sense for other media organizations, even beyond making money. So long as the organization's leader is clear in the group's mission, she can build a staff that both respects and is loyal to that goal. For instance, if an organization's mission is to turn out vast quantities of media product in the short term, there is a particular "type" that might be an ideal fit for this job. This "type" must be willing to put in physically demanding hours that will likely blur lines between private time and work time. If the mission is to do long-term, in-depth collaborative research/teamwork/etc., there might exist another "type" of fit, one who would glean command fewer physical and even psychological obstacles. Moreover, this structure could also benefit creative organizations that depend upon individual productivity as well as some collaborative work. To reach a high level of productivity that is consistent, the organization must institute a leader who exercises emotional intelligence. This leader must be able to navigate the relationships with people both "above" her and "below" her in whatever kind of hierarchy exists. In other words, she must be able to efficiently and effectively confer with all members of the organization, while utilizing all different forms of communication (face-to-face, phone, email, IM). While the main communicative tool may be CMC, she must be accomplished with all communication measures. This delicate balance also reveals the potential failure of this sort of enterprise. The three levels of the organization - front line, middle level and top-level employees – must all fit together. A breakdown within or between any of these levels could cause a collapse of the system. For instance, Deuze (2007) writes that most creative industry employees do not perceive management, business and commerce as entirely opposite to quality, culture or creativity. But if a front line employee, such as a writer, outwardly resists a manager's implementation of creative direction that might benefit the company's bottom line, the system becomes at risk. It therefore depends primarily on the middle level to resolve such a conflict. This could mean negotiating with the employee for a reconstructed fit or replacing that employee with someone who is better suited altogether. But even these negotiations must be articulated to the top-level employees to ensure cohesiveness.

Thus, the ultimate success of this enterprise depends on the group's leader. While the group's fluid dynamics stem from informal and formal structures, it is again the leader's responsibility to manage the balance of personalities, in addition to her normal task-related responsibilities. So while organizational structure or content ideas are important, perhaps the most critical decision top-level executives make is, who will be the most effective leader? Certainly, there will be scholars who are unconvinced by my cross-disciplinary approach, however, I believe the scope of evidence under analysis called for a framework, or rather frameworks that could holistically get to the essence of this culture.

NEW OPPORTUNITIES: A CALL FOR NEW DIRECTIONS

First and foremost, this chapter exemplifies the potential for new media researchers to adopt a cross-disciplinary approach to their analysis. As old models for understanding media cease to support the complex structures of new organizations, we must look to other frameworks for additional guidance. Accordingly, this research illustrates how being receptive to other means of data interpretation can lead to rich explanatory power. Other findings from this case study, many of which

are not explored within this chapter, propose that future research should examine the economic implications of new media organizations testing innovative ways of conducting media work. While some may believe news workers such as those employed by *Gawker Media* are in control of their work situations, others may conclude that the organization is taking unfair advantage of its employees by prioritizing output over personal health and wellbeing. How might these new organizational models have an effect on incoming generations of media workers and what could this mean for the industry as a whole?

Similarly, from a practical perspective, while the old media model is falling apart, it would be useful to understand what types of skills are necessary for young journalists entering this new world of media work. As frequently implied, this research indicates that a new employee must be willing to forgo a nine-to-five schedule in lieu of often-grueling work hours. Media reports (Richtel, 2008) of bloggers acquiring sometimes-deadly health problems due to time stress underscore the fact that this new world of media work is challenging to both the body and the mind. In addition to accepting such time commitments, a new journalist should have a functioning knowledge of progressive technology, although extensive technological experience is not a requirement. For example, many of the media workers in this research entered the workplace with only rudimentary knowledge of the technology and then became socialized to the mechanics of the job. What is mandatory, however, is a willingness to adapt to unconventional media making processes.

CONCLUSION

This chapter has attempted to describe the cross-disciplinary conceptual frameworks used to examine a popular American entertainment website that employs a virtual newsroom utilizing instant messaging as its primary means of communication. The research is derived from a case study that utilized a combination of organizational theory and newsroom sociology frameworks to consider how organizational structure and routines shape the media product. With the emerging technology and increasing collaborative environments, researchers will be continually confronted with a myriad of possible frameworks to utilize. With such opportunity can also come confusion, and it is my opinion that researchers in this arena exercise the intellectual freedom to choose a framework they feel best responds to the nature of phenomena being studied. In this case, I merged frameworks that captured elements of media production with organizational culture and leadership. Another researcher studying this topic might have chosen differently, and their analysis would have likely reflected a slightly different picture. However, given that any scholarly research places importance on both subjective and objective data, it is my belief that the overall representation of the site would remain consistent.

REFERENCES

Ahmadi, M., Helms, M., & Ross, T. (2000). Technological developments: Shaping the telecommuting work environment of the future. *Facilities, 18*(1/2), 83–89. doi:10.1108/02632770010312204

Akkirman, A., Harris, D., & Drew, L. (2005). Organizational communication satisfaction in the virtual workplace. *Journal of Management Development, 24*(5), 397–409. doi:10.1108/02621710510598427

Berkowitz, D. (1992). Non-routine news and newswork: Exploring a what-a-story. *The Journal of Communication, 42*(1), 82–93. doi:10.1111/j.1460-2466.1992.tb00770.x

Blanton, K. (2005, October 16). Home work. *The Boston Globe*. Retrieved October 8, 2007, from http://www.boston.com/news/globe

Breed, W. (1955). Social control in the newsroom. *Social Forces, 33*, 326–335. doi:10.2307/2573002

Clark, H. (1992). *Arenas of language use*. Chicago: University of Chicago Press.

Dellinger, K. (2004). Masculinities in safe and embattled organizations: Accounting for pornographic and feminist magazines. *Gender and Society, 18*(5), 545-566.Denison, D.R. (1996). What is the difference between organizational culture and organizational climate? A native's point of view on a decade of paradigm wars. *Academy of Management Review, 21*(3), 619–654.

Deuze, M. (2007). *Media work*. Cambridge: Polity.

Diamond, M., & Allcorn, S. (2003). The cornerstone of psychoanalytic organizational analysis: Psychological reality, transference and counter-transference in the workplace. *Human Relations, 56*(4), 491–514. doi:10.1177/0018726703056004005

Farmer, L. A. (2005). Situational leadership: A model for leading telecommuters. *Journal of Nursing Management, 13*, 483–189. doi:10.1111/j.1365-2934.2005.00573.x

Fen, J., Lazar, J., & Preece, J. (2004). Empathy and online interpersonal trust: A fragile relationship. *Behaviour & Information Technology, 23*(2), 97–106. doi:10.1080/01449290310001659240

Gamson (1994). *Claims to fame: Celebrity in Contemporary America*. Berkeley, CA: University of California Press.

Gandy, O. H. (1982). *Beyond agenda setting: Information subsidies and public policy*. Norwood, NJ: Ablex Publishing Company.

Gans, H. J. (1979). *Deciding what's news*. Evanston, IL: Northwestern University Press.

Gazanio, C., & Couson, D. C. (1988). Effect of newsroom management styles on journalists: A case study. *The Journalism Quarterly, 65*, 869–880.

Gibson, J., Blackwell, C., Dominicus, P., & Demerath, N. (2002). Telecommuting in the 21st century: Benefits, issues and a leadership model that will work. *The Journal of Leadership Studies, 8*(4), 75–86. doi:10.1177/107179190200800407

Giles, D. (2002). Parasocial interaction: A review of the literature and a model for future research. *Media Psychology, 4,* 279-305. Instant messaging. (2005). *The Computer Bulletin, 47*(3), 26.

Johnson, P., Heimann, V., & O'Neill, K. (2001). The wonderland of virtual teams. *Journal of Workplace Learning, 13*(1), 24–30. doi:10.1108/13665620110364745

Kets de Vries, M. (2001). *The leadership mystique: A user's manual for the human enterprise.* New York: Prentice Hall.

Kim, H., Kim, G. J., Park, H. W., & Rice, R. E. (2007). Configurations of relationships in different media: Ftf, email, instant messenger, mobile Phone, and SMS. *Journal of Computer-Mediated Communication, 12*(4), 2–24. doi:10.1111/j.1083-6101.2007.00369.x

Marshall, P. D. (1997). *Celebrity and power: Fame in contemporary culture.* Minneapolis: University of Minnesota Press.

Martinez, K. Z. (2004). Latina magazine and the invocation of a panethnic family: Latino identity as it is informed by celebrities and Papis Chulos. *Communication Review, 7*(2), 155–174. doi:10.1080/10714420490448697

Nardi, B. A. (2005). Beyond bandwidth: Dimensions of connection in interpersonal communication. *Computer Supported Cooperative Work, 14,* 91-130. Poynteronline. (2003, 10 April). *The face and mind of the American journalist.* Retrieved November 14, 2007, from: http://www.poynter.org/content/content_view.asp?id=28235

Quan-Haase, A., Cothrel, J., & Wellman, B. (2005). Instant Messaging for Collaboration: A Case Study of a High-Tech Firm. *Journal of Computer-Mediated Communication, 10*(4).

Reisner, A. E. (1992). The news conference: How daily newspaper editors construct the front page. *The Journalism Quarterly, 69*(4), 971–986.

Ryan, C. (2005). Struggling to survive: A study of editorial decision-making strategies at MAMM magazine. *Journal of Business and Technical Communication, 19*(3), 353–376. doi:10.1177/1050651905275643

Schein, E. H. (2004). *Organizational culture and leadership.* San Francisco: Jossey-Bass.

Schudson, M. (2003). *The sociology of news.* New York: W.W. Norton & Company.

Shoemaker, P. J., & Reese, S. D. (1996). *Mediating the message: Theories of influences on mass media content* (2nd ed.). White Plains, NY: Longman.

Sigelman, L. (1973). Reporting the news: An organizational analysis. *American Journal of Sociology, 77,* 660-670. Stacey, R. D. (1996). *Complexity and creativity in organizations.* San Francisco: Berrett-Koehler Publishers.

Singer, J. B. (1996). 'Virtual anonymity': Online accountability and the virtuous virtual journalist. *Journal of Mass Media Ethics, 11*(2), 95–106.

Singer, J. B., Tharp, M. P., & Haruta, A. (1999). Online staffers: Superstars or second-class citizens? *Newspaper Research Journal, 20*(3), 29–47.

Stapley, L. F. (1996). *The personality of the organization: A psycho-dynamic explanation of culture and change.* London: Free Association Books.

Steinem, G. (1994). Sex, lies and advertising. In Steinem, G. (Ed.), *Moving beyond words* (pp. 130–170). New York: Simon & Schuster.

Strom, D. (2006, April 5). I.M. generation is changing the way business talks. *The New York Times.*

Sumpter, R. S. (2000). Daily newspaper editors' audience construction routines: A case study. *Critical Studies in Media Communication, 17*(3), 334–346. doi:10.1080/15295030009388399

Ter Hofte, G. H., Mulder, I., & Verwijs, C. (2006). Close encounters of the virtual kind: A study on placed-based presence. *AI & Society, 20,* 151–168. doi:10.1007/s00146-005-0013-6

Tuchman, G. (1978). *Making news: A study in the construction of reality.* New York: The Free Press.

Vos, P., & van der Voordt, T. (2001). Tomorrow's offices through today's eyes: Effects of innovation in the working environment. *Journal of Corporate Real Estate, 4*(1), 48–65. doi:10.1108/14630010210811778

White, D. M. (1950). The 'Gatekeeper': A case study in the selection of news. *The Journalism Quarterly, 27,* 383–390.

Zach, M. H. (1994). Electronic messaging and communication effectiveness in an ongoing work group. *Information and Management Systems, 26,* 231–241.

Chapter 11
Sharing Information about the Pain:
Patient–Doctor Collaboration in Therapy and Research

Richard Chalfen
Harvard Medical School, USA

Michael Rich
Harvard Medical School, USA

ABSTRACT

The chapter presents findings from recent studies that feature a model of doctor-patient collaboration called Video Intervention/Prevention Assessment (VIA), a research methodology that engages patient-participants in sharing their life stories on video, communicating their concerns and teaching their doctors what it means to live with a chronic illness. Patients are collaborators in creating a comprehensive understanding of illness that expands the medical community's definition of disease. This chapter focuses on visual narratives made by young patients with Cystic Fibrosis and Spina Bifida as they experience their transitions from pediatric to adult-oriented medicine care. Collaboration in research facilitates more effective ownership of and accountability for their illness, facilitating adherence to treatment plans and improved quality of life. Our chapter concludes with an evaluation of the pros and cons of VIA as a collaborative information methodology.

INTRODUCTION

"I think that's really cool that someone actually takes the time to watch it [my videos] -- I respect your job a lot. The thing with doctors is they think they know everything." (Male participant with Spina Bifida)

Although the professional practice of medicine has always been collaborative, in the sense that the doctor depends on information and cooperation from the patient, the doctor-patient relationship has traditionally been approached and experienced as paternalistic. Patients and doctors develop phenomenological constructions of each other, of

DOI: 10.4018/978-1-61520-797-8.ch011

disease, and of the illness experience by contributing information through a range of verbal and non-verbal communications, including medical and psychosocial histories, physical examinations, and laboratory evaluations. The rarely achieved ideal collaboration between patient and doctor uses ongoing open communication to seek similarities and address differences in these conditions, to find a common understanding of the illness, to share responsibility for treatment plans and outcomes. Patient-doctor interactions are marked by mutual requests for sharing information from two experts, the patient as owner and custodian of a particular illness and the doctor who possesses diagnostic, therapeutic, and prognostic knowledge of diseases (Cordella, 2004; Heritage & Maynard, 2006).

Current states of medical economics and informatics are exerting an impact on modes of collecting information that are fundamental to successful collaborations. Doctors obtain better anatomic and physiologic data, but have sacrificed rich psychological and socio-cultural information. The demise of the house call has dramatically shifted how doctors know their patients. The contexts of information-gathering are not part of the patients' worlds, but sterile clinical settings such as emergency rooms, clinics, hospital rooms, and doctors' offices. Office visits and hospital admissions, opportunities to observe the patient and the disease process are becoming shorter. The trend is clear. Technologically advanced testing both increases and improves anatomical imaging and physiological metrics.

In other ways, however, the quality of medical data is diminished as knowledge of illness-in-the-home-context is no longer available. Assessment of patient behavior and disease signs is now relegated to collapsed periods of time or replaced by medical tests that examine the structure and function of single organs, diminishing opportunities for learning the psychosocial and cultural information that define the whole patient. Because patients suffer their disease processes in the context of their lives and their worlds in which they live, their illnesses cannot be fully understood and their quality of life cannot be effectively addressed without doctors learning about and responding to how their diseases are experienced by individual patients within the context of their lives.

Long seen by both patient and doctor as the passive supplicant, the patient has a great deal to contribute to a collaboration in diagnosis and healing, filling blind spots in the doctor's observational and diagnostic methods. Not only does the patient bring intimate knowledge and constant monitoring of her body, herself, and her life to the collaboration, but she can share and work with her rich experience with illness and wellness. Her personally realized knowledge of a particular illness, her theories of its origin, contagion, persistence, and the meaning of living with it -- what Arthur Kleinman has described as the "explanatory model" (Kleinman, 1988) -- are all important diagnostic evidence and potentially powerful therapeutic tools. How can we open channels of communication so that patients can express and doctors can hear this important information? We simply asked patients to teach their doctors about their lives with illness, their experience, concerns, and needs, implicitly and explicitly linking collaboration and communication.

To engage patients in a more equitable collaborative relationship with their clinicians, an innovative research methodology has been developed at the Center on Media and Child Health at Children's Hospital Boston. Video Intervention/ Prevention Assessment (VIA) is a research methodology that asks patient-participants to use video technology to reveal their own medical conditions and communicate how they see themselves living with those conditions in their own physical and social environments. VIA is built on the assumption that patient-participants are collaborators who offer direct and intimate portrayals of their illness experiences, co-creating with their doctors a comprehensive understanding of illness and working together to devise and implement a strategy for wellness.

CAMERA-ASSISTED COLLABORATIVE EFFORTS

The components of the VIA patient-doctor collaboration are not new. Filmmakers have historically developed collaborative relationships and techniques with their subjects to enable the emergence of new information provided "from the inside out." In documentary films and videos, the on-camera interview is a familiar example, sometimes scripted, but many times spontaneous. Filmmakers have asked their subjects to cooperate by giving them access to private domains, living spaces, sensitive relationships, and personal interactions. The common objective has been revelation, to gain authentic looks-behind-the-scenes by probing key informants for new information, offering viewers unusual views of life, and using the synergy between observed and observer to find fresh understandings of the human condition.

Other strands of influence on VIA can be found in ethnographic film and video formats familiar to both visual anthropology and visual sociology. Some projects have consisted of a filmmaker and an anthropologist collaborating with one another, working in separate roles to produce an ethnographic film. Alternatively an individual social scientist becomes trained in both a social science and documentary filmmaking, with the objective of combining knowledge and production skills to produce culturally sensitive and ethnographically valid documents. In both cases, the project objectives have been to produce ethnographic portraits of people as they lived everyday life in their own familiar social contexts, as a way of communicating an unfamiliar culture to the filmmaker's home culture. The "outsider-looking-in" perspective was limited however, and some social scientists felt they could generate a better way of seeing and knowing a culture if they asked members of that culture to make the images themselves, to provide a subjective "insider-looking-out" perspective. Seeking to explore the illness experience through the eyes and mind of the patient-participant, we

developed VIA methodology and practice as a creative integration of collaborative information behavior and participant media research.

Most examples of collaborative media and insider participation focus on the ways that interested parties participate in the image-making process and how different tasks are shared to produce a series of photographs, a film, or a video. A visiting researcher or filmmaker can request cooperation in different ways (Banks 2001, Pink 2008) – these may include:

- Asking subjects of the photographs, film, or video to re-enact aspects of their lives along a pre-planned theme or storyline (Flaherty, 1922);
- Asking subjects to indicate what subject matter they want filmed, why they want it, and which material they want included in the final product (NB: more often, than not, community members propose a selection of subject matter for purposes of local improvement in physical, social or political conditions) (Elder, 1995; Kennedy 1971, 1982);
- Asking subjects to collaborate in editing or otherwise organizing a film, including asking them for preferred meanings of particular scenes and overall meaning of the visual documentation. (MacDougall, 1992; Asch, 1991)

One fundamental distinction in collaborative media is based on who is actually holding the camera, creating images, and deciding on content to be included – outsiders looking in at subjects living their lives or insiders looking out at their lives and worlds. The model of collaboration is dramatically changed when a researcher or filmmaker selects subjects whose lives are being documented to make their own pictures, a collaborative relationship that has been called participant media. Variations of participant media include auto-photographic method (Ziller, 1990), hermeneutic photography (Hagedorn, 1994, 1996), visual narratives (Rich & Chalfen, 1999; Chalfen & Rich, 2007), pictorial diaries (Holliday 2004a & 2004b), bio-documentary film (Worth, 1966), socio-documentary film (Chalfen, 1981 & 1992; Chalfen & Haley, 1971), "participative video" (Prosser & Loxley, 2008), photo/video therapy (Weiser, 1999; Furman, 1990) among others. These efforts are occasionally referred to as subject-generated images or indigenous media (Ginsburg, 1991) and may be developed as research, a form of applied work (Pink 2008), or "participatory action research."

A central aim of the participatory visual media process is to create pictorial narratives that convey what respondents want to communicate in the manner they wish it communicated. Participatory media projects center on an individual or small group of people using borrowed cameras to produce visual texts following their own incentives, ideas, and objectives. Because they ultimately control the flow of images and information, those studied are no longer just subjects of the visual media, they are participants in the project, collaborating with the outside researchers in the collection of images and data. Visual anthropologists and visual sociologists, in both domestic and international projects, have asked members of different social groups to create their own images to elucidate and answer research questions. Work has been done with the Navajo (Worth, Adair & Chalfen, 1997) as well as groups living in East Africa (Bellman & Jules-Rosette, 1977), Australia (Michaels, 1985), and South America (Turner, 1991; Asch, 1991; Aufderheide, 1995).

With significant variation in the degree of instruction, direction, and intervention, the project director (PD) or principal investigator (PI) motivates image-making by participants, receives the images participants generate, and may even involve participants in the shaping of the final product.

- Depending on the type of data wanted, the PD/PI may simply provide the tools and technical instructions required to make images or may offer varying amounts of narrative, visual, and/or aesthetic instruction for camera use (shooting strategy, camera technique) or editing (shot juxtaposition, sequencing) following different cinematic traditions.

- In some cases, the PD/PI may question and/or coach the image-makers at different points in the process in order to ensure obtaining enough images to "tell the story", to stay on track to meet the project objectives, to obtain participant perspectives on both the process and product, to develop strategy, and to optimize anticipated outcomes.

- On some projects, the PD/PI may want to feed the images created back to individual participants or community members in an iterative process to understand and validate what is revealed, to enrich it with participant observations, interpretations, and commentary about locally realized meanings, and to involve participants in shaping results and drawing conclusions (Chalfen, 2007).

All of these variations are found in projects directed toward better knowing young people and, in some cases, learning about their medical problems. These include Fotokids started by Nancy McGirr in 1991; Kids with Cameras founded by Zana Briski in 2002; Shooting Back created Jim Hubbard In 1989; Visible Voice projects initiated by Vincent O'Brien, 2002-06; and The Literacy Through Photography Workshop pioneered by Wendy Ewald (1985).

Health-Related Collaborations

The uniqueness of VIA methodology and research goals becomes clearer when we consider the broad range of collaborative techniques that have been applied to health concerns and questions. Carolyn Wang and colleagues describe Photovoice (Wang, 1999; Wang & Burris, 1994, 1996), a participatory action methodology which they developed and first directed toward public health education in China:

As an educational tool, the practice of photovoice *has three main goals: (1) to empower rural women to record and reflect their lives, especially health needs, from their own point of view; (2) to increase their collective knowledge about women's health status; and (3) to inform policymakers and the broader society about health and community issues that are of greatest concern to rural women (Wang, Burris and Xiang, 1996).*

Photovoice has been used widely by other researchers, exemplified by Laura Lorenz's elicitation of perspectives of brain injury survivors (Lorenz, 2006; Lorenz, Webster & Foley, 2007) and Ellen Lopez's study of quality of life issues among African American breast cancer survivors (Lopez, Eng, Randall-David & Robinson, 2005). Other medically-related projects have asked patients to use still cameras to explain their feelings about being hospitalized (Radley, 2002; Radley & Taylor, 2003a, 2003b), undergoing chemotherapy (Frith & Harcourt, 2007), living with poor cardiovascular health (Fitzpatrick, Tu, Steinman & Suin, 2007), and attempting to understand family alcoholism (Evans, 1979), among others.

VIA Research as Collaboration

VIA selectively draws upon the participant media tradition of study. In 1994, Michael Rich, an Adolescent Medicine physician and former film producer, saw the potential for using cameras, otherwise regarded as objective scopic technology, to elicit the subjective expression of young people's experiences living with and managing chronic illnesses. He was joined by Richard Chalfen, a visual anthropologist with an extensive history

in participant media research, having previously collaborated with Navajo living in Pine Springs, Arizona (Worth, Adair & Chalfen, 1997), and several groups of teenagers living in Philadelphia (Chalfen, 1972; Chalfen, 1981). VIA quickly became the cornerstone of the Center on Media and Child Health (www.cmch.tv) at Children's Hospital Boston, an interdisciplinary group that investigates the positive and negative effects of media on physical, mental, and social health.

VIA was established from the beginning as an interdisciplinary method, combining perspectives and skills from medicine, public health, anthropology, psychology, and social work. We established a collaborative team approach to designing research, training and guiding participants to collect visual data, and analyzing the results. Since 1994, the VIA collaborative strategy has been applied to investigate the illness experiences of children and adolescents with asthma (Rich, Lamola & Chalfen, 1998; Rich & Chalfen, 1999; Rich, Lamola, Amory & Schneider, 2000; Rich, Taylor & Chalfen, 2000; Rich, Patashnick & Chalfen 2002; Chalfen & Rich 2007), diabetes (Buchbinder et al., 2005), obesity (Rich, Huecker, & Ludwig, 2001; Rich, Patashnick, Huecker & Ludwig, 2002), and the health care transition experiences of adolescents with chronic, function-limiting conditions such as spina bifida, cystic fibrosis, sickle cell disease, and perinatally acquired HIV (Rich, Patashnick & Kastelic, 2005). Examples of data from VIA participants living with spina bifida and cystic fibrosis will be used to illustrate the collaborative VIA process.

VIA Models of Collaboration: Fieldwork Protocol

While the diagnoses and medical circumstances of each project may vary, VIA data are consistent – participant-created audiovisual documentation of day-to-day life experiences with illness from the perspective of the patient. Each VIA participant is asked to record what is personally important about their illness experience, how it makes them feel, and how they respond to illness, their medical care and treatment plans, and the physical and psychosocial contexts in which they live with and try to manage their chronic disease.

Each VIA participant is loaned a lightweight handheld video camcorder and asked to "teach your doctor about your life with [your medical condition]." Understanding the request to tell their own stories in their own ways, participants are encouraged to document their lives with illness, recording anything and everything they feel reveals their lives, dreams, successes, and frustrations. Each participant is provided with suggestions of universally shared situations and scenes to document, including getting up in the morning, going to school, extracurricular activities, hanging out with friends, eating a meal, working, showing their homes and neighborhoods, and visiting doctors and other health care professionals. Participants are asked to interview family, friends, and anyone else who knows them and their medical condition. Finally, we ask VIA participants to set up the camera and talk to it on a daily basis, as a "personal monologue", reflecting on the day's events and sharing their thoughts and feelings about what they have experienced, as well as their anticipations of and concerns about the future.

Children and adolescents who meet eligibility criteria for the medical condition being studied are recruited from primary care and specialty clinics at Children's Hospital Boston and its affiliated community health centers. We describe VIA and the study expectations to each potential participant. If the patient (and parent, if the patient is under 18) wants to participate, s/he (or the parent) is asked to sign a written informed consent. The VIA Field Coordinator instructs each participant in the technical aspects of operating the study camcorder, but does not teach any video technique, visual style, aesthetics, or conventions of visual representation. During the six to ten weeks that a participant typically needs to complete his/her visual narrative, the Field Coordinator meets

weekly with the participant in his/her home or at a clinic visit, in order to collect finished tapes, provide blank tapes, talk about how the project is going, and offer support, encouragement, and brainstorming with the participant about what s/he may wish to tape in the coming week. The participant's visual narrative is deemed complete when the Field Coordinator and participant agree that all facets of the project have been satisfactorily completed. At that point, the Field Coordinator retrieves all VIA video equipment, provides the participant with a complete, unedited copy of his/her visual narrative, provides a written release form for the participant (or parent, if participant is a minor) to sign if s/he wishes to allow the use of any or all of his/her visual narrative in research publications and presentations, and remunerates the participant for the time invested in creating the visual narrative. (For a more detailed description of the VIA method, see http://www.cmch.tv/via/home/.)

VIA Method: Data Analysis

VIA visual narratives are mastered and converted to a format accessible to the analysis team (originally VHS tapes, now digitized to a secure computer server). In archiving the visual narratives, each frame of video is assigned a dedicated number, indicating the study participant, the date and time it was recorded, and video time code to facilitate quick location and common reference for the VIA analysis team.

Logging the video is the first step of VIA visual narrative analysis. Analogous to a transcription of an audio tape, a VIA log is a guide to the audiovisual data, text documentation of what is observable on each tape. It provides a simplified, indexable guide with which to find certain scenes, situations, or concepts. Although the pilot VIA project was logged by hand on paper logsheets, we are now using better data management tools and techniques to log directly on computers. In the logs, scenes and shots are differentiated by distinct styles of text, the dedicated numerical video location code, and who is controlling the camcorder. The content of each scene is logged in parallel streams of "objective" and "subjective" descriptions. For purposes of clarity and reliability of the VIA logging and analysis, objective content is defined as that which is concretely visible or audible, with all speculation, assumption, and emotion removed, so the description is reproducible by any observer. The subjective stream of the log carries the emotional tone of the scene and the logger's assessment of the VIA participant's attitudes, beliefs, and motivations. Since the subjective logging stream can vary with the logger's gender, age, culture, and life experiences, all VIA visual narratives are independently logged by at least two loggers and the logs compared for inter-rater reliability.

Loggers meet with the full interdisciplinary research team on a regular basis to relate, compare, and discuss findings. Techniques derived from ethnography, participant observation, and visual anthropology are used to analyze the content of the visual narratives. Grounded theory (Glaser, 1992; Glaser & Strauss, 1967) is used to identify and develop emerging themes that unify the participants' illness experiences. The resultant themes are compared and contrasted within and among participants' visual narratives.

In recent projects, we have used Transana software to log the visual narratives directly, following the video data on a split screen beside the ongoing logging document. Once the logs have been completed, they are exported from Transana and imported into NVivo, a qualitative analysis software program that allows VIA logs to be analyzed with a maximum of flexibility, while retaining the richness and depth of the original data (Patashnick & Rich, 2005).

Once the visual narrative data are coded and structured using NVivo, the interdisciplinary research team collaborates to examine them through each discipline's theoretical framework. Taking the different disciplinary perspectives of medicine, public health, anthropology, psychology, and clinical social work on the same audiovisual data allows us to triangulate on our findings. Finding analyses that are consistent with all disciplinary perspectives increases rigor, as each discipline illuminates expands, and sometimes challenges the findings of the others, as we work to characterize and understand the patient's illness experience[1]

VIA Personal Monologue as Diary

The VIA methodology draws on diary traditions of personal expression. With the increased availability of digital technology, methods utilizing photo diaries (Latham, 2004; Dinsmore, 1996) represent another thread of social science research relevant to VIA methodology; particularly important are examples focused on medical issues (Harrison, 2002; Gibson, 2005; Radley & Taylor, 2003b).

For the diary-like component of VIA, the personal monologue, participants are asked to make audiovisual entries by facing and talking into a camera on a nightly basis. Here is an opportunity for participants to reflect on their experiences and articulate their confidential thoughts about their lives, their hopes, their fears, and most often, the hardships and difficulties of living with their particular illness. One example of diaristic expression in a VIA personal monologue comes from a 22-year old participant with spina bifida, a congenital disorder of the spinal cord that results in paralysis and dysfunction of the lower half of the body:

You know I have my really weird days, I have my serious days. It's like everybody. Everybody has their serious days, everybody has their shitty days. But you know, I think I was telling you earlier about this band-aid stuff. I don't want these pills to keep telling me that everything's okay. I mean... I don't want to be programmed. Like, "Oh lets put a band-aid on a wound and tell this guy that he's not sad anymore." I don't want some pill to tell me I'm not sad or make my problems go away. I mean, regardless of whatever pill I've taken, all the shit's that happened in my past has happened. No pill's going to take that away and erase it. I've had a lot of problems in certain schools I've went to, being made fun of for being disabled. I've had things happen to me sexually when I was younger. I'm on medication because I used to have thoughts of suicide. I've done some things in my life that would surprise you. I'm not always Mister Funny Guy.

VIA personal monologues serve as rich sources of information and insight. The young people who participate in VIA studies share a cultural understanding that a diary is a confidential communication of and with oneself. VIA benefits from participants' expectation of confidentiality which lowers their resistance to self-revelation, but we have found that VIA participants' enthusiasm for making their visual narratives is as much because they know that someone who cares will listen and respond while respecting their autonomy and privacy. We found that degrees of collaboration increase as we move away from the traditional intrapersonal communication model of diary writing toward a more interpersonal one, when participants know someone will be seeing and hearing their diary entries.

Patient Views of VIA Collaboration

The comments that VIA participants have made on the kinds of collaboration this method offered them, their perceptions of our offer of partnership as co-producer and co-researcher, offer valuable insights into how they see and understand the VIA experience. Research participants often expressed an appreciation for being asked to be a collaborator in, rather than a passive subject of research. They frequently called attention to themselves and their lives as individuals, saying, "This is my life" or establishing the framework of "This is a day in the life of me." We heard, "I'm doing this documentary to show you what it is like to be me. So, hope you like it." In another example we heard:

I have cystic fibrosis and this is my life. This is a part of my life and for you to truly get an idea of what it is like, you need to know this. You need to think about [this]. Well, you don't need to think about it, but you need to know. I need to tell you so you know...

One key component of successful collaboration was grounded in the model of communication that VIA offers. Participants realized their discourse was meaningful, that someone was going to listen and take their narrative seriously. One patient with spina bifida offered:

But this project's helped me through a lot. I'm grateful for the project, I'm grateful for this camera. I'm grateful to know you, [VIA Field Coordinator]... I'm glad that other people are going to eventually see this when I sign papers. I'm not ashamed of anything. I didn't do this for no reason. So, if anybody wants to learn, let them learn.

We learned how much our participants appreciated being assigned the role of teacher, feeling that doctors really need to hear what they knew about themselves and their lives. One cystic fibrosis patient said, "I think that's really cool that someone actually takes the time to watch it. I respect your job a lot. The thing with doctors is they think they know everything." The importance to participants of this elevation to the status of expert, teacher, and research collaborator was revealed to us by a spina bifida participant:

It's a fun project, we got a good friend out of the deal [the VIA Staff as audience]. I got to help you out of the deal, I hope. I hope I got to teach you a bit.... Talking to the camera and telling you my life history and whatever and past, sometimes I'm being funny, sometimes I'm being serious, but ultimately I like telling you things in my life and I feel comfortable. Maybe it's because I'm just talking to myself and talking to the camera, but I know someone out there is going to be watching it and understand it. Or at least try to understand it.

In one sign-off message at the end of a visual narrative, we heard, "I hope you have learned something, at least one thing, from me. I hope I wasn't too boring. I hope you can better understand what my life is like living with CF. Thank you for giving me the opportunity to do this project. Bye."

In some cases, VIA visual narratives showed that a parent, usually a mother, connected with her disabled child in close and complex ways, took on the role of partner in self-expression and acts as a spokesperson for the pair. One mother of a spina bifida participant said:

But first I'm going to go back to what I want to say to the doctors out there about why we need help. I told [VIA Field Coordinator] that I've had fantasies for a while about being able to address doctors and telling them what we have been going through since J__ was born 17 years ago. And now you're giving me the opportunity to do that, I hope I can do a good job...

In this example of psychological enmeshment, the mother goes beyond the first person plural to designate herself as her son's voice, signified by her use of the first person singular. The same mother said:

Thank you, Dr. Rich, for adapting things to let me say something out here, and anything I can do to help, it makes my life meaningful to do this for J__, and it makes my life meaningful if I can help other families or other kids now. I don't mean to be self-important... but if I can ever do that or if there is anything else I can ever do, I'd love to do it, and thanks for listening.

VIA participants reflected on their freedom to express themselves in this collaborative model of communication. Some considered the camcorder a benevolent observer and listener, while others were frustrated by its inability to respond, as revealed by this conversation between a 16-year old participant with cystic fibrosis and her brother:

*Brother: I gotta mumble so the camera can't hear me... How can you talk to a f*****' camera, seriously?*

Participant: It lets out a lotta stress you know.

Brother: How do you figure, you sit there and talk to this thing?

Participant: Because it can't talk back and they can't tell people what you're talking about.

Brother: So it's not good, because, you always need an opinion. The camera can't give you a fucking opinion.

A participant with spina bifida elaborated on this idea:

But when I do want to be in a serious mood, I really do feel like I can talk to the camera. Like I really... I talk nice about how I feel. I know [the Field Coordinator] is watching. I know that she's going to hear it. And that's okay, because you know somebody's going to hear you, you know what I mean. So, at that particular time, it's like looking at a machine and talking to yourself, but you know that you're safe because someone's on the other end, you know what I mean. And I know that the someone on the other end isn't just someone I'm doing a project with, it's someone that I've befriended.

The tacit understanding of a watching, listening, and learning audience was important to participants. They appreciated the built-in benefits of having an audience-at-a-distance. Perhaps as a welcome relief from family and friends, each participant could speak freely without risking being interrupted by an annoying argument or hostile criticism. One participant was explicit, "See that's what it's [the camera] for. They don't care what we say. They don't care what we do. We could tell it to fuck off, say whatever we want on it."

On occasion, however, enthusiastic participants found themselves on the border of wanting to do a thorough job of showing their lives and deciding what might be inappropriate for display to the camera, in spite of our claim to their freedom of expression. Participants appreciated the offer and ability to "say anything" on their tapes, implying that it was okay, even though an adult would be listening. But could they say and show anything and expect it to remain confidential? The Field Coordinator reinforced their expressive freedom, but discouraged nudity and exhibitionist behaviors inspired by the presence of the camcorder. We heard one spina bifida patient state there are certain lines he did not want to cross in his videos, like bowel care. He said he hopes that others are sharing things that he does not, because he wants to tell VIA as much as he can:

Back in the bathroom again. I feel like this is all I've been doing lately. I dunno, my friends don't really want to be on the camera and stuff. I'm gonna actually show you how to insert this thing…I guess you said, "Do what you gotta do on here and show you how stuff works." I will show you how I actually insert this catheter.

Later we heard:

It's about 6:45 in the morning and I'm about to get some sleep…I just wanted to film, and try to get this project rolling…. you're going to know that I need a little more assistance… I don't know, like you said, "You do your everyday, you know, living on this tape." I mean, I wanna know how do I take a shower on tape?…How do I do that

without steaming up the camera? The camera will get all steamy and out of focus. Do you want me to film when I go to bed? It will only be on for an hour…The thing is…how personal is that? I know you want your everyday living on there. I want to do the best that I can for the project. I want to do a good job for you.

Several participants reflected on how their participation in the VIA project had empowered them to make changes for themselves or contribute to the wellbeing of others, while others remained skeptical, questioning, even cynical. Looking forward at the conclusion of his visual narrative, an introspective and enthusiastic participant living with cystic fibrosis turned the camera toward himself and said, "It's kind of weird that this is done. It's been fun, it's been great. It's… at its end. I don't know. I'm off to get my health in shape, just think longevity, just continue on with my life." Some VIA participants voiced appreciation for the opportunity to make a positive difference in the lives of others with similar health conditions. Another cystic fibrosis participant said, "It's been a rough road and I hope that I can teach somebody something doing this project." A third participant with cystic fibrosis said he feels

…blessed to be a part of something that could be something in the future…. A way the doctors treat patients, a way a doctor treats human beings, let alone patients. I'm literally blessed that I can do this… to have a chance to be a part of something that could mean something in this world means so much to me.

Other cystic fibrosis participants were not without some skepticism. "I think this is a very good study. It's probably not going to cure cystic fibrosis, but I don't know. I think this is a really good study…" Equal parts of skepticism, cynicism and conspiracy theory, a combination not unfamiliar to adolescent years, were heard in the following conversation between an adolescent girl with cystic fibrosis, her brother, and a friend:

Brother: A documentary on yourself because you're going to be dead soon... Why do you do this? They don't need to know...

Participant: It's not yours, its mine.

Friend: You never know. They could discover a cure for it tomorrow.

Brother: They already have a cure, they just aren't giving it out.

Ultimately, several participants felt transformed by their collaboration as co-researchers and by the VIA process of self-examination, reflection, and self-revelation:

I definitely feel like I'm a different person, I should say more of a more at ease person, more the person I want to be now, than what I was when I first started the study.

What does the VIA Model of Collaboration Provoke?

We discovered important parallels between how adolescents and young adults with chronic diseases collaborated on their VIA research project and how they collaborated on their health and treatment plans. Being a co-producer in a symbolic world of generating and sharing information has its counterparts in health care in the form of staying active and taking charge of one's health and taking a pro-active approach to medical treatment. Several key factors contributed to this parallel development and to how successful VIA was at eliciting valuable information:

- Our patient-participants found themselves promoted to the role of teacher, a source of information, knowledge, wisdom, and experience. In acknowledging patients' expertise and strength, VIA leveled the traditional power differential between doctor and patient, recognizing patients as equals in the knowledge exchange. With this significant shift in power relations, patients were not "just" listeners and learners – they were speakers and teachers.

- The participants came to be appreciated for what they knew, what they had experienced, and what they had mastered. Because of their hard-won expertise, others wanted to know about their lives and they had a commodity that was sought by representatives of the adult world.

- Participants felt they could help other young people in similar personal and medical circumstances, that they could at least contribute to improving the quality of life of fellow patients.

- Participants knew what they said and did was confidential, meant for members of their medical team and related health care professionals. They were not making tapes or video clips for distribution via the internet, YouTube, or for broadcast television – their visual narratives were serious and important documents.

- Participants were being listened to with respect by those who could make a difference. Participants were articulating the problems and troubles in their lives as constructive criticism aimed at improving the health care delivery system. Appreciated for what they had to offer, participants appeared relieved to transition from always being talked at and talked about to the talker to whom others listen.

Patient-Researcher Collaboration

The collaboration we sought required the patient-participants to take another position in the communications paradigm, a shift, which, in turn, signaled another set of changes in both role and status. They were asked to move from their very familiar role of consumer of media to the producer of media. Much is regularly said about how each successive generation of young people grows up in a more visually rich, media-saturated world. In this case, we have seen one example of how their familiarity with media can be harnessed to activate collaborative information behavior and answer previously unasked questions. The children and adolescents who participated in VIA pursued the creation of their visual narratives with considerable ease and enthusiasm. They were adept and comfortable with the camcorders, understood what we wanted, moved seamlessly from behind the camera to on-camera, and generated spontaneous, genuine, and often unexpected audiovisual data.

Patient-Doctor Collaboration

The collaboration we established with VIA as a research method had a second, and very much related, set of consequences. One of the remarkable, and somewhat unexpected, findings from the initial VIA pilot project with asthma was that asthma patients who had been VIA participants showed a significant improvement in their asthma-specific quality of life after completing their visual narratives, but before either researchers or participants viewed their visual narratives (Rich, Lamola, Gordon & Chalfen, 2000). In exploring this surprising, but welcome finding that VIA had therapeutic effects, we found that: (1) the VIA process of self-examination led participants to see how their day-to-day lifestyles were inconsistent with what they knew to be best for their asthma, so they actively confronted these discrepancies and self-corrected, and, more importantly, (2) mastering VIA, a process that they imagined to be complex and out-of-reach when most of them started, built their self-efficacy, the sense that they can take control of the uncontrollable, so they learned from the metaphor of VIA and

took control of their lives with their newfound confidence and competence.

With several of the VIA research participants, we found a similar phenomenon – the collaboration between participants and researchers in the VIA process fostered improved collaborations and partnerships of the VIA participants with their doctors. Collaborations can be contagious, even generative. While much lip service has been paid by the health care community toward the concept of developing physician-patient partnerships in care, little of substance has been done to realize that ideal.

When a clinician asks a patient to teach him what it is like to live with a medical condition with the intention of hearing and responding to the information, patients take new ownership and control of their own medical conditions clearly indicating critical features of their condition, challenges they face in its management, and ideas and motivations for improving their functional status, establishing themselves as legitimate partners in their health care. With improved self-efficacy in the collaborative process, patients can take ownership of their condition, partner more assertively and effectively with their doctors, establish more responsibility for and control of the illness experience, and take charge of their own medical management and healing process.

Common Factors

The sharing of power has always had significant implications. It is no surprise that we found links between collaboration and power-sharing in both the symbolic domain of research and the real life of medical practice. A sense of empowerment is particularly important to adolescent patients as they must navigate a series of often unfamiliar and problematic power relationships in both private and public realms of life.

When patients are asked to be co-researchers, co-producers and co-healers, they are empowered as individuals and patients, but the implications of both the VIA process and its findings extend to the larger communities of doctors and patients. The collaborative VIA research process generates images and information that, as doctors and other clinicians have said, "we never get to see." VIA participants have related that their participation has let them say things "they never get to say."

The origins of the VIA methodology were based, in part, on improving patient-clinician communication, understanding, and cooperation. The VIA model of collaboration addresses the limitations of the acknowledged power inequity of the patient-doctor interaction. VIA sought a communicative channel to facilitate an improved flow of information and to gain a better understanding of the relationships between illness as experienced by patients and disease as understood by doctors. Access to more complete knowledge of how an illness works within the life of a patient can lead to improved medical and social interventions. VIA offers knowledge of important variables and unknown details of life behind a patient's clinic appearance, thus improving chances for better adherence to treatment plans and, in turn, improved life conditions for both patients and doctors.

ACKNOWLEDGMENT

This research was supported by grant #K23 HD01296 from the National Institute of Child Health and Human Development, as well as condition-specific grants from the Deborah Munroe Noonan Foundation, the William F. Milton Foundation, and the Christopher Reeve Paralysis Foundation. We extend our sincere thanks to the participants for their enthusiastic participation; the clinicians and staff of Children's Hospital Boston for their assistance in identifying and recruiting VIA study participants; Jennifer Patashnick for her intern supervision and coding, Julie Polvinen for serving as Field Coordinator, Laura Sherman for transcription and editing help, Brady King and Isabel Lopes for reference searches.

REFERENCES

Asch, T., Cardozo, J. I., Cabellero, H., & Bortoli, J. (1991). The story we now want to hear is not ours to tell: Relinquishing control over representation: Toward sharing visual communication skills with The Yanomami. *Visual Anthropology Review, 7*(2), 102–106. doi:10.1525/var.1991.7.2.102

Aufderheide, P. (1995). The video in the villages project: Videomaking with and by Brazilian Indians. *Visual Anthropology Review, 11*(2), 82–93. doi:10.1525/var.1995.11.2.83

Bellman, B., & Jules-Rosette, B. (1997). *A Paradigm for looking: Cross-cultural research with visual media.* New York: Ablex.

Buchbinder, M. H., Detzer, M. J., Welsch, R. L., Christiano, A. S., Patashnick, J. L., & Rich, M. (2005). Assessing adolescents with insulin-dependent diabetes mellitus: a multiple perspective pilot study using visual illness narratives and interviews. *Journal of Adolescent Health, 36*(1), 71.e79 –71.e13.

Chalfen, R. (1981). A Sociovidistic approach to children's filmmaking: The Philadelphia Project. *Studies in Visual Communication, 7*(1), 2–33.

Chalfen, R. (1992). Picturing culture through indigenous imagery: A telling story. In Crawford, P., & Turton, D. (Eds.), *Film as Ethnography* (pp. 222–241). Manchester: University of Manchester Press.

Chalfen, R. (1997). Foreword and Afterword. In Worth, S., Adair, J., & Chalfen, R. (Eds.), *Through Navajo eyes: An exploration in film communication and anthropology* (2nd rev. ed.). Albuquerque, NM: University of Mexico Press.

Chalfen, R. (2007). *Variations of bio-documentary representation: Kids make pictures.* Paper presented at the Annual Meetings of the International Visual Sociology Association, New York.

Chalfen, R., & Haley, J. (1971). Reaction to socio-documentary film research in a mental health clinic. *The American Journal of Orthopsychiatry*, *41*(1), 91–100.

Chalfen, R., & Rich, M. (2007). Combining the applied, the visual and the medical: patients teaching physicians with visual narratives. In Pink, S. (Ed.), *Visual Interventions: Applied Visual Anthropology* (pp. 53–70). New York: Berghan Books.

Cordella, M. (2004). *The Dynamic consultation: A discourse analytical study of doctor-patient communication*. Amsterdam, Philadelphia: John Benjamin.

Dinsmore, S. (1996). Strategies for self-scrutiny: Video diaries 1990-1993. *New Scholarship From BFI Research*, 41-57.

Elder, D. (1995). Collaborative filmmaking: An open space for making meaning, A moral ground for ethnographic film. *Visual Anthropology Review*, *11*(2), 94–101. doi:10.1525/var.1995.11.2.94

Evans, G. B., Steer, R. A., & Fine, E. W. (1979). Alcohol value clarification in sixth graders:" a film-making project. *Journal of Alcohol and Drug Education*, *24*(2), 1–10.

Ewald, W. (1985). *Portraits and dreams: Photographs and stories by children of the Appalachians*. New York: Writers and Readers Publications.

Fitzpatrick, A. L., Tu, S. P., Steinmen, L., & Suin, M. K. (2007). *Using photovoice to understand perceptions of cardiovascular health in multicultural settings*. Paper presented at the American Public Health Association 135th Annual Meeting and Expo, Washington, DC.

Flaherty, R. J. (1922). *Nanook of the north*. New York: Révillon Frères.

Frith, H., & Harcourt, D. (2007). Using photographs to capture women's experiences of chemotherapy: reflecting on the method. *Qualitative Health Research*, *17*(10), 1340–1350. doi:10.1177/1049732307308949

Furman, L. (1990). Video therapy: An alternative for the treatment of adolescents. Special Issue: The creative arts therapies with adolescents. *The Arts in Psychotherapy*, *17*, 165–169. doi:10.1016/0197-4556(90)90027-N

Gibson, B. E. (2005). Co-producing video diaries: The presence of the 'absent' researcher. *International Journal of Qualitative Methods*, *4*(3), 1–9.

Ginsburg, F. (1991). Indigenous media: Faustian contract of global village? *Cultural Anthropology*, *6*(1), 92–112. doi:10.1525/can.1991.6.1.02a00040

Glaser, B. G. (1992). *Basics of grounded theory analysis*. Mill Valley, CA: Sociology Press.

Glaser, B. G., & Strauss, A. L. (1967). *The Discovery of grounded theory: Strategies for qualitative research*. Hawthorne, NY: Aldine de Gruyter.

Hagedorn, M. (1994). Hermeneutic photography: an innovative esthetic technique for generating data in nursing research. *ANS. Advances in Nursing Science*, *17*(1), 44–50.

Hagedorn, M. I. (1996). Photography: an aesthetic technique for nursing inquiry. *Issues in Mental Health Nursing*, *17*(6), 517–527. doi:10.3109/01612849609006530

Harrison, H. (2002). Seeing health and illness worlds: Using visual methodologies in a sociology of health and illness: a methodological review. *Sociology of Health & Illness*, *24*(6), 856–872. doi:10.1111/1467-9566.00322

Heritage, J., & Maynard, D. W. (Eds.). (2006). *Communication in medical care: Interaction between primary care physicians and patients*. Cambridge, UK: Cambridge University Press. doi:10.1017/CBO9780511607172

Holliday, R. (2004a). Filming "The Closet": The role of video diaries in researching sexualities. *The American Behavioral Scientist*, *47*(12), 1597–1616. doi:10.1177/0002764204266239

Holliday, R. (2004b). Reflecting the self. In Knowles, C., & Sweetman, P. (Eds.), *Picturing the social landscape: Visual methods and the sociological imagination* (pp. 49–65). London: Routledge.

Kennedy, T. (1971). The Skyriver Project: The story of a process. *National Film Board of Canada Challenge for Change Program, 12*, 3–21.

Kennedy, T. (1982). Beyond advocacy: A facilitative approach to public participation. *Journal of the University Film and Video Association, 34*(3), 33–46.

Kleinman, A. (1988). *The Illness narratives: Suffering, healing and the human condition.* New York: Basic Books.

Latham, A. (2004). Researching and writing everyday accounts of the city: An introduction to the diary-photo diary interview process. In Knowles, C., & Sweetman, P. (Eds.), *Picturing the social landscape: Visual methods and the sociological imagination* (pp. 117–131). London: Routledge.

Lopez, E. D. S., Eng, E., Randall-David, E., & Robinson, N. (2005). Quality-of-Life concerns of African American breast cancer survivors within rural North Carolina: Blending the techniques of photovoice and grounded theory. *Qualitative Health Research, 15*(1), 99–115. doi:10.1177/1049732304270766

Lorenz, L. S. (2006). *Living without connections: Using narrative analysis of photographs and interview text to understand living with traumatic brain injury and facilitators and barriers to recovery from the patient's perspective.* Paper presented at the European Sociological Association, Mid-Term Conference, Cardiff, Wales.

Lorenz, L. S., Webster, B., & Foley, L. (2007). *Making visible the invisible: Using photovoice to understand living with brain injury.* Paper presented at the 26th Annual Conference, Brain Injury Association of Massachusetts, Marlborough, MA.

MacDougall, D. (1991). Whose story is it? *Visual Anthropology Review, 7*(2), 2–10. doi:10.1525/var.1991.7.2.2

Michaels, E. (1985). How video has helped a group of aborigines in Australia. *Media Development, 1*, 16–18.

Patashnick, J. L., & Rich, M. (2005). Researching human experience: Video Intervention/Prevention Assessment (VIA). *Australasian Journal of Information Systems, 12*(2), 103–111.

Pink, S. (Ed.). (2008). *Visual interventions: Applied visual anthropology.* New York: Berghahn Books.

Prosser, J., & Loxley, A. (2008). *Introducing visual methods.* ESRC National Center for Research Methods. [NCRM Review Paper/010]

Radley, A. (2002). Portrayals of suffering: on looking away, looking at, and the comprehension of illness experience. *Body & Society, 8*(3), 1–23. doi:10.1177/1357034X02008003001

Radley, A., & Taylor, D. (2003). Images of recovery: A photo-elicitation study on the hospital ward. *Qualitative Health Research, 13*(1), 77–99. doi:10.1177/1049732302239412

Radley, A., & Taylor, D. (2003). Remembering one's stay in hospital: A study in photography, recovery and forgetting. *Health (London), 7*(2), 129–159. doi:10.1177/1363459303007002872

Rich, M., & Chalfen, R. (1999). Showing and telling asthma: Children teaching physicians with visual narratives. *Visual Sociology, 14*, 51–71. doi:10.1080/14725869908583802

Rich, M., Huecker, D., & Ludwig, D., S. (2001). Obesity in the lives of children and adolescents: Inquiry through patient-created visual narratives. *Pediatric Research, 49*, 7A.

Rich, M., Lamola, S., Amory, C., & Schneider, L. (2000). Asthma in life context: Video Intervention/ Prevention Assessment (VIA). *Pediatrics, 105*(3), 469–477. doi:10.1542/peds.105.3.469

Rich, M., Lamola, S., Gordon, J., & Chalfen, R. (2000). Video Intervention/Prevention assessment: A patient-centered methodology for understanding the adolescent illness experience. *The Journal of Adolescent Health, 27*(3), 155–165. doi:10.1016/S1054-139X(00)00114-2

Rich, M., Patashnick, J., & Kastelic, E. (2005). Achieving independence: the role of parental involvement with adolescents with spina bifida. *The Journal of Adolescent Health, 36*(2), 129. doi:10.1016/j.jadohealth.2004.11.070

Rich, M., & Patashnick, J. L. (2002). Narrative research with audiovisual data: Video Intervention/ Prevention Assessment (VIA) and NVivo. *International Journal of Social Research Methodology, 5*(3), 245–261. doi:10.1080/13645570210166373

Rich, M., Patashnick, J. L., Huecker, D., & Ludwig, D. (2002). Living with obesity: visual narratives of overweight adolescents [abstract]. *The Journal of Adolescent Health, 30*(2), 100. doi:10.1016/ S1054-139X(01)00361-5

Rich, M., Polvinen, J., & Patashnick, J. L. (2005). Visual narratives of the pediatric illness experience: Children communicating with clinicians through video. [Special issue on Child Psychiatry and the Media]. *Child and Adolescent Psychiatric Clinics of North America, 14*(3), 571–587. doi:10.1016/j.chc.2005.02.013

Terence, T. (1991). The social dynamics of video media in an indigenous society: The cultural meaning and the personal politics of videomaking in Kayapo communities. *Visual Anthropology Review, 7*(2), 68–76. doi:10.1525/var.1991.7.2.68

Wang, C., & Burris, M. A. (1997). Photovoice: Concept, methodology, and use for participatory needs assessment. *Health Education & Behavior, 24*(3), 369–387. doi:10.1177/109019819702400309

Wang, C., Burris, M. A., & Xiang, Y. P. (1996). Chinese village women as visual anthropologists: a participatory approach to reaching policymakers. *Social Science & Medicine, 42*(10), 1391–1400. doi:10.1016/0277-9536(95)00287-1

Wang, C. C. (1999). Photovoice: a participatory action research strategy applied to women's health. *Journal of Women's Health, 8*(2), 185–192. doi:10.1089/jwh.1999.8.185

Weiser, J. (1999). *Phototherapy techniques: Exploring the secrets of personal snapshots and family albums*. Vancouver, BC, Canada: Photo-Therapy Centre Press.

Worth, S. (1966). Film as non-art: An approach to the study of film. *The American Scholar, 35*(2), 322–334.

Worth, S., Adair, J., & Chalfen, R. (1997). *Through Navajo eyes: an exploration in film communication and anthropology*. Albuquerque, NM: University of New Mexico Press.

Ziller, R. C. (1990). *Photographing the self: Methods for observing personal orientations*. Newbury Park, CA: Sage.

ADDITIONAL READING

Barbara, H. (2002). Seeing health and illness worlds; Using visual methodologies in a sociology of health and illness: a methodological review. *Sociology of Health & Illness, 24*(6), 856–872. doi:10.1111/1467-9566.00322

Ewald, W. (2001). *I wanna take me a picture: Teaching photography and writing to children*. Boston, MA: Beacon Press.

Kleinman, A. (1988). *The illness narratives: Suffering, healing and the human condition*. New York: Basic Books.

Pink, S. (Ed.). (2008). *Visual interventions: Applied visual anthropology.* Oxford, UK: Berghahn Books.

Prosser, J. (1998). *Image-based research.* London: Falmer Press.

Thomson, P. (Ed.). (2008). *Doing visual research with children and young people.* London: Routledge.

White, S. A. (2003). *Participatory video: Images that transform and empower.* London: Sage.

Worth, S., Adair, J., & Chalfen, R. (1997). *Through Navajo eyes: an exploration in film communication and anthropology.* Albuquerque, NM: University of New Mexico Press.

ENDNOTE

[1] In addition, several of our VIA studies have assessed participants with clinical interviews and standardized health-related quality of life (HRQL) instruments before making visual narratives of their illness experience and after the project. The visual narratives have then been coded and triangulated with the data derived from clinical interviews and HRQL instruments for areas of congruence and dissonance.

Chapter 12
Informing Traces:
The Social Practices of Collaborative Informing in the Midwifery Clinic

Pamela J. McKenzie
The University of Western Ontario, Canada

ABSTRACT

The concept of "traces" is useful for understanding the collaborative practices of informing. Readers of documents leave traces of their use, and institutional talk embeds traces of collaborative work, including work done and elsewhere and at other times. This chapter employs a multifaceted qualitative strategy of analytic bracketing to analyze traces in midwives' and clients' discussions of clinical results. Results are used to identify and evaluate trends in relation to the current case or to universal norms. Conflicting forms of evidence may need to be negotiated. Barriers may arise when results or sources are inadequate or unavailable. Midwives and women manage these barriers by flexibly assigning the role of information provider in official and unofficial ways. The analysis of traces provides insight into the hows and whats of collaborative work and reveals it to be a complex set of practices that go well beyond the immediately visible contributions of others.

INTRODUCTION

The concept of "traces" or "footprints" is a useful one for the study of the collaborative practices of informing (see, for example, Foster, 2006, pp. 340-347). Documents may be seen to carry the traces of the subjects and objects they describe (Frohmann, 2008), and users of physical or digital documents may leave behind evidence of their use that is taken up by subsequent users as informative. Through the inscriptions made by previous authors and readers, documents used in collaborative environments can record, mediate, and co-ordinate the work of those who are invested in a single project though they may be responsible for different tasks, located in different places, and held to different timelines (Davies & McKenzie, 2004).

Although they may not be preserved in documentary form, traces are also evident in interper-

DOI: 10.4018/978-1-61520-797-8.ch012

sonal interactions, as when speakers invoke past experiences or outside sources as informative for the present occasion. The objective of this chapter is to analyze the ways that midwives and child-bearing women produce, take up, call on, and use references to people, places and events outside of their here-and-now interaction as they collaborate in presenting, discussing, and interpreting clinical findings. Analyzing institutional talk can reveal traces of work done in other places or at other times (Smith, 1990; McKenzie, 2006) and can show how the institutional work of informing is necessarily collaborative even when it appears not to be (McKenzie, 2009). The analysis of traces provides insight into both the *hows* and the *whats* (Holstein & Gubrium, 2005) of "the intertwined, institutionally disciplined, documentary and non-documentary practices from which 'information' emerges as an effect" (Frohmann, 2004, p. 198).

BACKGROUND

Several LIS studies have considered the work of people who gather together over time in formal and informal groups such as departments, communities of practice, task forces, crews, and teams. LIS researchers have attended to the temporal situatedness of information-related activities (Solomon, 1997; Savolainen, 2006) and have considered the development of collaborative projects over time (e.g., Hyldegård, 2006). Traces become useful for participants to situate themselves in the ongoing trajectory of the collaborative endeavour (e.g., Sonnenwald, Maglaughlin, & Whitton, 2004; Hertzum, 2008). They also allow those not physically present to contribute to the business at hand, as people, institutions, and interests may be brought into the conversation through spoken invocation (McKenzie & Oliphant, 2010) or through documentary traces such as the medical record (Davies & McKenzie, 2004).

A visit to a health care provider's clinic is a single occasion but is also a member both of a

longer series of such occurrences and of a more extensive set of social relations (Smith, 1990). Research on clinical interaction shows that health care providers and their clients provide and use traces of the encounter's place in a larger series of events in many and diverse ways. Both providers and clients orient to their past and future dealings together and situate the current discussion in relation to the previous knowledge that each is held to have. Robinson (2006) showed how a doctor's invitation to a patient to present a concern contains cues about the history of the relationship and reminders about who knows what about what has taken place before. Failing to attend to the visit's position in the ongoing physician-patient relationship (for example, by asking "What can we do for you today?" rather than "And how has the pain been this week?") has implications for the effectiveness of the interaction. Heritage and Robinson (2006) found that, in order to show that they have made all reasonable attempts to solve a problem before seeking the doctor's assistance, patients may provide a narrative of self-diagnosis and problem solving that begins in the past and culminates in the present of this visit to the doctor. Maynard (2003) analyzed the ways that people in clinical and everyday settings establish an announcement or a diagnosis as "news" by presenting and responding to it in particular ways. The news delivery sequence may include a pre-announcement that not only alerts the hearer to expect news, but prepares him or her for its positive or negative valence (e.g., "I have some good news about your test results"). Serious communication problems can arise when the newsworthiness or the valence are not taken up in the same way by speaker and hearer. West (2006) found that clinicians do the work of providing "continuity of care" partly through closing visits by making arrangements for what should happen next between the participants. Even sociable non-instrumental talk bears traces of the interpersonal relationship between care provider and client (Ragan, 2000).

LIS research on collaborative information seeking in medical settings has largely been set in critical or emergency care contexts (e.g., Gorman et al., 2000; McKnight, 2007; Reddy & Jansen, 2008; Reddy & Spence, 2008). Not surprisingly, therefore, these studies have focused on the work of health care providers and not on the contributions of patients. This chapter will build on this research by showing how practitioners and clients collaborate to bring the interaction into being, and how their work links to work done elsewhere (Smith, 1990). For example, diagnosis and treatment recommendation are often considered to be the work of the health care provider. However, conversation analytic research has shown that the patient is an active collaborator in both processes (Brooks-Howell, 2006; Stivers, 2006), and that her or his seemingly inconsequential responses can have important implications for the way they proceed. The simple receipt token "Oh," when used instead of "Mhmm," can serve the interactional function of indicating that a hearer treats what has been said as news and is now, for the purposes of this interaction, informed on this issue (Maynard, 2003, p. 101; McKenzie, 2009).

Rather than looking at the ways that "information tasks" are "performed in collaboration with others" (Foster, 2006, p.350), I start from the premise that "information" itself is constituted out of social practices – the interaction of people and documents, co-present and absent, past and future (Davenport & Cronin, 1998; Frohmann, 2004; Smith, 1990). I therefore take an approach that allows for an analysis of what Holstein and Gubrium (2005) call "interpretive practice":

the constellation of procedures, conditions, and resources through which reality is apprehended, understood, organized, and conveyed in everyday life.... Interpretive practice engages both the **hows** *and the* **whats** *of social reality; it is centered in both how people methodically construct their experiences and their worlds, and in the configurations of meaning and institutional life that inform and shape their reality-constituting activity (p. 484, emphasis in original).*

This chapter will demonstrate how interactional traces, defined here as direct or indirect reference to people, organizations, or interests outside the confines of the here-and-now clinical interaction, serve as a) resources for participants in doing the work of presenting and discussing clinical findings; and b) evidence for researchers analyzing the *hows* and *whats* of the practices that enable people to collaborate in doing institutionally mandated information work.

METHODOLOGICAL PROBLEMS AND SOLUTIONS

Theoretical Issues and Controversies

Several recent studies of collaborative information seeking (Foster 2006, p. 350) have used contextual qualitative methods. Holstein and Gubrium (2005) describe the strengths and limitations of two contextual qualitative approaches that focus on the "the interactional, institutional, and cultural variabilities" (p. 492) of the constitution of social life in and through discourse.

Ethnomethodologically-informed analysis pays close attention to the *hows* of social life: "the mechanisms by which social forms are brought into being in everyday life" (p. 484). Developed by Harold Garfinkel (1967), ethnomethodology "arguably has been the most analytically radical and empirically productive in specifying the actual procedures through which social order is accomplished" (Holstein & Gubrium, 2005, p.483). Ethnomethodological approaches focus on how people "do" social life and on the kinds of socially contingent, practical reasoning they use to do so (Holstein & Gubrium, 2005, p. 485). Methods attend closely to naturally-occurring talk. An indifferent stance to members' methods means that ethnomethodologists accept members' practical reasoning as adequate to the task at hand rather than critiquing it against some external criterion (Holstein & Gubrium, 2005, p. 487). Holstein and Gubrium (2005) caution that this indifferent focus on the *hows* of talk-in-interaction means that ethnomethodological analysis fails to attend to the meaningful *whats*: "the massive resources that are taken up in, and that guide, the operation of conversation, or... the consequences of producing particular results and not others, each of which is an important ingredient of practice" (p. 492).

Foucauldian discourse analysis, on the other hand, attends to the *whats* (Holstein & Gubrium, 2005): how historically and culturally located practices -- "discourses" -- "systematically form the objects of which they speak" (Foucault, 1972, p.48). Discourses in the Foucauldian sense are not simply rhetorical constructions, but broad systems of power/knowledge. For example, the physical design of the penitentiary and its documentary apparatus of timetables and regulations constructs inmates as the objects of moral discipline and rehabilitation (Foucault, 1995). Foucauldian analysis therefore makes visible the results and conditions of possibility of discourses, but pays little attention to real-time talk and social interaction and "provides little or no sense of the *everyday* technology by which [the birth of new discursive formations] is achieved" (Holstein & Gubrium, 2005, p. 491).

While Holstein and Gubrium concede that these two perspectives come from different intellectual traditions and work in different registers -- and are often presented as mutually exclusive (e.g., Budd, 2006) -- they contend that qualitative research would be enriched by an "analytics of interpretive practice" that retains ethnomethodology's sensitivity to the *hows* of interaction while attending to "both the constitutive and constituted *whats* of everyday life" (Holstein and Gubrium, 2005, p. 489).

Methodological Solutions

Holstein and Gubrium (2005) advocate a form of what they call "analytic bracketing," a "skilled juggling act, alternatively concentrating on the myriad *hows* and *whats* of everyday life" (2005, pp. 495-496). Analytic bracketing requires the researcher alternately to focus on both facets of interpretive practice, "documenting each in turn, and making informative references to the other in the process" (Holstein & Gubrium, 2005, p. 496).

In this chapter I use three analytic strategies to bring Holstein and Gubrium's (2005) analytics of interpretive practice to the domain of LIS. This methodological approach can provide new understanding of both the *hows* and the *whats* of collaborative practices of informing in an institutional setting. This chapter will demonstrate how passages of naturally-occurring talk contain traces to past and future times and to the activities of other people in other places. The analysis of both provides insight into the ways that traces contribute to participants' business at hand and serves as an analytic model for identifying traces in other settings and contexts.

Data Collection

Data come from transcripts of audio-recordings of 40 midwifery clinic visits. Midwifery in Ontario is a licensed and publicly-funded direct-entry profession (i.e. midwives are not required to be nurses, Bourgeault & Fynes, 1997; Bourgeault, 2006). Ontario midwives provide continuous care to low-risk women through pregnancy, home or hospital birth, and for six weeks postpartum (Association of Ontario Midwives, n.d.). Informed choice and continuity of care are foundational to the midwifery model (College of Midwives of Ontario, 2004). These principles have important implications for the study of collaborative information seeking. First, midwives are mandated to inform childbearing women to support women's decision-making (McKenzie, 2009). At the same time, the woman is taken to be the expert on her own body, situation, and preferences, and has the right to inform her midwife on these issues. Second, this mandated informing takes place within a developing relationship between the woman and her primary and backup midwives.

I purposively selected Ontario communities to include a range of populations. I contacted all practices in each selected community. Fifteen agreed to participate: five from the city of Toronto (population > 2 million), two from large cities (population > 300,000), five from medium-sized cities (population 50,000- 300,000), and three from small towns and rural areas (population < 50,000). In order to be included, both a midwife and one or more of her clients had to be willing to participate. I therefore accepted all willing midwife-client pairs, a total of 40 clients and 31 midwives.

I audio-recorded one clinic visit between each participating woman and her midwife. While video recording would have produced a richer data set, I decided against it for several reasons. First, participants moved around the examining room over the course of the visit: a videographer would be required. Most examining rooms were very small and partners, children, and midwifery students frequently attended with the midwife and woman. Few visit rooms would accommodate an extra person. Second, videorecording in such close quarters would have been obtrusive to the point of disruptiveness. Many participants noted that they had forgotten the presence of the audio recorder. This would not have been the case with video equipment. Finally, much of what took place in the visits was physically intimate (e.g. internal pelvic examinations). While all participants were happy to have an audio recorder continue to record through their entire visit, it is likely that some might have been unwilling to have their visit videorecorded or would have asked that the recording equipment turned off for portions of the visit.

The 37 pregnant clients ranged from 14 to 40 weeks gestation, and the three postpartum visits took place between 2 and 4 weeks after the birth. Midwives - all women - had between 6 months and more than 20 years of experience. Eighteen of the women were first-time mothers and 22 had given birth before. Of these, 11 had been attended by the present midwife in one or more previous pregnancies and 11 had been with other midwives in the current practice, midwives at another practice, or with physicians. Audio-recordings of visits have been transcribed. Data collection and analysis conform to ethical guidelines on research on human subjects of Social Science and Humanities Research Council of Canada (CIHR, NSERC, & SSHRC, 2003) and the study was approved by the Non-Medical Research Ethics Board at The University of Western Ontario. All participants are identified by code.

Data Analysis

I went through the 40 transcripts line by line to identify traces of people, events, and situations that predated or existed outside of the current interaction. Traces may be explicit or very subtle. In many cases temporal words (modifiers like again, still, next, last, before, after; the use of past tense) signalled their presence. However, a midwife's parting request to "Say hi to the girls for me!" also embeds traces. This request displays knowledge that the woman has daughters and positions the midwife as someone who may legitimately claim sufficient familiarity to make such a request (Harré & van Langenhove, 1999). The woman neither refused the midwife's request nor challenged her knowledge claim (e.g., "I have boys, not girls"). Both speakers therefore contributed to this positioning: the woman's response is integral to understanding the midwife's request in its interactional context (Heritage, 2004).

In this chapter I analyze the traces embedded in a particular work task (Heritage, 2004): the presentation, discussion, and evaluation of clinical findings. Clinical findings were reported in all 40 visits, and reporting them is a mandated part of woman-midwife interaction.

In conducting an analysis that attends to the multiple foci required by analytic bracketing, I have selected three analytic strategies. The first is conversation analysis (CA), particularly as it is applied to the study of institutional interaction (e.g., Heritage, 2004). The second is discourse analysis as practised in social psychology (e.g., Potter, 1996), and the third is relational analysis of the kind that forms part of institutional ethnography (e.g., Smith, 1990). I have previously used each of these analytic approaches on its own with the midwifery data set. This chapter brings the three together in ways that show the interplay among locally constitutive interactional practices and broader structural and discursive constraints.

An initial example[1] will serve to ground the introduction of each of the three analytic strategies. The example is a presentation of a clinical finding that occurs very frequently in midwife-woman visits, the reporting of blood pressure. This example was chosen because it is very typical of this kind of talk:

M: Good! [velcro sound of the blood pressure cuff being removed] One-ten over seventy-four. [clattering] That's a good blood pressure. [sounds of movement.] It's been good all along with you hasn't it?

W: Yup.

The description of each analytic strategy will include a brief example of the kind of analysis it can provide of this example. The findings sections will then focus on showing the possibilities of an analytics that oscillates among perspectives.

1. Conversation analysis (CA): CA is one form of ethnomethodologically-inspired analysis that focuses closely on the ways that speakers sequentially and methodically do things together through interactional practice. CA is based on a number of fundamental theoretical assumptions (Heritage, 2004; Wooffitt, 2005). First, conversation analysts argue that social interaction itself has institutional characteristics with associated rights and obligations independent of any individual characteristics of speakers. This "interaction order" both underlies and mediates the operation of all other social institutions (Heritage, 2004, p.222). Second, CA assumes that participants manage their interaction on a turn-by-turn basis so focuses on the *sequential* organization of talk. Third, conversation analysts argue that turns of talk perform actions (Heritage & Maynard, 2006a, pp. 9-10) such as news giving (Maynard, 2003) and accomplishing institutionally-mandated informed choice (McKenzie, 2009). CA is useful for breaking an interaction down to its constituent parts and showing the incremental steps by which speakers accomplish it as a particular kind of talk (Heritage, 2004; McKenzie, 2009). Conversation analysis has been generally criticized for restricting its scope too narrowly on the mechanics of interaction, although CA studies of institutional interaction (e.g., Heritage, 2004) also reveal aspects of the broader institutional context (Holstein & Gubrium, 2005, p.488). CA, particularly in its application to institutional interaction, can answer questions such as: Within what institutionally-relevant tasks are traces subsumed? (Heritage, 2004; McKenzie, 2009). Who is framed as the information provider and who as the person to be informed? What information is each participant taken to have or not have? (Labov & Fanshel, 1977) What is made explicit among speakers and what is left unsaid? How are traces used interactionally? How do participants take up traces as constituents of the work of informing? (McKenzie, 2009). CA requires a careful analysis of what action each turn of talk accomplishes and how it relates to previous turns. Individual instances and subsections are then compared to identify patterns,

consistencies and deviations. By analyzing these patterns turn-by-turn a researcher can identify the interactional and institutional "fingerprint" of the talk and can demonstrate how each component contributes to the sequential accomplishment of the business at hand (Heritage, 2004; McKenzie, 2009). CA can, for example, identify the blood-pressure excerpt as an example of a news-delivery sequence (Maynard, 2003), where the midwife is treated as knowing and being able to evaluate the result and the woman is treated as the recipient of the good news.

2. Discourse analysis (DA) of the type used by Jonathan Potter (1996) and other social psychologists, is a method identified by Holstein and Gubrium (2005) as attending to something of both *how* and *what*. This form of analysis is concerned with the ways that accounts are constructed as credible and factual and with the rhetorical functions accounts perform within their broader interactional contexts. It is therefore useful for showing the ways speakers use traces to make and contest claims and to work up or challenge sources of evidence as credible and authoritative (McKenzie, 2003; McKenzie & Oliphant, 2006). It can answer questions such as:

What sources of evidence do speakers reference on when calling on traces? What discursive functions do traces perform? (Potter, 1996). A DA analysis requires looking closely at talk itself as artfully constructed rather than as a simple and transparent representation of some external truth or of the speaker's mental state. Analysis proceeds through a close study of variations in the construction of talk, both within and across accounts, to identify both the discursive building blocks speakers use when producing an account and the discursive functions that account might be serving (Potter, 1996). DA of the blood pressure excerpt might focus on the kind of evidence used in working up an evaluation as "good": the midwife calls on the woman's previous blood pressure readings ("all along") to invoke a series of independent observations that together suggest an objectively observable trend.

3. Relational analysis: Of the three forms of analysis used here, this one attends most directly to the *whats* of interpretive practice (Holstein & Gubrium, 2005, p. 495). Smith argues that work done in a local setting bears "the threads and shreds of the relations it is organized by and organizes" (1990, pp. 3-4). While Smith acknowledges the importance of Foucauldian discourses, she argues they do not have an overriding power; that local interaction affords "play and interplay" (Smith, 1990, p. 202; Holstein & Gubrium, p. 495). Relational analysis addresses questions such as: What kind of knowledge is required in order to make a particular statement, claim, or request (Smith, 1990) and what resources are required for the statement to be accepted as legitimate? How does a trace hook the work done here and now into work done at other times and in other places? To what times/places/people/sources does the trace hook in (Smith, 1990)? Specifically, how does local midwifery work hook into the broader biomedical and neoliberal consumerist discourses within which midwifery must negotiate its egalitarian feminist ethos (Sharpe, 2004a; Spoel, 2007; Thachuk, 2007)?

Analysis within this perspective focuses, not on how talk is constructed, but on where traces lead. Attention therefore extends beyond a consideration of the talk itself. By identifying the people, places, documents, and organizations whose work is linked to what is going on in the present moment, the analysis can show how the talk, text, and work happening here are connected, and are visible as constituents of, larger social relations (Smith, 1990, p.210). Relational analysis of the blood pressure example might focus on where standards of "good" blood pressure come from: what organizations are charged with developing, communicating, and enforcing such standards, and how such standards come to be accepted and reproduced within clinical practice (e.g., McKenzie, 2006).

Although analytic bracketing has no set procedures, it has procedural implications. Holstein and

Gubrium (2005) caution that analytic bracketing must be more than the simple application of multiple analytic strategies. Like drivers of a vehicle with a manual transmission, researchers must constantly shift between perspectives, constantly turning their attention in more than one direction. The analyst must oscillate between *how* and *what*, now being indifferent to members' practices, and now considering them in relation to their broader institutional and discursive contexts. In this case, familiarity with each of the three analytic strategies enabled me to look at each excerpt from a variety of perspectives, as demonstrated by the blood pressure example above. As is evident from that excerpt, even a small and routine bit of talk is a rich site that affords glimpses of both the constraints that the structural and discursive context place on the presentation of clinical findings and the artful ways that individual women and midwives work within and around these constraints.

The Findings section will first describe the characteristics of talk about clinical results and will show how it exhibits traces of past interactions among the present speakers as well as interactions with other agencies and care providers. Next, I will describe a function that talk about clinical results can perform: identifying and evaluating trends. Multiple forms of conflicting evidence may need to be brought together in order to achieve a resolution. Finally, I will address the ways that midwives and women respond to barriers when results or resources are inadequate or unavailable.

FINDINGS

Reporting Clinical Results

The reporting and interpretation of clinical results is a mandated form of talk in a clinician-client encounter, and each participant has institutionally-mandated roles. Although participants may discuss the clinician's health in their friendly talk together, the institutional mandate is almost universally given to talk about the *client's* clinical results. Three kinds of clinical results were discussed in midwifery visits. First were the results of clinical assessments made as part of the visit itself. These included the prenatal physical examination of the woman (weight, urine tests for glucose and protein, blood pressure, fetal heart rate, abdominal palpation to assess fetal size and position) and postpartum examination of the woman and infant (e.g., infant weight, measurement, breathing and heart function; maternal blood pressure). Talk about these kinds of results therefore embedded traces of collaboration between this woman and midwife, and possibly among them and other midwives and students caring for the woman during previous visits. The second kind of results came from tests and procedures that were requisitioned or ordered (and data perhaps collected) in the course of a clinic visit, but which were analyzed by an external lab or consultant. Procedures of this kind include diagnostic ultrasound, screening for gestational diabetes, urine testing for bacteria, and blood work for disease antibodies or hemoglobin levels. Official clinical results therefore came back to the midwife in the form of formal reports to be taken up with the client at later visits, and talk references collaboration among the midwife, the external providers, and possibly the administrative staff of both (McKenzie, 2006). The third kind of results came from tests or procedures ordered by the obstetricians, family doctors, or midwives who attended women's previous pregnancies, or by the medical specialists treating women's pre-existing conditions or pregnancy-related complications. In these cases it would be the other care provider who first discussed clinical findings with the woman. Sometimes other care providers automatically forwarded reports to the midwife and at other times -- for example, when specialist care predated the current pregnancy -- they did not, and midwives wanting access to these findings needed to acquire the reports. Talk about this type of result therefore embeds all traces of collaboration evident in talk about the other two kinds of result, but here it is the consultant clinician, not the present midwife, who is taken to hold administrative responsibility for the results and records.

As it is the health care provider who receives consultants' reports and test results, she or he is generally taken to hold prior knowledge about the findings. In talk about clinical results, the practitioner is therefore institutionally understood to be the information provider while the client is placed in the role of person to be informed. A health care provider is likewise institutionally taken to have both the professional knowledge and the authority to diagnose and to prescribe next courses of action (Lee & Garvin, 2003; Heritage & Maynard, 2006, p.354; Elwyn, Gwyn, Edwards, & Grol, 1999). Ontario midwifery, however, espouses a woman-centered model of care which, at least in ideal form, actively and consciously rejects provider dominance. The midwifery model posits care to be egalitarian, relational and empowering (College of Midwives of Ontario, 1994; Spoel, 2007; Thachuk, 2007); women's experience and knowledge ideally determine midwifery knowledge and practice (Bourgeault 2006; MacDonald, 2006), and the woman is understood to be the primary decision-maker about her own care (College of Midwives of Ontario, 2005). This means that, in some cases, the midwifery client is institutionally understood to "own" the knowledge of her clinical results and therefore takes the role of information provider while the midwife is the person to be informed. The reporting of clinical results therefore takes one of two interactional forms, depending on who is held to have prior knowledge.

Labov and Fanshel (1977) classified talk according to the presumed prior knowledge of speakers. In a conversation where speaker A talks to hearer B,

A-events are events to which the speaker has privileged access, and about which he [sic] cannot reasonably be contradicted, since they typically concern A's own emotions, experience, personal

biography.... B-events are, similarly, events about which the hearer has privileged knowledge." (Stubbs, 1983, 118-119)

AB-events are taken to be known to both A and B (Labov and Fanshel, 1977, p.100). The discussion of clinical findings may therefore be treated as being properly A- or B-event talk, depending on who raises the issue and who is entitled to claim prior knowledge.

In presenting results arising from data collected by the midwife in the course of the visit or from external reports received by her, usual practice is for the midwife to raise the issue as an A-event topic. Midwives and the midwifery students working under their supervision consistently provided an immediate verbal report of the results of their physical examination,

S: It's nice and low, it's ninety-four over fifty-six.

W: It's

S: So-.

W: always been low.

S: Yeah. [laughs]

M: [paper rustles] And, did I tell you last time that [the baby's] thyroid test and her p.k.u. test came back normal?

W: Umm, yeah I think so.

M: Okay. So all that tested normal.

In both cases, the midwife/student presented herself as knowledgeable about the procedure and result and the woman accepted this presentation.

Some kinds of clinical data are collected by the woman herself as an acknowledgement of the woman's right to active involvement in her care. As Hawkins and Knox (2003) observe, this practice highlights a fundamental difference between midwifery and medical care:

Many women note with surprise and relief that their midwives do not stand over them as they weigh themselves.... Most clients can note the numbers on a scale and differentiate between the colours on a [urine] test strip.... Many women prefer this opportunity to test themselves, report the results and consult with the midwives if results appear unusual. (p. 93)

In the clinics where I collected data, women generally checked weight and urine immediately upon arrival, and a urine-and-weight report was almost universally the first or second order of business in a prenatal visit. If a woman did not offer an A-event report, the midwife made a B-event query which generally elicited a report of the number in pounds or kilograms:

M: And did you weigh yourself?

W: Yeah. One, forty? What was I be//fore?// Last time?

....//M: Good.//

M: Last time? One thirty-three.

W: Oh my God. That's a **lot!**

M: Well you were pretty tiny before this pregnancy.

W: Yeah but. Oh well. [laughs]

Although these three examples are routine and very ordinary, each embeds multiple traces of work done in other times and places. The "weight" example directly references the woman's work of getting on scale and reading a number, but it also embeds traces of the work of midwives negotiating a woman-centered practice model. Here, the woman "owns" her own weight, for the present at least, and is taken as the information provider. Once the midwife has recorded the datum, however, responsibility for holding it and the authority to know about it might pass to her. The woman's request for her weight from "last time" references this authority and she treats the midwife as legitimately knowledgeable about, and herself as ignorant of, her previous weight.

These routine exchanges therefore provide clues about the ways that professional responsibility, ownership of "facts," the authority to construct occurrences as facts, and the right to take on the role of information provider are negotiated in midwifery care. They also contain evidence of documentary practices. The "thyroid" excerpt's reference to results that have "come back" links to a set of practices completely external to this visit (McKenzie, 2006; Yakel, 2001) but contributing to it. The work of lab technicians is inscribed onto a report which may be transferred through further inscription to a check box or text field in the woman's chart for later retrieval by this or subsequent midwives.

Although the midwifery model seeks to disrupt a hegemonic biomedical discourse, midwifery practice is embedded within the organizational structure of the Ontario healthcare system and is subject to its licensing and regulatory practices. The Antenatal Record (Ontario Ministry of Health and Long-Term Care, 2005) is a central organizing document in Ontario pregnancy care. It was developed by a subcommittee of the Ontario Medical Association, who indicates that its use is "not mandatory," (Ontario Medical Association Subcommittee, 2000). Sharpe, however, characterizes its use as "required" for midwives (2004a, p. 160). The Antenatal Record functions as a boundary object (Star & Griesemer, 1989) that both coordinates and embeds traces of the work of the midwives and possibly other practitioners providing care for each client (Davies & McKenzie, 2004). It is here that midwives inscribe measurements taken and the results of clinical tests and procedures. Midwives' inscriptions are therefore subject to the biomedical discourses that organize Ontario healthcare: "clinical relevance" is institutionally defined in biomedical terms (Spoel, 2007). For example, although the choice of home or hospital birth is a basic tenet of midwifery care, the Antenatal Record does not include this in its list of discussion topics (Ontario Ministry of Health and Long-term Care, 2005; see also McKenzie, 2006).

Identifying Trends

Once a clinical result has been reported, it may be taken up as a constituent of a trend. In order for a trend to be identified and evaluated, a new datum needs to be reported, as described above. The new datum must then be compared with one or more previous data, and a trend reported. The trend may then be evaluated or extrapolated into the future as a prediction. Data for the establishment of trends could be either local, related to this one woman over time:

M: So the baby's heart rate was one forty-six.

W: Okay, that's lower than it was last time.

M: Yeah, so I can show you where [paper rustling] your growth has been. So today's yeah. So I'm

right on that fiftieth percentile so that's perfect. And right what we'd be [paper rustling] expecting.

W: Mmmkay.

Inscriptions made at this visit are thus linked to norms and standards developed elsewhere and are themselves carried through the record into the future of the midwife-client relation (Smith, 1990).

Norms were never far away, and new observations were commonly evaluated in relation to both local trends and universal norms. In some cases, local and universal measures converged on a single evaluation:

M: And that's another centimetre. Compared to last week you're right on track. You're measuring thirty-nine centimetres for thirty-nine weeks. [movement sound] And last time you were, thirty-eight [cm] at thirty-eight [weeks]!

W: Yeah. [laughs]

In other cases, local and universal assessments were not congruent, and midwife and woman were required to negotiate which should apply in this case. This negotiation involved gathering multiple forms of evidence and evaluating each with respect to the others. Midwife and woman might agree that one form of evidence won out, or they might have to negotiate their own perspectives relative to competing sources (McKenzie & Oliphant, 2010). In the "weight" example discussed above, the woman and midwife negotiated the appropriateness of a local trend in relation to universal standards:

M: And did you weigh yourself?

W: Yeah. One, forty? What was I be//fore?// Last time?

...................................//M: Good.//

M: Last time? One thirty-three.

W: Oh my God. That's a **lot**!

M: Well you were pretty tiny before this pregnancy.

W: Yeah but. Oh well. [laughs]

The woman questioned the appropriateness of the weight gain, evaluating it in relation to some suggested but unstated standard and aligning herself in agreement, if not in physical compliance, with it. The midwife rejected the woman's evaluation and substituted her own, presenting a local trend as counterevidence. She invoked the woman's pre-pregnancy size as an AB-event, known to both. The woman did not contest this framing, and ruefully accepted the midwife's reconfigured evaluation. This excerpt therefore references the exercise of professional judgement: although a woman is recognized as the primary decision-maker, it is the midwife who has the institutional right and responsibility to make the definitive clinical evaluation.

Overcoming Barriers

Several sources were potentially available to the midwife and woman in presenting and evaluating clinical results: documentary evidence from the Antenatal Record and other reports, physical evidence from an examination of the woman's body, verbal evidence from someone else, and lived, personal first-hand knowledge (Wilson, 1983). Occasionally one of these sources was missing or deficient, and midwives and women developed strategies for working around these deficiencies.

Three midwives in my data set were either meeting their clients for the very first time or having the first substantive visit with a newly-pregnant woman. Although these midwives had no shared history or first-hand knowledge of the woman to draw upon (Wilson, 1983), they made use of other resources at their disposal. On the surface, the next excerpt appears very similar to the other "weight gain" example -- the midwife evaluates the woman's weight gain and the woman accepts her right to do so. However, this talk embeds a rather different set of traces as it took place within the first meeting between the two:

M: So the visit **before** that you'd hardly gained any weight, at all. And this visit //you made// up for it

...................................//W: Yeah, ((suddenly))// [both laugh]

M: You had a bit of a //growth spurt.//

...................//W: Apparently.// Yeah.

The midwife's statement about the woman's previous weight gain is therefore a B-event claim rather than an AB-event claim, but the woman contests neither the correctness of the claim nor the midwife's right to make it. This passage embeds traces of a system of official documentation including the Antenatal Record but also references the standard role of a licensed midwife. Although much literature emphasizes the importance of the ongoing caring relationship between a woman and her primary midwife (e.g., Sharpe, 2004b), the complex of clinical records and the documentary practices of licensing and practice management make it possible for a new midwife to step into a woman's care midstream and make authority claims that are indistinguishable in type from those made by the midwife in the first weight gain example. Here the woman accords the new midwife authority over B-events that is functionally equivalent to the first-hand authority of the midwife she has replaced. This midwife's ability to step into the breach is supported by a large amount of unseen collaborative information work, from the collective recordkeeping of midwives in the practice to the weekly meetings where each midwife may be brought up to speed on what has taken place.

In other cases, midwives and women used their own and one another's first-hand knowledge to work around record-keeping deficiencies. The Antenatal Record might not record everything, and midwives commonly "checked in" with women, temporarily assigning them the role of information provider and themselves the role of person to be informed, to confirm whether she or another midwife had discussed a result with the woman:

M: [paper rustles] And, did I tell you last time that her thyroid test and her p.k.u test came back normal?

W: Umm, yeah I think so.

M: Okay. So all that tested normal.

Explicit or implicit references to record-keeping deficiencies or failures are a particularly rich site for identifying and following traces. These deficiencies illustrate the flexible ways that midwives and women assigned and reassigned the role of information provider and the corresponding authority and prior knowledge of a clinical result. In the next example, the woman had gone for an ultrasound examination to confirm the position of her baby, who was suspected to be lying in a nonstandard head-up (breech) position. Ultrasound technicians are not authorized to communicate diagnoses with clients. They refer the image to a radiologist for interpretation and the radiologist's office sends the report to the primary care provider for discussion. However, pregnant women are generally physically positioned so that they can see the ultrasound image and they may infer some diagnoses on their own.

M: Where's the baby Sybilla?

W: [indicates breech position with her hand on her abdomen] Head, bum, feet.

M: You know for sure? The ul, they did the ultrasound?

W: Yeah. Did they not send you the results?

M: I haven't seen the results yet. [rustling papers]

W: Oh really, oh I was hoping that //((we wouldn't have a)) wait.//

···//M: No, let's get//
No, w, [can hear dial tone on speaker phone: M is calling to request that the report be faxed to her]

M: uhh [monotone blips of keying in the phone number] wasn't actually sure //that they//

···//W:
It was// very clear. But not, not engaged [in the pelvis].

M: But not engaged. Yeah so ((it's a breech // okay))//

....//*W: Yeah.*// *Yes. So far.*

Both the midwife and the woman knew that the woman had gone for the ultrasound, and both expected the midwife to have received the report and to explain it at this visit. The report's absence constituted a potential barrier to officially informing the woman about the state of her pregnancy. However, the two overcame this barrier by switching roles: by asking the woman about the baby's position, the midwife presented herself as ignorant and the woman as knowledgeable on this question and relinquished the role of information provider, which the client took up. Even as she called to request the official report, the midwife accepted the woman's report as authoritative, and the two went on to discuss options before the fax arrived. This excerpt illustrates the midwife's parallel strategies of going through prescribed channels to get the official report while supplementing with an unofficial but adequate-for-the-moment report from the woman. The collaborative efforts of the midwife, client, ultrasound technician, radiologist, and administrative staff (as well as the ultrasound system itself and the various regulations and protocols associated with its use) were all therefore required in order to accomplish an evaluation of the baby's position.

Another conscious departure from a paternalistic biomedical model is midwifery's practice of giving the woman physical custody of her original Antenatal Record (McKenzie, 2006) as her due date approaches. With this physical transfer comes a symbolic transfer of formal authority over the record. In the final example, a midwife, woman and a midwifery student had been discussing the woman's previous birth, a caesarian section attended by midwives and doctors in another city:

M: Okay, so what we like to do is we would like to request thee um, the C-section [report] from the hospital so I have a chance to sort of review that.

W: Okay. [...] Um, is that anything I would have? Cause I still have all my paperwork and everything from, from her birth.

S: From the clinic, //the midwifery// clinic at, at

.........................//*W: Yeah//*

S: Yeah.

W: Midwifery clinic and from [hospital in other city]

S: She might, //you might// have it, yeah.

...............//*M: Okay.//*

M: Yeah. //Can you look it up? It, it would say// "operative report."

...............//*W: I'll look, I'll look through my file and see ((if there's anything)).//*

W: Okay [...]

M: [to student] Just make a note that we have requested a, [paper rustling] copy of the um, operative report from her. So then we have to follow that up. [to woman] If we don't have it then, we have to ask you to sign an authorization and we'll fax it down to the hospital //and then// we have to request [a copy of the report from the hospital].........//*W: Sure//*

While the woman in the ultrasound example temporarily became the best-source-for-now until the official report could be obtained, the woman in the C-section example became the primary source of official documentation about her previous birth. The midwife would only go to the prescribed source if this strategy were unsuccessful.

Although the midwife is most often positioned as the information provider in reporting clinical findings, there are many official and unofficial exceptions. By flexibly assigning this role, woman and midwife can overcome barriers that might otherwise prove insurmountable. These work-arounds may temporarily upset the established way of doing things and pose small challenges to the dominant discourse.

FUTURE RESEARCH DIRECTIONS

Analytic bracketing offers LIS researchers a new way to analyze and understand collaboration. This strategy has identified some of the interactional *hows* of collaboration as well as providing insight into the more deeply embedded discursive *whats* that underlie the institutionally mandated work of informing. As a new analytic strategy for LIS researchers, it offers much promise for identifying the traces of collaborative work embedded in naturally-occurring talk in institutional settings.

While conversation analysis, discourse analysis, and relational analysis each offer a single view of the dynamics of reporting clinical findings, Holstein and Gubrium's (2005) notion of analytic bracketing offers a means of playing off one form of analysis against another. Holstein and Gubrium caution against a simple analytic integration and argue instead for an "oscillating indifference to the realities of everyday life" that highlights the *interplay* of institutional discourse and local artfulness (2005, p. 495). Holstein and Gubrium propose that an oscillating focus on *what* and *how* can begin to address some of the *whys* of social life. Discursive practice "provides the footing for answering why recognizable constel-

lations of social order take on locally distinctive shapes" (2005, p. 498). This chapter has taken some initial steps in this direction, considering what combinations of physical, verbal, documentary, and first-hand evidence are brought into play in making claims and identifying and evaluating trends; what is the origin of universal data against which individual cases are to be evaluated; who is understood to hold what knowledge and what authority to provide what evidence; who exercises what rights to make claims, diagnoses, evaluations, predictions, and recommendations, to identify trends or to interpret evidence; what resources are available and to whom; what conflicts and barriers arise and how are these negotiated and resolved; what work-arounds are developed and what are the consequences of these; how and under what circumstances rights, knowledge, and authority claims are made, contested and negotiated; how people knowingly and unknowingly collaborate with their past and future selves and with others in other places and at other times; what traces of these collaborations are embedded in their current interaction.

Future use of analytic bracketing can expand on this analysis by unpacking other kinds of institutional practice with informing as a mandate. In addition, analytic bracketing is well-suited to the analysis of other forms of collaborative endeavour, including: how both discussion topics and "information needs" are interactionally negotiated as legitimate; how "informing" as an institutionally mandated form of interaction is enacted in practice; how dominant and alternative discourses are invoked in the provision of evidence and the making of claims; what the analysis of traces shows about the history of a relation and its development over time.

CONCLUSION

The analysis in this chapter demonstrates that even the most routine interactions embed traces of collaborative work, some done here and now and some done at other times and/or in other places. Indeed, Smith (1990) argues that any institutional interaction embeds traces of extralocal work. Identifying and analyzing how such traces are produced can provide insight into the interactional *hows*, and following traces leads to the discursive *whats* of institutionally mandated informing. This chapter has shown that naturally-occurring talk in institutional settings is a rich site, and that analytic bracketing is a flexible methodological approach, through which to reveal collaboration as a complex and multifaceted set of practices that go well beyond the visible contributions of others present and absent.

ACKNOWLEDGMENT

This research was funded by an internal research grant from the Faculty of Information and Media Studies of The University of Western Ontario and a Standard Research Grant from the Social Sciences and Humanities Research Council of Canada. The author wishes to acknowledge the support of Jacquelyn Burkell, co-investigator on the internal research grant, of the research assistants who assisted in transcribing the data, and of the participants for their generosity.

REFERENCES

Association of Ontario Midwives. (n.d.) *What is a midwife?* Retrieved May 10, 2010, from http://www.aom.on.ca/Midwifery_Care/What_is_a_Midwife.aspx

Bourgeault, I. L. (2006). Push! The struggle for midwifery in Ontario. Montreal, PQ: McGill Queen's University Press.

Bourgeault, I. L., & Fynes, M. (1997). Integrating lay and nurse-midwifery into the U.S. and Canadian health care systems. *Social Science & Medicine, 44*(7), 1051–1063. doi:10.1016/S0277-9536(96)00290-0

Brookes-Howell, L. C. (2006). Living without labels: the interactional management of diagnostic uncertainty in the genetic counselling clinic. *Social Science & Medicine, 63*(12), 3080–3091. doi:10.1016/j.socscimed.2006.08.008

Budd, J. (2006). Discourse analysis and the study of communication in LIS. *Library Trends, 55*(1), 65–82. doi:10.1353/lib.2006.0046

Burkell, J., & McKenzie, P. J. (2005). Information provision for informed prenatal decision making. In L. Vaughan (Ed.), *Data, information, and knowledge in a networked world.* Canadian Association for Information Science 2005 Annual Conference June 2-4, 2005. Retrieved May 10, 2010 from http://www.cais-acsi.ca/proceedings/2005/burkell_2005.pdf

Canadian Institutes of Health Research. Natural Sciences and Engineering Research Council of Canada, &. Social Sciences and Humanities Research Council of Canada. (2003). *Tri-Council policy statement: Ethical conduct for research involving humans.* Ottawa, ON: Public Works and Government Services Canada. Retrieved May 10, 2010 from http://www.pre.ethics.gc.ca/policy-politique/tcps-eptc/docs/TCPS%20October%202005_E.pdf

College of Midwives of Ontario. (1994). *Philosophy of midwifery care in Ontario.* Retrieved May 10, 2010, from http://www.cmo.on.ca/downloads/communications/standards/G01-Philosophy%20of%20Midwifery%20Care%20Jan94.pdf

College of Midwives of Ontario. (2005). *Informed choice standard*. Retrieved May 10, 2010, from http://www.cmo.on.ca/downloads/communications/standards/G14-Informed%20Choice%20Standard%20Sept%2005.pdf

Davies, E., & McKenzie, P. J. (2004). Preparing for opening night: temporal boundary objects in textually-mediated professional practice. *Information Research, 10*(1). Retrieved May 10, 2010, from http://informationr.net/ir/10-1/paper211.html

Elwyn, G., Gwyn, R., Edwards, A., & Grol, R. (1999). Is shared decision-making feasible in consultations for upper respiratory tract infections? Assessing the influence of antibiotic expectations using discourse analysis. *Health Expectations, 2*(2), 105–117. doi:10.1046/j.1369-6513.1999.00045.x

Foster, J. (2006). Collaborative information seeking and retrieval. In Cronin, B. (Ed.), *Annual Review of Information Science and Technology* (*Vol. 40*, pp. 329–356). Medford, NJ: Information Today.

Foucault, M. (1972). *The archaeology of knowledge*. New York: Pantheon.

Foucault, M. (1995). *Discipline & punish, the birth of the prison* (2nd ed.). New York: Vintage Books.

Frohmann, B. (2004). *Deflating information: from science studies to documentation*. Toronto, ON: University of Toronto Press.

Frohmann, B. (2008, September). *Biopolitics and the body's documentality*. Brown Bag lecture presented at the Faculty of Information and Media Studies, The University of Western Ontario.

Garfinkel, H. (1967). *Studies in ethnomethodology*. Englewood Cliffs, NJ: Prentice-Hall.

Gill, V. T., & Maynard, D. W. (2006). Explaining illness: patients' proposals and physicians' responses. In Heritage, J., & Maynard, D. W. (Eds.), *Communication in medical care: Interaction between primary care physicians and patients* (pp. 115–150). Cambridge, UK: Cambridge University Press. doi:10.1017/CBO9780511607172.007

Gorman, P., Ash, J., Lavelle, M., Lyman, J., Delcambre, L., & Maier, D. (2000). Bundles in the wild: managing information to solve problems and maintain situation awareness. *Library Trends, 49*(2), 266–289.

Gwyn, R., & Elwyn, G. (1999). When is a shared decision not (quite) a shared decision? Negotiating preferences in a general practice encounter. *Social Science & Medicine, 49*(4), 437–447. doi:10.1016/S0277-9536(99)00067-2

Harré, R., & van Langenhove, L. (1999). *Positioning theory*. Oxford: Blackwell.

Hawkins, M., & Knox, S. (2003). *The midwifery option: A Canadian guide to the birth experience*. Toronto, ON: HarperCollins.

Heritage, J. (2004). Conversation analysis and institutional talk: analysing data. In Silverman, D. (Ed.), *Qualitative research: Theory, method and practice* (2nd ed., pp. 222–245). Thousand Oaks, CA: Sage.

Heritage, J., & Maynard, D. W. (2006). Problems and prospects in the study of physician patient interaction: 30 years of research. *Annual Review of Sociology, 32*, 351–374. doi:10.1146/annurev.soc.32.082905.093959

Heritage, J., & Robinson, J. D. (2006). The structure of patients' presenting concerns: physicians' opening questions. *Health Communication, 19*(2), 89–102. doi:10.1207/s15327027hc1902_1

Hertzum, M. (2008). Collaborative information seeking: the combined activity of information seeking and collaborative grounding. *Information Processing & Management, 44*(2), 957–962. doi:10.1016/j.ipm.2007.03.007

Holstein, J. A., & Gubrium, J. F. (2005). Interpretive practice and social action. In Denzin, N., & Lincoln, Y. S. (Eds.), *The Sage handbook of qualitative research* (3rd ed., pp. 483–505). Thousand Oaks, CA: Sage.

Hyldegård, J. (2006). Collaborative information behaviour--exploring Kuhlthau's Information Search Process model in a group-based educational setting. *Information Processing & Management, 42*(1), 276–298. doi:10.1016/j.ipm.2004.06.013

Labov, W., & Fanshel, D. (1997). *Therapeutic discourse: Psychotherapy as conversation.* New York: Academic Press.

Lee, R. G., & Garvin, T. (2003). Moving from information transfer to information exchange in health and health care. *Social Science & Medicine, 56*(3), 449–464. doi:10.1016/S0277-9536(02)00045-X

MacDonald, M. (2006). Gender expectations: natural bodies and natural births in the new midwifery in Canada. *Medical Anthropology Quarterly, 20*(2), 235–256. doi:10.1525/maq.2006.20.2.235

Maynard, D. W. (2003). *Bad news, good news: conversational order in everyday talk and clinical settings.* Chicago, IL: University of Chicago Press.

McKenzie, P. J. (2003). Justifying cognitive authority decisions: discursive strategies of information seekers. *The Library Quarterly, 73*(3), 261–288. doi:10.1086/603418

McKenzie, P. J. (2004). Positioning theory and the negotiation of information needs in a clinical midwifery setting. *Journal of the American Society for Information Science and Technology, 55*(8), 685–694. doi:10.1002/asi.20002

McKenzie, P. J. (2006). Mapping textually-mediated information practice in clinical midwifery care. A. Spink, & C. Cole (Editors), New directions in human information behaviour (pp. 73-92). Dordrecht: Springer.

McKenzie, P. J. (2009). Informing choice: the organization of institutional interaction in clinical midwifery care. *Library & Information Science Research, 31*(3), 163–173. doi:10.1016/j.lisr.2009.03.006

McKenzie, P. J., & Oliphant, T. (2010). Informing evidence: claimsmaking in midwives' and clients' talk about interventions. *Qualitative Health Research, 20*(1), 29–41. doi:10.1177/1049732309355591

McKnight, M. (2007). A grounded theory model of on-duty critical care nurses' information behavior: the patient-chart cycle of informative interactions. *The Journal of Documentation, 63*(1), 57–73. doi:10.1108/00220410710723885

Ontario Medical Association Subcommittee on the Antenatal Record. (2000, March). A guide to the Revised Antenatal Record of Ontario. *Ontario Medical Review*, 1–6.

Ontario Ministry of Health and Long-term Care. (2003). *Public information, midwifery in Ontario. What is a midwife?* Retrieved May 10, 2010, from http://www.health.gov.on.ca/english/public/program/midwife/midwife_mn.html

Ontario. Ministry of Health and Long-term Care. (2005). *Antenatal record 2.*

Potter, J. (1996). *Representing reality: Discourse, rhetoric and social construction.* Thousand Oaks, CA: Sage.

Ragan, S. L. (2000). Sociable talk in women's health care contexts: two forms of non-medical talk. In Coupland, J. (Ed.), *Small talk* (pp. 241–264). London: Longman.

Reddy, M. C., Dourish, P., & Pratt, W. (2001). Coordinating heterogeneous work: information and representation in medical care. In *Proceedings of the European Conference on Computer supported Cooperative Work (ECSCW '01)* (pp. 239-258). Dordrecht: Kluwer.

Reddy, M. C., & Jansen, B. J. (2008). A model for understanding collaborative information behavior in context: A study of two healthcare teams. *Information Processing & Management, 44*(1), 256–273. doi:10.1016/j.ipm.2006.12.010

Reddy, M. C., & Spence, P. R. (2008). Collaborative information seeking: A field study of a multidisciplinary patient care team. *Information Processing & Management, 44*(1), 242–255. doi:10.1016/j.ipm.2006.12.003

Robinson, J. D. (2006). Soliciting patients' presenting concerns. In Heritage, J., & Maynard, D. W. (Eds.), *Communication in medical care: Interaction between primary care physicians and patients* (pp. 22–47). Cambridge, UK: Cambridge University Press. doi:10.1017/CBO9780511607172.004

Savolainen, R. (2006). Time as a context of information seeking. *Library & Information Science Research, 28*(1), 110–127. doi:10.1016/j.lisr.2005.11.001

Sharpe, M. (2004a). Exploring legislated midwifery: texts and ruling relations. In Bourgeault, I. L., Benoit, C., & Davis-Floyd, R. (Eds.), *Reconceiving Midwifery* (pp. 150–166). Montreal, Canada: McGill-Queen's University Press.

Sharpe, M. J. D. (2004b). *Intimate business: woman-midwife relationships in Ontario, Canada.* Unpublished doctoral dissertation, Ontario Institute for Studies in Education, University of Toronto.

Smith, D. E. (1990). *Texts, facts and femininity: Exploring the relations of ruling.* New York: Routledge.

Solomon, P. (1997). Discovering information behavior in sense making. I. Time and timing. *Journal of the American Society for Information Science American Society for Information Science, 48*(12), 1097–1108. doi:10.1002/(SICI)1097-4571(199712)48:12<1097::AID-ASI4>3.0.CO;2-P

Sonnenwald, D., Maglaughlin, K. L., & Whitton, M. C. (2004). Designing to support situation awareness across distances: an example from a scientific collaboratory. *Information Processing & Management, 36*, 461–479. doi:10.1016/S0306-4573(99)00039-4

Spoel, P. (2007). A feminist rhetorical perspective on informed choice in midwifery. *Rhetor: Journal of the Canadian Society for the Study of Rhetoric, 2*. Retrieved May 10, 2010, from http://uregina.ca/~rheaults/rhetor/2007/spoel.pdf

Star, S. L., & Griesemer, J. R. (1989). Institutional ecology, translations and boundary objects: amateurs and professionals In Berkeley's Museum of Vertebrate Zoology, 1907-1939. *Social Studies of Science, 19*(3), 387–420. doi:10.1177/030631289019003001

Stivers, T. (2006). Treatment decisions: negotiations between doctors and parents in acute care encounters. In Heritage, J., & Maynard, D. W. (Eds.), *Communication in medical care: Interaction between primary care physicians and patients* (pp. 279–312). Cambridge, UK: Cambridge University Press. doi:10.1017/CBO9780511607172.012

Stubbs, M. (1983). *Discourse analysis: The sociolinguistic analysis of natural language.* Chicago: University of Chicago Press.

Thachuk, A. (2007). Midwifery, informed choice, and reproductive autonomy: a relational approach. *Feminism & Psychology, 17*(1), 39–56. doi:10.1177/0959353507072911

West, C. (2006). Coordinating closings in primary care visits: producing continuity of care. In Heritage, J., & Maynard, D. W. (Eds.), *Communication in medical care Interaction between primary care physicians and patients* (pp. 379–415). Cambridge, UK: Cambridge University Press. doi:10.1017/CBO9780511607172.015

Wilson, P. (1983). *Second hand knowledge: An inquiry into cognitive authority*. Westport, CT: Greenwood.

Yakel, E. (2001). The social construction of accountability: radiologists and their record-keeping practices. *The Information Society, 17*(4), 233–245. doi:10.1080/019722401753330832

ADDITIONAL READING

Arminen, I. (2005). *Institutional interaction: Studies of talk at work*. Burlington, VT: Ashgate.

Budd, J. (2006). Discourse analysis and the study of communication in LIS. *Library Trends, 55*(1), 65–82. doi:10.1353/lib.2006.0046

Campbell, M., & Gregor, F. (2002). *Mapping social relations: A primer in doing institutional ethnography*. Aurora, ON: Garamond.

Davenport, E., & Cronin, B. (1998). Texts at work: some thoughts on 'just for you' service in the context of domain expertise. *Journal of Education for Library and Information Science, 39*(4), 264–274.

Drew, P. D., & Heritage, J. (1992). *Talk at work: Interaction in institutional settings*. Cambridge: Cambridge University Press.

Frohmann, B. (2004). *Deflating information: From science studies to documentation*. Toronto, ON: University of Toronto Press.

Garfinkel, H. (1967). *Studies in ethnomethodology*. Englewood Cliffs, NJ: Chap. Prentice-Hall.

Heritage, J., & Maynard, D. W. (Eds.). (2006a). *Communication in medical care: Interaction between primary care physicians and patients*. Cambridge: Cambridge University Press. doi:10.1017/CBO9780511607172

Heritage, J., & Maynard, D. W. (2006b). Problems and prospects in the study of physician-patient interaction: 30 years of research. *Annual Review of Sociology, 32*, 351–374. doi:10.1146/annurev.soc.32.082905.093959

Holstein, J. A., & Gubrium, J. F. (2005). Interpretive practice and social action. N. Denzin, & Y. S. Lincoln (Editors), The Sage handbook of qualitative research (3rd ed., pp. 483-505). Thousand Oaks, CA: Sage.

Potter, J., & Wetherell, M. (1987). *Discourse and social psychology; beyond attitudes and behaviour*. London: Sage.

Savolainen, R. (2007). Information behavior and information practice. reviewing the "umbrella concepts" of information seeking studies. *The Library Quarterly, 77*(2), 109–132. doi:10.1086/517840

Smith, D. E. (1987). *The everyday world as problematic: A feminist sociology*. Toronto, ON: University of Toronto Press.

Smith, D. E. (1990). *The conceptual practices of power: A feminist sociology of knowledge*. Toronto: University of Toronto Press.

Smith, D. E. (1990). *Texts, facts and femininity: Exploring the relations of ruling*. New York: Routledge.

Solomon, P. (1997). Conversation in information-seeking contexts: a test of an analytical framework. *Library & Information Science Research, 19*(3), 217–248. doi:10.1016/S0740-8188(97)90014-1

Star, S. L., & Griesemer, J. R. (1989). Institutional ecology, "translations" and boundary objects: amateurs and professionals In Berkeley's Museum of Vertebrate Zoology, 1907-1939. *Social Studies of Science*, *19*(3), 387–420. doi:10.1177/030631289019003001

Stooke, R. (2005). Institutional Ethnography. In K. E. Fisher, Erdelez, S. & McKechnie. E. F. (Eds.) Theories of information behavior: A researcher's guide (pp. 210-214). Medford, NJ: Information Today.

Talja, S., & McKenzie, P. J. (2007). Editors' introduction: special issue on discursive approaches to information seeking in context. *The Library Quarterly*, *77*(2), 97–108. doi:10.1086/517839

Talja, S., Tuominen, K., & Savolainen, R. (2005). "Isms" in information science: constructivism, collectivism, and constructionism. *The Journal of Documentation*, *61*(1), 79–101. doi:10.1108/00220410510578023

Tuominen, K., & Savolainen, R. (1996). A social constructionist approach to the study of information use as a discursive action. In P. Vakkari, R. Savolainen, & B. Dervin (eds), Information seeking in context: Proceedings of an international conference in information needs, seeking and use in different contexts, 14-16 August, 1996, Tampere, Finland (pp. 81-96). London: Taylor Graham.

Tuominen, K., Talja, S., & Savolainen, R. (2002). Discourse, cognition, and reality: toward a social constructionist metatheory for library and information science. *Emerging frameworks and methods: CoLIS 4. Proceedings of the Fourth International Conference on Conceptions of Library and Information Science* (pp. 271-283). Greenwood Village, Colo.: Libraries Unlimited.

Wetherell, M., Taylor, S., & Yates, S. J. (2001). *Discourse as data: A guide for analysis*. London: Sage.

Wetherell, M., Taylor, S., & Yates, S. J. (2001). *Discourse theory and practice: A reader*. London: Sage.

Wooffitt, R. (2005). *Conversation analysis and discourse analysis: A comparative and critical introduction*. Thousand Oaks, CA: Sage.

Yakel, E. (2001). The social construction of accountability: radiologists and their record-keeping practices. *The Information Society*, *17*(4), 233–245. doi:10.1080/019722401753330832

APPENDIX: TRANSCRIPTION STANDARDS (KEY)

M:	Conversational turns are prefaced by an initial identifying the speaker (**Midwife**, **Woman**, **Student**), and a colon.
//	Marks overlapping talk.
(())	Inaudible.
[]	Nonverbal elements such as laughter, physical gestures, changes in tone, or to indicate the removal or identifying details or the editing of the excerpt for this article.
…	Indicates the approximate length of a pause in seconds.
? !	Punctuation indicates both grammatical sentence-ends and emphatic or interrogative intonation, syntax, or intent.

Chapter 13

Collaboration as Co-Constructed Discourse:
Developing a Coding Guide for the Analysis of Peer Talk During Educational Information Seeking

Jonathan Foster
University of Sheffield, UK

ABSTRACT

This chapter presents a coding guide for the analysis of peer talk during educational information seeking. The guide is an outcome of a structuring content analysis of learners' dialogues as they seek, evaluate, and use information on a collaborative basis. The analysis is informed by a language-based theory of learning and the sequential organization of spoken discourse. The generic steps of a structuring content analysis are described first; before each step, sequence, exchange, and move type identified in the dialogues are described. Illustrative examples of each unit and type of talk are provided, so as to aid in the precise and reliable assignment of the categories and codes in further studies. The chapter concludes with implications of the coding guide, and the broader study of which it is a part, for research in educational information seeking.

INTRODUCTION

Educational settings are one of a range of contexts in which studies of collaborative information behavior have been conducted. In such settings students are often presented with a learning activity designed to motivate them to seek, evaluate, and use information on a collaborative basis. Designing and facilitating learning activities that encourage collaboration during information seeking transforms the relationship between learners and information by introducing the role of the peer as an important influence on the identification and negotiation of information needs, the development of search strategies, and the sharing, evaluation, and use of the information once retrieved. In doing so a new set of factors enters into the student-information relationship. These include the deployment of social and interpersonal skills, discussion skills, and the use of technology that enable learners to search, share, evaluate, and present information on a collaborative basis.

One of the mediating tools that learners use to seek, evaluate and present information together is talk. This is because it is through talk that learners interpret and negotiate their information needs, de-

DOI: 10.4018/978-1-61520-797-8.ch013

velop their search terms and strategies; and evaluate the pertinence of the documents found to the task at hand. While a number of studies have explored the role of talk in information seeking (e.g. Belkin & Vickery, 1985; Saracevic, Spink, & Wu, 1997; Ellis et al., 2002; Wu, 2005), there have been very few empirical analyses of talk in settings of collaborative information seeking (Foster, 2009). At the core of such analyses is the task of coding and categorization. A choice facing the discourse analyst at this point is whether the codes and categories are informed by a pre-established set of theoretical categories and codes; or whether the codes and categories are developed from the ground up on the basis of an examination of the materials. The decision made will be influenced of course by the goals and methodology of the particular research study. Foster (2009) presented an analysis of the functions and forms of talk used by learners as they collectively reviewed information shared and interpreted as part of a collaborative learning activity. The study took the form of a structuring content analysis of the learners' dialogues; and was informed by an analytical framework called the "sequential organization of spoken discourse" (see Wells (1999) for the original framework; and Appendix A for a revision of the framework used in the current study). This chapter elaborates on the study by presenting a coding guide for the analysis of peer talk during educational information seeking. After an overview of the generic steps of a structuring content analysis, the chapter focuses on a detailed description of the codes and categories used in analyzing the organization of peer talk during educational information seeking. The chapter concludes with remarks on the implications of the guide, and the study of which it is a part, for analyzing talk during educational information seeking.

STRUCTURING CONTENT ANALYSIS

The aim of a structuring content analysis is to filter out and (re-) assemble certain themes, content, and aspects from the materials used. The content of the materials is (re-) structured, ordered, and analyzed in accordance with a theoretically informed system of categories, and a coding guide results that enables the precise coding of similar materials in the future. The technique can be described in the following way:

"Structuring content analysis seeks to filter out particular aspects of the material and to make a cross-section of the material under ordering criteria that are strictly determined in advance, or to assess the material according to particular criteria. This involves formal, content-focused, typologizing and scaling procedures, depending on the type of structuring dimensions that have been developed in accordance with some theory, and these are then subdivided into individual categories. The basic idea in this is the exact formulation of definitions, typical textual passages ('key examples') and coding rules which will result in a coding guide that makes the task of structuring very precise" (Mayring, 2004: 269).

As this definition implies it is possible to conduct different structuring content analyses depending on the theoretical criteria used to inform an analysis of the materials. In this instance a framework developed for the analysis of educational discourse informed the task of coding and categorization.

An overview of the generic steps of a structuring content analysis is provided here (see Mayring (2003) for a diagrammatic presentation of the steps). At Step 1 the content analyst determines the materials to be used. In this instance the materials used originate from a study investigating the functions and forms of talk used by students when seeking information as part of a collaborative learning activity known as group investigation (Sharan & Sharan, 1992). Group investigation is a cooperative learning method that encourages students to acquire knowledge within a social context of accountability. A typical group investigation will proceed through six stages. Stage 1: class determines subtopics; Stage 2: groups plan their investigations; Stage 3: groups carry out their investigations; Stage 4: groups plan their presentations; Stage 5: groups make their presentations; Stage 6: teacher and students evaluate their projects. Each stage also incorporates an information task (Foster, 2007, 2009). The module in which the group investigation was implemented was an undergraduate *Information Management and Strategy* module, with a curriculum organised around the themes of information policy, information audit, and information strategy. The materials used for the structuring content analysis, and the study of which it was a part, are taken from transcripts of audio-recordings of nine student dialogues at Stage 4 of their group investigations i.e. the plan presentation stage (Sharan & Sharan, 1992). At Step 2 the main content-related categories that are to be applied to the materials are identified. In this instance the analysis was informed by a language-based theory of learning and the discourse content categories of step, sequence, exchange and move (Wells, 1999). At Step 3 the characteristics of the categories established at Step 2 are determined; and a system of individual categories is compiled. The characteristics of the discourse content categories used here were once again informed by Wells' (1999) framework, and its theorization of educational discourse as sequential and co-constructed. In view of the nature of the materials, i.e. peer dialogues, the characteristics of one of the categories, that of exchange, was also informed by a previous study of the use of dialogical peer talk in an educational setting (Mercer & Wegerif, 1997). At Step 4 the content analyst provides definitions, root examples, and coding rules for the system of categories; and a detailed description of this step in the shape of a coding guide. At Step 5 the analyst works through the materials, coding up the places of discovery. At Step 6 the analyst works through the same materials, processing and extracting the places of discovery that have been coded. Step 7 consists of a re-visiting, and if necessary, amendment of the category system. This will be necessary in the light of testing the initial set of theoretically informed categories against the materials used. In so doing new characteristics of the categories are identified and the category schema is revised accordingly. At Step 8 the coded and extracted materials are paraphrased. At Step 9 the materials are summarized according to each individual category; and at Step 10 the materials are summarized according to each main category. In sum Steps 1- 3 are concerned with determining the

materials and the initial set of categories; while Steps 4-10 are concerned with data making, the grounding and revision of the initial categories in a particular context, and paraphrasing and summarising the content. An analysis of the data is then conducted. For a fuller description of the context and purposes of the study, its methodology and findings see Foster (2009). The coding guide developed in the course of the original study is now described.

DEVELOPMENT OF THE CODING GUIDE

This section contains examples of each of the categories used to code and categorize the content of the learners' dialogues i.e. step, sequence, exchange and move. Each of the categories is enumerated and a definition and illustrative example provided for each type of step, sequence, exchange, and move. Before the examples are presented a note on the logic and organization of the section is also warranted. This relates to the different perspectives that can be taken on the discourse materials. From the perspective of the discourse analyst, the initial task is to segment the dialogues in a systematic and orderly way; in this case into collective, hence co-constructed, units of talk. Bearing this in mind the student dialogues were first segmented first into content related to each step of Stage 4 of a group investigation i.e. review information, interpret information, and plan a presentation. The content of each of these steps was then segmented into sequences; each sequence was then segmented and coded into its constituent exchanges (e.g. nuclear, dependent). Finally codes were assigned to the smallest unit of talk out of which exchanges are constituted, i.e. individual discourse moves. From the perspective of the discourse user, the appropriate logic would be to proceed from the ground up i.e. first assigning a code to the individual moves of each speaker; and then proceeding to code and categorize the exchanges and the sequences out of which each step of the instructional activity was co-constructed. In view of the chapter's purpose in acting as a coding guide for discourse analyses the perspective of the discourse analyst has been adopted. A final word on the structure of each illustrative example. Each example is organized as follows: Col 1: line number; Col 2: speaker; Col 3: utterance; Col 4: exchange type; Col 5: utterance position; Col 6: move type.

Steps

In keeping with Wells' (1999) framework, the first and largest unit of talk into which the learners' dialogues were segmented was the step. These steps corresponded to the instructions handed to students for Stage 4 of their investigations. These instructions were: (a) to review their searches (b) to develop a shared response to the question under investigation and (c) to plan a presentation to their classmates. Rather than present the entire discourse content of each step the initial exchanges only—sufficient for the identification of the opening of the step—are presented. While the beginning of a step can be explicitly identified, the completion of a step is inferred by identifying the beginning of the next step in the dialogue. Three types of step were initially identified: share information; interpret information; and completion.

Step A. Share Information

Table 1 presents the opening moves from the initial sequence of one of the student group's 'Share Information' steps. The beginning of the step is identified by a preparatory exchange during which the students negotiate their turns at sharing information. The preparatory exchange is followed by a nuclear exchange that signals the beginning of the sequence during which Student A. shares information.

Step B. Interpret Information

Table 2 and Table 3 present the opening moves of the initial sequences of the 'Interpret Information' steps of two separate student dialogues. Table 2 illustrates the Interpret step being initiated by a student expressing her opinion on the content of the search results. This opinion is supported by a justification in the student's next discourse move (lines 6-7). In contrast Table 3 illustrates an example of the Interpret step being initiated not by a reference to the content of the information but through an implied reference to the Interpret phase of the instructions for Stage 4 of the group investigations.

Table 1. Share information step (excerpt)

(1)	E:	Who wants to go first?	Pre.	I	REQ NOM
(2)	A:	Well, I'll go first of that's alright	Pre.	R	BD
(3)		Well, basically I found a lot of quotes	Nuc.	I	IN
(4)		Regarding information policy [...]			

Table 2. Interpret information step (excerpt)

(1)	K:	Well, it seemed to me that the company ones	Nuc.	I	OP
(2)		Were focusing on gaps and inconsistencies			
(3)		And the academic ones were more about			
(4)		I don't know, mind you that Susan Henschel,			
(5)	A:	I think			
(6)	K:	Gaps and inconsistencies ()	Nuc.	I	JU
(7)		They seem to talk more about information flows			
(8)	A:	Yeh	Nuc.	R	AC
(9)	K:	Stuff like that.			

Table 3. Interpret information (excerpt)

(1)	J:	() we're going to have to try to interpret this.	Nuc.	I	IN
(2)		There seem to be a number of factors ()	Nuc.	I	OP

Table 4. Completion step (excerpt)

(1)	J:	We've got, I mean from what I've got,	Pre.	I	OP
(2)		I think we've got like enough of the benefits			
(3)	A:	Yeh	Pré.	R1	AC
(4)	M:	Um	Pre.	R2	AC
(5)		In terms of tangible and intangible	Pre.	I	EXT O
(6)	C:	Yep.	Pré.	R	AC
(7)	J:	Is there any way that, we could try	Nuc.	I	SU
(8)		And may be put a few bullet points			
(9)		About conclusions?			

Step C. Completion

Table 4 and Table 5 present the opening moves of the initial sequences of two separate completion steps. It is during this phase that students engage in planning their presentations. In both examples one of the students initiates the step by giving a suggestion that is intended to advance the activity in the direction of its completion. In Table 4 the suggestion is prefaced however by a preparatory exchange during which the students agree on the completion of the preceding Interpret step.

Sequences

While each of the steps provides the students with a sequential task structure that organizes their discussion, it is the sequence of talk that is the key unit through which the business of Stage 4 of the group investigation gets done:

"In understanding the role of talk in joint activity it is this unit which is of greatest functional significance. For it is in the succession of moves that occurs in following through on the expectations set up by the initiating move in a nuclear exchange that the "commodity' being exchanged—some form of goods or services, or some form of information—is introduced, negotiated, and brought to completion" (Wells, 1999: 236).

Table 6 presents an example of a sequence extracted from the Interpret step of one of the dialogues. The example illustrates the two-part structure of a sequence; comprising a nuclear exchange (lines 1-5), and a dependent exchange (lines 6-22). The expectations or actions for the sequence are introduced at the head of the sequence in the nuclear exchange;

Table 5. Completion step (excerpt)

(1)	D:	Shall we start	Nuc	I	SU
(2)	M:	Yeh	Nuc	R	AC
(3)	D:	To try and plan ()			
(4)		Start (to) list the main sort of factors	Nuc	I	JU
(5)	L:	Oh, okay	Nuc	R	AC

223

while these expectations or actions are negotiated or completed in the dependent exchange. In this example it is expectations for opinion giving that are established in the nuclear exchange (lines 1-5); and these opinions are given and taken up in the dependent exchange (lines 6-22).

A range of possible expectations or actions can be established in a nuclear exchange. What these expectations or actions might be can be identified with reference to the possible set of discourse moves that can be made. These are described below following a description of the unit of talk out of which sequences, as has been mentioned, are constituted: the exchange.

Exchanges

The two-part structure of a sequence serves to illustrate how the discourse of the students is co-con-structed through nuclear and dependent exchanges. While the sequence is the key unit of co-construction for learning, it is not the only unit of talk that is co-constructed. The minimal unit of co-construction is the exchange. Wells (1999) identifies four types of exchange: a nuclear exchange; a dependent exchange; an embedded exchange; and a preparatory exchange. A nuclear exchange is self-standing; while dependent, embedded and preparatory exchanges are known as 'bound' exchanges, since they are bound in some way to the nuclear exchange. Examples of these exchange types are presented here.

Nuclear Exchange

A nuclear exchange can be a self-standing exchange, i.e. comprised of a speaker's initial move 'I' and a hearer's response move 'R'. All that needs to happen is that the exchange contributes new content to the

Table 6. Sequence

(1)	J:	Um, I mean what do we think	Nuc	I	REQ OP
(2)		If we were in our organization			
(3)		Why would we			
(4)	C:	Yeh	Nuc	R	AK
(5)	J:	Be using an information audit?			
(6)	M:	I suppose like, it would probably	Dep	R	OP
(7)		Be like, short term benefits			
(8)		You've got to see that first.			
(9)	J:	I think,	Dep	I	OP
(10)		Yeh	Emb.	R	AC
(11)		I remember in the lecture Jon	Dep	I	EXT O
(12)		Was saying about, y'know,			
(13)		Even if it is ultimately for			
(14)		The long term benefits			
(15)	M:	Yeh	Dep	R	AK
(16)	J:	You need to may be, as I said,	Dep	I	JU
(17)		Gain support from people,			
(18)		Support from stakeholders.			
(19)		And you need to have			
(20)		The short-term benefits			
(21)		And the tangible benefits as well			
(22)	A:	Yes	Dep	R	AC

Table 7. Nuclear exchange

(1)	J:	Um, I mean what do we think	**Nuc.**	I	REQ OP
(2)		If we were in our organization			
(3)		Why would we			
(4)	C:	Yeh	**Nuc.**	R	AK
(5)	J:	Be using an information audit?			

Table 8. Dependent exchange

(1)	M:	I suppose like, it would probably	Dep	R	OP
(2)		Be like, short term benefits			
(3)		You've got to see that first.			
(4)	J:	I think,	Dep	I	OP
(5)		Yeh	Emb.	R	AC
(6)		I remember in the lecture Jon	Dep	I	EXT O
(7)		Was saying about, y'know,			
(8)		Even if it is ultimately for			
(9)		The long term benefits			
(10)	M:	Yeh	Dep	R	AK
(11)	J:	You need to may be, as I said,	Dep	I	JU
(12)		Gain support from people,			
(13)		Support from stakeholders.			
(14)		And you need to have			
(15)		The short-term benefits			
(16)		And the tangible benefits as well			
(17)	A:	Yes	Dep	R	AC

current discourse. More typically a nuclear exchange will form the initial exchange in a longer sequence of talk that comprises the nuclear exchange with a series of dependent exchanges, the content of which 'follows up' on the expectations or actions established in the nuclear exchange. Table 7 presents an example of a nuclear exchange extracted from the sequence presented in Table 6.

In this instance the nuclear exchange functions specifically to establish the expectation among the students that each gives an opinion on the current topic.

Dependent Exchange

The dependent exchange forms the 'tail' of a sequence of talk. Its general function is to follow

through on the expectations or actions introduced in a nuclear exchange. Table 8 presents an example of a dependent exchange extracted from the sequence presented in Table 6. In this exchange the students follow-up on and in doing so satisfy the expectations for opinion-giving that are contained in the sequence's nuclear exchange.

How a commodity or in this study information is exchanged, evaluated, and used is of particular interest in an educational context. On the one hand an item of information e.g. an opinion can be exchanged with no comment; on the other hand an opinion can be engaged with, explored and/or challenged. Given the educational context the dependent exchanges in the students' dialogues were further differentiated with reference to the types of collaborative talk that they contained. A definition and illustrative example of each type of collaborative talk is presented here.

Cumulative Talk

Cumulative talk can be characterized as talk where "speakers build positively but uncritically on what the other has said" (Mercer & Wegerif, 1997). Hence when using cumulative talk information will be exchanged, or some other action is performed or agreed upon, by the students in an orderly, but uncritical, way. Table 9 contains an example of a dependent exchange (lines 5-12) that is characterized by cumulative talk. The sequence within which the cumulative exchange occurs is taken from the Completion step of one of the student dialogues. The sequence begins with a student seeking confirmation as to the content and the division of labor of their upcoming presentation. The other students provide this confirmation through acknowledgements and confirmations. Therefore the sequence functions to establish publicly and officially, what had previously existed only implicitly i.e. common ground on presentation content and division of labour—in an orderly and uncritical way.

It is also worth noting that in cumulative exchanges, the initiation and direction of the dialogue tends to be under the unilateral control of one speaker;

with other speakers providing acknowledgements, acceptances, and confirmations.

Exploratory Talk

When using exploratory talk information is exchanged among the participants, or some other action is performed or agreed upon, again in an orderly but also more meaningful and critical way. It is a collaborative form of talk where "partners engage critically but constructively with each other's ideas" (Mercer & Wegerif, 1997). The occurrence of exploratory talk is characterized by the use of opinions, support for these opinions, e.g. justifications, explanations, and constructive engagement by partners with the views and opinions of others. Table 10 presents an example of a dependent exchange (lines 5-14) that can be characterized as exploratory talk. The sequence within which the exploratory exchanges occur is taken from the Interpret step of one of the students' dialogues. The question that this group is investigating is: "What are the benefits of conducting information audits?" And the current task in which the students are engaged is categorizing the benefits identified in the documents found. The sequence begins with one of the students identifying a benefit (lines 1-4), and expressing an opinion as to the category into which this benefit should fall. What

Table 9. Cumulative talk

(1)	A:	Right, so, OK.	Nuc.	I	TR
(2)		First part before we come to here.	Nuc.	I	IN
(3)	M:	Yeh.	Nuc.	R1	AK
(4)	E:	Yeh.	Nuc.	R2	AK
(5)	A:	First part we talk about.	Dep.	I	REQ CO
(6)		I'll talk about this.			
(7)		Murryam'll talk about this.			
(8)	M:	Yeh.	Dep.	R	CO
(9)	A:	And you're going to talk about,	Dep.	I	REQ CO
		Like the examples			
(10)	E:	Yeh.	Dep.	R	CO
(11)	A:	And the countries	Dep.	I	REQ CO
(12)	E:	Yeh.	Dep.	R	CO

defines the dependent exchange as exploratory is the way in which the other students (lines 7-8; and lines 10-14) take up the student's opinion, building and extending on it in a constructive and meaningful way. Engagement in exploratory talk is particularly valuable in an educational context where tutors are seeking meaningful dialogue between students as a tool for learning.

Disputational Talk

In contrast to both cumulative and exploratory exchanges, disputational talk works to undermine the expectations or actions established in the nuclear exchange. Whereas cumulative and exploratory exchanges reinforce or extend these expectations respectively; in disputational talk the initial expectations are challenged in a critical and potentially conflicting way. Mercer and Wegerif (1997) define disputational talk as talk "characterized by disagreement and individualized decision-making". Table 11 presents an example of a dependent exchange (lines 4-16) that can be categorized as disputational talk. The sequence within which the series of disputational exchanges occurs is extracted again from the Interpret step of one of the student dialogues. The sequence begins with one of the students suggesting a method for categorizing the benefits of

conducting information audits (lines 1-3). In this example however the initial suggestion is rejected, and an alternative method for categorizing is proposed (lines 4-9). Yet another student then offers a resolution of the two conflicting suggestions (lines 10-16). In doing so common ground between the students is eventually accomplished but in a less orderly way than if either cumulative or exploratory talk had been used.

Preparatory Exchange

As the name implies a preparatory exchange performs a function that is preparatory to the exchange or actions of the main sequence. Table 12 presents an example of this exchange type.

The example given is the initiating exchange of one of the student dialogues. Through it the students are negotiating turns at sharing information. Deciding on this is clearly preparatory to collective information sharing; and the exchange is therefore coded as a pre-exchange.

Embedded Exchange

Problems in the uptake of a move in the current exchange are dealt with in an embedded exchange

Table 10. Exploratory talk

(1)	J:	What—did anybody pick up this objective	Nuc.	I	REQ PN
(2)		in Orna, risk avoidance?			
(3)	A:	Yeh	Nuc.	R1	YN
(4)	M:	Yeh	Nuc.	R2	YN
(5)	J:	Short-term	Dep	I	IN
(6)		So, I mean, that could be—	Dep.	I	OP
(7)	M:	Could go into making information	Dep.	I	EXT O
(8)		More accessible and usable for the—			
(9)	A:	Yeh	Emb.	R	AK
(10)		Orna said about risk avoidance.	Dep.	I	EXT O
(11)		And then () said about			
(12)		Draws attention to problem areas			
(13)		Which kind of same thing isn't it,	Dep.	I	REQ OP
(14)		When you get () avoids risk			

Table 11. Disputational talk

(1)	J:	Could we try and pick out	Nuc.	I	SU
(2)		The tangible then first?			
(3)		And write that down?			
(4)	C:	I don't know if it's going	Nuc.	R1	RJ
(5)	A:	()	Nuc.	R2	()
(6)	C:	To be easier.			
(7)		It might be easier to listen,	Dep.	I	SU-C
(8)		And then write, put 'T' next			
(9)		To that one.			
(10)	A:	() split the page in two.	Dep.	I	SU
(11)	C:	Alright	Dep.	R	AC
(12)	A:	And then say (),	Dep.	I	EXT S
(13)		Say, y'know,			
(14)		Say, 'oh', that's a tangible			
(15)		And then put it in that column			
(16)		And we can (probably take it from there?)	Dep.	I	SU

Table 12. Preparatory exchange

(1)	E:	Who wants to go first?	**Pre**	I	REQ NOM
(2)	A:	Well, I'll go first if that's alright.	**Pre**	R	BD

(Wells, 1999). Table 13 presents an example of an embedded exchange.

This example is extracted from a sequence of talk (see Table 39) in which one of the students is acting as an information giver, and another student is acting as a recorder. All the students in the group are attempting to categorize the benefits of conducting an information audit. The problem addressed in the embedded exchange arises because the recorder's attention has been distracted by writing. The problem is resolved through a repetition request.

Discourse Moves

In this section examples are presented of the smallest unit of talk that can be coded and categorized using this framework: the individual discourse move. Unlike a 'sequence' and an exchange, the individual discourse move is not a collective unit. Nevertheless it represents the smallest unit of co-construction and is located either in an initiating or responding position within a larger exchange. An illustrative example for each discourse move is provided, along with any explanatory commentary that aids in its reliable assignment to empirical talk. Each of the moves performs an individual function in the dialogues. For ease of understanding however the moves are grouped here according to their common function in the student dialogues. Therefore, some discourse moves aid in structuring the direction of the dialogue e.g. suggestions; others function to give information and opinions etc; others aid in eliciting information e.g. request information, request opinion; while others aid in establishing and maintaining common ground between the participants e.g. request repetition, check for understanding, confirming, and extending. It should be borne in mind however that each individual move could equally exist as a

Table 13. Embedded exchange

(1)	C:	Say again, comprehensive database	Emb	I	REQ RP
(2)	M:	Will have a comprehensive database of	Emb	R	RP

Table 14. Give suggestion (SU)

(1)	A:	We should come up with our own definition	Nuc	I	**SU**
(2)		I think			
(3)	M:	Yeh	Nuc	R1	AC
(4)	E:	OK	Nuc	R2	AC

freestanding move, outside of a category scheme purposefully developed for the analysis of student talk during educational information seeking.

Structuring Moves

In a cooperative learning activity that involves students collaborating on the seeking, evaluation, and presentation of information, both tutor and students will have a joint responsibility for progressing the activity through its constituent stages. Hence, although responsibility for designing the activity rests with the tutor, initial responsibility for ongoing structuring of the stages of the activity will rest with the students. In the absence of a tutor who is structuring their activity on a moment-by-moment basis a key move in the students' dialogues will be the 'give suggestion' move (see Table 14). A 'give suggestion' move then is to be interpreted as a suggestion for advancing the activity, or one of its constituent stages, in some way.

The example in Table 14 illustrates the location of a give suggestion move in the exchange initial position 'I' of a nuclear exchange at the head of a sequence extracted from the Interpret step of one of the dialogues. In this example the student is suggesting that rather than extract a definition [of information strategy] from the assembled documents, they should attempt to arrive at their own definition. A suggestion may be accepted and taken up by the other participants, or it may be rejected. In this case the suggestion is accepted, and subsequently followed up.

Informing Moves

A group of moves function to aid in the giving of information, opinions etc. Examples of these types of move are presented here. Table 15 presents an example of a 'give information' move (lines 3-5). The example illustrates the location of the informing move in the exchange-response position of a nuclear exchange. This is in response to a specific 'request information' move (lines 1-2). Equally, a give information move could occur in an exchange-initial position.

In seeking information as part of a cooperative learning exercise it will be important for the students to move beyond the exchange and sharing of information *per se* to interpreting and evaluating the information and applying it to the question at hand. Table 16 presents an example of a 'give opinion' move (lines 1-3). The student is expressing an opinion on the current state of the investigation; and having secured agreement with this opinion (lines 4-6), suggests the next course of action.

As mentioned when discussing exploratory talk, a suggestion or an opinion will often be accompanied by support for that suggestion or opinion. Table 17 illustrates the use of a 'give justification/explanation' move. In this example the student gives a justification/explanation (lines 6-7) in support of her suggestion (line 1) to initially present individually.

Along with providing a justification or explanation, support for suggestions made or opinions given can take the form of giving a relevant example. Table 18 illustrates this discourse move. The example is

Table 15. Give information (IN)

(1)	L:	So, what have we got there	Nuc.	I	REQ IN
(2)		() example ()			
(3)	E:	Copyright ()	Nuc.	R	IN
(4)		Then () information manager's perspective	Nuc		IN
(5)		May be, a little bit			

Table 16. Give opinion (OP)

(1)	J:	We've got, I mean from what I've got	Pre.	I	**OP**
(2)		I think we've got like, the list which is			
(3)		Enough of the benefits.			
(4)	A:	Yeh	Pre.	R1	AC
(5)	M:	Um.	Pre.	R2	AC
(6)		In terms of tangible and intangible			EXT O
(7)	J:	Is there anyway that we could try	Nuc.	I	SU
(8)		And may be put a few bullet points			
(9)		About conclusions?			

extracted, like the example in Table 17, from a sequence occurring within the final Completion step, where the students are planning their presentation. In this sequence the students are coordinating their content for the presentation (line 1). In support of this one of the students identifies their contribution through the provision of relevant examples (line 11-14; 16).

The simplest informing move is that of a yes (positive) or no (negative) response. Table 19 presents an example of this move (line 5) in exchange-response position as part of an elicitation exchange.

Elicitation Moves

During the course of a cooperative learning activity, students will want to seek suggestions, information, opinions, and justifications from other students. This section provides examples of these types of move. Ongoing structuring of the activity can take place either through a student making a suggestion; or through a student inviting suggestions from other students. Table 20 presents an example of a 'request suggestion' move. In this example the students have re-formulated and settled on a focus for their

Table 17. Give justification/explanation (JU)

(1)	M:	We can separate up like first	Nuc	I	SU
(2)	E:	You mean start off individually like.	Dep.	I	EXT O
(3)		And then move on to the next person.			
(4)		And then we go through the presentation.			
(5)	M:	Yeh.	Dep.	R	AC
(6)		Because then at least, it shows like.	Dep.	I	**JU**
(7)		Even though we have similar stuff.			

Table 18. Give relevant example (EX)

(1)	D:	So, shall (we) divide things up?	Nuc.	I	SU
(2)		So now you're saying ()		I	EXT
(3)		Then we can sort of			
(4)		Meet up altogether and			
(5)	L:	Okay	Nuc	R	AC
(6)	D:	Try and work it like that	Dep	I	EXT
(7)	L:	Well I'll, I'll do	Dep	I	SU
(8)	D:	You do	Dep	I	SU
(9)	L:	I'll write this up	Dep	I	SU
(10)	D:	Yeh	Dep	R	AC
(11)	L:	Um, then maybe	Dep	I	SU
(12)		If I point out a few that,			
(13)		Enabling factors of			
(14)		Like London University	Dep.	I	EX
(15).	D:	Um	Dep.	R	AC
(16)	L:	And University of Glasgow ()	Dep	I	EX
(17)	M:	Um	Dep	R	AC

Table 19. Give yes/no answer (P/N)

(1)	C:	We've got the academic ones.	Nuc.	I	IN
(2)		Glamorgan wasn't it?	Dep.	I	CH
(3)	A:	Um	Dep.	R	CL
(4)	C:	Did you find? What, Sunderland?	Dep	I	REQ PN
(5)	B:	Um.	Dep.	R	Y
(6)		It's a bit, um, it's a bit	Dep	I	IN
(7)		It's quite detailed			
(8)	C:	Um	Dep	R	AK
(9)	B:	I don't know about this	Dep	I	OP

presentation. Having made an initial suggestion for what should be included in the presentation (lines 1-5), and with no other suggestions forthcoming, the current speaker requests suggestions from the other students (line 7).

Some features of the general and specific contexts of the move are worth mentioning, when helping to identify the move as a 'request suggestion' rather than a 'request opinion' for example. Although not part of the extract presented here, the sequence is preceded by general discussion among the members of the student group as to how to advance the activity; while the question "Anything else we think's important?" is immediately preceded by a suggestion from the current speaker. Table 21 presents an example of a 'request information' move. In keeping with other request moves, the move is designed to elicit a specific rather than a general response from their partners in the dialogue. In this instance the elicitation is used to request a description (line 1) of the content of a document.

As mentioned earlier an expected feature of the

Table 20. Request suggestion (REQ SU)

(1)	K:	Well,	Nuc.	I	SU
(2)		I think one of the important things	Nuc.	I	
(3)		We should have in			
(4)		Is the fact that it's a set of attitudes			
(5)		Not necessarily a report from JISC.			
(6)		I think that's—	Nuc.	I	OP
(7)		Anything else we think's important?	Nuc.	I	**REQ SU**
(8)	J:	It's a process	Dep.	R1	SU
(9)	E:	It's a set of attitudes	Dep.	R2	SU
(10)	K:	Yes	Dep.	F	AC
(11)	J:	Not a document	Dep.	I	EXT O

Table 21. Request information (REQ IN)

(1)	L:	So, what have we got there?	Nuc.	I	**REQ IN**
(2)		() example ()			
(3)	E:	Copyright ()	Nuc.	R	IN
(4)		Then () information manager's perspective	Nuc		IN
(5)		May be, a little bit.			

student dialogues from an educational perspective will be the presence of talk intended to interpret and evaluate the information, rather than simply synthesize it. Table 22 presents an example of the 'request opinion' move.

In this example a participant makes a specific request for an opinion. Again for the purposes of consistency in coding, it is worth noting the general and specific contexts of the move. In this instance the general context is of the inviting of an opinion on a

suggestion already proposed; and more specifically the speaker's justification and qualification for their opinion should also be noted. Table 17 provided an example of a 'give justification/explanation' move, supplied in support of a suggestion. A justification/explanation can also be requested. Table 23 presents an example of a 'request justification/explanation' move. In this example a student invites other students (line 6) to interpret and give an explanation of the meaning of 'scaling the information process' (line 1).

Table 22. Request opinion (REQ OP)

(1)	K:	Do you think we should talk about it	Dep	I	**REQ OP**
(2)		In terms of organizational context as well?			
(3)		Depends on our definition	Dep	I	JU
(4)		And how it fits in.			
(5)		I mean at the end of the day	Dep	I	QU
(6)		Its all relative to that one organization.			
(7)		But I don't know if that's like			
(8)	A:	I think the broader definition	Dep	R	OP

Table 23. Request justification/explanation (REQ JU)

(1)	M:	Scaling the information process	Nuc	I	IN
(2)		So no we kind of	I	OP	
(3)		Covered that one anyway			
(4)	J:	Um	Nuc	R	AC
(5)	M:	I suppose, I suppose we've kind of	Dep	I	QU
		Covered that one anyway			
(6)	J:	What do you think it means by that?	Dep.	I	**REQ JU**
(7)	M:	I think scaling the information process	Dep.	R	JU
(8)		I think it's just like um			
(9)		I suppose informational flows			
(10)		And y'know through formal	Dep	R	EXT S
(11)		And informal channels			

Table 24. Request yes/no answer (REQ P/N)

(1)	J:	What—did anybody pick up this objective	Nuc.	I	**REQ P/N**
(2)		in Orna, risk avoidance?			
(3)	A:	Yeh	Nuc	R1	Y
(4)	M:	Yeh	Nuc.	R2	Y

Table 24 presents an example of the simplest elicitation move: a request for a yes/no answer. In this example a student is requesting a yes/no answer (lines 1-2) in relation to common identification of a specific item of information.

In a group setting students will need to identify an orderly way of taking turns at talk. This can occur either publicly and officially or tacitly. Table 25 presents an example of a 'request nomination' move extracted from the initial sequence of the first step of one of the dialogues i.e. as part of the initial 'review information' step. In this example, which takes the form of a preparatory exchange, one of the students invites the others to nominate themselves to share information first (line 1). The request is taken up by one of the other students (line 2). The exchange contrasts with a typical classroom setting, where the tutor rather than a fellow student would initiate the exchange.

Table 26 presents an example of a 'request repetition' move. In this example one of the students is acting as a recorder for their discussions and, pre-occupied with drawing up this record, does not initially hear what another student has said; and requests a repetition for the purposes of drawing up a record of their agreed points (line 13).

Table 25. Request to speak (REQ NOM)

(1)	E:	Who wants to go first?	Pre.	I	**REQ NOM**
(2)	A:	Well, I'll go first if that's alright.	Pre.	R	BD
(3)	A:	Well, basically, I found a lot of quotes	Nuc.	I	IN
(4)		Regarding information policy [...]			

Table 26. Request repetition (REQ RP)

(1)	M:	Um.	Nuc	I	IN
(2)		OK.			
(3)		If I start off with the () magazine.			
(4)		Er. Em.			
(5)		I think this'll be a tangible one.	Dep		OP
(6)		Because it's a comprehensive database	Dep.	I	JU
(7)		Of the of the organization's			
(8)		Information resources.			
(9)	J:	So may be organizing,	Dep.	I	REF
(10)		Organizing tangible information better ()			
(11)	M:	Um	Dep.	R	AK
(12)	J:	I think that's what they mean, isn't it?	Dep.	I	REQ OP
(13)	C:	Say again, comprehensive database	Emb.	I	**REQ RP**
(14)	M:	Will have a comprehensive database of	Emb.	R	RP
(15)		Its information resources			

Grounding Moves

Informing and elicitation moves relate to the sharing, exchange, interpretation, and evaluation of information. Since the information seeking will take place as part of a cooperative learning exercise, a significant aspect of the students' activity will be geared to establishing and maintaining common ground about information shared, contributions made, and decisions taken (Clark, 1996). Therefore a crucial feature of the dialogues will be the presence of 'grounding' moves that are intended to establish and maintain the development of common ground in an orderly way. This grounding applies both to the current exchange e.g. acknowledgements of information received, acceptances of opinions given; as well as over the course of the activity as the students develop a common pool of knowledge in response to the question

Table 27. Acknowledge (AK)

(1)	L:	Are we just going to have	Nuc.	I	REQ SU
(2)		One set of purposes then?			
(3)		() encompass like, all what		I	JU
(4)		An information audit is,			
(5)		Or just centre it around say		I	SU
(6)		Say we can split up by saying TFPL			
(7)		'Cause this what their purposes		I	JU
(8)		Of an information audit is			
(9)	E:	Yeh	Nuc.	R	**AK**
(10)	L:	And then, Susan Henschel,	Dep	I	EXT
(11)		This is what her purpose of			
(12)	D:	Um	Dep	R	**AK**

Table 28. Accept previous contribution (AC)

(1)	J:	Should we start off,	Dep	I	SU
(2)		We could start off			
(3)		With Or, Orna			
(4)		Um, talk about her definition			
(5)	K:	Uh, uh	Dep	R	AK
(6)	J:	Because that's what everybody else	Dep	I	JU
(7)		Knows about.			
(8)		Then we could go on about () NHS	Dep	I	SU
(9)		And then () JISC	Dep	I	SU
(10)	K:	Yeh	Dep	R	**AC**
(11)	J:	And then, come up with,	Dep	I	EXT S
(12)		How the same () relates to the organization		I	
(13)	E:	Um	Dep	R	**AC**

Table 29. Repeat own contribution (RP)

(1)	M:	Um.	Nuc	I	IN
(2)		OK.			
(3)		If I start off with the () magazine.			
(4)		Er. Em.			
(5)		I think this'll be a tangible one.	Dep		OP
(6)		Because it's a comprehensive database	Dep.	I	JU
(7)		Of the of the organization's			
(8)		Information resources.			
(9)	J:	So may be organizing,	Dep.	I	REF
(10)		Organizing tangible information better ()			
(11)	M:	Um	Dep.	R	AK
(12)	J:	I think that's what they mean, isn't it?	Dep.	I	REQ OP
(13)	C:	Say again, comprehensive database	Emb.	I	**REQ RP**
(14)	M:	Will have a comprehensive database of	Emb.	R	RP
(15)		Its information resources			

guiding their group investigation. Examples of these grounding moves are presented here.

Two types of response moves can be used by hearers to feedback to the current speaker that an item of information has been received Table 27 presents an example of the 'acknowledge' move used by hearers to validate the speaker's utterance. In this example a student is requesting and making suggestions for organizing the upcoming presentation (lines 1-8).

In response the other students acknowledge rather than necessarily accept, the suggestions that have been given (line 9; 12).

Table 28 presents an example of a slightly stronger form of validation: an 'accept' move. In this example the current speaker is making a suggestion for organizing the presentation (lines 1-4). This suggestion is supported by a justification (lines 6-9). Whereas in Table 26 the current speaker's

Table 30. Check for understanding (CH)

(1)	M:	Em, and then, em	Pre.	I	TR
(2)		I think this is an intangible ()	Nuc.	I	OP
(3)		Identify the dynamic information	Nuc.	I	IN
(4)		Of the organization			
(5)	J:	Is that the information flows?	Emb.	I	**CH**
(6)	M:	Yeh, I think it is.	Emb.	R	CL
(7)	J:	Could be both couldn't it?	Dep.	I	OP

Table 31. Clarify own previous contribution (CL)

(1)	J:	Er, so then what, what is	Nuc.	I	REQ SU
(2)		What is our overall conclusion			
(3)		Do we think?			
(4)	E:	About is this everything ()	Emb.	I	CH
(5)		About audit, policy, and strategy?			
(6)	J:	No, strategy, what is,	Emb.	R	**CL**
(7)		What is strat–			
(8)		What is information strategy			

utterance is merely acknowledged, in this example the speaker's utterance receives greater validation through an acceptance of what has been said. As can be seen from the transcriptions in Tables 27 and 28 the same response, i.e. 'Yeh', can be coded either as an acknowledgement (Table 27, line 9) or as an acceptance (Table 28, line 10). Assignment of the appropriate code will require reference to other features of the utterance e.g. intonation and emphasis (with an acceptance receiving stronger emphasis than an acknowledgement).

Grounding between partners in the dialogue can also be established through repetition. Table 29

presents an example of the use of a 'repetition' move. In this example the speaker (lines 14-15) repeats her original contribution (lines 6-8) in response to a repetition request from another student.

In order for common ground to be established between the participants, it can be necessary on occasion for hearers to check that a speaker's contribution has been correctly received or interpreted. Table 30 presents an example of a 'check' move. The example illustrates how some of the content of the contribution (lines 1-4) is not fully grounded; and a student proceeds to check (line 5) that their interpretation of the phrase 'understand the dynamic

Table 32. Qualify previous contribution (QU)

(1)	M:	Scaling the information process	Nuc	I	IN
(2)		So no we kind of		I	OP
(3)		Covered that one anyway			
(4)	J:	Um	Nuc	R	AC
(5)	M:	I suppose, I suppose we've kind of	Dep	I	**QU**
		Covered that one anyway			

Table 33. Reformulate (REF)

(1)	J:	Er, so then,	Nuc	I	REQ SU
(2)		What, what is our overall conclusion			
(3)		Do we think?			
(4)	E:	About, is this everything ()	Emb.	I	CH
(5)		About audit, policy and strategy?			
(6)	J:	No strategy, what is,	Emb.	R1	CL
(7)		What is strat, what is information strategy?			
(8)	K:	Or what do we think's important	Emb.	R2	**REF**
(9)		About information strategies? I think			
(10)	J:	No, what is, what is an.	Emb.	I	REJ
(11)		If that's a definition.			CL
(12)	K:	Yeh.	Emb.	R	AC
(13)		What is an.		I	RP

Table 34. Evaluate previous contribution (EVA)

(1)	D:	May be not to the same extent.	Dep	I	EXT
(2)		As a knowledge management company			
(3)		But it's still sort of slightly (used)			
(4)	L:	Yeh.	Dep	R	AC
(5)		So	Dep	I	
(6)	E:	That's a good point actually	Dep	I	**EVA**
(7)		Because it's bandied around a lot		JU	
(8)		Knowledge management			
(9)		I can see it being taken on			
(10)		In organizations.			

information of the organization' is held in common. It should also be noted that this grounding exchange is coded as an embedded exchange, since it stands to one side of the main flow of the expectations for the sequence, which concern the categorization of benefits [of conducting an information audit].

As the example in Table 30 illustrates (line 6), the response to a check move is a clarification. Table 31 provides a further example of a check-clarification combination. In this example, a student checks (lines 4-5) her understanding of the phrase 'What is our overall conclusion?' In response the speaker clarifies the meaning implicit in his previous contribution (lines 6-8).

In a manner similar to a give justification/explanation move (see Table 17), a speaker can use a qualification move to follow up on their previous contribution. Table 32 presents an example of this move. At lines (1-3) the student expresses the opinion that a particular benefit of conducting information audits has already been categorized. At lines (4-5) this opinion is qualified with the statement "I suppose, I suppose we've kind of covered that one anyway". The impact of this qualification is to weaken the strength of the previous opinion.

The grounding moves described thus far largely revolve around the establishment of common ground in relation to information exchange i.e. information receipt, checks and clarifications. Participants can also use other moves to comment more directly on the meaning of the information exchanged. These range from simple reformulations of the content of

Table 35. Reject previous contribution (RJ)

(1)	J:	Could we try and pick out	Nuc.	I	SU
(2)		The tangible then first?			
(3)		And write that down?			
(4)	C:	I don't know if it's going	Nuc.	R1	**RJ**
(5)	A:	()	Nuc.	R2	()
(6)	C:	To be easier.			
(7)		It might be easier to listen,	Dep.	I	SU-C
(8)		And then write, put 'T' next			
(9)		To that one.			

Table 36. Extend previous contribution (EXT)

(1)	M:	We can separate up like first	Nuc	I	SU
(2)	E:	You mean start off individually like.	Dep.	I	**EXT**
(3)		And then move on to the next person.			
(4)		And then we go through the presentation.			
(5)	M:	Yeh.	Dep.	R	AC
(6)		Because then at least, it shows like.	Dep.	I	JU
(7)		Even though we have similar stuff […].			

what another speaker has said, to evaluating, and extending the suggestions, ideas or actions expressed by another speaker. These moves are considered here.

Table 33 presents an example of the content of a student's contribution subsequently being reformulated by another student. In this example the sequence begins with one student inviting the others to agree on a conclusion for their shared response to the question guiding their group investigation (lines 1-3). Specifying the focus of this conclusion provokes a series of clarificatory exchanges (lines 4-13); exchanges that include one student (lines 8-9) that reformulating the content of a previous contribution (lines 6-7).

Table 34 presents an example of a student moving beyond reformulation to evaluation of a previous contribution. In this example a student provides a positive evaluation (line 6), an evaluation supported by a justification (lines 7-10), of the contribution provided by the student at (lines 1-3). The effect of this positive evaluation is to add to the common ground among the students.

Of course previous contributions can not only be accepted, and positively evaluated; they can also be rejected. Table 35 provides an example of a 'reject previous contribution' move. In this sequence taken from the 'Interpret' step of the talk, a student makes a suggestion for how to approach the task of categorizing the benefits of conducting an information audit (lines 1-3). The next speaker rejects this suggestion (lines 4, 6), before offering her own counter-suggestion (lines 7-9). The pivotal move that provides evidence of the positive establishment and development of common ground between the participants is the 'extend' move. A move that is key is to identification of exploratory exchanges. Table 36 presents an example of the extend move.

The sequence is initiated by one of the first speaker by making a suggestion (line 1) for the organization of the content of the presentation. This suggestion is taken up and extended on by the second speaker (lines 2-4). The first speaker accepts the second speaker's extension of her suggestion (line 5) providing further justification for their agreed course of action (lines 6-7).

Table 37. Give confirmation (CO)

(1)	C:	So	Pre.	I	
(2)		We're going to start with like, saying that,	Nuc.	I	REQ CO
(3)		The benefits can be gained from			
(4)		The good information audit			
(5)		And explain that it has to be continuous			
(6)	A:	Yeh	Nuc.	R1	CO
(7)	M:	Um	Nuc.	R2	CO

Table 38. Focus formulation substep (initiating sequence)

(1)	J:	() we're going to have to try to interpret this.	Nuc.	I	IN
(2)		There seem to be a number of factors ()	Nuc.	I	SU
(3)	C:	Um	Nuc.	R1	AK
(4)	M:	Yeh	Nuc.	R2	AK
(5)	C:	I don't know whether it would be better	Dep.	I	RJ
(6)		To try and sort of make a big long list	Dep.	I	SU
(7)		And literally go through			
(8)		'cause as we say, y'know	Dep.	I	JU
(9)		A lot of them overlap			
(10)	M:	Yeh	Dep.	R1	AK
(11)	A:	Yeh	Dep.	R2	AK
(12)	M:	And then like categorize them	Dep.	I	EXT O
(13)		Like into p'rhaps the short term			
(14)		And the long term			
(15)	C:	Yeh	Dep.	R	AK
(16)	M:	And also the tangible and the intangible	Dep.	I	EXT S
(17)	J:	Yeh	Dep.	R	AK
(18)	M:	Just so like, if we started off with a big list	Dep.	I	EXT O
(19)		'cause then covering actually	Dep.	I	JU
(20)	C:	Yeh	Dep.	R1	AK
(21)	A:	Um	Dep.	R2	AK
(22)	M:	Everything, I s'ppose	Dep.	I	EXT S

A move found quite often in the student dialogues was a 'give confirmation' move. This move occurred almost exclusively during sequences summarizing the state of the group's emerging and summative response to their investigation. In this example the 'give confirmation' move (lines 6, 7) occurs in response to a request confirmation move (line 2); as one student seeks to co-construct confirmation of the content their presentation.

REVISION OF CATEGORY SYSTEM

As indicated by the steps of a structuring analysis, it is likely that the initial category system will require revision in the light of its application to the materials. In this study a number of revisions and amendments were made to the category system at each level of the 'sequential organization of discourse' framework.

Table 39. Information collection substep (initiating sequence)

(1)	M:	Um.	Nuc	I	IN
(2)		OK.			
(3)		If I start off with the () magazine.			
(4)		Er. Em.			
(5)		I think this'll be a tangible one.	Dep		OP
(6)		Because it's a comprehensive database	Dep.	I	JU
(7)		Of the of the organization's			
(8)		Information resources.			
(9)	J:	So may be organizing,	Dep.	I	REF
(10)		Organizing tangible information better ()			
(11)	M:	Um	Dep.	R	AK
(12)	J:	I think that's what they mean, isn't it?	Dep.	I	REQ
(13)	C:	Say again, comprehensive database	Emb.	I	REQ RP
(14)	M:	Will have a comprehensive database of	Emb.	R	RP
(15)		Its information resources.			
(16)		And then it just goes to say	Dep.	I	IN
(17)		Like a complete inventory,			
(18)		Existing information resources, systems,			
(19)		People, technology, equipment.			
(20)		So, that's () tangible ()	Dep.	I	OP

Table 40. Coordinating exchange

(1)	D:	Start off with…what Orna says	Nuc	I	SU
(2)	M:	Yeh	Nuc	R1	AC
(3)	L:	Um	Nuc	R2	AC
(4)	D:	So you start off with Orna…	Dep	I	RP
(5)	M:	Yeh	Dep	R	AC
(6)	D:	At the end you put, at the end	Dep.	I	SU
(7)	M:	[…] And then at the end	Dep.	I	SU
(8)		We can have like how			
(9)		To incorporate how			
(10)		How what we found, and how Orna, Orna's			
(11)	D:	…compare what we	Dep.	I	SU
(12)	M:	…compare…	Dep.	R	RP
(13)		These are…you know	Dep.	I	JU
(14)		And these are all exactly			
(15)		Successful (or) constraining			
(16)		And then	Dep.	I	OP
(17)		And that's it.			

Table 41. Discourse move: extension self

(1)	J:	Should we start off,	Dep	I	SU
(2)		We could start off			
(3)		With Or, Orna			
(4)		Um, talk about her definition			
(5)	K:	Uh, uh	Dep	R	AK
(6)	J:	Because that's what everybody else	Dep	I	JU
(7)		Knows about.			
(8)		Then we could go on about () NHS	Dep	I	EXT S
(9)		And then () JISC	Dep	I	SU
(10)	K:	Yeh	Dep	R	AC
(11)	J:	And then, come up with,	Dep	I	EXT S
(12)		How the same () relates to the organization		I	
(13)	E:	Um	Dep	R	AC

Steps

Segmentation of the dialogues into their constituent steps revealed that the Interpret step could be further segmented into two sub-steps: a series of sequences bound by content relating to the development of an agreed focus for the group's response (Table 38); and a series of sequences bound by content relating to the collection of evidence in support of the agreed focus (Table 39). Following Kuhlthau (1991; 2004)

these groups of bound sequence were categorized as 'focus formulation' and 'information collection' steps. The initial sequences of a focus formulation and an information collection step are presented here.

The opening exchange signals the beginning of the Interpret step. In this sequence the students begin to formulate the method by which they will categorize the benefits of conducting an information audit. The dependent exchange is characterized by disputational talk (lines 5-22) as alternative perspec-

Table 42. Discourse move: extension other

(1)	J:	What—did anybody pick up this objective	Nuc.	I	REQ PN
(2)		in Orna, risk avoidance?			
(3)	A:	Yeh	Nuc.	R1	Y
(4)	M:	Yeh	Nuc.	R2	Y
(5)	J:	Short-term	Dep	I	IN
(6)		So, I mean, that could be—	Dep.	I	OP
(7)	M:	Could go into making information	Dep.	I	**EXT O**
(8)		More accessible and usable for the—			
(9)	A:	Yeh	Emb.	R	AK
(10)		Orna said about risk avoidance.	Dep.	I	**EXT O**
(11)		And then () said about			
(12)		Draws attention to problem areas			
(13)		Which kind of same thing isn't it,	Dep.	I	REQ OP
(14)		When you get () avoids risk			

Table 43. Discourse move: counter suggestion

(1)	J:	Could we try and pick out	Nuc.	I	SU
(2)		The tangible then first?			
(3)		And write that down?			
(4)	C:	I don't know if it's going	Nuc.	R1	RJ
(5)	A:	()	Nuc.	R2	()
(6)	C:	To be easier.			
(7)		It might be easier to listen,	Dep.	I	**SU-C**
(8)		And then write, put 'T' next			
(9)		To that one.			
(10)	A:	() split the page in two.	Dep.	I	SU
(11)	C:	Alright	Dep.	R	AC
(12)	A:	And then say (),	Dep.	I	EXT S
(13)		Say, y'know,			
(14)		Say, 'oh', that's a tangible			
(15)		And then put it in that column			
(16)		And we can (probably take it from there?)	Dep.	I	SU

tives are provided as to how to do this. Once this focus has been resolved succeeding sequences in this sub-step are characterized by exploratory exchanges.

This example of the initiating sequence of an information collection sub-step (Table 39) is ex-

tracted from the same Interpret step. The focus for their response has been formulated and agreed; and the content of the sequence relates to the process of reviewing the documents at hand, identifying the benefits, and categorizing these into an agreed

Table 44. Discourse move: rebuttal

(1)	D:	You just do the slides for that, and then	Dep.	I	SU
(2)		We all chip in on them			
(3)	L:	Um	Dep.	I	AK
(4)	D:	And then at the end, overall review of what	Dep.	I	SU
(5)	L:	Um	Dep.	I	AK
(6)	D:	How it links to Orna's and our definition	Dep.	I	JU
(7)	L:	Alright	Dep.	R	AC
(8)		I just felt it would be easier	Dep.	I	SU-C
(9)		If we kind of like put down			
(10)		What we found um			
(11)		And then give a definition in Orna's			
(12)		And then, this is what our.			
(13)		Do you know what I mean?	Dep.	I	REQ OP
(14)	D:	Yeh.	Dep.	R	AK
(15)		Thing is that they're	Dep.	I	**RB**
(16)		These are what we found.			

schema of tangible and intangible benefits.

Sequences

By identifying the function contained in the nuclear exchange it was also possible to group the sequences that occurred during the learners' dialogues into the following categories: structuring, informing, eliciting, and summarizing sequences. Foster (2009) provides further discussion of these categories.

Exchanges

Based on the type of collaborative talk that they contained, the initial category scheme categorized dependent exchanges into three types: exploratory, disputational and cumulative exchanges. A further type of dependent exchange was identified in the dialogues: coordinating exchanges. This type of dependent exchange occurred mainly in the final Completion step, during which students organized the content of their presentations; and defined their roles. Such sequences are characterized by an emphasis on action, and a mainly uncritical acceptance of the initial action suggested. Table 40 presents an example of this type of dependent exchange.

Discourse Moves

Testing of the initial category scheme against the materials led to the identification of a number of moves not incorporated in the initial schema. First it became apparent that it is possible to distinguish between two types of extension (EXT) move. On the one hand this move can function to follow up on the content of the current speaker's own talk i.e. an extension self move (EXT S); on the other hand the move can also function to follow up on the talk of others (EXT O). When evaluating the quality of the talk, the latter was considered to lead to a more collaborative form of talk than the former (see Foster, 2009 for further commentary). Tables 41 and 42 present examples of these uses of the 'extension' move. Table 41 illustrates how the speaker extends his own initial contribution (lines 1-4) twice, at line 8 and at line 11.

In contrast the example in Table 42 illustrates two students extending not their own contribution (at lines

7-8 and lines 1-12 respectively), but the previous contribution of a fellow student (lines 5-6).

Two further moves were identified in the dialogues that were not incorporated in the initial category system. Both of these moves aid in the identification and characterization of disputational exchanges. Suggestions are extended to include counter-suggestions, and rebuttals are also identified. In Table 43 the sequence begins with a student making a suggestion for how to categorize the benefits [of conducting information audits] (lines 1-3). The initial suggestion is rejected (lines 4, 6) before a counter-suggestion is proposed (lines 7-9).

Table 44 presents an example of a rebuttal. In this example, taken from a completion step, the sequence is structured as suggestion, counter-suggestion, rebuttal. The sequence begins with a student making a suggestion for how the content of the presentation should be structured (lines 1-2; 4; 6). The next student presents a counter-suggestion (lines 7-12); a suggestion that is acknowledged but rebutted by the first student (lines 15-16).

After revision of the category system is complete the analyst is now ready to apply the system to an analysis of the discourse materials. *Appendix A* presents the revised category system; and *Appendix B* presents the full list of discourse categories and codes used in coding and categorizing the learners' dialogues.

CONCLUSION

This chapter has presented a coding guide that aids the analysis of learners' dialogues during educational information seeking. Underpinning the organization of the guide is a language-based theory of learning that structures educational content in accordance with the sequential and nature of spoken discourse. This framework specifies a range of collective units of talk i.e. step, sequence, exchange, along with individual discourse moves, that makes it possible to speak of classroom discourse as co-constructed. Emphasis has also been placed on the need to revise the initial category system in the light of its' testing against the empirical materials at hand: understanding information exchange in educational settings; learner engagement; and communications sharing. By drawing on a language-based theory of learning and the sequential nature of discourse, it becomes clear that understanding information seeking as a matter of the seeking, retrieval, and exchange of information is a simplistic view. Language is not only used by learners to describe information; language and its use is also constitutive of information. When information seeking occurs as part of a broader collaborative learning activity, the co-constructed nature of talk and information seeking also becomes apparent. By drawing on a language-based theory of learning it is also clear that learner engagement with information at all stages of information seeking draws on a far wider repertoire of actions than is implied by the categories of information need, seeking, retrieval and use. Analysis of learners' talk will reveal for example that when information is discussed, a range of actions are applied to that information e.g. the giving and eliciting of opinions, justifications/explanations, and examples etc, that transform information into knowledge as that information becomes embedded in users' activities and tasks. Finally when looking for information involves collaboration this points to the mediating roles played not only by activities, technology, and other users, but also by language. From a discourse perspective the tool of communications sharing *par excellence* remains language and talk.

REFERENCES

Belkin, N., & Vickery, A. (1985). *Interaction in information systems: A review of the research from document retrieval to knowledge-based systems*. London: The British Library.

Clark, H. H. (1996). *Using language*. Cambridge, UK: Cambridge University Press. doi:10.1017/CBO9780511620539

Ellis, D. (2002). Information seeking and mediated searching, part 5: User-intermediary interaction. *Journal of the American Society for Information Science and Technology, 53*(11), 883–893. doi:10.1002/asi.10133

Foster, J. (2009). Understanding interaction in information seeking and use as a discourse: A dialogic approach. *The Journal of Documentation, 65*(1), 83–105. doi:10.1108/00220410910926130

Foster, J., Wu, M.-M., & Lin, A. (2009, November). Collaborative information seeking and sharing in educational settings: identifying the challenges. In N. Caidi, S. Y. Rieh, & G. Oyarce (Chairs), *Collaborative Information seeking and Sharing*. Symposium conducted at the SIGUSE meeting of the American Society for Information Science and Technology, Vancouver, Canada.

Kuhlthau, C. C. (1991). Inside the search process: Information seeking from the user's perspective. *Journal of the American Society for Information Science American Society for Information Science, 42*, 361–371. doi:10.1002/(SICI)1097-4571(199106)42:5<361::AID-ASI6>3.0.CO;2-#

Kuhlthau, C. C. (2004). *Seeking meaning: A process approach to library and information services*. Westport, CT: Libraries Unlimited.

Mayring, P. (2004). Qualitative content analysis. In Flick, U., von Kardoff, E., & Steinke, L. (Eds.), *A companion to qualitative research* (pp. 266–269). London: Sage.

Mercer, N., & Wegerif, R. (1997). A dialogical framework for researching peer talk. In Wegerif, R., & Scrimshaw, P. (Eds.), *Computers and talk in the primary classroom* (pp. 49–61). Bristol, UK: Multilingual Matters.

Saracevic, T., Spink, A., & Wu, M.-M. (1997). Users and intermediaries in information retrieval: what are they talking about? In A. Jameson, C. Paris, C., & C. Tasso (Eds.). *Proceedings of the 6th International Conference on User Modeling,* 2-5 June, Chia Languna, Sardinia, Italy (pp. 43-54).

Sharan, Y., & Sharan, S. (1992). *Expanding cooperative learning through group investigation*. New York: Teachers College Press.

Wells, G. (1999). *Dialogic inquiry: Toward a sociocultural practice and theory of education*. Cambridge, UK: Cambridge University Press. doi:10.1017/CBO9780511605895

Wu, M.-M. (2005). Understanding patrons' micro-level information-seeking (MLIS) in information retrieval situations. *Information Processing & Management*, *41*, 929–947. doi:10.1016/j.ipm.2004.08.007

Mayring, P. (2003). *Qualitative inhaltsanalyse: Grundlagen and techniken* (6th ed.). Basel, Germany: Beltz Verlag.

Wu, M.-M., & Foster, J. (2010). Exploring factors for collaborative group investigation. *Journal of Educational Media & Library Sciences*, *47*(2), 123–146.

ADDITIONAL READING

Foster, J. (2006). Collaborative information seeking and retrieval. In Cronin, B. (Ed.), *Annual Review of Information Science and Technology* (*Vol. 40*, pp. 329–356). Medford, NJ: Information Today.

APPENDIX A. REVISED CATEGORY SYSTEM

Figure 1.

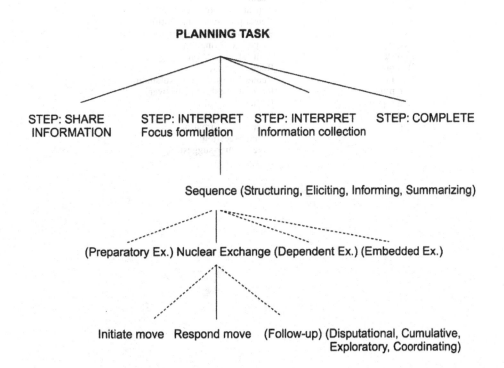

PLANNING TASK

STEP: SHARE INFORMATION   STEP: INTERPRET Focus formulation   STEP: INTERPRET Information collection   STEP: COMPLETE

Sequence (Structuring, Eliciting, Informing, Summarizing)

(Preparatory Ex.) Nuclear Exchange (Dependent Ex.) (Embedded Ex.)

Initiate move   Respond move   (Follow-up) (Disputational, Cumulative, Exploratory, Coordinating)

APPENDIX B. DISCOURSE CATEGORIES AND CODES

Steps	
SI	Sharing information
IN	Interpret
CO	Completion
Sub steps	
FF	Focus formulation
IC	Information collection
Sequences	
ST	Structuring
IN	Informing
EL	Eliciting
SU	Summarizing
Moves	
I	Initial
R	Response
R1	Response 1
R2	Response 2
Ak	Acknowledge
Acc	Accept previous contribution
Bid	Request to speak
Ch	Check for understanding
Cl	Clarify own previous contribution
Co	Give confirmation
Eva	Evaluate previous contribution
Ex	Give relevant example
Ext. s	Extend own previous contribution
Ext. o	Extend other previous contribution
In	Give information
Ju	Give justification/explanation
Nom	Nominate next speaker
Op	Give opinion
Pos/neg	Give "Yes" or "No" answer
Qu	Qualify previous contribution
Rb	Rebuttal
Rep	Repeat own previous contribution
Rej	Reject previous contribution
Ref	Reformulate previous contribution
Req in	Request information
Req su	Request suggestion
Req op	Request opinion
Req ju	Request justification/explanation
Req p/n	Request "Yes"/"No" answer
Req rep	Request repetition
Req nom	Request nomination
Req co	Request confirmation
Su	Give suggestion
Su-c	Give counter-suggestion

Compilation of References

Abraham, R. (2007). Mobile phones and economic development: Evidence from the fishing industry in India Indian School of Business, Hyderabad, India. *Information Technologies and International Development, 4*(1).

Ackerman, M. S. (2000). The Intellectual Challenge of CSCW: The Gap Between Social Requirements and Technical Feasibility. *Human-Computer Interaction, 15*(2-3), 181–205.

Ackerman, M. S., & McDonald, D. W. (1996). Answer Garden 2: Merging Organizational Memory with Collaborative Help. In *Proc of ACM Conf. on Computer Supported Cooperative Work* (CSCW '96) (pp. 97-105). Boston, MA: ACM Press.

Adesope, O., Olubunmi, S., & McCracken, J. (2007). Implementing mobile learning in developing countries: Prospects and challenges. In Montgomerie, C., & Seale, J. (Eds.), *Proceedings of world conference on educational multimedia, hypermedia and telecommunications 2007* (pp. 1249–1254). Chesapeake, VA: AACE.

Adler, A., Nash, J. C., & Noël, S. (2006). Evaluating and implementing a collaborative office document system. *Interacting with Computers, 18*(4), 665–682. doi:10.1016/j.intcom.2005.10.001

Ahmadi, M., Helms, M., & Ross, T. (2000). Technological developments: Shaping the telecommuting work environment of the future. *Facilities, 18*(1/2), 83–89. doi:10.1108/02632770010312204

Akkirman, A., Harris, D., & Drew, L. (2005). Organizational communication satisfaction in the virtual workplace. *Journal of Management Development, 24*(5), 397–409. doi:10.1108/02621710510598427

Amershi, S., & Morris, M. R. (2008, April 5-10). CoSearch: a system for co-located collaborative Web search. In *Proceedings of SIGCHI Conference on Human Factors in Computing Systems* (pp. 1647-1656). Florence, Italy.

Aminuzzaman, S., Baldersheim, H., & Jamil, I. (2003). Talking back: Empowerment and mobile phones in rural Bangladesh: A study of the village pay phone of Grameen Bank. *Contemporary South Asia, 12*(3), 327–348. doi:10.1080/0958493032000175879

Anderson, J. L. (2006). A structured approach for bringing mobile telecommunications to the world's poor. *Electronic Journal of Information Systems in Developing Countries, 27*(2), 1–9.

Anderson, P. (1999). Complexity Theory and Organization Science. *Organization Science, 10*(3), 216–232. doi:10.1287/orsc.10.3.216

Anderson, R. J. (1994). Representations and requirements: The value of ethnography in system design. *Human-Computer Interaction, 9*(2), 151–182. doi:10.1207/s15327051hci0902_1

Andrews, D., Nonnecke, B., & Preece, J. (2003). Electronic survey methodology: a case study in reaching hard-to-involve Internet users. *International Journal of Human-Computer Interaction, 16*(2), 185–210. doi:10.1207/S15327590IJHC1602_04

Aouiche, K., Lemire, D., & Godin, R. (2008). Collaborative OLAP with tag clouds: Web 2.0 OLAP formalism and experimental evaluation. In *Proceedings of the 4th International Conference on Web Information Systems and Technologies (WEBIST 2008)*, Funchal, Madeira, Portugal (pp. 5-12).

Ardichvili, A., Page, V., & Wentling, T. (2003). Motivation and barriers to participation in virtual knowledge-sharing communities of practice. *Journal of Knowledge Management, 7*(1), 64–77. doi:10.1108/13673270310463626

Asch, T., Cardozo, J. I., Cabellero, H., & Bortoli, J. (1991). The story we now want to hear is not ours to tell: Relinquishing control over representation: Toward sharing visual communication skills with The Yanomami. *Visual Anthropology Review, 7*(2), 102–106. doi:10.1525/var.1991.7.2.102

Association of Ontario Midwives. (n.d.) *What is a midwife?* Retrieved May 10, 2010, from http://www.aom.on.ca/Midwifery_Care/What_is_a_Midwife.aspx

Aufderheide, P. (1995). The video in the villages project: Videomaking with and by Brazilian Indians. *Visual Anthropology Review, 11*(2), 82–93. doi:10.1525/var.1995.11.2.83

Austin, A. E., & Baldwin, R. G. (1991). *Faculty collaboration: Enhancing the quality of scholarship and teaching.* San Francisco: Jossey-Bass.

Avery, P., & Foster, I. (2000). The GriPhyN Project: Towards petascale virtual-data grids. *GryPhyn Report 2000-1.* Retrieved February 9, 2009, from http://www.griphyn.org/documents/document_server/uploaded_documents/doc--501--proposal_all.doc

Baecker, R. M. (1995). *Readings in Human-Computer Interaction: Towards the Year 2000.* San Francisco: Morgan Kaufmann.

Bakeman, R., & Gottman, J. M. (1986). *Observing interaction: An introduction to sequential analysis.* Cambridge, UK: Cambridge University Press.

Baliamoune-Lutz, M. (2003). An analysis of the determinants and effect of ICT diffusion in developing countries. *Information Technology for Development, 10,* 151–169. doi:10.1002/itdj.1590100303

Bandura, A. (1977). *Social learning theory.* New York: General Learning Press.

Bayes, A. (2001). Infrastructure and rural development: Insights from a Grameen bank village phone initiative in Bangladesh. *Agricultural Economics, 25*(2–3), 261–272. doi:10.1111/j.1574-0862.2001.tb00206.x

Baym, N. K. (1997). Interpreting soap operas and creating community: inside an electronic fan culture. In Kiesler, S. (Ed.), *Culture of the Internet* (pp. 103–120). Mahwah, NJ: Lawrence Erlbaum Associates.

Beamish, A. (2008). *Learning from work: designing organizations for learning and communication.* Stanford, CA: Stanford University Press.

Belkin, N., & Vickery, A. (1985). *Interaction in information systems: A review of the research from document retrieval to knowledge-based systems.* London: The British Library.

Bell, G. (2005). The age of the thumb: A cultural reading of mobile technologies from Asia. In Glotz, P., Bertschi, S., & Locke, C. (Eds.), *Thumb culture: The meaning of mobile phones for society* (pp. 67–88). Bielefeld, Germany: Transcript Verlag.

Bellman, B., & Jules-Rosette, B. (1997). *A Paradigm for looking: Cross-cultural research with visual media.* New York: Ablex.

Benkler, Y. (2006). *How Social Production transforms Markets and Freedom.* New Haven, CT: Yale University Press.

Berger, P. L., & Luckmann, T. (1966). *The social construction of reality: A treatise in the sociology of knowledge.* Garden City, NY: Anchor Books.

Berkowitz, D. (1992). Non-routine news and newswork: Exploring a what-a-story. *The Journal of Communication, 42*(1), 82–93. doi:10.1111/j.1460-2466.1992.tb00770.x

Bird, C., Pattison, D., D'Souza, R., Filkov, V., & Davanbu, P. (2008). *Latent Social Structure in Open Source Projects.* Paper presented at the SIGSOFT 2008, Atlanta, GA.

Bishop, J. (2007). Increasing participation in online communities: A framework for human–computer interaction. *Computers in Human Behavior, 23,* 1881–1893. doi:10.1016/j.chb.2005.11.004

Blackwell, A. F., Stringer, M., Toye, E. F., & Rode, J. A. (2004). Tangible interface for collaborative information retrieval. In *Proceedings of SIGCHI Conference on Human Factors in Computing Systems* Vienna, Austria (pp. 1473-1476).

Blake, C., & Pratt, W. (2006). Collaborative information synthesis: a model of information behaviors of scientists in medicine and public health. *Journal of the American Society for Information Science and Technology, 57*(13), 1740–1749. doi:10.1002/asi.20487

Blanton, K. (2005, October 16). Home work. *The Boston Globe.* Retrieved October 8, 2007, from http://www.boston.com/news/globe

Bobrow, D. G., & Whalen, J. (2002). Community Knowledge Sharing in Practice: The Eureka Story. *Reflections-Society for Organizational Learning, 4*(2), 47–59.

Bongey, S. B., Cizadlo, G., & Kalnbach, L. (2006). Explorations in course-casting: podcasts in higher education. *Campus-Wide Information Systems, 23*(5), 350–367. doi:10.1108/10650740610714107

Bourgeault, I. L. (2006). Push! The struggle for midwifery in Ontario. Montreal, PQ: McGill Queen's University Press.

Bourgeault, I. L., & Fynes, M. (1997). Integrating lay and nurse-midwifery into the U.S. and Canadian health care systems. *Social Science & Medicine, 44*(7), 1051–1063. doi:10.1016/S0277-9536(96)00290-0

Bray, D., Croxson, K., Dutton, W., & Konsynski, B. (2008). *Sermo: An Authenticated, Community-Based, Knowledge Ecosystem* (OII DPSN Working Paper No. 7). Oxford, UK: University of Oxford, Oxford Internet Institute. Retrieved from http://ssrn.com/abstract=1016483.

Breed, W. (1955). Social control in the newsroom. *Social Forces, 33*, 326–335. doi:10.2307/2573002

Brookes-Howell, L. C. (2006). Living without labels: the interactional management of diagnostic uncertainty in the genetic counselling clinic. *Social Science & Medicine, 63*(12), 3080–3091. doi:10.1016/j.socscimed.2006.08.008

Brown, J. S., & Duguid, P. (2001). Knowledge and organization: a social-practice perspective. *Organization Science, 12*(2), 198–213. doi:10.1287/orsc.12.2.198.10116

Bruce, H., Fidel, R., Pejtersen, A., Dumais, S., Grudin, J., & Poltrock, S. (2003). A comparison of the collaborative information retrieval behaviors of two design teams. *New Review of Information Behaviour Research: Studies of Information Seeking in Context, 4*(1), 139–153. doi:10.1080/14716310310001631499

Buchbinder, M. H., Detzer, M. J., Welsch, R. L., Christiano, A. S., Patashnick, J. L., & Rich, M. (2005). Assessing adolescents with insulin-dependent diabetes mellitus: a multiple perspective pilot study using visual illness narratives and interviews. *Journal of Adolescent Health, 36*(1), 71.e79 –71.e13.

Budd, J. (2006). Discourse analysis and the study of communication in LIS. *Library Trends, 55*(1), 65–82. doi:10.1353/lib.2006.0046

Burkell, J., & McKenzie, P. J. (2005). Information provision for informed prenatal decision making. In L. Vaughan (Ed.), *Data, information, and knowledge in a networked world.* Canadian Association for Information Science 2005 Annual Conference June 2-4, 2005. Retrieved May 10, 2010 from http://www.cais-acsi.ca/proceedings/2005/burkell_2005.pdf

Butler, B. S. (2001). Membership size, communication activity, and sustainability: a resource-based model of online social structures. *Information Systems Research, 12*(4), 346–362. doi:10.1287/isre.12.4.346.9703

Butler, D. (2005). Science in the web age: Joint efforts. *Nature, 438*, 548–549. doi:10.1038/438548a

Butler, D. (2007). Data sharing: The next generation. *Nature, 446*, 10–11. doi:10.1038/446010b

Caffarella, R. S., & Zinn, L. F. (1999). Professional development for faculty: a conceptual framework of barriers and supports. *Innovative Higher Education, 23*(4), 241–254. doi:10.1023/A:1022978806131

Cairncross, F. (1997). *The death of distance: How the communications revolution will change our lives.* Boston, MA: Harvard University Business School Press.

Canadian Institutes of Health Research. (2007). *Access to research outputs.* Retrieved February 9, 2009, from http://www.cihr-irsc.gc.ca/e/34846.html

Canadian Institutes of Health Research. Natural Sciences and Engineering Research Council of Canada, &. Social Sciences and Humanities Research Council of Canada. (2003). *Tri-Council policy statement: Ethical conduct for research involving humans.* Ottawa, ON: Public Works and Government Services Canada. Retrieved May 10, 2010 from http://www.pre.ethics.gc.ca/policy-politique/tcps-eptc/docs/TCPS%20October%202005_E.pdf

Carr, N. (2008). *The Big Switch: Rewiring the World, From Edison to Google.* London: W. W. Norton and Company.

Case, D. (2006). Information seeking. *Annual Review of Information Science & Technology, 40*, 293–327. doi:10.1002/aris.1440400114

Cassarino, I., & Geuna, A. (2008). *Distributed Film Production: Artistic Experimentation or Feasible Alternative? The Case of a Swarm of Angels* (OII DPSN Working Paper No. 14). Oxford, UK: University of Oxford, Oxford Internet Institute. Retrieved from http://ssrn.com/abstract=1326510.

Cassarino, I., & Richter, W. (2008). Swarm creativity. The legal and organizational challenges of open content film production (DIME Working Paper No. 45). In Andersen, B. (Ed.), *DIME Working Papers on Intellectual Property Rights.* London: Birkbeck College.

Castells, M., Qiu, J. L., Fernández-Ardévol, M., & Sey, A. (2007). *Mobile communication and society: A global perspective (information revolution and global politics).* Cambridge, MA: MIT Press.

Cerf, V. G., Cameron, A., Lederberg, J., Russel, C., Schatz, B., & Shames, P. (1993). *National Collaboratories: Applying Information Technologies for Scientific Research.* Washington, DC: National Academy Press.

Chalfen, R. (1981). A Sociovidistic approach to children's filmmaking: The Philadelphia Project. *Studies in Visual Communication, 7*(1), 2–33.

Chalfen, R. (1992). Picturing culture through indigenous imagery: A telling story. In Crawford, P., & Turton, D. (Eds.), *Film as Ethnography* (pp. 222–241). Manchester: University of Manchester Press.

Chalfen, R. (1997). Foreword and Afterword. In Worth, S., Adair, J., & Chalfen, R. (Eds.), *Through Navajo eyes: An exploration in film communication and anthropology* (2nd rev. ed.). Albuquerque, NM: University of Mexico Press.

Chalfen, R. (2007). *Variations of bio-documentary representation: Kids make pictures.* Paper presented at the Annual Meetings of the International Visual Sociology Association, New York.

Chalfen, R., & Haley, J. (1971). Reaction to socio-documentary film research in a mental health clinic. *The American Journal of Orthopsychiatry, 41*(1), 91–100.

Chalfen, R., & Rich, M. (2007). Combining the applied, the visual and the medical: patients teaching physicians with visual narratives. In Pink, S. (Ed.), *Visual Interventions: Applied Visual Anthropology* (pp. 53–70). New York: Berghan Books.

Chambers, E. (1992). Work load and the quality of student learning. *Studies in Higher Education, 17*(2), 141–153. doi:10.1080/03075079212331382627

Charmaz, K. (2003). Qualitative Interviewing and Grounded Theory Analysis. In Holstein, J. A., & Gubrium, J. F. (Eds.), *Inside Interviewing: New Lenses, New Concerns* (pp. 311–330). Thousand Oaks, CA: Sage Publications.

Cheng, R., & Vassileva, J. (2005). User- and Community-Adaptive Rewards Mechanism for Sustainable Online Community. In Ardissono, L., Brna, P., & Mitrovic, A. (Eds.), *Lecture Notes in Computer Science* (pp. 332–336). Berlin: Springer-Verlag.

Chrislip, D. D., & Larson, C. E. (1994). *Collaborative leadership: How citizens and civic leaders can make a difference.* San Francisco: Jossey-Bass.

Chui, M., Johnson, B., & Manyika, J. (2009). *Distributed Problem-Solving Networks: An Introduction and Overview* (OII DPSN Working Paper No. 18). Oxford, UK: University of Oxford, Oxford Internet Institute. Retrieved from http://ssrn.com/abstract=1411739.

Chung, K. H., & Cox, R. A. K. (1990). Patterns of productivity in the finance literature: A study of the bibliometric distributions. *The Journal of Finance, 45*(1), 301–309. doi:10.2307/2328824

Cicourel, A. V. (1990). The Integration of Distributed Knowledge in Collaborative Medical Diagnosis. In Galegher, J., Kraut, R. E., & Egido, C. (Eds.), *Intellectual Teamwork* (pp. 221–242). Hillsdale, NJ: Lawrence Erlbaum Associates.

Clark, H. (1992). *Arenas of language use*. Chicago: University of Chicago Press.

Clark, H. H. (1996). *Using language*. Cambridge, UK: Cambridge University Press. doi:10.1017/CBO9780511620539

Clauson, K. A., Polen, H. H., Boulos, M. N. K., & Dzenowagis, J. H. (2008). Scope, completeness, and accuracy of drug information in Wikipedia. *The Annals of Pharmacotherapy*, *42*(12), 1814. doi:10.1345/aph.1L474

College of Midwives of Ontario. (1994). *Philosophy of midwifery care in Ontario*. Retrieved May 10, 2010, from http://www.cmo.on.ca/downloads/communications/standards/G01-Philosophy%20of%20Midwifery%20Care%20Jan94.pdf

College of Midwives of Ontario. (2005). *Informed choice standard*. Retrieved May 10, 2010, from http://www.cmo.on.ca/downloads/communications/standards/G14-Informed%20Choice%20Standard%20Sept%2005.pdf

Constant, D., Sproull, L., & Kiesler, S. (1999). The kindness of strangers: the usefulness of electronic weak ties for technical advice. In Desanctis, G., & Fulk, J. (Eds.), *Shaping organization form: Communication, connection, and community* (pp. 415–444). Thousand Oaks, CA: Sage Publications, Inc.

Cordella, M. (2004). *The Dynamic consultation: A discourse analytical study of doctor-patient communication*. Amsterdam, Philadelphia: John Benjamin.

Courtright, C. (2007). Context in information behavior research. *Annual Review of Information Science & Technology*, *41*, 273–306. doi:10.1002/aris.2007.1440410113

Cronin, B., & Davenport, E. (1993). Social intelligence. [ARIST]. *Annual Review of Information Science & Technology*, *29*, 3–44.

Cross, R., Davenport, T., & Cantrell, S. (2003). The Social Side of High Performance. *Sloan Management Review*, *45*(1), 20–24.

Crowston, K., & Howison, J. (2005). The Social Structure of Free and Open Source Software Development. *First Monday*, *10*(2).

Daft, R., & Wiginton, J. (1979). Language and Organization. *Academy of Management Review*, *4*(2), 179–191. doi:10.2307/257772

David, P., & Spence, M. (2003). *Towards an institutional infrastructure for e-Science: the scope of the challenge* (Research Report No. 2). Oxford, UK: University of Oxford, Oxford Internet Institute. Retrieved from http://ssrn.com/abstract=1325240.

Davies, E., & McKenzie, P. J. (2004). Preparing for opening night: temporal boundary objects in textually-mediated professional practice. *Information Research*, *10*(1). Retrieved May 10, 2010, from http://informationr.net/ir/10-1/paper211.html

de Souza, C. S., & Preece, J. (2004). A framework for analyzing and understanding online communities. *Interacting with Computers*, *16*, 579–610. doi:10.1016/j.intcom.2003.12.006

Dee, C., & Blazek, R. (1993). Information needs of the rural physician: a descriptive study. *Bulletin of the Medical Library Association*, *81*(3), 259–264.

Deepak, P., & Bhamidipaty, A. (2007). Optimizing on mobile usage cost for the lower income group: Insights and recommendations. In C. Baranauskas, P. Palanque, J. Abascal, S. Diniz, & J. Barbosa, (Eds.), Human–computer interaction—Proceedings of Interact 2007: 11th IFIP TC 13 international conference, Rio de Janeiro, Brazil, September 10–14, 2007 (pp. 339–342). New York: Springer Verlag.

Dellinger, K. (2004). Masculinities in safe and embattled organizations: Accounting for pornographic and feminist magazines. *Gender and Society*, *18*(5), 545-566. Denison, D.R. (1996). What is the difference between organizational culture and organizational climate? A native's point of view on a decade of paradigm wars. *Academy of Management Review, 21*(3), 619–654.

Dennen, V. P. (2008). Pedagogical lurking: Student engagement in non-posting discussion behavior. *Computers in Human Behavior, 24*(4), 1624–1633. doi:10.1016/j.chb.2007.06.003

Denning, P. J., & Yaholkovsky, P. (2008, April). Getting to We. *Communications of the ACM, 51*(4), 19–24. doi:10.1145/1330311.1330316

Dervin, B. (1992). From the Mind's Eye of the User: The Sense-Making Qualitative-Quantitative Methodology. In Glazer, J. D., & Powell, R. R. (Eds.), *Qualitative Research in Information Management* (pp. 61–82). Englewood, CO: Libraries Unlimited, Inc.

Descy, D. E. (2007). Browser-based online applications: Something for everyone! *TechTrends: Linking Research and Practice to Improve Learning, 51*(2), 3–5.

Detlefsen, E. G. (1998). The information behaviors of life and health scientists and health care providers: characteristics of the research literature. *Bulletin of the Medical Library Association, 86*(3), 385–390.

Deuze, M. (2007). *Media work.* Cambridge: Polity.

Diamond, M., & Allcorn, S. (2003). The cornerstone of psychoanalytic organizational analysis: Psychological reality, transference and counter-transference in the workplace. *Human Relations, 56*(4), 491–514. doi:10.1177/0018726703056004005

Dignan, L. (2007). Salesforce.com rolls out customer data sharing; eyes 1 million subscribers. *ZDNet.* Retrieved February 9, 2009, from http://blogs.zdnet.com/BTL/?p=7239

Dinsmore, S. (1996). Strategies for self-scrutiny: Video diaries 1990-1993. *New Scholarship From BFI Research,* 41-57.

Donath, J. S., & Robertson, N. (1994, May 25-27). The sociable web. In *Proceedings of WWW Conference.* Geneva, Switzerland: CERN.

Donner, J. (2007). The rules of beeping: Exchanging messages via intentional missed calls on mobile phones. *Journal of Computer-Mediated Communication, 13*(1), 1–22. doi:10.1111/j.1083-6101.2007.00383.x

Dourish, P., & Bellotti, V. (1992). Awareness and coordination in shared workspaces. In *Proceedings of ACM Computer-Supported Cooperative Work (CSCW)* (pp. 107-114). Toronto, Ontario.

Dourish, P., & Belotti, V. (1992a). Awareness and coordination in shared workspaces. In *Proc of the 1992 ACM Conference on Computer Supported Cooperative Work (CSCW'92)* (pp: 107-115). New York: ACM.

Durkheim, E. (1893). *The division of labor in society.* New York: Free Press.

Durkheim, E. (1897). *Suicide: A study in sociology.* New York: Free Press.

Dutton, W. H. (2008). The Wisdom of Collaborative Network Organizations: Capturing the Value of Networked Individuals. *Prometheus, 26*(3), 211–230. doi:10.1080/08109020802270182

Dutton, W. H., & Eynon, R. (2009). Networked Individuals and Institutions: A Cross-Sector Comparative Perspective on Patterns and Strategies in Government and Research. *The Information Society, 25*(3), 198–207. doi:10.1080/01972240902848914

Edwards, K., Mynatt, E., Petersen, K., Spreitzer, M., Terry, D., & Theimer, M. (1997). Designing and Implementing asynchronous collaborative applications with Bayou. In P*roc. of 10th Annual ACM Symp. on User Interface Software and Technology* (UIST'97), Banff, Alberta, Canada (pp. 119-128).

Eisenhardt, K. (1989). Making Fast Strategic Decisions in High-Velocity Environments. *Academy of Management Journal, 32*(3), 543–576. doi:10.2307/256434

Elder, D. (1995). Collaborative filmmaking: An open space for making meaning, A moral ground for ethnographic film. *Visual Anthropology Review, 11*(2), 94–101. doi:10.1525/var.1995.11.2.94

Ellis, D. (2002). Information seeking and mediated searching, part 5: User-intermediary interaction. *Journal of the American Society for Information Science and Technology, 53*(11), 883–893. doi:10.1002/asi.10133

Ellis, D., & Haugan, M. (1997). Modeling the Information Seeking Patterns of Engineers and Research Scientists in an Industrial Environment. *The Journal of Documentation, 53*(4), 384–403. doi:10.1108/EUM0000000007204

Ellis, D., Cox, D., & Hall, K. (1993). A comparison of the information seeking patterns of researchers in the physical and social sciences. *The Journal of Documentation, 49*(4), 356–369. doi:10.1108/eb026919

Elwyn, G., Gwyn, R., Edwards, A., & Grol, R. (1999). Is shared decision-making feasible in consultations for upper respiratory tract infections? Assessing the influence of antibiotic expectations using discourse analysis. *Health Expectations, 2*(2), 105–117. doi:10.1046/j.1369-6513.1999.00045.x

Erickson, F. (1977). Some approaches to inquiry in school-community ethnography. *Anthropology & Education Quarterly, 8*(2), 58–69. doi:10.1525/aeq.1977.8.2.05x1396r

Erickson, T., & Kellogg, W. A. (2000). Social Translucence: An Approach to Designing Systems that Support Social Processes. *ACM Transactions on Computer-Human Interaction, 7,* 59–83. doi:10.1145/344949.345004

Ertzscheid, O. (2001). An attempt to identify and manage collective practices involved in information retrieval. In *Proc of 5th World Multi conference on Systemics, Cybernetics and Informatics* (SCI / ISAS 2001), Orlando, FL.

Evans, B. M., & Chi, E. H. (2008, June 20). Towards a model of understanding social search. In *Proceedings of IEEE/ACM JCDL 2008 Collaborative Exploratory Search,* Pittsburgh, PA. Retrieved from http://workshops.fxpal.com/jcdl2008/submissions/tmpDE.pdf

Evans, G. B., Steer, R. A., & Fine, E. W. (1979). Alcohol value clarification in sixth graders:" a film-making project. *Journal of Alcohol and Drug Education, 24*(2), 1–10.

Ewald, W. (1985). *Portraits and dreams: Photographs and stories by children of the Appalachians.* New York: Writers and Readers Publications.

Farmer, L. A. (2005). Situational leadership: A model for leading telecommuters. *Journal of Nursing Management, 13,* 483–189. doi:10.1111/j.1365-2934.2005.00573.x

Farooq, U., Ganoe, C. H., Carroll, J. M., & Giles, C. L. (2009). Designing for e-science: Requirements gathering for collaboration in CiteSeer. *International Journal of Human-Computer Studies, 67,* 297–312. doi:10.1016/j.ijhcs.2007.10.005

Fen, J., Lazar, J., & Preece, J. (2004). Empathy and online interpersonal trust: A fragile relationship. *Behaviour & Information Technology, 23*(2), 97–106. doi:10.1080/01449290310001659240

Fidel, R., Bruce, H., Pejtersen, A. M., Dumais, S., Grudin, J., & Poltrock, S. (2000). Collaborative Information Retrieval (CIR). *The New Review of Information Behaviour Research: Studies of Information Seeking in Context, 1*(1), 235–247.

Fidel, R., Pejtersen, A. M., Cleal, B., & Bruce, H. (2004). A Multidimensional Approach to the Study of Human-Information Interaction: A Case Study of Collaborative Information Retrieval. *Journal of the American Society for Information Science American Society for Information Science, 55*(11), 939–953.

Findley, L. G. R., & Inge, L. G. J. (2005). North American defence and security in the aftermath of 9/11. *Canadian Military Journal, 6*(1), 9–16.

Fisher, K., & Julien, H. (2009). Information behavior. *Annual Review of Information Science & Technology, 43,* 317–358.

Fitzpatrick, A. L., Tu, S. P., Steinmen, L., & Suin, M. K. (2007). *Using photovoice to understand perceptions of cardiovascular health in multi-cultural settings.* Paper presented at the American Public Health Association 135th Annual Meeting and Expo, Washington, DC.

Flaherty, R. J. (1922). *Nanook of the north.* New York: Révillon Frères.

Forsythe, D. E., Buchanan, B. G., Osheroff, J. A., & Miller, R. A. (1992). Expanding the concept of medical information: An observational study of physicians' information needs. *Computers and Biomedical Research, an*

International Journal, 25(2), 181–200. doi:10.1016/0010-4809(92)90020-B

Forte, A., & Bruckman, A. (2005). *Why do people write for Wikipedia? Incentives to contribute to open-content publishing.* Paper presented at the *GROUP* workshop "Sustaining community: The role and design of incentive mechanisms in online systems", Sanibel Island, FL. Retrieved February 9, 2009, from http://www.cc.gatech.edu/~aforte/ForteBruckmanWhyPeopleWrite.pdf

Foster, J. (2006). Collaborative information seeking and retrieval. In Cronin, B. (Ed.), *Annual Review of Information Science and Technology* (*Vol. 40*, pp. 329–356). Medford, NJ: Information Today.

Foster, J. (2009). Understanding interaction in information seeking and use as a discourse: A dialogic approach. *The Journal of Documentation, 65*(1), 83–105. doi:10.1108/00220410910926130

Foster, J., Wu, M.-M., & Linm, A. (2009, November). Collaborative information seeking and sharing in educational settings: identifying the challenges. In N. Caidi, S. Y. Rieh, & G. Oyarce (Chairs), *Collaborative Information seeking and Sharing*. Symposium conducted at the SIGUSE meeting of the American Society for Information Science and Technology, Vancouver, Canada.

Foucault, M. (1972). *The archaeology of knowledge.* New York: Pantheon.

Foucault, M. (1995). *Discipline & punish, the birth of the prison* (2nd ed.). New York: Vintage Books.

Frith, H., & Harcourt, D. (2007). Using photographs to capture women's experiences of chemotherapy: reflecting on the method. *Qualitative Health Research, 17*(10), 1340–1350. doi:10.1177/1049732307308949

Frohmann, B. (2004). *Deflating information: from science studies to documentation.* Toronto, ON: University of Toronto Press.

Frohmann, B. (2008, September). *Biopolitics and the body's documentality.* Brown Bag lecture presented at the Faculty of Information and Media Studies, The University of Western Ontario.

Fu, X., Kelly, D., & Shah, C. (2007, July 23-27,). Using collaborative queries to improve retrieval for difficult topics. In *Proceedings of ACM SIGIR,* Amsterdam, The Netherlands (pp. 879-880).

Furman, L. (1990). Video therapy: An alternative for the treatment of adolescents. Special Issue: The creative arts therapies with adolescents. *The Arts in Psychotherapy, 17,* 165–169. doi:10.1016/0197-4556(90)90027-N

Galbraith, J. (1982). Designing the Innovating Organization. *Organizational Dynamics, 10*(3), 4–25. doi:10.1016/0090-2616(82)90033-X

Gamson (1994). *Claims to fame: Celebrity in Contemporary America.* Berkeley, CA: University of California Press.

Gandy, O. H. (1982). *Beyond agenda setting: Information subsidies and public policy.* Norwood, NJ: Ablex Publishing Company.

Gans, H. J. (1979). *Deciding what's news.* Evanston, IL: Northwestern University Press.

Garbacz, C., & Thompson, H. G. (2007). Demand for telecommunication services in developing countries. *Telecommunications Policy, 31*(5), 276–289. doi:10.1016/j.telpol.2007.03.007

Garcia, A., Dawes, M. E., Kohne, M. L., Miller, F. M., & Groschwitz, S. F. (2006). Workplace studies and technological change. *Annual Review of Information Science & Technology, 40,* 393–437. doi:10.1002/aris.1440400117

Garfinkel, H. (1967). *Studies in ethnomethodology.* Englewood Cliffs, NJ: Prentice-Hall.

Gartner Inc. (2007, January 30). *Business intelligence market will grow 10 percent in EMEA in 2007 according to Gartner* [Press release]. Retrieved February 9, 2009, from http://www.gartner.com/it/page.jsp?id=500680

Gazanio, C., & Couson, D. C. (1988). Effect of newsroom management styles on journalists: A case study. *The Journalism Quarterly, 65,* 869–880.

Gerosa, L., Giordani, A., Ronchetti, M., Soller, A., & Stevens, R. (2004, October 6-9). Symmetric synchronous collaborative navigation. In *Proceedings of the 2004 IADIS International WWW/Internet Conference,* Madrid, Spain (pp. 1-7).

Gibson, B. E. (2005). Co-producing video diaries: The presence of the 'absent' researcher. *International Journal of Qualitative Methods, 4*(3), 1–9.

Gibson, C., & Cohen, S. (Eds.). (2003). *Knowledge Sharing and Shared Understanding in Virtual Teams.* San Francisco, CA: Jossey-Bass.

Gibson, J., Blackwell, C., Dominicus, P., & Demerath, N. (2002). Telecommuting in the 21st century: Benefits, issues and a leadership model that will work. *The Journal of Leadership Studies, 8*(4), 75–86. doi:10.1177/107179190200800407

Giles, D. (2002). Parasocial interaction: A review of the literature and a model for future research. *Media Psychology, 4,* 279-305. Instant messaging. (2005). *The Computer Bulletin, 47*(3), 26.

Gill, V. T., & Maynard, D. W. (2006). Explaining illness: patients' proposals and physicians' responses. In Heritage, J., & Maynard, D. W. (Eds.), *Communication in medical care: Interaction between primary care physicians and patients* (pp. 115–150). Cambridge, UK: Cambridge University Press. doi:10.1017/CBO9780511607172.007

Ginsburg, F. (1991). Indigenous media: Faustian contract of global village? *Cultural Anthropology, 6*(1), 92–112. doi:10.1525/can.1991.6.1.02a00040

Glaser, B. G. (1992). *Basics of grounded theory analysis.* Mill Valley, CA: Sociology Press.

Glaser, B. G., & Strauss, A. L. (1967). *The Discovery of grounded theory: Strategies for qualitative research.* Hawthorne, NY: Aldine de Gruyter.

Gloor, P. (2005). *Swarm Creativity, COIN.* Boston, MA: MIT Press.

Göldi, A. (2007). *The Emerging Market for Web-based Enterprise Software.* Unpublished master's thesis, Massachusetts Institute of Technology, Boston, MA.

Golovchinsky, G., Pickens, J., & Back, M. (2008). A taxonomy of collaboration in online information seeking. In *11th International Workshop on Collaborative Information Retrieval, JCDL 2008,* June 20, 2008.

Golovchinsky, G., Pickens, J., & Back, M. (2008, June 20). A taxonomy of collaboration in online information seeking. In *Proceedings of IEEE/ACM JCDL 2008 Collaborative Exploratory Search,* Pittsburgh, PA.

Golovchinsky, G., Qvarfordt, P., & Pickens, J. (2009, March). Collaborative information seeking. *Computer,* 47–51. doi:10.1109/MC.2009.73

Goodman, J. (2007). Linking mobile phone ownership and use to social capital in rural South Africa and Tanzania. *Moving the Debate Forward: The Vodafone Policy Paper Series #3 2005.* Retrieved February 1, 2009, from http://www.vodafone.com/etc/medialib/attachments/cr downloads.Par.78351.File.tmp/GPP. SIM paper 3.pdf

Gorman, P. N., Ash, J., Lavelle, M., Lyman, J., Delcambre, L., & Maier, D. (2000). Bundles in the Wild: Managing Information to Solve Problems and Maintain Situation Awareness. *Library Trends, 49*(2), 266–289.

Gray, B. (1989). *Collaborating: Finding common ground for multiparty problems.* San Francisco: Jossey-Bass.

Green, T. J., Karvounarakis, G., Taylor, N. E., Biton, O., Ives, Z. G., & Tannen, V. (2007). ORCHESTRA: Facilitating collaborative data sharing. In *Proceedings of the ACM International Conference on Management of Data (SIGMOD'07),* Beijing, China (pp. 1131-1133).

Grippa, F., Zilli, A., Laubacher, R., & Gloor, P. (2006). E-mail may not reflect the social network. In *Proceedings of the 2006 International Sunbelt Social Network Conference,* Vancouver, BC, Canada.

Grudin, J. (1988). Problems in the Design and Evaluation of Organisational Interfaces. In *CSCW '88* (pp. 85–93). Portland, Oregon: Why CSCW Applications Fail.

Grudin, J. (1994, January). Groupware and social dynamics: eight challenges for developers. *Communications of the ACM, 37*(1), 92–105. doi:10.1145/175222.175230

Grudin, J. (1995). Groupware and Social Dynamics, 762-774. In R. M. Baecker, J. Grudin, W. A. S. Buxton & S. Greenberg (Eds.), Readings in Human-Computer Interaction: Toward the Year 2000. San Francisco, CA: Morgan Kaufmann.

GSM Association. (2006, June). *Universal access: How mobile can bring communications to all* [Policy Paper 2006023].

Gwyn, R., & Elwyn, G. (1999). When is a shared decision not (quite) a shared decision? Negotiating preferences in a general practice encounter. *Social Science & Medicine, 49*(4), 437–447. doi:10.1016/S0277-9536(99)00067-2

Hagedorn, M. (1994). Hermeneutic photography: an innovative esthetic technique for generating data in nursing research. *ANS. Advances in Nursing Science, 17*(1), 44–50.

Hagedorn, M. I. (1996). Photography: an aesthetic technique for nursing inquiry. *Issues in Mental Health Nursing, 17*(6), 517–527. doi:10.3109/01612849609006530

Hall, H. (2001). Input-friendliness: motivating knowledge across intranets. *Journal of Information Science, 27*(3), 139–146. doi:10.1177/016555150102700303

Hall, H., & Graham, D. (2004). Creation and recreation: motivating collaboration to generate knowledge capital in online communities. *International Journal of Information Management, 24*, 235–246. doi:10.1016/j.ijinfomgt.2004.02.004

Han, R., Perret, V., & Naghshineh, M. (2000). WebSplitter: A Unified XML Framework for Multi-Device Collaborative Web Browsing. In *Proceedings of ACM Computer-Supported Cooperative Work (CSCW)*, Philadelphia, Pennsylvania, USA (pp. 221-230).

Hansen, P., & Jarvelin, K. (2005). Collaborative Information Retrieval in an information-intensive domain. *Information Processing & Management, 41*, 1101–1119. doi:10.1016/j.ipm.2004.04.016

Hardy, A. (1980). The role of the telephone in economic development. *Telecommunications Policy, 4*(4), 278–286. doi:10.1016/0308-5961(80)90044-0

Harré, R., & van Langenhove, L. (1999). *Positioning theory*. Oxford: Blackwell.

Harris, K. (1999). The online life of communities: nurturing community activity in the information society. In Pantry, S. (Ed.), *Building community information networks: strategies and experiences* (pp. 61–83). London: London Association Publishing.

Harrison, H. (2002). Seeing health and illness worlds: Using visual methodologies in a sociology of health and illness: a methodological review. *Sociology of Health & Illness, 24*(6), 856–872. doi:10.1111/1467-9566.00322

Hartley, J., & Branthwaite, A. (1989). The psychologist as wordsmith: A questionnaire study of the writing strategies of productive British psychologists. *Higher Education, 18*(4), 423–452. doi:10.1007/BF00140748

Havenstein, H. (2003). BI vendors seek to tap end-user power. *InfoWorld, 25*(22).

Hawkins, M., & Knox, S. (2003). *The midwifery option: A Canadian guide to the birth experience*. Toronto, ON: HarperCollins.

Henri, F., & Pudelko, B. (2003). Understanding and analysing activity and learning in virtual communities. *Journal of Computer Assisted Learning*, (19): 474–487. doi:10.1046/j.0266-4909.2003.00051.x

Heritage, J. (2004). Conversation analysis and institutional talk: analysing data. In Silverman, D. (Ed.), *Qualitative research: Theory, method and practice* (2nd ed., pp. 222–245). Thousand Oaks, CA: Sage.

Heritage, J., & Maynard, D. W. (2006). Problems and prospects in the study of physician patient interaction: 30 years of research. *Annual Review of Sociology, 32*, 351–374. doi:10.1146/annurev.soc.32.082905.093959

Heritage, J., & Maynard, D. W. (Eds.). (2006). *Communication in medical care: Interaction between primary care physicians and patients*. Cambridge, UK: Cambridge University Press. doi:10.1017/CBO9780511607172

Heritage, J., & Robinson, J. D. (2006). The structure of patients' presenting concerns: physicians' opening questions. *Health Communication, 19*(2), 89–102. doi:10.1207/s15327027hc1902_1

Hertzum, M. (2008). Collaborative information seeking: the combined activity of information seeking and collaborative grounding. *Information Processing & Management, 44*(2), 957–962. doi:10.1016/j.ipm.2007.03.007

Hiltz, R., & Turoff, M. (1978). *The Network Nation*. Reading, MA: Addison-Wesley.

Hirsh, S., & Dinkelacker, J. (2004). Seeking information in order to produce information: An empirical study at Hewlett Packard Labs. *Journal of the American Society for Information Science and Technology, 55*(9), 807–817. doi:10.1002/asi.20024

Holliday, R. (2004a). Filming "The Closet": The role of video diaries in researching sexualities. *The American Behavioral Scientist, 47*(12), 1597–1616. doi:10.1177/0002764204266239

Holliday, R. (2004b). Reflecting the self. In Knowles, C., & Sweetman, P. (Eds.), *Picturing the social landscape: Visual methods and the sociological imagination* (pp. 49–65). London: Routledge.

Holstein, J. A., & Gubrium, J. F. (2005). Interpretive practice and social action. In Denzin, N., & Lincoln, Y. S. (Eds.), *The Sage handbook of qualitative research* (3rd ed., pp. 483–505). Thousand Oaks, CA: Sage.

Horst, H., & Miller, D. (2006). *The cell phone: An anthropology of communication*. Oxford: Berg.

Huysman, M., & de Wit, D. (2004). A critical evaluation of knowledge management practices. In Ackerman, M., Pipek, V., & Wulf, V. (Eds.), *Sharing Expertise: Beyond Knowledge Management* (pp. 27–55). Cambridge: MIT Press.

Huysman, M., & Wulf, V. (2006). IT to Support Knowledge Sharing in Communities, Towards a Social Capital Analysis. *Journal of Information Technology,* (21): 40–51. doi:10.1057/palgrave.jit.2000053

Hyldegard, J. (2006). Collaborative information behavior - exploring Kuhlthau's Information Search Process model in a group-based educational setting. *Information Processing & Management, 42*(1), 276–298. doi:10.1016/j.ipm.2004.06.013

Hyldegard, J. (2009). Beyond the search process – Exploring group members' information behavior in context. *Information Processing & Management, 45*(1), 142–158. doi:10.1016/j.ipm.2008.05.007

IBM, Inc. (2007). *Many Eyes*. Retrieved February 9, 2009, from http://manyeyes.alphaworks.ibm.com/manyeyes/

Ikeya, N., & Okada, M. (2007) Doctors' Practical Management of Knowledge in the Daily Case Conference. In S. Hester & D. Francis (Eds.), *Orders of Ordinary Action: Respecifying Sociological Knowledge* (pp. 69-89). Aldershot, UK: Ashgate.

Ikeya, N., & Vinkhuyzen, E. (in press). Designing beyond the meeting: accommodating collaborative problem solving and risk management. In Szymanski, P. (Ed.), *Making Work Visible: Ethnographically grounded case studies of work practice*. Cambridge, UK: Cambridge University Press.

International, Q. S. R. (n.d.). *N6 Software*. Retrieved July 19, 2008, from http://www.qsrinternational.com/products_previous-products_n6.aspx

Ioannidis, J. P. (2005). Why most published research findings are false. *PLoS Medicine, 2*(8), e124. doi:10.1371/journal.pmed.0020124

Islam, M. S., & Grönlund, A. (2007). Agriculture market information e-service in Bangladesh: A stakeholder-oriented case analysis. In M. Wimmer (Ed.), Electronic government, proceedings of the 6th international EGOV conference, Regensburg, Germany, September 3–7.

Ito, M. (2004). *Personal portable pedestrian: Lessons from Japanese mobile phone use*. Paper presented at Mobile Communication and Social Change, the 2004 International Conference on Mobile Communication in Seoul, Korea.

Ito, M. (2005). Mobile phones, Japanese youth, and the re-placement of social contact. In Ling, R., & Pedersen, P. E. (Eds.), *Mobile communications: Re-negotiation of the social sphere* (pp. 131–148). London: Springer.

Ito, M., Horst, H., Bittanti, M., Boyd, D., Herr-Stephenson, B., & Lange, P. G. (2008). *Living and learning with new media: Summary of findings from the digital youth project.* The John D. & Catherine T. MacArthur Foundation Reports on Digital Media and Learning.

Ito, M., Okabe, D., & Anderson, K. (2007). Portable objects in three global cities: The personalization of urban places. Forthcoming in L. Rich & C. Scott (Eds.), The mobile communication research annual volume 1: The reconstruction of space & time through mobile communication practices. NJ: Transaction Publishers.

Järvelin, K., & Ingwersen, P. (2004). Information seeking research needs extension towards tasks and technology. Information Research, 10(1), paper 212 [Available at http://InformationR.net/ir/10-1/paper212.html].

Javid, P. S., & Parikh, T. S. (2006, May). *Augmenting rural supply chains with a location-enhanced mobile information system.* Paper presented at International Conference on Information and Communication Technologies and Development, Berkeley, CA.

Johansen, R. (1988). *Groupware: Computer Support for Business Teams.* New York: The Free Press.

Johnson, P., Heimann, V., & O'Neill, K. (2001). The wonderland of virtual teams. *Journal of Workplace Learning, 13*(1), 24–30. doi:10.1108/13665620110364745

Jones, C. (2007). Intelligence reform: The logic of information sharing. *Intelligence and National Security, 22*(3), 384–401. doi:10.1080/02684520701415214

Joyce, E., & Kraut, R. E. (2006). Predicting Continued Participation in Newsgroups. *Journal of Computer-Mediated Communication, 11*(3), 723–747. doi:10.1111/j.1083-6101.2006.00033.x

Kameda, T., Ohtsubo, Y., & Takezawa, M. (1997). Centrality in socio-cognitive networks and social influence: An illustration in a group decision-making context. *Journal of Personality and Social Psychology, 73,* 296–309. doi:10.1037/0022-3514.73.2.296

Karamuftuoglu, M. (1998). Collaborative Information Retrieval: Towards a Social Informatics View of IR interaction. *Journal of the American Society for Information Science American Society for Information Science, 49*(12), 1070–1080. doi:10.1002/(SICI)1097-4571(1998)49:12<1070::AID-ASI3>3.0.CO;2-S

Katz, J. (1998). Luring the lurkers. *Retrieved March 10, 2009 from* http://slashdot.org/features/98/12/28/1745252.shtml.

Kavoori, A., & Chadha, K. (2006). The cell phone as a cultural technology: Lessons from the Indian case. In Kavoori, A., & Arceneaux, N. (Eds.), *The cell phone reader: Essays in social transformation* (pp. 227–240). New York: Peter Lang.

Keator, D. B., Grethe, J. S., Marcus, D., Ozyurt, B., Gadde, S., & Murphy, S. (2008). A national human neuroimaging collaboratory enabled by the Biomedical Informatics Research Network (BIRN). *IEEE Transactions on Information Technology in Biomedicine, 12*(2), 162–172. doi:10.1109/TITB.2008.917893

Kennedy, T. (1971). The Skyriver Project: The story of a process. *National Film Board of Canada Challenge for Change Program, 12,* 3–21.

Kennedy, T. (1982). Beyond advocacy: A facilitative approach to public participation. *Journal of the University Film and Video Association, 34*(3), 33–46.

Kets de Vries, M. (2001). *The leadership mystique: A user's manual for the human enterprise.* New York: Prentice Hall.

Kim, H., Kim, G. J., Park, H. W., & Rice, R. E. (2007). Configurations of relationships in different media: Ftf, email, instant messenger, mobile Phone, and SMS. *Journal of Computer-Mediated Communication, 12*(4), 2–24. doi:10.1111/j.1083-6101.2007.00369.x

Kittur, A., & Kraut, R. (2008). *Harnessing the Wisdom of Crowds in Wikipedia: Quality Through Coordination.* Paper presented at the CSCW 2008, San Diego, CA.

Kittur, A., Suh, B., Pendleton, B. A., & Chi, E. H. (2007). *He Says, She Says: Conflict and Coordination in Wikipedia.* Paper presented at the CHI 2007, San Jose, CA.

Kleinman, A. (1988). *The Illness narratives: Suffering, healing and the human condition.* New York: Basic Books.

Kling, R. (1980). Social Analyses of Computing: Theoretical Perspectives in Recent Empirical Research. *Computing Surveys, 12*(1), 61–110. doi:10.1145/356802.356806

Kling, R. (1991). Cooperation, Coordination and Control in Computer-Supported Work. *Communications of the ACM, 34*(12), 83–88. doi:10.1145/125319.125396

Knobloch, L. K., & Solomon, D. H. (2002). Information seeking beyond initial interaction: Negotiating relational uncertainty within close relationships. *Human Communication Research, 28*, 243–257. doi:10.1093/hcr/28.2.243

Kolko, B. E., Rose, E. J., & Johnson, E. J. (2007, May). *Communication as information-seeking: The case for mobile social software for developing regions.* Paper presented at 16th international conference on the World Wide Web (WWW), Banff, Alberta, Canada.

Kollock, P., & Smith, M. (1996). Managing the virtual commons: Cooperation and conflict in computer communities. In Herring, S. (Ed.), *Computer-mediated communication: Linguistic, social, and cross-cultural perspectives.* Amsterdam: John Benjamins.

Kouzes, R. T., Myers, J. D., & Wulf, W. A. (1996). Collaboratories: Doing science on the Internet. *Computer, 29*(8), 40–46. doi:10.1109/2.532044

Kuhlthau, C. C. (1989). The information search process of high-middle-low achieving high school seniors. *School Library Media Quarterly, 17*, 224–228.

Kuhlthau, C. C. (1991). Inside the search process: Information seeking from the user's perspective. *Journal of the American Society for Information Science American Society for Information Science, 42*(5), 361–371. doi:10.1002/(SICI)1097-4571(199106)42:5<361::AID-ASI6>3.0.CO;2-#

Kuhlthau, C. C. (2004). *Seeking meaning: A process approach to library and information services.* Westport, CT: Libraries Unlimited.

Labov, W., & Fanshel, D. (1997). *Therapeutic discourse: Psychotherapy as conversation.* New York: Academic Press.

Laine, C., Goodman, S. N., Griswold, M. E., & Sox, H. C. (2007). Reproducible research: Moving toward research the public can really trust. *Annals of Internal Medicine, 146*(6), 450–453.

Lambropoulos, N. (2005, July). *Paradise Lost? Primary Empathy in Online Communities of Interest and Ways of Use.* Paper presented at the 11th International Conference on Human-Computer Interaction, Las Vegas, NV.

Larson, J. R., Foster-Fishman, P. G., & Keys, C. B. (1994). Discussion of shared and unshared information in decision-making groups. *Journal of Personality and Social Psychology, 67*, 446–461. doi:10.1037/0022-3514.67.3.446

Latham, A. (2004). Researching and writing everyday accounts of the city: An introduction to the diary-photo diary interview process. In Knowles, C., & Sweetman, P. (Eds.), *Picturing the social landscape: Visual methods and the sociological imagination* (pp. 117–131). London: Routledge.

Leckie, G. J., Pettigrew, K. E., & Sylvain, C. (1996). Modeling the Information Seeking of Professionals: A General Model Derived from Research on Engineers, Health Care Professionals, and Lawyers. *The Library Quarterly, 66*(2), 161–193. doi:10.1086/602864

Lee, R. G., & Garvin, T. (2003). Moving from information transfer to information exchange in health and health care. *Social Science & Medicine, 56*(3), 449–464. doi:10.1016/S0277-9536(02)00045-X

Lerner, J., & Tirole, J. (2002). Some Simple Economics of Open Source. *The Journal of Industrial Economics, 50*(2), 197–234.

Lerner, J., & Tirole, J. (2005). The Economics of Technology Sharing: Open Source and Beyond. *The Journal of Economic Perspectives, 19*(2), 99–120. doi:10.1257/0895330054048678

Lie, M., & Sørensen, K. H. (1996). Making technology our own? Domesticating technology into everyday life. In Lie, M., & Sørensen, K. H. (Eds.), *Making Technology our Own? Domesticating Technology into Everyday Life* (pp. 1–30). Oslo: Scandinavian University Press.

Liechti, O., & Sumi, Y. (2002). Awareness and the WWW. *International Journal of Human-Computer Studies, 56*(1), 1–5. doi:10.1006/ijhc.2001.0512

Lindsay, B. (2008). Breaking university rules. *Australian Universities Review, 50*(1), 37–39.

Livny, M., Ramakrishnan, R., Beyer, K., Chen, G., Donjerkovic, D., Lawande, S., et al. (1997). DEVise: Integrated querying and visual exploration of large datasets. In *Proceedings of the ACM International Conference on Management of Data (SIGMOD'97)* (301-312).

Ljungberg, J. (2000). Open Source movements as a model for organizing. *European Journal of Information Systems, 9*(4), 208–216. doi:10.1057/palgrave/ejis/3000373

London, S. (1995, November). *Collaboration and community*. Retrieved April 9, 2008, from http://scottlondon.com/reports/ppcc.html

Lopez, E. D. S., Eng, E., Randall-David, E., & Robinson, N. (2005). Quality-of-Life concerns of African American breast cancer survivors within rural North Carolina: Blending the techniques of photovoice and grounded theory. *Qualitative Health Research, 15*(1), 99–115. doi:10.1177/1049732304270766

Lorenz, L. S. (2006). *Living without connections: Using narrative analysis of photographs and interview text to understand living with traumatic brain injury and facilitators and barriers to recovery from the patient's perspective*. Paper presented at the European Sociological Association, Mid-Term Conference, Cardiff, Wales.

Lorenz, L. S., Webster, B., & Foley, L. (2007). *Making visible the invisible: Using photovoice to understand living with brain injury*. Paper presented at the 26th Annual Conference, Brain Injury Association of Massachusetts, Marlborough, MA.

Lotka, A. J. (1926). The frequency distribution of scientific productivity. *Journal of the Washington Academy of Sciences, 16*(12), 317–324.

Lucas, U. (2000). Worlds apart: students' experiences of learning introductory accounting. *Critical Perspectives on Accounting, 11*(4), 479–504. doi:10.1006/cpac.1999.0390

Lund University Libraries. (2003). *Directory of open access journals*. Retrieved February 9, 2009, from http://www.doaj.org/

Ma, K.-L. (2007). Creating a collaborative space to share data, visualization and knowledge. *ACM SIGGRAPH Computer Graphics Quarterly, 41*(4).

MacDonald, M. (2006). Gender expectations: natural bodies and natural births in the new midwifery in Canada. *Medical Anthropology Quarterly, 20*(2), 235–256. doi:10.1525/maq.2006.20.2.235

MacDougall, D. (1991). Whose story is it? *Visual Anthropology Review, 7*(2), 2–10. doi:10.1525/var.1991.7.2.2

Maekawa, T., Hara, T., & Nishio, S. (2006). A collaborative web browsing system for multiple mobile users. In *Proceedings of IEEE Conference on Pervasive Computing and Communications (PERCOM)*, Pisa, Italy.

Malone, T. W. (1988, February). *What is coordination theory?* (Tech. Rep. No. SSM WP # 2051-88). Boston, MA: Massachusetts Institute of Technology.

Malone, T. W., Grant, K. R., Turbak, F. A., Brobst, S. S., & Cohen, M. D. (1987). Intelligent information sharing systems. *Communications of the ACM, 30*(5), 390–402. doi:10.1145/22899.22903

Mann, S. J. (2001). Alternative perspectives on the student experience: alienation and engagement. *Studies in Higher Education, 26*(1), 7–19. doi:10.1080/03075070020030689

March, J. (1991). Exploration and Exploitation in Organizational Learning. *Organization Science, 2*(1), 71–87. doi:10.1287/orsc.2.1.71

Mark, G., Abrams, S., & Nassif, N. (2003). Group-to-Group Distance Collaboration: Examining the Space Between. In *Proc. of the 8th European Conference of Computer-Supported Cooperative Work (ECSCW'03)*, Helsinki, Finland (pp. 99-118).

Marker, P., McNamara, K., & Wallace, L. (2002). *The significance of information and communication technologies for reducing poverty. Development Policy Department, DFID Final Report*. London: DFID.

Markoff, J. (2009, February 17). The cellphone, navigating our lives. *The New York Times*, p. D1.

Marshall, C. C., Shipman, F. M. III, & McCall, R. J. (1995). Making large-scale information resources serve communities of practice. *Journal of Management Information Systems: JMIS, 11*(4), 65–86.

Marshall, P. D. (1997). *Celebrity and power: Fame in contemporary culture*. Minneapolis: University of Minnesota Press.

Marsick, V. J., & Watkins, K. E. (1990). *Informal and incidental learning in the workplace*. London: Routledge.

Martinez, K. Z. (2004). Latina magazine and the invocation of a panethnic family: Latino identity as it is informed by celebrities and Papis Chulos. *Communication Review, 7*(2), 155–174. doi:10.1080/10714420490448697

Maynard, D. W. (2003). *Bad news, good news: conversational order in everyday talk and clinical settings*. Chicago, IL: University of Chicago Press.

Mayring, P. (2004). Qualitative content analysis. In Flick, U., von Kardoff, E., & Steinke, L. (Eds.), *A companion to qualitative research* (pp. 266–269). London: Sage.

McDonald, D. W., & Ackerman, M. S. (1998). Just Talk to Me: A Field Study of Expertise Location. In *Proc. of the ACM Conference on Computer-Supported Cooperative Work* (CSCW'98), Seattle, WA (pp. 315-324).

McFadden, M., & Munns, G. (2002). Student engagement and the social relations of pedagogy. *British Journal of Sociology of Education, 23*(3), 357–366. doi:10.1080/0142569022000015409

McKenzie, P. J. (2003). Justifying cognitive authority decisions: discursive strategies of information seekers. *The Library Quarterly, 73*(3), 261–288. doi:10.1086/603418

McKenzie, P. J. (2004). Positioning theory and the negotiation of information needs in a clinical midwifery setting. *Journal of the American Society for Information Science and Technology, 55*(8), 685–694. doi:10.1002/asi.20002

McKenzie, P. J. (2006). Mapping textually-mediated information practice in clinical midwifery care. A. Spink, & C. Cole (Editors), New directions in human information behaviour (pp. 73-92). Dordrecht: Springer.

McKenzie, P. J. (2009). Informing choice: the organization of institutional interaction in clinical midwifery care. *Library & Information Science Research, 31*(3), 163–173. doi:10.1016/j.lisr.2009.03.006

McKenzie, P. J., & Oliphant, T. (2010). Informing evidence: claimsmaking in midwives' and clients' talk about interventions. *Qualitative Health Research, 20*(1), 29–41. doi:10.1177/1049732309355591

McKnight, M. (2007). A grounded theory model of on-duty critical care nurses' information behavior: the patient-chart cycle of informative interactions. *The Journal of Documentation, 63*(1), 57–73. doi:10.1108/00220410710723885

McLaughlin, M. L., Osborne, K. K., & Smith, C. B. (1995). Standards of conduct on Usenet. In Jones, S. G. (Ed.), *CyberSociety: Computer-mediated communication and society* (pp. 90–111). Thousand Oaks, CA: Sage Publications.

Mengis, J., & Eppler, M. (2005). *Understanding and enabling knowledge sharing in conversations: a literature review and management framework*. 2nd Annual Conference on Knowledge Management in the Asian Pacific (KMAP), Wellington (New Zealand).

Mercer, N., & Wegerif, R. (1997). A dialogical framework for researching peer talk. In Wegerif, R., & Scrimshaw, P. (Eds.), *Computers and talk in the primary classroom* (pp. 49–61). Bristol, UK: Multilingual Matters.

Michaels, E. (1985). How video has helped a group of aborigines in Australia. *Media Development, 1*, 16–18.

Mitchell, A. (1996). *Communication and Shared Understanding in Collaborative Writing*. Unpublished Master's Thesis, Computer Science Department, University of Toronto.

Moran, T. P., & Carroll, J. M. (Eds.). (1996). *Design Rationale: Concepts, Techniques, and Use*. Mahwah, NJ: Lawrence Erlbaum Associates, Inc.

Morris, M. R. (2008, April 5-10,). A survey of collaborative web search practices. In *Proceedings of ACM SIGCHI Conference on Human Factors in Computing Systems,* Florence, Italy (pp. 1657-1660).

Morris, M. R., & Horvitz, E. (2007). SearchTogether: An Interface for Collaborative Web Search. In *Proc. of ACM Conf on User Interface Software and Technology* (UIST'07) Newport, RI (pp. 3-12).

Morris, M. R., Paepcke, A., & Winograd, T. (2006). TeamSearch: Comparing Techniques for Co-Present Collaborative Search of Digital Media. In *First IEEE International Workshop on Horizontal Interactive Human-Computer Systems (TABLETOP '06)*, Adelaide, South Australia (pp. 97-104).

Narayan, D., Chambers, R., Shah, M. K., & Petesch, P. (2000). *Voices of the poor: Crying out for change.* New York: Oxford University Press. doi:10.1596/0-1952-1602-4

Nardi, B. A. (2005). Beyond bandwidth: Dimensions of connection in interpersonal communication. *Computer Supported Cooperative Work, 14*, 91-130. Poynteronline. (2003, 10 April). *The face and mind of the American journalist.* Retrieved November 14, 2007, from: http://www.poynter.org/content/content_view.asp?id=28235

Nardi, B., Whittaker, S., & Schwarz, H. (2002). NetWORKers and their Activity in Intentional Networks. *Computer Supported Cooperative Work, 11*, 205–242. doi:10.1023/A:1015241914483

Nash, J., Adler, A., & Smith, N. (2004). TellTable spreadsheet audit: From technical possibility to operating prototype. In *Proceedings 2004 Conference European Spreadsheet Interest Group* (pp. 45-56).

Niu, J. (2006). *Incentive study for research data sharing.* Retrieved February 9, 2009, from http://icd.si.umich.edu/twiki/pub/ICD/LabGroup/fieldpaper_6_25.pdf

Noël, S., & Robert, J.-M. (2004). Empirical study on collaborative writing: What do co-authors do, use and like? *Computer Supported Cooperative Work, 13*(1), 63–89. doi:10.1023/B:COSU.0000014876.96003.be

Nokia's Expanding Horizon Magazine (2008, January). *Affordability key in bringing digital inclusion.* 12.

Nokia's Expanding Horizon Magazine (2009, January). *A roadmap to affordable mobility in emerging markets.* 13.

Nonnecke, B., & Preece, J. (2000). *Lurker demographics: Counting the silent.* Paper presented at the Conference on Human Factors in Computing Systems, The Hague.

Nonnecke, B., & Preece, J. (2001). *Why lurkers lurk.* Paper presented at the Americas Conference on Information Systems, Boston.

Nonnecke, B., Andrews, D., & Preece, J. (2006). Non-public and public online community participation: Needs, attitudes and behavior. *Electronic Commerce Research, 6*(1), 7–20. doi:10.1007/s10660-006-5985-x

O'Neill, P. D. (2003). The 'poor man's mobile telephone': Access versus possession to control the information gap in India. *Contemporary South Asia, 12*(1), 85–102. doi:10.1080/0958493032000123380

Ochoa, X., & Duval, E. (2008). *Quantitative analysis of user-generated content on the Web.* Web Science Workshop WebEvolve.

Okada, K. I., Maeda, F., Ichikawaa, Y., & Matsushita, Y. (1994). Multiparty videoconferencing at virtual social distance: MAJIC design. In *Proceedings 1994 ACM conference on Computer supported cooperative work* (pp. 385-393).

Olson, G. M., Olson, J. S., Carter, M. R., & Storrosten, M. (1992, February). Small group design meetings: An analysis of collaboration. *Human-Computer Interaction, 7*(4), 347–374. doi:10.1207/s15327051hci0704_1

Olson, G., & Olson, J. (2000). Distance Matters. *Human-Computer Interaction, 15*, 139–179. doi:10.1207/S15327051HCI1523_4

Olson, J. S., Olson, G. M., Storrøsten, M., & Carter, M. (1993, October). Groupwork close up: a comparison of the group design process with and without a simple group editor. *ACM Transactions on Information Systems, 11*(4), 321–348. doi:10.1145/159764.159763

Ontario Medical Association Subcommittee on the Antenatal Record. (2000, March). A guide to the Revised Antenatal Record of Ontario. *Ontario Medical Review,* 1–6.

Ontario Ministry of Health and Long-term Care. (2003). *Public information, midwifery in Ontario. What is a midwife?* Retrieved May 10, 2010, from http://www.health.gov.on.ca/english/public/program/midwife/midwife_mn.html

Ontario. Ministry of Health and Long-term Care. (2005). *Antenatal record 2.*

Orlikowski, W. J. (1992). Learning from Notes: Organizational Issues in Groupware Implementation. In *CSCW 92* (pp. 362–369). Toronto: ACM Press.

Orr, J. E. (1996). *Talking about machines: An ethnography of a modern job.* Ithaca, NY: ILR Press/ Cornell University Press.

Ovum. (2006). *The economic benefit of mobile services in India.* January. GSM Association Asia Pacific, Oxford: Oxford University Press.

Paepcke, A. (1996). Information Needs in Technical Work Settings and Their Implications for the Design of Computer Tools. *Computer Supported Cooperative Work: The Journal of Collaborative Computing, 5,* 63–92. doi:10.1007/BF00141936

Papert, S. (1970). *Teaching children thinking* (AI Memo No.247 and Logo Memo No. 2). Cambridge, MA: MIT Artificial Intelligence Laboratory.

Papert, S. (1980). *Mindstorms: Children, computers and powerful ideas.* New York: Basic books.

Patashnick, J. L., & Rich, M. (2005). Researching human experience: Video Intervention/Prevention Assessment (VIA). *Australasian Journal of Information Systems, 12*(2), 103–111.

Pavitt, C. (1993). Does communication matter in social influence during small group discussion? Five positions. *Communication Studies, 44,* 216–227.

Pedersen, E. R., McCall, K., Moran, T. P., & Halasz, F. G. (1993). Tivoli: An electronic whiteboard for informal workgroup meetings. In *Proceedings SIGCHI conference on Human factors in computing systems* (pp. 391-398).

Pettigrew, K. a. (2001). Conceptual frameworks in information behavior. *Annual Review of Information Science & Technology, 35,* 43–78.

Pheiffer, G., Holley, D., & Andrew, D. (2006). Developing thoughtful students: using learning styles in an HE context. *Education + Training, 47*(6), 422–431. doi:10.1108/00400910510617042

Pickens, J., & Golovchinsky, G. (2007, October 23). Collaborative Exploratory Search. In *Proceedings of Workshop on Human-Computer Interaction and Information Retrieval* (pp. 21-22). Cambridge, MA: MIT CSAIL.

Pink, S. (Ed.). (2008). *Visual interventions: Applied visual anthropology.* New York: Berghahn Books.

Piwowar, H. A., Day, R. S., & Fridsma, D. B. (2007). Sharing Detailed Research Data Is Associated with Increased Citation Rate. *PLoS ONE, 2*(3). doi:10.1371/journal.pone.0000308

Plant, R. (2004). Online communities. *Technology in Society, 26*(1), 51–65. doi:10.1016/j.techsoc.2003.10.005

Poltrock, S., Grudin, J., Dumais, S., Fidel, R., Bruce, H., & Pejtersen, A. (2003). Information seeking and sharing in design teams. In *Proceedings of the 2003 international ACM SIGGROUP conference on Supporting group work* (pp. 239-247). New York: ACM.

Posner, I., & Baecker, R. M. (1993). How people write together. In Baecker, R. M. (Ed.), *Readings in Groupware and Computer-Supported Cooperative Work: Assisting Human-Human Collaboration* (pp. 239–250). San Mateo, CA: Morgan Kaufman.

Potter, J. (1996). *Representing reality: Discourse, rhetoric and social construction.* Thousand Oaks, CA: Sage.

Powell, K. R., & Albers, H. E. (2006). Center for Behavioral Neuroscience: A prototype multi-institutional collaborative research center. *Journal of Biomedical Discovery and Collaboration, 1*(1), 9. doi:10.1186/1747-5333-1-9

Preece, J. (1999). Empathic communities: balancing emotional and factual communication. *Interacting with Computers, 12*(1), 63–77. doi:10.1016/S0953-5438(98)00056-3

Preece, J. (2001). Sociability and usability in online communities: Determining and measuring success. *Behaviour & Information Technology, 20*(5), 347–356. doi:10.1080/01449290110084683

Preece, J., Nonnecke, B., & Andrews, D. (2004). The top five reasons for lurking: Improving community experiences for everyone. *Computers in Human Behavior, 20*(2). doi:10.1016/j.chb.2003.10.015

Propp, K. M. (1999). Collective information processing in groups. In Frey, L. R. (Ed.), *The handbook of group communication theory and research* (pp. 225–250). Thousand Oaks, CA: Sage.

Prosser, J., & Loxley, A. (2008). *Introducing visual methods.* ESRC National Center for Research Methods. [NCRM Review Paper/010]

Quan-Haase, A., Cothrel, J., & Wellman, B. (2005). Instant Messaging for Collaboration: A Case Study of a High-Tech Firm. *Journal of Computer-Mediated Communication, 10*(4).

Raban, D. R., & Rafaeli, S. (2007). Investigating ownership and the willingness to share information online. *Computers in Human Behavior, 23*, 2367–2382. doi:10.1016/j.chb.2006.03.013

Radley, A. (2002). Portrayals of suffering: on looking away, looking at, and the comprehension of illness experience. *Body & Society, 8*(3), 1–23. doi:10.1177/1357034X02008003001

Radley, A., & Taylor, D. (2003). Images of recovery: A photo-elicitation study on the hospital ward. *Qualitative Health Research, 13*(1), 77–99. doi:10.1177/1049732302239412

Radley, A., & Taylor, D. (2003). Remembering one's stay in hospital: A study in photography, recovery and forgetting. *Health (London), 7*(2), 129–159. doi:10.1177/1363459303007002872

Ragan, S. L. (2000). Sociable talk in women's health care contexts: two forms of non-medical talk. In Coupland, J. (Ed.), *Small talk* (pp. 241–264). London: Longman.

Randall, D., Harper, R., & Rouncefield, M. (2007). *Fieldwork for design: theory and practice.* London: Springer-Verlag.

Reddy, M. C., & Jansen, B. J. (2008). A model for understanding collaborative information behavior in context: A study of two healthcare teams. *Information Processing & Management, 44*(1), 256–273. doi:10.1016/j.ipm.2006.12.010

Reddy, M. C., & Spence, P. R. (2008). Collaborative information seeking: A field study of a multidisciplinary patient care team. *Information Processing & Management, 44*(1), 242–255. doi:10.1016/j.ipm.2006.12.003

Reddy, M. C., Dourish, P., & Pratt, W. (2001). Coordinating heterogeneous work: information and representation in medical care. In *Proceedings of the European Conference on Computer supported Cooperative Work (ECSCW '01)* (pp. 239-258). Dordrecht: Kluwer.

Reddy, M., & Dourish, P. (2002). A finger on the pulse: temporal rhythms and information seeking in medical work. In *CSCW '02: Proceedings of the 2002 ACM conference on Computer supported cooperative work* (pp. 344-353). New York: ACM.

Reddy, M., & Spence, P. R. (2006). Finding Answers: Information Needs of a Multidisciplinary Patient Care Team in an Emergency Department. In *Proc. of American Medical Informatics Association Fall Symposium (AMIA'06)*, Washington, DC (pp. 649-653).

Reddy, M., Jansen, B. J., & Krishnappa, R. (2008). The Role of Communication in Collaborative Information Searching. In Proc. of American Society of Information Sciences and Technology (ASIST'08), Columbus, OH.

Reed, D. A. (2003). Grids, the TeraGrid, and Beyond. *Computer, 36*(1), 62–68. doi:10.1109/MC.2003.1160057

Reed, D. A., Giles, R. C., & Catlett, C. E. (1997). Distributed data and immersive collaboration. *Communications of the ACM, 40*(11), 38–48. doi:10.1145/265684.265691

Reidpath, D. D., & Allotey, P. A. (2001). Data Sharing in Medical Research: An Empirical Investigation. *Bioethics, 15*(2), 125–134. doi:10.1111/1467-8519.00220

Reisner, A. E. (1992). The news conference: How daily newspaper editors construct the front page. *The Journalism Quarterly, 69*(4), 971–986.

Rhodes, C., & Nevill, A. (2004). Academic and social integration in higher education: a survey of satisfaction and dissatisfaction within a first-year education studies cohort at a new university. *Journal of Further and Higher Education, 28*(2), 179–193. doi:10.1080/0309877042000206741

Rich, M., & Chalfen, R. (1999). Showing and telling asthma: Children teaching physicians with visual narratives. *Visual Sociology, 14*, 51–71. doi:10.1080/14725869908583802

Rich, M., & Patashnick, J. L. (2002). Narrative research with audiovisual data: Video Intervention/Prevention Assessment (VIA) and NVivo. *International Journal of Social Research Methodology, 5*(3), 245–261. doi:10.1080/13645570210166373

Rich, M., Huecker, D., & Ludwig, D., S. (2001). Obesity in the lives of children and adolescents: Inquiry through patient-created visual narratives. *Pediatric Research, 49*, 7A.

Rich, M., Lamola, S., Amory, C., & Schneider, L. (2000). Asthma in life context: Video Intervention/Prevention Assessment (VIA). *Pediatrics, 105*(3), 469–477. doi:10.1542/peds.105.3.469

Rich, M., Lamola, S., Gordon, J., & Chalfen, R. (2000). Video Intervention/Prevention assessment: A patient-centered methodology for understanding the adolescent illness experience. *The Journal of Adolescent Health, 27*(3), 155–165. doi:10.1016/S1054-139X(00)00114-2

Rich, M., Patashnick, J. L., Huecker, D., & Ludwig, D. (2002). Living with obesity: visual narratives of overweight adolescents [abstract]. *The Journal of Adolescent Health, 30*(2), 100. doi:10.1016/S1054-139X(01)00361-5

Rich, M., Patashnick, J., & Kastelic, E. (2005). Achieving independence: the role of parental involvement with adolescents with spina bifida. *The Journal of Adolescent Health, 36*(2), 129. doi:10.1016/j.jadohealth.2004.11.070

Rich, M., Polvinen, J., & Patashnick, J. L. (2005). Visual narratives of the pediatric illness experience: Children communicating with clinicians through video. [Special issue on Child Psychiatry and the Media]. *Child and Adolescent Psychiatric Clinics of North America, 14*(3), 571–587. doi:10.1016/j.chc.2005.02.013

Ridings, Catherine M., Gefen, D. & Arinze, B. (2006). Psychological Barriers: Lurker and Poster Motivation and Behavior in Online Communities. *Communications of the Association for Information Systems*, (18): 329–354.

Roberts, N. C., & Bradley, R. T. (1991, June). Stakeholder collaboration and innovation: a study of public policy initiation at the state level. *The Journal of Applied Behavioral Science, 27*(2), 209. doi:10.1177/0021886391272004

Robinson, J. D. (2006). Soliciting patients' presenting concerns. In Heritage, J., & Maynard, D. W. (Eds.), *Communication in medical care: Interaction between primary care physicians and patients* (pp. 22–47). Cambridge, UK: Cambridge University Press. doi:10.1017/CBO9780511607172.004

Rodden, T. (1991). A Survey of CSCW Systems. *Interacting with Computers, 3*(3), 319–353. doi:10.1016/0953-5438(91)90020-3

Rodden, T., & Blair, G. (1991, September 25-27). CSCW and distributed systems: the problem of control. In *Proceedings of ECSCW*, Amsterdam, The Netherlands (pp. 49—64).

Roldan, G., Helmersen, P., & Wong, A. (2007). *Connecting the Unconnected: Examining Local Needs, Exploring Service Opportunities in Bangladesh*. Telenor research paper.

Romano, N., Roussinov, D., Nunamaker, J., & Chen, H. (1999). Collaborative Information Retrieval Environment: Integration of Information Retrieval with Group Support Systems. In *Proc of the 32nd Hawaii International Conference on System Sciences* (HICCS'99), Hawaii (pp. 1-10).

Roth, S. (2004). Capstone Address: Visualization as a medium for capturing and sharing thoughts. In *Proceedings IEEE InfoVis 2004* (pp. 8).

Ruiz-Molina, M. E., & Cuadrado-Garcia, M. (2008). E-learning in a university interdisciplinary and bilingual context: Analysis of students' participation, motivation and performance. *Multicultural Education & Technology Journal, 2*(3), 156–169. doi:10.1108/17504970810900450

Rutgers. (2009). *Rutgers DISCIPLE project*. Retrieved March 7, 2009, from http://www.caip.rutgers.edu/disciple

Ryan, C. (2005). Struggling to survive: A study of editorial decision-making strategies at MAMM magazine. *Journal of Business and Technical Communication, 19*(3), 353–376. doi:10.1177/1050651905275643

Saracevic, T., Spink, A., & Wu, M.-M. (1997). Users and intermediaries in information retrieval: what are they talking about? In A. Jameson, C. Paris, C., & C. Tasso (Eds.). *Proceedings of the 6th International Conference on User Modeling,* 2-5 June, Chia Languna, Sardinia, Italy (pp. 43-54).

Savolainen, R. (2006). Time as a context of information seeking. *Library & Information Science Research, 28*(1), 110–127. doi:10.1016/j.lisr.2005.11.001

Savolainen, R. (2009). Epistemic work and knowing in practice as conceptualizations of information use. Information Research, 14(1), paper 392. [Available at http://InformationR.net/ir/14-1/paper392.html]

Savolainen, R., & Kari, J. (2004). Placing the Internet in Information Source Horizons. A Study of Information Seeking by Internet Users in the Context of Self Development. *Library and Information Research, 26,* 415–433. doi:10.1016/j.lisr.2004.04.004

Scacchi, W. (2007). *Free/Open Source Software Development: Recent Research Results and Emerging Opportunities.* Paper presented at the ESEC/FSE 2007, Cvtat, Croatia.

Schein, E. H. (2004). *Organizational culture and leadership.* San Francisco: Jossey-Bass.

Schoberth, T., Heinzl, A., & Preece, J. (2006). Exploring Communication Activities in Online Communities: A Longitudinal Analysis in the Financial Services Industry. *Journal of Organizational Computing and Electronic Commerce, 16*(3-4), 247–265. doi:10.1207/s15327744joce1603&4_5

Schudson, M. (2003). *The sociology of news.* New York: W.W. Norton & Company.

Schuler, D. (1996). *New community networks: Wired for change.* Reading, MA: Addison-Wesley Publishing.

Schultz, N., & Beach, B. (2004). *From lurkers to posters* Australian National Training Authority. Retrieved March 10, 2009, from http://74.125.47.132/custom?q=cache:Vq8ieWkntgUJ:www.flexiblelearning.net.au/resources/lurkerstoposters.pdf+From+lurkers+to+posters&cd=2&hl=en&ct=clnk&gl=us&client=google-coop-np.

Schwenk, T. L., & Green, L. A. (2006). The Michigan Clinical Research Collaboratory: Following the NIH roadmap to the community. *Annals of Family Medicine, 4*(1), 49–54. doi:10.1370/afm.538

Scott, N. (2008). An evaluation of enhanced student support (including podcasting) on assessed course work achievement and student satisfaction. *Learning and Teaching in Action,* 7(1). Retrieved September 16, 2009, from http://www.celt.mmu.ac.uk/ltia/issue15/scott.php

Seddon, K., Skinner, N., & Postlethwaite, K. (2008). Creating a model to examine motivation for sustained engagement in online communities. *Education and Information Technologies, 13*(1), 17–34. doi:10.1007/s10639-007-9048-2

Senge, P. (1990). *The fifth discipline: The art and practice of the learning organization.* New York: Doubleday/Currency.

Shah, C. (2008). Toward Collaborative Information Seeking (CIS). *Proceedings of the Collaborative Exploratory Search Workshop.*

Shah, C. (2008, June 20). Toward Collaborative Information Seeking (CIS). In *Proceedings of JCDL 2008 Collaborative Exploratory Search,* Pittsburgh, PA. Available from http://workshops.fxpal.com/jcdl2008/submissions/tmpE1.pdf

Shah, C. (2009, May 10). Lessons and Challenges for Collaborative Information Seeking (CIS) Systems Developers. In *GROUP 2009 Workshop on Collaborative Information Behavior,* Sanibel Island, Florida.

Available from http://www.personal.psu.edu/sap246/ Shah_CIB_Workshop.pdf.

Shah, C., Marchionini, G., & Kelly, D. (2009, April 4-9). Learning design principles for a collaborative information seeking system. In *Proceedings of ACM SIGCHI Conference on Human Factors in Computing Systems*, Boston, MA.

Shapira, B., Kantor, P. B., & Melamed, B.The effect of extrinsic motivation on user behaviour in a collaborative information finding system. *Journal of the American Society for Information Science and Technology, 52*(11), 879–887. doi:10.1002/asi.1148

Sharan, Y., & Sharan, S. (1992). *Expanding cooperative learning through group investigation.* New York: Teachers College Press.

Sharpe, M. (2004a). Exploring legislated midwifery: texts and ruling relations. In Bourgeault, I. L., Benoit, C., & Davis-Floyd, R. (Eds.), *Reconceiving Midwifery* (pp. 150–166). Montreal, Canada: McGill-Queen's University Press.

Sharpe, M. J. D. (2004b). *Intimate business: woman-midwife relationships in Ontario, Canada.* Unpublished doctoral dissertation, Ontario Institute for Studies in Education, University of Toronto.

Sharpe, R., Benfield, G., Roberts, G., & Francis, R. (2006, October). *The undergraduate experience of blended e-learning: a review of UK literature and practice.* Retrieved September 16, 2009, from http://www.heacademy.ac.uk/assets/York/documents/ourwork/research/literature_reviews/blended_elearning_full_review.pdf

Sherer, P. D., Shea, T. P., & Kristensen, E. (2003). Online communities of practice: A catalyst for faculty development. *Innovative Higher Education, 27*(3), 183–194. doi:10.1023/A:1022355226924

Shoemaker, P. J., & Reese, S. D. (1996). *Mediating the message: Theories of influences on mass media content* (2nd ed.). White Plains, NY: Longman.

Sigelman, L. (1973). Reporting the news: An organizational analysis. *American Journal of Sociology, 77*, 660-670.Stacey, R. D. (1996). *Complexity and creativity in organizations.* San Francisco: Berrett-Koehler Publishers.

Silverstone, R. (1994). *Television and everyday life.* London: Routledge.

Silverstone, R. (Ed.). (2005). *Media, technology and everyday life in Europe. From information to communication.* Aldershot: Ashgate.

Silverstone, R. Hirsch, E., & Morley, D. (1999). Information and communication technologies and the moral economy of the household. In R. Silverstone, & E. Hirsch (Eds.). Consuming technologies: Media and information in domestic spaces (pp. 15–31). London: Routledge.

Silverstone, R., & Haddon, L. (1998). Design and the domestication of information and communication technologies: Technical change and everyday life. In Silverstone, R., & Mansell, R. (Eds.), *Communication by design: The politics of information and communication technologies* (pp. 44–74). Oxford: Oxford University Press.

Singer, J. B. (1996). 'Virtual anonymity': Online accountability and the virtuous virtual journalist. *Journal of Mass Media Ethics, 11*(2), 95–106.

Singer, J. B., Tharp, M. P., & Haruta, A. (1999). Online staffers: Superstars or second-class citizens? *Newspaper Research Journal, 20*(3), 29–47.

Smeaton, A. F., Lee, H., Foley, C., & Givney, S. M. (2006). Collaborative video searching on a tabletop. *Multimedia Systems Journal, 12*(4), 375–391. doi:10.1007/s00530-006-0064-7

Smith, D. E. (1990). *Texts, facts and femininity: Exploring the relations of ruling.* New York: Routledge.

Smith, M. A. (1999). Invisible crowds in cyberspace. In Smith, M. A., & Kollock, P. (Eds.), *Communities in cyberspace* (pp. 195–219). New York: Routledge.

Solomon, P. (1997). Discovering information behavior in sense making. I. Time and timing. *Journal of the American Society for Information Science American Society for Information Science, 48*(12), 1097–1108. doi:10.1002/(SICI)1097-4571(199712)48:12<1097::AID-ASI4>3.0.CO;2-P

Sonnenwald, D. H. (1996, July). Communication roles that support collaboration during the design process. *Design Studies*, *17*(3), 277–301. doi:10.1016/0142-694X(96)00002-6

Sonnenwald, D. I. H. (1999). Evolving Perspectives of Human Information Behavior: Contexts, Situations, Social Networks and Information Horizons. In Wilson, T., & Allen, D. (Eds.), *Exploring the Contexts of Information Behavior* (pp. 176–190). London: Taylor Graham.

Sonnenwald, D. I. H. (2005). Information Horizons. In K. Fischer, S. Erdelez, & L. E. F. McKechnie (Eds.), Theories of Information Behavior (pp. 191-197). Medford, NJ: Asis&t.

Sonnenwald, D. I. H., & Pierce, L. G. (2000). Information Behavior in Dynamic Group Work Contexts: Interwoven Situational Awareness, Dense Social Networks and Contested Collaboration in Command and Control. *Information Processing & Management*, *36(3)*, 461–479. doi:10.1016/S0306-4573(99)00039-4

Sonnenwald, D. I. H., & Wildemuth, B. M. (2001). *Investigating Information Seeking Behavior Using the Concept of Information Horizons.* Paper presented at the ALISE Methodology Paper Competition.

Sonnenwald, D. I. H., Whitton, M. C., & Maglaughlin, K. L. (2003). Evaluating a Scientific Collaboratory: Results of a Controlled Experiment. *ACM Transactions on Computer-Human Interaction*, *10*(2), 150–176. doi:10.1145/772047.772051

Sonnenwald, D., Maglaughlin, K. L., & Whitton, M. C. (2004). Designing to support situation awareness across distances: an example from a scientific collaboratory. *Information Processing & Management*, *36*, 461–479. doi:10.1016/S0306-4573(99)00039-4

Spence, P. R., Reddy, M., & Hall, R. (2005). A Survey of Collaborative Information Seeking of Academic Researchers. In *Proc. of ACM Conf. on Supporting Group Work* (*GROUP'05*), Sanibel Island, FL (pp. 85-88).

Spence, P., & Reddy, M. (2007). The Active Gatekeeper in Collaborative Information Seeking Activities. In *Proc.* *of ACM Conf. on Supporting Group Work* (GROUP'07), Sanibel Island, FL (pp. 277-280).

Spink, A., & Cole, C. (2006). Human information behavior: Integrating diverse approaches and information use. *Journal of the American Society for Information Science and Technology*, *57*(1), 25–35. doi:10.1002/asi.20249

Spoel, P. (2007). A feminist rhetorical perspective on informed choice in midwifery. *Rhetor: Journal of the Canadian Society for the Study of Rhetoric*, *2*. Retrieved May 10, 2010, from http://uregina.ca/~rheaults/rhetor/2007/spoel.pdf

Sproull, L., & Faraj, S. (1997). Atheism, sex, and databases: The net as a social technology. In Kiesler, S. (Ed.), *Culture of the internet* (pp. 35–51). Mahwah, NJ: Lawrence Erlbaum Associates.

Sproull, L., & Kiesler, S. (1995). Computer, Networks, and Work. In Baecker, R. M., Grudin, J., Buxton, W. A. S., & Greenberg, S. (Eds.), *Readings in Human-Computer Interaction: Toward the Year 2000* (pp. 755–761). San Francisco, CA: Morgan Kaufmann.

Stapley, L. F. (1996). *The personality of the organization: A psycho-dynamic explanation of culture and change.* London: Free Association Books.

Star, S. L., & Griesemer, J. R. (1989). Institutional ecology, translations and boundary objects: amateurs and professionals In Berkeley's Museum of Vertebrate Zoology, 1907-1939. *Social Studies of Science*, *19*(3), 387–420. doi:10.1177/030631289019003001

Stein, L. D., Mungall, C., Shu, S. Q., Caudy, M., Mangone, M., & Day, A. (2002). The Generic Genome Browser: A building block for a model organism system database. *Genome Research*, *12*, 1599–1610. doi:10.1101/gr.403602

Steinem, G. (1994). Sex, lies and advertising. In Steinem, G. (Ed.), *Moving beyond words* (pp. 130–170). New York: Simon & Schuster.

Stivers, T. (2006). Treatment decisions: negotiations between doctors and parents in acute care encounters. In Heritage, J., & Maynard, D. W. (Eds.), *Communica-*

tion in medical care: Interaction between primary care physicians and patients (pp. 279–312). Cambridge, UK: Cambridge University Press. doi:10.1017/CBO9780511607172.012

Story, M.-A., Cheng, L.-T., Bull, I., & Rigby, P. (2006). *Shared Waypoints and Social Tagging to Support Collaboration in Software Development.* Paper presented at the CSCW '06, Banff, Alberta Canada.

Strauss, A., & Corbin, J. (1990). *Basics of Qualitative Research: Grounded Theory Procedures and Techniques.* Newbury Park, CA: Sage Publications.

Strom, D. (2006, April 5). I.M. generation is changing the way business talks. *The New York Times.*

Stubbs, M. (1983). *Discourse analysis: The sociolinguistic analysis of natural language.* Chicago: University of Chicago Press.

Stubbs, M., & Martin, I. (2003). Blended learning: one small step. *Learning and Teaching in Action, 2*(3). Retrieved September 16, 2009, from http://www.celt.mmu.ac.uk/ltia/issue6/stubbsmartin.shtml

Suchman, L. A. (1987). *Plans and situated actions: The problem of human-machine communication.* Cambridge, UK: Cambridge University Press.

Sumpter, R. S. (2000). Daily newspaper editors' audience construction routines: A case study. *Critical Studies in Media Communication, 17*(3), 334–346. doi:10.1080/15295030009388399

Sun, C., Xia, S., Sun, D., Chen, D., Shen, H., & Cai, W. (2006). Transparent adaptation of single-user applications for multi-user real-time collaboration. *ACM Transactions on Computer-Human Interaction, 13*(4), 531–582. doi:10.1145/1188816.1188821

Surowiecki, J. (2004). *The Wisdom of Crowds: Why the Many Are Smarter Than the Few and How Collective Wisdom Shapes Business, Economies, Societies, and Nations.* New York, NY: Doubleday.

Swan, K., & Shih, L. F. (2006). On the nature and Development of Social Presence in Online Course Discussions. *Journal of Asynchronous Learning Networks.*

Swivel, Inc. (2007). *Swivel.* Retrieved February 9, 2009, from http://www.swivel.com

Symon, G., Long, K., & Ellis, J. (1996). The Coordination of Work Activities: Cooperation and Conflict in a Hospital Context. *Computer Supported Cooperative Work, 5*(1), 1–31. doi:10.1007/BF00141934

Talja, S., & Hansen, P. (2005). Information Sharing. In Spink, A., & Cole, C. (Eds.), *New Directions in Human Information Behavior* (pp. 113–134). Dordrect, Netherlands: Springer. doi:10.1007/1-4020-3670-1_7

Taylor, A., & Richard, H. (2003). The gift of the gab?: A design oriented sociology of young people's use of mobiles. *Computer Supported Cooperative Work, 12,* 267–296. doi:10.1023/A:1025091532662

Taylor, N. E., & Ives, Z. G. (2006). Reconciling while tolerating disagreement in collaborative data sharing. In *Proceedings of the ACM Conference on Management of Data (SIGMOD '06)* (pp. 13-24).

Ter Hofte, G. H., Mulder, I., & Verwijs, C. (2006). Close encounters of the virtual kind: A study on placed-based presence. *AI & Society, 20,* 151–168. doi:10.1007/s00146-005-0013-6

Terence, T. (1991). The social dynamics of video media in an indigenous society: The cultural meaning and the personal politics of videomaking in Kayapo communities. *Visual Anthropology Review, 7*(2), 68–76. doi:10.1525/var.1991.7.2.68

Thachuk, A. (2007). Midwifery, informed choice, and reproductive autonomy: a relational approach. *Feminism & Psychology, 17*(1), 39–56. doi:10.1177/0959353507072911

Torrance, H. (2007). Assessment as learning? How the use of explicit learning objectives, assessment criteria and feedback in post-secondary education and training can come to dominate learning. *Assessment in Education, 14*(3), 281–294. doi:10.1080/09695940701591867

Tuchman, G. (1978). *Making news: A study in the construction of reality.* New York: The Free Press.

Tutt, D., Hindmarsh, J., & Fraser, M. (2007). The distributed work of local action: Interaction amongst virtually collocated research teams. In *Proceedings of the European Conference on Computer-Supported Cooperative Work (ECSCW 2007)* (pp. 199-218).

Twidale, M. B., & Nichols, D. M. (1996). Collaborative browsing and visualisation of the search process. In *Proceedings of Aslib* (Vol. 48, p. 177-182). Available from http://www.comp.lancs.ac.uk/computing/research/cseg/projects/ariadne/docs/elvira96.html

Twidale, M. B., Nichols, D. M., & Paice, C. D. (1995). Supporting collaborative learning during information searching. In *Proceedings of Computer Supported Collaborative Learning* (pp. 367–374). Bloomington, Indiana: CSCL.

Twidale, M., & Nichols, D. M. (1998). Designing Interfaces to Support Collaboration in Information Retrieval. *Interacting with Computers, 10*(2), 177–193. doi:10.1016/S0953-5438(97)00022-2

Twidale, M., Nichols, D. M., & Paice, C. D. (1997). Browsing is a Collaborative Activity. *Information Processing & Management, 33*(6), 761–783. doi:10.1016/S0306-4573(97)00040-X

Vakkari, P. (2003). Task-based information searching. *Annual Review of Information Science & Technology, 37*, 413–464. doi:10.1002/aris.1440370110

Viégas, F. B., Wattenberg, M., McKeon, M., van Ham, F., & Kriss, J. (2008). Harry Potter and the meat-filled freezer: A case study of spontaneous usage of visualization tools. In *Proceedings HICSS 2008* (pp. 159).

Viégas, F. B., Wattenberg, M., van Ham, F., Kriss, J., & McKeon, M. (2007). A site for visualization at internet scale. In *Proceedings Infovis 2007* (pp. 1121–1128). Many Eyes.

Vishwanath, A., & Chen, H. (2008, May). *Personal communication technologies as an extension of the self: A cross-cultural comparison of people's associations with technology and their symbolic proximity with others.* Paper presented at the annual meeting of the International Communication Association, Montreal, Quebec, Canada.

von Krogh, G., Ichijo, K., & Nonaka, I. (2000). *Enabling knowledge creation: How to unlock the mystery of tacit knowledge and release the power of innovation.* Oxford, UK: Oxford University Press.

Vos, P., & van der Voordt, T. (2001). Tomorrow's offices through today's eyes: Effects of innovation in the working environment. *Journal of Corporate Real Estate, 4*(1), 48–65. doi:10.1108/14630010210811778

Wagner, C., & Prasarnphanich, P. (2007). Innovating collaborative content creation: The role of altruism and wiki technology. In *Proceedings HICSS 2007, 40*(1), 278.

Waldrop, M. M. (2008). Science 2.0 - Is Open Access Science the Future? *Scientific American.* Retrieved February 9, 2009, from http://www.sciam.com/article.cfm?id=science-2-point-0

Wang, C. C. (1999). Photovoice: a participatory action research strategy applied to women's health. *Journal of Women's Health, 8*(2), 185–192. doi:10.1089/jwh.1999.8.185

Wang, C. C., & Lai, C. Y. (2006). Knowledge Contribution in the Online Virtual Community: Capability and Motivation. In by J. Lang, F. Lin and J. Wang (Ed.), Lecture Notes in Computer Science (pp. 442-453). Berlin: Springer-Verlag.

Wang, C., & Burris, M. A. (1997). Photovoice: Concept, methodology, and use for participatory needs assessment. *Health Education & Behavior, 24*(3), 369–387. doi:10.1177/109019819702400309

Wang, C., Burris, M. A., & Xiang, Y. P. (1996). Chinese village women as visual anthropologists: a participatory approach to reaching policymakers. *Social Science & Medicine, 42*(10), 1391–1400. doi:10.1016/0277-9536(95)00287-1

Wasko, M. M., & Faraj, S. (2000). "It is what one does": Why people participate and help others in electronic communities of practice. *The Journal of Strategic Information Systems, 9*(2-3), 155–173. doi:10.1016/S0963-8687(00)00045-7

Wasko, M. M., & Faraj, S. (2005). Why should I share? Examining social capital and knowledge contribution in electronic networks of practice. *Management Information Systems Quarterly, 29*(1), 35–57.

Wattenberg, M. (2005). Baby names, visualization, and social data analysis. In Proceedings Infovis 2005 (pp. 1-7).

Waverman, L., Meloria, M., & Melvyn, F. (2005, March). The impact of telecoms on economic growth in developing countries. *Vodafone Policy Paper Series, 2*.

Weber, S. (2004). *The Success of Open Source*. Cambridge, MA: Harvard University Press.

Wei, C., & Kolko, B. (2005, July). *Studying mobile phone use in context: Cultural, political, and economic dimensions of mobile phone use*. Paper presented at International Professional Communication Conference, Limerick, Ireland.

Weick, K., & Roberts, K. (1993). Collective Mind in Organizations: Heedful Interrelating on Flight Decks. *Administrative Science Quarterly, 38*(3), 357–381. doi:10.2307/2393372

Weilenmann, A., & Catrine, L. (2002). Local use and sharing of mobile phones. In B. Brown, N. Green, & R. Harper (Eds.). Wireless world: Social and interactional aspects of the mobile age (pp. 92 107). London: Springer-Verlag.

Weiser, J. (1999). *Phototherapy techniques: Exploring the secrets of personal snapshots and family albums*. Vancouver, BC, Canada: PhotoTherapy Centre Press.

Wells, G. (1999). *Dialogic inquiry: Toward a sociocultural practice and theory of education*. Cambridge, UK: Cambridge University Press. doi:10.1017/CBO9780511605895

Wenger, E. (1998). *Communities of practice: Learning, meaning, and identity*. New York: Cambridge University Press.

Wenger, E., McDermott, R., & Snyder, W. M. (2002). *Cultivating communities of practice: A guide to managing knowledge*. Boston: Harvard Business School Press.

West, C. (2006). Coordinating closings in primary care visits: producing continuity of care. In Heritage, J., & Maynard, D. W. (Eds.), *Communication in medical care Interaction between primary care physicians and patients* (pp. 379–415). Cambridge, UK: Cambridge University Press. doi:10.1017/CBO9780511607172.015

Whalen, M., Whalen, J., Moore, R. J., Raymond, G. T., Szymanski, M. H., & Vinkhuyzen, E. (2004). Studying workscapes. In *Discourse & technology: multimodal discourse analysis* (pp. 208–229). Washington, DC: Georgetown University Press.

White, D. M. (1950). The 'Gatekeeper': A case study in the selection of news. *The Journalism Quarterly, 27*, 383–390.

Wilbanks, J., & Boyle, J. (2006). *Introduction to Science Commons*. Retrieved February 23, 2009, from http://sciencecommons.org/wp-content/uploads/ScienceCommons_Concept_Paper.pdf

Wilbur, S. B., & Young, R. E. (1988, April 20-22). The COSMOS project: a multi-disciplinary approach to design of computer supported group working. In R. Speth (Ed.), EUTECO 88: Research into Networks and Distributed Applications. Vienna, Austria.

Wilson, P. (1983). *Second hand knowledge: An inquiry into cognitive authority*. Westport, CT: Greenwood.

Wilson, T. (2000). Human information behavior. *Informing Science, 3*(2), 49–56.

Wilson, T. (2008). Activity Theory and Information Seeking. *Annual Review of Information Science & Technology, 37*, 119–161. doi:10.1002/aris.2008.1440420111

Wilson, T. D. (1981). On User Studies and Information Needs. *The Journal of Documentation, 37*(1), 3–15. doi:10.1108/eb026702

Wong, A. (2007). The local ingenuity: Maximizing livelihood through improvising current communication access technology. In *Ethnographic Praxis in Industry Conference Proceedings* (Vol. 1, pp. 104–114). American Anthropological Association.

Worth, S. (1966). Film as non-art: An approach to the study of film. *The American Scholar, 35*(2), 322–334.

Worth, S., Adair, J., & Chalfen, R. (1997). *Through Navajo eyes: an exploration in film communication and anthropology*. Albuquerque, NM: University of New Mexico Press.

Wu, C. G., Gerlach, J. H., & Young, C. E. (2007). An empirical analysis of open source software developers' motivations and continuance intentions. *Information & Management*, *44*(3), 253–262. doi:10.1016/j.im.2006.12.006

Wu, M.-M. (2005). Understanding patrons' micro-level information-seeking (MLIS) in information retrieval situations. *Information Processing & Management*, *41*, 929–947. doi:10.1016/j.ipm.2004.08.007

Yakel, E. (2001). The social construction of accountability: radiologists and their record-keeping practices. *The Information Society*, *17*(4), 233–245. doi:10.1080/019722401753330832

Yang, B. (2005). *Social networks and individualism: The role of the mobile phone in today's social transformation in urban China.* Presented at the International Conference on Mobile Communication and Asian Modernities II.

Yang, S. C. (2003). Creating an Internet theatre in gender education. *Journal of Computer Assisted Learning*, *19*(1), 249–251. doi:10.1046/j.1365-2729.2003.00251.x

Zach, M. H. (1994). Electronic messaging and communication effectiveness in an ongoing work group. *Information and Management Systems*, *26*, 231–241.

Ziller, R. C. (1990). *Photographing the self: Methods for observing personal orientations.* Newbury Park, CA: Sage.

About the Contributors

Jonathan Foster is a lecturer in Information Management at the Information School, University of Sheffield. Prior to this he worked in a London-based electronic publishing house. His research interests are in information management and educational informatics. He has worked on a number of research projects in the areas of computer based collaborative group work and learning. He is currently investigating the implementation and evaluation of interactive archives for new media artworks.

* * *

Norihisa Awamura is a doctoral student at Graduate School of Library and Information Science, Keio University and a Research Fellow of Japan Society for Promotion of Science (DC2). He specializes in User Study in Library and Information Science. The focus of his doctoral research is to establish a research framework to understand, analyze, and describe how practical management of knowledge is accomplished as a part of work activity, with a specific focus on situated information-related actions in actual settings. He is specifically interested in the area of collaborative information behavior and ethnomethodological studies of work and workplace. He has been conducting fieldwork by participating in PARC's ethnographic research projects with two IT companies. He obtained his M.A. and B.A. in Library and Information Science from Keio University in Japan.

Anne Beamish is a Research Scientist in the Design Laboratory at MIT. She teaches classes in the Department of Urban Studies and Planning and the Media Lab within the School of Architecture and Planning and is the Creative Director of ArchNet. From 2002-2007, she was Assistant Professor in the graduate Community and Regional Planning Program in the School of Architecture, the University of Texas at Austin. She received her Ph.D. from the Department of Urban Studies and Planning at MIT. An architect and urban planner by training, her research and teaching interests include the social and spatial aspects of information and communication technologies; the design of online environments to support physical and virtual communities; organizational and practice-based learning; public art; and urban public space.

David A. Bray deployed in 2009 for 120-days to Afghanistan to help NATO and U.S. Forces "think differently" about inter-organizational strategies among military and humanitarian organizations in the region. He previously served as IT Chief for the Bioterrorism Preparedness and Response Program at the U.S. Centers for Disease Control from 2000-2005. He led the technology aspects of the program in response to 9/11, anthrax, West Nile, SARS, and other major outbreaks; later receiving the CDC Director's Award for Information Services. He holds a PhD from the Goizueta Business School, Emory University and subsequently served as a Post-Doctoral Research Associate with MIT's Center for Collective Intelligence and the Harvard Kennedy School. He also served as a Visiting Associate at the University of Oxford's Internet Institute. David's work and research focuses on grassroots collaborations within and across organizations, particularly for national security and crisis response.

Richard Chalfen, Ph.D. is currently Senior Scientist at the Center on Media and Child Health at Children's Hospital Boston/Harvard Medical School and Emeritus Professor of Anthropology, Temple University, continuing to teach at the Japan campus in Tokyo. He is past-president of the American Anthropological Association's Society of Visual Anthropology and former Chair of Temple's Department of Anthropology. He is the author of over 100 publications some of which have been translated into Italian, Hungarian, German and Russian. Current interests include applied visual studies, comparative studies of visual culture (US and Japan), health and participatory media research, and cross-cultural home media.

William H. Dutton (B.A. University of Missouri; M.A., PhD. SUNY Buffalo, 1974) is Director of the Oxford Internet Institute, Professor of Internet Studies, University of Oxford, and a Professorial Fellow of Balliol College. Bill is also Principal Investigator of the Oxford e-Social Science (OeSS) Project of the UK's National Centre for E-Social Science (NCeSS), and Principal Investigator of the Oxford Internet Surveys (OxIS). He is currently working on the potential for the emergence of a Fifth Estate enabled by the Internet, the rise of Collaborative Network Organizations (CNOs), and the diffusion and implications of innovations in e-Research — the use of advances in the Internet and related ICTs in research across the disciplines. In addition to his academic roles, he was appointed in February 2009 to chair Ofcom's Advisory Committee for England and to represent the South East within the committee.

Sanda Erdelez is an Associate Professor at the University of Missouri, U.S.A., School of Information Science and Learning Technologies and the founder of the Information Experience Laboratory (http://ielab.missouri.edu). She obtained bachelors and masters degrees from the University of Osijek, Croatia; and a Ph.D. from Syracuse University, where she studied as a Fulbright Scholar. Dr. Erdelez conducts research, teaching, and consulting in human information behavior, Internet search behavior, and usability evaluation. Her research in accidental aspects of information behavior (information encountering) has been funded by SBC Communication and Dell Inc., and she also served as a research team member and a co-PI on research projects funded by the U.S. Department of Education and the National Science Foundation. Dr. Erdelez co-edited (with K. Fisher and L. McKechnie) the Theories of Information Behavior (Information Today, 2005) and authored more than 80 research papers and presentations.

Sean P. Goggins is an Assistant Professor at Drexel University, U.S.A., College of Information Science and Technology. He obtained a bachelors degree from the University of Wisconsin-Madison, a masters degree from the University of Minnesota and a Ph.D. from the University of Missouri. Dr. Goggins conducts research and teaching in social computing, collaborative information behavior and the uptake and use of information and communication technologies that support distributed work and learning groups. Dr. Goggins has worked on research projects examining context awareness tools in online environments, usability of 3D Virtual Environments and the development of small groups who come together exclusively online. Dr. Goggins has 15 years of industry experience researching, designing and implementing collaborative technology solutions.

Elizabeth Meyers Hendrickson's primary interests involve the organizational communication systems found within various mediums. Her studies have examined the relationship between magazine editor and celebrity publicists during booking negotiations, as well as how media framing can recast politicians as celebrities. Recent work has studied how computer mediated communication can work as an organizational tool for media, while also considering the interpersonal dynamic ramifications of such instruments. She has published in the journal *Journalism Practice* and *Journal of Magazine and New Media Research*, has written chapters for books on celebrity culture and media ethics and reviews regularly for a range of other journals and academic publishers. She is a member of Kappa Tau Alpha, AEJMC and ICA. Dr. Hendrickson was an entertainment editor at magazines such as Ladies' Home Journal, Glamour and First for Women before obtaining her graduate degrees.

Nozomi Ikeya is a research scientist at Palo Alto Research Center (PARC). Her interest is in "practical management of knowledge" - how knowledge is created, shared, transferred, and used as part of activities. She studies "knowledge in action" in social settings from an ethnomethodological perspective. She has conducted ethnographic studies of work in various professional work settings, library services, particularly service design practices and reference service interactions; emergency medical practice at hospitals and call centers; project management of software engineering; and IT hardware designers' work practices. She was formerly Associate Professor of the Sociology Department at Toyo University in Japan, and she received M.A. in Library and Information Science from Keio University in Japan, and Ph.D. in Sociology from University of Manchester in the United Kingdom.

Bernard J. Jansen - Dr. Jim Jansen is an assistant professor in the College of Information Sciences and Technology at The Pennsylvania State University. Jim has more than 150 publications in the area of information technology and systems, with articles appearing in a multi-disciplinary range of journals and conferences. His specific areas of expertise are Web searching, sponsored search, and personalization for information searching. He is co-author of the book, Web Search: Public Searching of the Web and co-editor of the book Handbook of Weblog Analysis. Jim is a member of the editorial boards of six international journals. He has received several awards and honors and six application development awards, along with other writing, publishing, research, and leadership honors. Several agencies and corporations have supported his research. He is actively involved in teaching both undergraduate and graduate level courses, as well as mentoring students in a variety of research and educational efforts. He also has successfully conducted numerous consulting projects.

Daniel Lemire is a Full Professor of Computer Science at the University of Quebec at Montreal (UQAM) and an Adjunct Professor at the University of New Brunswick. He is a member of the research center in Cognitive Computer Science LICEF. Previously, he was a research officer at the National Research Council of Canada (NRC) where he led the e-Health Research Group, and an assistant professor at Acadia University. He was also a post-doctoral fellow at the Biomedical Engineering Institute. He has a B.Sc. and M.Sc. in Mathematics from the University of Toronto, and a Ph.D. in Engineering Mathematics from the Ecole Polytechnique and the Université de Montréal. His research interests include Collaborative Data Management, Information Filtering and Retrieval, Database Theory, e-Learning, and Data Warehousing.

Pam McKenzie is Associate Professor and Assistant Dean, Research at the Faculty of Information and Media Studies at The University of Western Ontario. Her research focuses on the ways that individuals in local settings collaboratively construct information needs, seeking, and use. She is interested in temporal, textual and interactional aspects of information practices, in the intersections of information work and caring work, and in gendered and embodied information practices and spaces.

Sylvie Noël, PhD, is a research scientist for the Communications Research Centre of Canada. She has worked at the CRC for the past ten years on the human factors of computer-supported cooperative work and collaborative virtual worlds. Her research projects have included the development of collaborative editing tools, the support of quality of experience during video conferencing, the use of tags in online social applications, and the impact of adding haptics and emotions to virtual worlds. Previously she worked at the Department of Psychology of the University of Western Australia in Perth, Australia, on a computer-supported learning project. Her research interests also include collaborative data analysis, sensors and ubiquitous computing, tangible interfaces, and small screen interactions.

Madhu C. Reddy is an Assistant Professor in the College of Information Sciences and Technology at Penn State University. He received his Ph.D. in Information and Computer Science from the University of California, Irvine. Dr. Reddy's primary research interests are at the intersections of Medical Informatics, Computer Supported Cooperative Work (CSCW), and Information Sciences. He is especially interested in the design, implementation and adoption of collaborative healthcare technologies such as electronic patient records. Dr. Reddy's current research is focused on how well these and other technologies support information behavior and decision-making in multidisciplinary patient-care teams. He has published his research in a variety of leading journals in different fields such as medical informatics and information sciences.

Michael Rich, MD, MPH is Associate Professor of Pediatrics at Harvard Medical School, Associate Professor in Society, Human Development and Health at Harvard School of Public Health. At Children's Hospital Boston, he practices adolescent medicine and is founder and Director of the Center on Media and Child Health. Dr. Rich has authored numerous research reports and reviews for the peer-reviewed medical and public health literature, chapters in books on media and their effects of health and practice policy statements for the American Academy of Pediatrics (AAP). He received the New Investigator Award from the Society for Adolescent Medicine for developing Video Intervention/Prevention Assessment (VIA) and the Holroyd-Sherry Award from the AAP for his contributions to the understanding of the influence of media on the health of children and adolescents.

Wolf Richter joined the Oxford Internet Institute as a DPhil student in October 2006 to study the economic and legal impact of the Internet on the production and distribution of digital media. For his DPhil thesis, he was involved in a cooperation with Tsinghua University in Beijing and the Berkman Center at Harvard University to study blanket licensing models for on-campus file-sharing networks. His recent research includes the role of intellectual property law in distributed problem-solving networks, open content film production, and the performance of online news aggregators. Wolf is a strategy consultant with McKinsey & Company on academic leave. He holds Masters degrees in Intellectual property law from Swiss Federal Institute of Technology in Zurich and Computer Sciences from Humboldt University in Berlin.

Shinichiro Sakai is a Ph.D candidate at the Graduate School of Sociology, Rikkyo University in Japan. His research interests lie in Ethnomethodology, sociology of media and studies of work and workplace in particular. Over the last couple of years he has been conducting fieldwork in a Japanese corporation. Prior to that he was involved in a three-year project on a workplace study of the activity of plumbers. He is currently a visiting researcher at Palo Alto Research Center.

Philip Scown has a background in cognitive psychology and computer science. His PhD, carried out at Loughborough University, researched the knowledge needs of agents, people or software based, working collaboratively and simultaneously in real-time systems. Such systems are, for example, found in process control, aviation, and international banking. Since then he has worked on the use of multimedia podcasts as both a collaborative activity and a tool for assessment in Higher Education. Other research interests include quantifying the user experience of modern consumer devices. Outside of the University system Philip has worked both the public and private sectors: in banking, telecommunications, electricity supply.

Chirag Shah is an assistant professor in School of Communication & Information (SC&I) at Rutgers, The State University of New Jersey. He received his PhD from the School of Information & Library Science (SILS) at University of North Carolina (UNC) at Chapel Hill. He holds an MS in Computer Science from UMass Amherst. He has also worked at many world-renowned research laboratories, such as FXPAL in California and National Institute of Informatics in Tokyo, Japan. His dissertation was focused on collaborative information seeking. He is also interested in social search and question-answering, social medias, and contextual information extraction. He has developed several tools for exploratory information seeking and extraction, including "Coagmento" for collaborative information seeking, and "ContextMiner" for capturing contextual information from multiple online sources.

Patricia Ruma Spence is an experienced IT consultant currently pursuing a PhD in the College of Information Sciences and Technology at The Pennsylvania State University – University Park. Her research focuses on the collaborative information use of multidisciplinary teams. As a native of Missouri, she received her B.S. in Engineering Management and her M.S. in Information Science & Technology, both from Missouri University of Science & Technology (MS&T). Before returning to graduate school, Patricia worked as a consultant at Andersen Consulting, LLP and The Extraprise Group, Inc. She has a solid background and experience in the strategic planning and implementation of information technologies, with strong emphasis in business analysis and change management. Patricia also has extensive experience in facilitation and communication at all levels of an organization, as well as the management, development and implementation of large-scale technologies.

Andrew Wong is a Senior Research Scientist at TRICAP (Telenor Research and Development Center Asia Pacific), part of the Telenor's Corporate Development Division. His research focuses on the role of information and communication technologies play in the developing countries, mainly in Telenor's Asia business units footprint. In addition he conducts research on the use of formal and informal financial services by the un-banked and un-served, mainly in Bangladesh, Pakistan, Thailand and India. Prior to joining the Telenor Group, Andrew worked with IDC (International Data Corporation), an advisory and market intelligence firm, with its headquarter in Boston, MA. Andrew holds a doctorate in Management from Multimedia University (Malaysia) and a Master in Business Administration from Cardiff University (United Kingdom).

Index

A

AOL instant messenger (AIM) 169
a priori 111, 114
ArchNet 37, 38, 39, 40, 41, 42, 46, 47, 48
Ariadne 76, 143, 150, 151
A Swarm of Angels (ASOA)
      4, 8, 9, 10, 11, 14
asynchronous collaboration 83, 130
asynchronous communication 36
asynchronous learning 129

B

BI market 56
BI systems 56
blended-learning 128, 129
blind spots 181
Business Intelligence (BI) 56, 64, 65, 68

C

childbearing women 198, 200
chronic illness 180
CIR prototype 80
clinical interaction 198, 199
clinical results 197, 204, 205
CNO Architecture 4
CNO ecology 12
Coagmento 147, 152, 153, 154, 158
co-browsing 143, 145
co-creating 1, 11, 13
co-creation 1, 3, 4, 8, 10
co-design 104
cognitive filtering 145
cognitive load 147, 148, 155

collaboration 1, 2, 3, 4, 10, 13, 36, 38,
      40, 49, 52, 109, 110, 112, 113, 114,
      115, 116, 117, 120, 121, 122, 123,
      124, 125, 141, 142, 143, 144, 145,
      146, 147, 148, 149, 150, 153, 154,
      155, 156, 157, 158, 180, 181, 182,
      187, 190, 191, 192, 243
collaboration tools 55
collaborative creation 2
collaborative exploratory search 143
collaborative filtering system 145
collaborative group workspaces 37
Collaborative Information Behavior (CIB) 73,
      74, 75, 76, 77, 78, 79, 80, 82, 83,
      84, 87, 89, 91, 92, 93, 94, 105, 107,
      109, 110, 111, 112, 114, 115, 116,
      117, 120, 121, 122, 123, 124, 125,
      141, 142, 143, 144, 145, 146, 147,
      148, 149, 150, 151, 153, 154, 155
collaborative information retrieval (CIR) sys-
      tems 73, 74, 75, 76, 79, 80, 82, 83,
      84, 85, 92, 143, 155, 156
collaborative information seeking (CIS) 74,
      75, 82, 92, 106, 143, 150, 152, 157,
      199, 200, 220
collaborative information synthesis 143
collaborative innovation network (COIN)
      110, 125
collaborative load 147, 155
Collaborative Network Organizations (CNO)
      1, 2, 3, 4, 7, 8, 11, 12, 13
collaborative research 55, 69
collaborative retrieval tools 76
collaborative talk 226, 240
collaborative work
      89, 92, 93, 94, 105, 109, 197